CONQUER

or

DIE!

WELLINGTON'S VETERANS AND THE LIBERATION
OF THE NEW WORLD

*Dedicated to the British volunteers
who fought and died in South America*

CONQUER
or
DIE!

WELLINGTON'S VETERANS AND THE LIBERATION
OF THE NEW WORLD

BEN HUGHES

OSPREY
PUBLISHING

First published in Great Britain in 2010 by Osprey Publishing,
Midland House, West Way, Botley, Oxford, OX2 0PH, UK
44-02 23rd Street, Suite 219, Long Island City, NY 11101, USA

E-mail: info@ospreypublishing.com

A CIP catalogue record for this book is available from the British Library

ISBN: 978 1 84908 183 2

Jacket and page layout by Myriam Bell Design, France
Index by Alison Worthington
Typeset in Cochin and 1786 GLC Fournier
Cartography by Peter Bull Art Studio
Originated by PPS Grasmere, Leeds, UK
Printed in China through Worldprint

10 11 12 13 14   10 9 8 7 6 5 4 3 2 1

Front Cover: Bridgeman Art Library and istockphoto.com

For a catalogue of all books published by Osprey please contact:

NORTH AMERICA
Osprey Direct, c/o Random House Distribution Center
400 Hahn Road, Westminster, MD 21157, USA

E-mail: uscustomerservice@ospreypublishing.com

ALL OTHER REGIONS
Osprey Direct, The Book Service Ltd., Distribution Centre, Colchester Road, Frating
Green, Colchester, Essex, CO7 7DW

E-mail: customerservice@ospreypublishing.com

Osprey Publishing is supporting the Woodland Trust, the UK's leading woodland
conservation charity, by funding the dedication of trees.

www.ospreypublishing.com

CONTENTS

MAPS AND BATTLEPLANS

Note: Where the author was unable to find definitive references to their exact positioning from the sources available, several military units are not named on the battle plans which are seen throughout the text.

THE ATLANTIC OCEAN

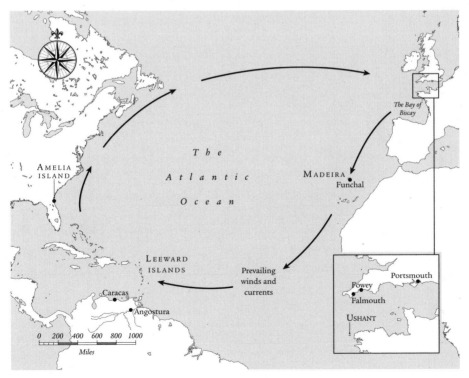

THE CARIBBEAN

VENEZUELA

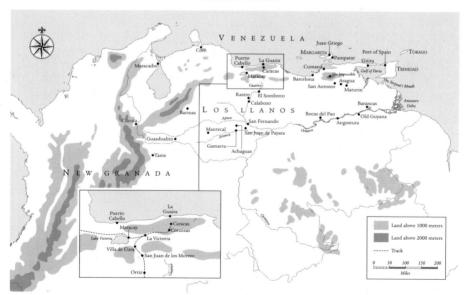

NEW GRANADA

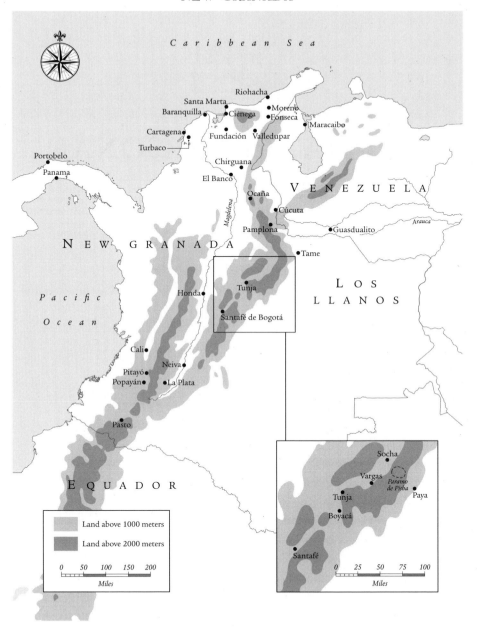

Caribbean Sea

Riohacha
Santa Marta
Baranquilla • Ciénega • Moreno • Fónseca
Cartagena • • Fundación Valledupar • Maracaibo
Turbaco
Chirguana
El Banco
Ocaña
Portobelo V E N E Z U E L A
Panama Cúcuta
Pamplona • Guasdualito
Arauca
N E W G R A N A D A Tame
L O S
L L A N O S
Pacific Honda
Ocean Tunja
Santafé de Bogotá
Cali
Neiva
Pitayó
Popayán • • La Plata
Pasto
E Q U A D O R

Socha
Vargas Páramo
de Pisba • Paya
Tunja
Boyacá
Land above 1000 meters
Land above 2000 meters Santafé

0 50 100 150 200   0   25   50   75   100
Miles   Miles

DRAMATIS PERSONAE

Ranks shown below are those held at the start of involvement in the campaign.

Alexander, Lieutenant Alexander (b.1782)
Veteran of the British Artillery. Attached to the Black Rifles after his arrival in Angostura in 1818.

Anzoátegui, Lieutenant-Colonel José (b.1789)
Foul-tempered Venezuelan patriot.

Arismendi, Juan Bautista (b.1775)
Patriot governor of the island of Margarita.

Barreiro, General José Maria (b.1793)
Inexperienced Spanish commander of the royalist 3rd Division, based in central New Granada.

Bermúdez, General José (b.1782)
Patriot guerrilla chief based in eastern Venezuela.

Blosset, Major John (dates unknown)
Napoleonic veteran of the 28th Foot's Egyptian campaign. Second in command of General English's British Legion.

Bolívar, Simón (b.1783)
The Liberator. Commander-in-chief of patriot forces in northern South America.

Brion, Admiral Luis (b.1782)
'A creole … rather advanced in years, of a commanding and stern deportment, dark penetrating eyes, and remarkably long black mustachios', Brion was the Curaçao-born mercenary admiral of the patriot fleet.[1]

Campbell, Colonel Peter (dates unknown)

Napoleonic veteran. Founder of the Black Rifles.

Cedeño, General Manuel (b.1780)

Venezuelan cavalry commander, fighting with the patriots since 1813.

Chesterton, Lieutenant George Laval (dates unknown)

Veteran of the 1812 War. Memoirist and officer of the British Legion.

Davy, Major William (dates unknown)

Senior officer in General English's British Legion.

Devereux, General John (b.1778)

Merchant, charlatan, founder and commander of the Irish Legion.

Elsom, Captain George (dates unknown)

Officer in Colonel Skeene's 2nd Venezuelan Lancers. Later was founder of the 2nd Venezuelan Rifles.

English, Captain James Towers (b.1782)

Former clerk and horse trader. Officer in Colonel Hippisley's 1st Venezuelan Hussars. Later was founder of the British Legion.

English, Mary (b.1789)

Captain English's wife.

Ferdinand VII (b.1784)

Tyrannical King of Spain.

Ferrier, Captain Thomas Idlerton (b.1785)

Officer in Colonel Gillmore's artillery. Later became commander of the British Legion.

Foley, Doctor Thomas (dates unknown)

Kerry-born. Originally part of Wilson's Red Hussars. Later became Bolívar's chief surgeon.

Gillmore, Colonel Joseph (dates unknown)

British Army veteran. Founder and commander of the 1st Venezuelan Artillery Regiment.

Grant, Captain Peter Alexander (b.1794)

British Army deserter. After working as a slave-driver on Demerara became an early independent volunteer. A 'specimen of eccentricity'.[2]

Hamilton, James (dates unknown)

Flamboyant Scottish merchant based in Angostura.

Hippisley, Captain Gustavus Butler (dates unknown)

Troublesome older son of Colonel Hippisley.

Hippisley, Colonel Gustavus Mathias (b.1768)

British Army veteran. Pompous martinet. Founder and commanding officer of 1st Venezuelan Hussars.

Johnstone, Captain John (dates unknown)

Originally a volunteer in Colonel Skeene's 2nd Venezuelan Lancers. Later joined Captain Elsom's Rifles.

MacDonald, Colonel Donald (dates unknown)

'An active vigorous man, in the prime of life.'[3] Napoleonic veteran who rose from the ranks to earn a commission. Founder and commanding officer of the 1st Venezuelan Lancers.

MacGregor, General 'Sir' Gregor (b.1786)

Napoleonic veteran. Early independent volunteer. Charismatic yet immoral. Married to Bolívar's niece.

McGuire, Lieutenant Laurence (b.1791)

'I would be quite happy if only I could pay … Mother, Brothers, and Sisters a visit now and again.'[4] Officer in Captain Elsom's Rifles.

Mackintosh, James (dates unknown)

London-based merchant and 'leading parliamentarian' who helped finance several expeditions to South America.[5]

Mackintosh, Major John (b.1798)

Brother of above. Volunteer in Colonel Wilson's 2nd Venezuelan Hussars. Efficient officer who was admired by his men. Later was second in command of Rooke's Rifles.

Manby, Captain Thomas (b.1801)

Napoleonic veteran. Later became officer in Captain Elsom's Rifles. 'Dearly love[d] women … and wine.'[6]

Mendéz, Luís López (b.1758)

Republican representative and recruiter based in London.

Minchin, Lieutenant Charles (b.1797)

One of four Irish brothers who volunteered for the patriots. Officer in Captain Elsom's Rifles. Later appointed captain in the British Legion.

Miranda, Francisco de (1750–1815)

Venezuelan libertine and revolutionary leader. Founder of the First Republic.

Morillo, General Pablo (b.1775)

Spanish Napoleonic veteran. Commander-in-chief of royalist forces in northern South America. An excellent tactician and ruthless soldier.

Murphy, Surgeon Richard (*c*.1785)

Volunteer in General English's British Legion.

Needham, Lieutenant-Colonel John (b.1792)

Commander of The Brussels' Lancers Corps.

O'Connor, Francis Burdett (b.1793)

Memoirist and second in command of the Irish Legion's 1st Lancers.

O'Leary, Coronet Daniel (b.1802)

The eighth of ten children born to a bankrupt Irish butter merchant, O'Leary was a studious and ambitious young man who joined Colonel Wilson's Red Hussars.

Páez, General José Antonio (b.1790)

'The Centaur of Los Llanos'. Caudillo chieftain and patriot commander. Uneducated and illiterate, Páez was an exceptional warrior.

Piar, General Manuel (b.1774)

Patriot commander who unwisely crossed Bolívar.

Piggot, Lieutenant-Colonel Robert (b.1774)

Second in command of Colonel Campbell's Black Rifles. 'He was the brother, the friend, [and] the companion of his officers, and the father' of his men.[7]

Popham, Admiral Sir Home (b.1762)

Over-zealous commander of the Royal Navy's Caribbean fleet.

Rafter, Colonel William (dates unknown)

A professional Napoleonic veteran, Rafter was commander of the 1st Rifles during General MacGregor's expedition to Portobelo.

Robinson, Surgeon James (*c*.1782)

Studied medicine at Edinburgh University. Served for ten years with the Royal Navy before joining Colonel Campbell's Black Rifles.

Rooke, Anna (b.1802)

A 'fascinating and elegant' mulatta of just 16 years of age.[8] Colonel Rooke's second wife.

Rooke, Lieutenant-Colonel James (b.1772)

'A huge, handsome, blue eyed blonde'.[9] Waterloo veteran and early volunteer. Commander of Bolívar's guard of honour.

Sámano, Viceroy Juan (b.1753)

Cruel and vindictive Spanish Viceroy of New Granada.

Sandes, Lieutenant Arthur (b.1793)

Kerry-born officer in Colonel Campbell's Black Rifles.

Santander, General Francisco de Paula (b.1792)

Machiavellian patriot commander from New Granada.

Skeene, Colonel Robert (dates unknown)
Founder of 2nd Venezuelan Lancers.

Urdaneta, General Rafael (b.1788)
Venezuelan-born, patriot commander 'of complying and intriguing disposition'.[10]

Valdés, Colonel Manuel (b.1767)
'Insolent and overbearing', Venezuelan patriot commander.[11]

Vowell, Lieutenant Richard Longeville (b.1795)
Oxford undergraduate of 'amiable but thoughtless disposition'.[12] Joined
Colonel MacDonald's 1st Venezuelan Lancers.

Walton, William (dates unknown)
London-based patriot agent and journalist for the *Morning Chronicle*.

White, William (dates unknown)
Patriot propagandist based in Port of Spain, Trinidad.

Wilson, Colonel Henry Croasdile (b.1785)
Napoleonic veteran. Founder of the Red Hussars. Arrogant and overbearing.

Wright, Lieutenant Thomas (b.1799)
Veteran naval officer of the 1812 War. Joined Colonel Campbell's Black Rifles.

PREFACE

Vencer o Morir! (to conquer or to die) was the motto of the British Legion, one of several bands of adventurers who served in the republican armies of Venezuela and New Granada (Colombia). Between 1817 and 1820, over 6,000 volunteers sailed from London, Dublin, Belfast and Liverpool to aid Simón Bolívar in liberating the colonies from their oppressors in Madrid. Although the contemporary media (fuelled by mercantile interest in an emerging market) followed their adventures closely, their memory soon faded once the war was won. Only a decade after large-scale recruitment had first taken place, one veteran was moved to write that 'few ... are ... aware of the number of Englishmen who have been sacrificed in this cause. It is therefore desirable, that some record should be left ... [to those] whose bravery ... contributed to some of the most distinguished successes ... of South American independence.'[1] As the 200th anniversary of these events draws closer, such sentiments ring truer than ever. The volunteers' role in the conflict has been played down in the countries they helped to liberate, and all but forgotten at home. *Conquer or Die!* is an attempt to redress this imbalance. *Conquer or Die!* is their story.

No other works about the volunteers have brought their adventures to the attention of the general public, nor done the tale's dramatic potential full justice. Hasbrouck's *Foreign Legionaries in South America*, published in 1928, is an entertaining account, but a little light in analysis and heavy on patriotic fervour. Lambert's *Voluntarios Británicos en la Gesta Bolivariana* is a far more involved study. Nevertheless, as it is only available in Spanish, stretches to three volumes and has a tendency to favour minutiae over atmosphere, it may alienate the general reader. The most recent publication, Matthew Brown's *Adventuring Through Spanish Colonies*, is meticulously researched and questions previous conclusions, but its thematic structure and lack of characterization ensure that it is more likely to be fully appreciated by the academic. *Conquer or Die!* gives flesh to the established bones of the story. It aims to bring these forgotten adventurers back to life.

Although the volunteers only represented a small fraction of those who fought and died in South America, their contribution to the primary source material is immense. Their memoirs, narratives and journals have all been used in this study. I have also drawn heavily on contemporary newspapers and unpublished documents. Some of these sources were written immediately after the events described. Others were composed decades later. A number are the testimonies of direct participants, several were written by eyewitnesses and a few by authors who merely met those involved. I have been selective when using sources composed by peripheral figures or those whose credibility is all too easy to doubt.

Reading *Conquer or Die!* one could be forgiven for supposing that South America's liberty was secured by foreigners alone. This would, of course, be an immense exaggeration. Although the British contribution was significant, the true authors of independence were the South Americans themselves, many of whom had been fighting for several years before the volunteers arrived in force. Whilst several of these key *Americanos* feature in this work, some do so only fleetingly. I make no apologies for this, even though some may consider it an outrageous omission. Nor is this work intended to be an encyclopaedic account of the conflict itself. The campaigns fought across Venezuela and New Granada involved countless engagements, ranging over a vast area. To cover all in detail would take a book much longer than this one. My principal aim is to tell the story through the eyes of the British volunteers. Above all, I have tried to portray what it was like to live through the triumphs and disasters, the fleeting glory, grinding misery, tragedy, rare moments of humour and outright farce, which characterized their contribution to the continent's independence.

Where possible, the terminology used is that favoured by the participants themselves. The British troops are 'volunteers', who fight for the 'patriots' or 'republicans' and are led by 'The Liberator', whilst the 'royalists' or 'Spaniards' are those they opposed. Although some modern spellings of proper nouns are used in the main body of the text, original spellings, punctuation and grammar have been kept in quotations. Where doubts exist concerning dates and numbers, an average of all those offered by credible primary sources is used.

Finally, I would like to acknowledge the proofreaders, professors, archivists and librarians without whom *Conquer or Die!* could never have been written. To the staff of the British Library's reading rooms and their peers in Ireland, Scotland, Venezuela and Colombia I owe an enormous debt of gratitude. Professor Matthew Brown, Jane and David Hughes, 'Red' Tim Dalrymple, Jamie Cowper, Richard Garey and Julia Weetman have all read and commented on drafts with enthusiasm and honesty. In the hamlet of Belencito in Boyacá, Colombia, Alonso Gil gave up an entire morning in search of the monastery where Colonel Rooke died, and Juan Soteto risked his boss's wrath by allowing me inside the Brazilian steelworks where the building now stands. Emilio Correa Calambas's local knowledge helped me orientate myself on the battlefield of Pitayó. Romaldo Criollo, a direct descendant of the Pastusos who defeated the British at Genoy, kindly shared the stories that his ancestors had passed down for generations and Julia Stiles provided some fascinating information on the latter-day adventures of Captain Richard Vowell.

As much as I owe to so many people, it is to the volunteers themselves that I dedicate this book. Their bravery, enthusiasm and perseverance inspired this project, and as a modern-day traveller and former resident of South America, I feel an affinity with their wanderlust. In today's globalized world where thousands embark on intercontinental travel every day, one can only imagine the sense of excitement and trepidation with which these brave adventurers set off across the Atlantic some 200 years ago.

PROLOGUE

MID-AFTERNOON, 16 MARCH 1818

A high mountain valley somewhere to the south-west of Caracas, Venezuela

Lieutenant Richard Vowell was certain his end had come. Left behind when his comrades had run in the face of the Spanish onslaught, the Englishman was soon to be surrounded by his enemies. He dropped to the ground and scrambled into the undergrowth. As his pursuers drew closer, he braced himself for the bayonet thrust he was convinced was only moments away. Luckily, the royalists were so intent on chasing the remnants of Bolívar's army, they failed to notice the cowering figure at their feet. With their footsteps receding up the slope, Vowell crawled further into the scrub, emerging onto a rock perched high above the valley. Peering through the smoke, he took in the battlefield spread out beneath him. Twisted bodies of men and horses had fallen throughout the entire valley. Where the routed troops had been crushed together as they fled down a narrow pass, they now lay piled on top of one another. A handful of patriot soldiers, entangled in thick thorn bushes and unable to escape, remained on the field. The royalists were firing volleys into the ever-decreasing mass. To the right, on a small rise near the brook that had divided the armies that morning, a group of Spanish officers were questioning prisoners. They were led forward one by one, interrogated and shot.

As Vowell absorbed the horror of the scene, the spirit of adventure that had inspired him to sail halfway round the world must have seemed hopelessly naive. Of the 80 volunteers who had enlisted in the 1st Venezuelan Lancers in London in the summer of 1817, only 18 remained the following February to join Bolívar's army. The fate of the rest was representative of what would happen to the 6,000 Britons who would sail for the continent over the next two years. One had died on the island of Saint Thomas's (Saint Thomas) as the result of a duel with a comrade. Two had been robbed and killed by Indians on their passage up the Orinoco. The rest had resigned, deserted or succumbed to typhus, malaria or yellow fever. After six weeks campaigning with the republicans, their numbers had dwindled even further. Several had been shot or bayoneted in a string of defeats, while others had been executed after capture. As he watched the sun sink beneath the far side of the valley, Lieutenant Richard Vowell, terrified, exhausted and alone, represented a quarter of all those that remained.

PART ONE

RAMBLING BROTHERS O' THE BLADE
1815–1818

Curse on the star, dear Harry, that betrayed
My choice from law, divinity or trade
To turn a rambling brother o' the blade!

Of all professions sure the worst is war.
How whimsical our future! How bizarre!
This week we shine in scarlet and in gold:
The next, the cloak is pawned – the watch is sold.

An Epistle from a Half-Pay Officer

Chapter 1

'FLAGS, BANNERS, GLORY AND RICHES'

On the morning of 19 June 1815, as the powder smoke dissipated above the battlefield of Waterloo, peace finally descended on Europe after 22 years of near constant conflict. In London the celebrations were unprecedented. Jubilant Britons thronged the streets singing 'God Save the King' and 'fêtes, operas, illuminations … [and] naval and military reviews, formed the order of the day and night'.[1] The Chancellor of the Exchequer, Nicolas Vansittart, proudly informed parliament that although the country had 'entered the conflict poor and feeble, she came out … rich and invincible'.[2] In the immediate aftermath of the battle, Britain had emerged as the single greatest power on the planet.[3]

Much of the country's prosperity was owed to an exceptional economic boost caused by the war for, during that time, the Royal Navy had blockaded the coastline of the continent and transatlantic trade had been concentrated in Britain's ports. When the fighting finished, however, this monopoly was abruptly brought to an end and the country was plunged into recession.[4] One of the institutions most affected was the army. Since 1792 Britain had seen mobilization on an unprecedented scale. By 1815 the army had swollen to a staggering 243,885 men, equating to 2½ per cent of the population.[5] After Waterloo, thousands of troops were needed for the occupation of France, but in 1817 they were called home. The army was split up and whole regiments disbanded. According to one contemporary observer, 40,000 troops were dismissed in the first year alone.[6] With no enemy to challenge or to provide prizes to capture at sea, the Royal Navy also went into decline. Hundreds of ships were decommissioned. The pride of Nelson's fleet was broken up and some ships ended their days as prison hulks anchored in the Thames. Thousands of sailors, marines, shipwrights, carpenters and sail-makers were laid off. Boatyards all along the south coast fell silent. With both the army and navy in decline, the munitions industry collapsed. Merchants who had grown rich supplying the troops went bankrupt. As recession took hold, unemployment spread across the land.

The introduction of the Corn Laws in 1815 only exacerbated the situation. Designed to protect landowners' profits by fixing grain prices at an artificially high level, this short-sighted legislation led to outbreaks of famine when the poor could no longer afford to make bread. To make matters worse, a string of unusually cold winters and wet summers caused consecutive harvests to fail.[7] A number of civil protests followed, culminating in a blood bath known as the Peterloo Massacre in an ironic nod to Wellington's victory four years earlier. The demonstration began peacefully, but when local yeomanry moved in to arrest the ringleaders, the situation degenerated into a riot. The crowd hurled bricks and stones and the 15th Hussars, who had been sent to police the event, tore into the protestors with sabres drawn.[8] Within ten minutes, 15 were dead and 500 had been wounded. In Ireland, home to over 40 per cent of Wellington's soldiers, the situation was even worse. Upon their return, veterans found the country blighted by poverty and crippled by draconian English laws. These brutalized men were desperate for work and eager for a new challenge. Although prospects of employment were bleak, political upheavals on the far side of the world were about to present them with an unlikely opportunity.

In South America, the wars of independence had been raging ever since Napoleon's invasion of the Iberian Peninsula in 1808, when Ferdinand VII had been forced into exile. Emboldened by the Spanish King's military humiliation and inspired by recent revolutions in the United States, France and Haiti, young idealists had risen up across Latin America to challenge the right of the Spanish interim government to rule them. In Chile, Bernado O'Higgins, the illegitimate son of an Irishman who had achieved high office in the region, gained prominence in the struggle for independence. José de San Martín led the republicans in the United Provinces of Rio de la Plata (Argentina), Miguel Hidalgo and José María Morelos rose up in New Spain (Mexico) and in New Granada the independence movement was headed by Antonio Nariño. Whilst Peru, Upper Peru (Bolivia) and Ecuador remained loyal to the Spanish crown, in Venezuela two key figures emerged for the patriots: Francisco de Miranda, a veteran of the American War of Independence and long-term advocate of revolution; and his protégé, the Caracas-born aristocrat, Simón Bolívar.[9] Together they had been defying the Spanish since 1810, when their troops first seized control of Caracas. Miranda was installed as president of the First Republic and Bolívar appointed lieutenant-colonel in the army. The revolutionaries had little support amongst the masses, however, and their efforts were soon overshadowed by a natural disaster of apocalyptic proportions, when, on 26 March 1812, a massive earthquake shook Caracas, killing 10,000.[10]

The royalist church sought political advantage from the catastrophe, claiming it was an act of divine retribution against those who dared depose God's chosen monarch.[11] Several patriot units defected and the tide began to turn against the revolution. Seeing his position crumble, Miranda started secret negotiations with the enemy, whilst at the same time preparing to escape to the Dutch-controlled island of Curaçao. The resulting pact was signed in San Mateo on 25 July 1812. Although offering protection to patriots and their property, the terms included the complete disbandment of the republican army. When he learnt of the deal, Bolívar wanted his fallen idol executed, but his co-conspirators favoured leniency. Duped into returning onshore, Miranda was chained up and left for the advancing royalists to do with as they saw fit. The Spaniards were delighted with the gift. Miranda was taken to Spain and thrown into La Carraca prison in Cádiz, where a British naval officer later saw him shackled to the walls of a damp cell.[12] He remained in custody until his death four years later, an ignominious end for a man who had travelled across four continents and mixed with kings, empresses and presidents in his unrelenting pursuit of liberty.[13] Back in Venezuela, the First Republic was in its death throes. Whilst the patriots bickered amongst themselves, the royalists seized control of Caracas and ousted Bolívar, who fled to neighbouring New Granada (modern-day Colombia). Known as 'The Liberator', Bolívar was a man of extraordinary tenacity, however. After raising more troops, he again took the capital in August 1813 and was proclaimed president of the Second Republic. But just when his glory seemed complete, developments across the Atlantic once again influenced South America's destiny.

In June that year, Wellington's redcoats had won a decisive victory at the battle of Vitoria in northern Spain. The French were driven back over the Pyrenees, and by the end of the year, King Ferdinand VII was restored to the throne. Unlike the interim government, whose willingness to compromise over the question of South American self-determination had been exploited by the republicans, the king would not countenance the thought of the colonies slipping from his grasp. In February 1815, he dispatched General Pablo Morillo with 10,000 veterans to restore control. Largely dependent on poorly trained conscripts, Bolívar could not compete with the largest Spanish force ever sent to the New World and was forced into exile once more.[14] After sailing to Haiti, he began planning a final homecoming. In exchange for a promise to abolish slavery, he received financial backing from Alexandre Pétion, one of the island's revolutionary leaders, and so launched another expedition, landing on the coast east of Caracas in late 1816. After taking the port of Barcelona, he pushed 300 miles up the Orinoco to join forces with General Manuel Piar, whose troops were besieging Angostura (now known as Cuidad Bolívar). As the provincial capital of Guyana, the city enjoyed lucrative trade links with the British Colonies in the West Indies. Its wealth and isolation from the royalist strongholds on the Caribbean coast were to make it the ideal base for the revolution.[15] On the verge of the city's capitulation, Bolívar's thoughts returned to a long-considered plan: to recruit Napoleonic veterans from Europe to professionalize his army and drive the Spanish from his homeland for good.[16] Previously, both the lack of funds and an established base had rendered the idea impractical, but with the wealth of Angostura now within reach, Bolívar wrote to his agent in London, Luís López Mendéz, ordering him to enlist the disbanded soldiers crowding the capital's streets without delay.

A sharp-featured, bespectacled man of scholarly appearance, Mendéz had been based at London's 27 Grafton Street since 1810, when the First Republic had sent a delegation to the capital hoping to gain Westminster's support. Although the mission had ended with the British government reiterating its alliance with Spain, Mendéz had not been idle in the intervening years. By 1817 he had fostered a network of patriot sympathizers across the capital, the most vocal of whom was William Walton, a journalist writing for the *Morning Chronicle*. Receiving financial support from the republicans for his efforts, Walton filled countless column inches extolling their virtues and printed biased reports of their progress in Guyana penned by William White, a British sympathizer based in nearby Trinidad.[17]

With little competition save occasional dispatches from India and accounts of Napoleon's failing health in exile on Saint Helena, the *Morning Chronicle*'s sabre-rattling propaganda was eagerly digested by the British public.[18] Bolívar's quest had romantic appeal for a people influenced by the Enlightenment and soon became the *cause célèbre* of the liberal left. Luminaries such as Byron and Keats and the pre-eminent political player of the day in Ireland, the lawyer and statesman Daniel O'Connell, were all equally vociferous in their support. Some evidence suggests that certain figures in the higher echelons of the British military were also sympathetic. When writing his memoirs in 1819, Gustavus Mathias Hippisley, one of Mendéz's first recruits, cryptically referred to 'the approbation of my friend, whose high rank in the army of Great Britain and … experience in military matters, was as distinguished as his name was honoured, loved and respected'.[19] Some historians have conjectured that this may have been a reference to Wellington himself, but the truth of such a claim remains impossible to verify.[20]

Westminster's Tory government, on the other hand, publicly disapproved of the 'insurgents' and backed a proclamation made by the Prince Regent in November 1817 prohibiting recruitment for the cause. The prince, who would be crowned George IV in 1820 (following his long-ailing father's terminal decline), was predictably unequivocal in his support for the royalists. The government's position, however, was not as clear as it first seemed. Whilst officially opposing recruitment and repeatedly informing the irate Spanish ambassador, the Duc de San Carlos, that they were doing all in their power to prevent it, in reality the policies pursued by the Foreign Secretary Lord Castlereagh, and other leading politicians were, according to the historian John Lynch, both 'diffident in … approach and vague in intent'.[21] Behind closed doors, Mendéz's activities were largely ignored, if not actively encouraged.[22] It is difficult to judge the extent of this 'tacit assent', however, for as it directly contravened official policy, little documentation survives.[23] Nevertheless, a letter filed in the Foreign Office archives suggests that certain elements in Westminster not only gave Mendéz their backing, but actually financed his activities with a secret 'yearly pension of £500' – a not insignificant sum in the early 19th century.[24]

Three factors motivated this clandestine approval. Firstly, an increased British presence in South America would both foil a Spanish resurgence and prevent a humbled but ever-ambitious France or an increasingly aggressive United States from gaining extra influence over the region. The second motivation was capital gain. Whilst recruitment briefly revived the stuttering munitions industry, far larger profits were to be made through trade with an independent Venezuela. The region produced Georgian Britain's three most popular indulgences (coffee, sugar and tobacco) and economists widely believed that it would eventually provide a significant market for manufactured European goods. Prior to Bolívar's capture of Angostura, this trade (with the exception of some smuggling operations) had been the exclusive domain of the Spanish crown. If Spain was defeated by the rebels, however, the country that would become the new republic's European trading partner would reap huge rewards. The government's final incentive was the chance to rid itself of some of the disbanded veterans crowding London's streets.[25] These disenchanted, brutalized men, who just three years earlier had been hailed as heroes, were now viewed as 'objects of horror, to be dreaded as depredators … [and] branded as culprits'.[26] If Bolívar wanted to bring about their removal 3,000 miles across the Atlantic, the British government was not about to prevent him.

Although a handful of individuals had joined the cause previously, recruitment began in earnest in mid-1817. Gustavus Mathias Hippisley, the first officer to raise an entire unit, agreed terms with Mendéz on 14 May. The *Morning Chronicle*'s William Walton witnessed the contract. A further five officers of varying suitability were then commissioned. All six were to receive the rank of colonel in the republican army of Venezuela. The 49-year old Hippisley, who formed the 1st Venezuelan Hussars, was an extremely wealthy man from a distinguished Somerset family that could trace its ancestry to Edward the Confessor.[27] After finishing his education at Saint Paul's in London, Hippisley had acquired a coronet's commission in the 9th Light Dragoons. He served with the regiment for seven years in Ireland, where he met and married Ellen Fitzgerald. A transfer accompanied by promotion then saw the couple posted to Britain's newly acquired colony at the Cape of Good Hope, where Hippisley rose to the post of major of brigade. After nine years in Africa, he retired on half pay and returned to England, later joining the West Mendip Militia as a captain. He remained with the regiment until it was demobilized shortly after Waterloo. Hippisley was a pompous disciplinarian and martinet. Unsuited to civilian life, he anticipated his new post in Venezuela with relish.

Henry Croasdile Wilson, the son of a protestant clergyman from Galway, formed a second cavalry regiment, which came to be known as the Red Hussars because of their brilliant scarlet uniforms.[28] Something of a child prodigy, Wilson had been sent to Oxford University in 1800 at the age of 15. After graduating, he joined the army, serving for four years with the 3rd Light Dragoons.[29] A brief interlude then saw him indulge his literary pretensions as the editor of 'a sort of French magazine' but when the project failed, Wilson fell upon hard times.[30] Boasting a fluent command of Spanish and claiming previous experience of South America, he believed he was the best qualified of the six colonels and thought himself Mendéz's favourite. Later events would show he was better suited to the ballroom than the battlefield, however, and his vanity and violent temper would actually prove detrimental to the cause.

A Scottish veteran named Donald MacDonald was commissioned to raise the 1st Venezuelan Lancers. 'An active vigorous man, in the prime of life', MacDonald had once served as a private in the British Army, later rising from the ranks to earn his commission.[31] After a subsequent promotion to captain, he served with distinction in the West Indies before joining the Portuguese Army in the Peninsular War as General Ballesteros's aide-de-camp.[32] Described by Hippisley as 'a soldier of fortune, with little or nothing left, save his honour or his sword', MacDonald was motivated by the chance to start afresh in the New World and leave his many creditors behind.[33]

Peter Campbell recruited an infantry regiment, which would come to be known as the Black Rifles.[34] Another Peninsular veteran, Campbell had served as a captain with the Buffs before retiring at the end of January 1818.[35] Little is known about him aside from an allusion Hippisley makes in his memoirs to his 'mercantile connexions', but judging from the regiment he raised, it seems he was a competent officer and fine judge of men.[36]

The position of colonel of the 1st Venezuelan Artillery Regiment was given to Joseph Gillmore, an Irishman who had also risen from the ranks. Beginning his career as a corporal in the West Indies, Gillmore had been promoted to ensign before returning to Europe and joining the Portuguese Mountain Artillery. He saw action at several set piece battles as the French retreated over the Pyrenees and he later returned to the British Army, serving as a lieutenant in the 27th Foot until his enforced retirement on 7 August 1817. Quietly capable, Gillmore was a professional soldier and enjoyed the respect of his men.

The last of the six colonels was Robert Skeene, a superb horseman commissioned to raise a second regiment of Lancers. Having started his career as a riding master training recruits in Maidstone, Skeene was 'well known in the British cavalry service' by the time he retired eight years later with the rank of lieutenant-colonel.[37]

Each of the six colonels had to recruit up to 50 officers and 100 non-commissioned officers (NCOs) to form the backbone of their regiments, the rank and file of which were to be conscripted in Venezuela. In the post-war climate of economic depression, enlistment proceeded swiftly. NCOs were 'hourly offering their services' and half pay officers were so keen to join that bribes were 'delicately offered on many occasions' to ensure a position.[38] Some had previously served with the colonels and others were known to them socially. Several 'young gentlemen who had never before held a regimental military commission' were made coronets and ensigns and Hippisley and Campbell even enlisted their sons.[39] Those applicants not known to the colonels were required to provide references. Some, such as James Towers English, who was made a captain in the 1st Venezuelan Hussars (and will later emerge as a key figure in this history), clearly faked their credentials. An ambitious yet amiable 36-year old opportunist, English assured Hippisley that he had served as a senior lieutenant in the 18th Light Dragoons, although it was later discovered that 'he never was higher than a senior clerk in the commissariat department', a fact subsequently confirmed by Home Office spies.[40]

Whilst the six colonels were recruiting, five smaller units, each totalling less than 50 men, were also being raised. The first set sail from London on the *Prince of Wales* in mid-1817. In August the second, led by Lieutenant-Colonel John Needham and consisting of just 11 officers and four NCOs, departed from Belgium on the *Parnasso*. Several of those on board were notable figures. Lieutenants James and Richard Stacey were first cousins to Lord Byron, and Captain Thomas Ferrier, a doctor's son from Manchester, would go on to play a decisive role in the war. The remaining three ships all sailed from Britain: 33 volunteers embarked on the *Gladwin* under Captain Eyre in the summer of 1817, the *Morgan Rattler* would leave from Portsmouth in November and the *Grace* would set sail from the Isle of Wight in January the following year.

The volunteers' backgrounds spanned the entire spectrum of 19th-century inequality. Oxbridge students and landed gentry rubbed shoulders with the poor and destitute. Those who were not veterans of the Napoleonic Wars had experienced a variety of occupations, ranging from labourers and weavers to accountants, lawyers and clerks.[41] Reflecting the make up of Wellington's army and the poverty blighting the isle, roughly 50 per cent were Irish.[42] Between 20 and 25 per cent were English, 5 per cent hailed from Scotland and the rest came from France, Italy, Poland, Germany and a host of other nations.[43] A significant minority were married and some had children. Although the average age was 28, the youngest volunteers were only 14 whilst the oldest were 40 years their senior.[44]

The volunteers were a product of their era. Late Georgian Britain was a notoriously debauched and brutal prelude to the strict moral code which would come into fashion in Victorian times.[45] Drinking, gambling, whoring and attending bare-knuckle prizefights were common pastimes that spanned the social divides. Pugilists such as Tom Molyneux, a former slave born in Virginia, and John Shaw, a hard-drinking trooper who had been killed at Waterloo, were household names famed for their exploits in the ring.[46] This was also Lord Byron's 'Age of Cant', when a veneer of respectability covered the sins of a generation. In public, women of class would 'go into fits at the bare mention of breeches, or expire if you were to name the thigh of a chicken', but details of their extramarital affairs were splashed across the pages of the capital's dailies and hundreds of child prostitutes solicited in the streets.[47] Equally, the philosophy of the Enlightenment and William Wilberforce's drive for emancipation attracted considerable public sympathy, yet racism, sexism and xenophobia were all an accepted and expected part of daily life. Following Waterloo, there was an unfailing belief in British superiority. Nelson and Wellington had done much to inflate an already exaggerated national pride and it seemed self-evident that the British were God's chosen people. John Bull was more than a match for any 'effeminate Frenchman', 'cruel, untrustworthy Spaniard' or 'uncouth American'. Many believed Britannia's mission was to educate the savages and free the world of tyrants like the 'Corsican upstart' by bringing ever-larger swathes of the globe under her benign mantle.

The upper classes, from which the majority of the volunteer officers were drawn, enjoyed a pampered, spoilt existence. Fabulously rich, their pleasures were feasting, fashion and the theatre, and men like the dandy George 'Beau' Brummell were heroes of the age. Gentlemen lived their lives by a strict code of personal honour. Originally a 16th-century import from Italy via France, the practice was thoroughly established by the Regency period and produced a particularly prickly mindset amongst the aristocracy, who carried handbooks to inform them of the correct response for every perceived slight. The often inescapable conclusion was the duel, a practice that was endemic amongst the elite.[48] The first quarter of the 19th century saw two prime ministers partake of 'grass before breakfast' and even members of the clergy were known to fight.[49]

The motivations of the volunteers were as varied as their backgrounds. One claimed 'emancipation of an oppressed and ... deserving people' as justification.[50] Another, who had served for nine years in the Napoleonic Wars, purported to less laudable, but perhaps more honest reasons when noting that 'a life of indolence … ill suited to one who … had been accustomed to the unceasing bustle of active service' had led him to take up the challenge.[51] Many younger recruits were drawn by the romantic lure of travel and adventure in a distant land. The fabled home of El Dorado was still largely unknown in Britain, and the recent publication of Alexander von Humboldt's narrative of his journeys in South America had awoken a wanderlust in many would-be explorers.[52] A restless spirit undoubtedly drove Richard Vowell, an idealistic young man of 'amiable but thoughtless disposition', to join MacDonald's 1st Lancers in the summer of 1817.[53] Born in Bath into an Anglo-Irish family, Vowell was the youngest of four children. His mother, Ann Hamilton, was the great-granddaughter of Viscount Boyne, and his father had been a major in the British Army, serving for many years in Jamaica before returning to Ireland as MP for Newbrough, County Wexford.[54] At 5ft 9in and with 'a robust frame', Vowell was physically suited to the life of a soldier.[55] Before he could emulate his father, however, he was expected to finish his education and in 1814 had been sent to Oxford University. At the age of 22, whilst still a Wadham undergraduate, he inherited £2,000 from 'a relative'.[56] The temptation to travel proved too much. Vowell gave up his studies and embarked on an adventure of a lifetime across the Atlantic.

A further motivation for many of the volunteers was the possibility of self-reinvention. Soldiers who had failed to attain promotion, academics and clerks who longed for adventure and men of low birth trapped by Britain's rigid class system were all presented with a second opportunity. Anything seemed possible in the New World and a role in Bolívar's revolution appeared to offer the chance to make their dreams come true. Although altruism, adventure and rebirth were all factors, money was the underlying incentive for the majority.[57] Ever since the cessation of hostilities, Britain had been suffering a general recession from which few had escaped unscathed. Only a fraction of the disbanded soldiers received pensions and the half pay issued to officers idling in semi-retirement was little more than the wage earned by a common labourer.[58] Many were unable to survive on such a meagre income and saw Mendéz's offer as a ticket out of penury.[59]

At first sight, the contracts drawn up at Grafton Street were extremely generous. The volunteers were promised wages of one-third more than those paid by the British Army and the officers were offered commissions one rank higher than they had previously held.[60] The latter was a particularly powerful inducement, as without the prospect of battlefield casualties there was little hope of promotion in Wellington's peacetime army.[61] As a final bonus, the officers were to receive a bounty of 200 pesos and the NCOs 80 pesos to be paid in Venezuela.[62] As the editor of *The Courier* commented in December 1817, 'the offer of such a reward in such bad times was not to be refused'.[63]

For those who agreed, however, nothing but a letter of introduction was supplied up front and the republicans later found Mendéz's promises difficult to keep.

Long before they received any pay, the officers had to buy their personal equipment. Sabres, saddles, paired pistols and fowling-pieces, telescopes, musket repair kits, compasses and fob watches were all purchased and packed ready for their adventure. The largest single expense was the uniform.[64] Whilst those of the Black Rifles were based on the sombre dark green coats, black shakoes (stiff cylindrical military dress hats) and breeches of their famed peers in the 95th Rifles, and the artillery wore similarly nondescript outfits, the cavalry units were ablaze with colour. Featuring such finery as 'figured gold lace round the collar and cuff', the uniforms for Hippisley's unit cost £40 each and an officer of the Red Hussars complained 'that his [brilliant scarlet] outfit amounted to upwards of two hundred guineas', the equivalent of an entire year's pay for an infantry major.[65] As well as being called upon to lend several of their officers the money for such purchases, the colonels were also required to provide for the needs of their NCOs. Hippisley, who had a considerable personal fortune, was able to cover these expenses. The others had little choice but to sink further into debt.[66]

Once their uniforms had been arranged, ships were procured to ferry the volunteers overseas. MacDonald's 80 men of the 1st Lancers embarked as fee-paying passengers aboard the *Two Friends* whilst the merchants who financed Skeene, Wilson and Gillmore chartered private vessels. Typically £25 per ton per month was charged.[67] Some was recovered by billing the officers £30, half to be paid up front and the rest on arrival. The remainder was shouldered by the merchants, who were promised the loan would eventually be repaid by the republic. The *Britannia*, the ship in which Gillmore's 90 artillerymen were to travel, was hired by William Graham, a well-known Glaswegian merchant based in the English capital. Graham also spent £35,000 on 18 cannon, several cases of muskets, and barrels of powder and ball which he intended to sell in South America.[68] Although Mendéz had assured him he would receive a good price, Mr John Ritchie, a financial agent known as a supercargo, was placed aboard to ensure the deal went through smoothly.[69]

Colonel Campbell chartered the frigate *Dowson*, 'a large roomy vessel', to transport the 163 men he had recruited for the Black Rifles.[70] On board was another supercargo, Mr Jones, who would oversee the sale of the 10,000 muskets stowed in the hold.[71] Colonel Wilson's Red Hussars, the smallest of the six regiments with just 77 men, would sail on the *Prince*.[72] Hippisley had previously rejected the vessel as being unseaworthy, but evidently Wilson's standards were less demanding. The largest ship was the 600-ton *Indian*. As well as providing berths for Colonel Skeene's 120 troops of the 2nd Lancers, it also took on board several strays who could find no space on their own regiments' boats.

Hippisley's 1st Hussars were financed by messrs Thompson and James Mackintosh, the latter a London-born merchant and 'leading parliamentarian'.[73] Instead of chartering a vessel to carry the 150 officers and men, they purchased the *Emerald* outright for £23,000.[74] Along with cases of rifles and pistols and barrels of powder, the merchants intended to sell the frigate to the Venezuelan Navy on arrival. To protect the investment, Mackintosh himself sailed on the *Prince*, sharing the best cabin with his fiancée, her sister and his younger brother John, a lieutenant in Colonel Wilson's Red Hussars who would later distinguish himself in South America.

The Archer sisters were not the only women to set sail. The *Indian* had room for 12 females and a single child and Colonel Wilson allowed four wives aboard the *Prince*, including the 'lovely' Maria Graham, married to the regiment's major, but coveted by many of his comrades.[75] In contrast, Colonel Hippisley issued an order forbidding passage to the spouses of officers, even though this resulted in several last-minute resignations. The colonel, perhaps with Mrs Hippisley in mind, suspected that others were not so troubled, claiming that he 'had at least the secret thanks of several of the married men for so wisely judging on their behalf'.[76] Bizarrely, whilst his officers were not allowed to take their wives, some NCOs were permitted to do so. Quartermaster-Sergeant Dobson, 'an old, intrepid and long tried soldier', even took his 19-year old daughter with him.[77] Several other non-combatants embarked. Each regiment had a surgeon, two assistants and a physician. Paymasters, farriers, quartermasters and clerks were also taken on board. Colonel MacDonald travelled with 'a young French criole' servant.[78] Mr Thomas Proctor, a printer promised employment in Angostura, sailed on the *Britannia* with his press, and the Black Rifles even took 'a fine bull-bitch' fighting dog on the *Dowson* as their regimental mascot.[79]

The first challenge faced by the volunteers was the voyage itself. By 1817 the route from England to South America was frequently travelled, but no less treacherous than when Columbus had set off into the unknown over three centuries earlier. It remained a perilous undertaking which many would not survive.

Chapter 2

'PROCEED TO SEA, BE THE WIND AND WEATHER AS THEY MIGHT'

The voyage began in London's East End, where the ships were docked around the Isle of Dogs and Blackwall. From there they would sail down the Thames to the Downs, a sheltered anchorage off the Kent coast, before steering west towards Portsmouth, Lymington or Falmouth. After picking up late arrivals, the ships would head into the treacherous currents of the Bay of Biscay, round the Iberian Peninsula and then turn south-west into the Atlantic. It would take between one and three weeks to reach the Portuguese colony of Madeira, where there was a final opportunity to stock up on fresh supplies before braving the open ocean. The trade winds would then carry them over 2,000 miles across the Atlantic to the Windward Islands of the Caribbean. In all, the voyage could take anything up to two months, although most would complete it in half that time.

Before setting sail, supplies and provisions were loaded. Cannon, muskets, pistols, rifles, barrels of gunpowder and lead shot, swords, lances and bayonets, uniforms, saddles, bridles and harnesses, squealing pigs, horses, sheep, chickens, ducks and hissing geese, barrels of salted pork, beef, herring, cheese, rice and hard-tack biscuits were hoisted, winched or carried on board, tethered on deck, led into pens and cages or packed into the airless hold below.[1] As the drinking water held in huge wooden butts was often less than sanitary, gallons of porter, wine, sherry and spirits were also taken on board.

A mess officer was appointed on each ship to keep careful accounts, as Mendéz had promised that the cost of provisioning the NCOs would be reimbursed in Venezuela. The officers, on the other hand, had to pay for their own supplies. On the *Two Friends* they were charged £40 per head, whereas Surgeon Henry White, the *Emerald*'s mess officer, asked the 1st Hussars for just £14 10s. Choosing White was the first of many mistakes

Colonel Hippisley was to make in command, for after collecting the money the surgeon deserted. It was later discovered that he was notorious in military circles, having been forced to resign his commission with the Surrey Militia due to unspecified bad conduct. Although White was later arrested, the money was never recovered and Hippisley was obliged to cover the cost of provisioning his own officers.[2]

The volunteers spent their last days in London sampling the capital's riotous nightlife. Despite the official illegality of their venture, Campbell's Black Rifle officers attended dances in full dress uniform, accompanied by their acclaimed 27-piece band. Taking full advantage of the 'extreme publicity … given to all their movements', they enjoyed themselves tremendously: drinking, dancing and gambling with the city's elite in fashionable Covent Garden, Soho and the West End.[3] Lieutenant Edward Poole had to borrow heavily to keep up. By the time the regiment left British shores, his wallet was already full of unpaid IOUs.[4]

After Surgeon White's arrest, the *Emerald* spent several weeks at anchor in Blackwall.[5] The area catered well for the tastes of a transient population of embarking soldiers and sailors and was notorious for its debauchery, even by Regency standards. Portuguese sailors, the Lascar crew of East Indiamen, Highlanders on leave and brightly uniformed cavalrymen were all to be seen amidst the filth and squalor of the back streets. Wherever such men were found, brothels, gin shops and taverns were more than happy to take their money. No doubt several of Hippisley's NCOs fully availed themselves of the pleasures on offer.

The six colonels, on the other hand, spent their final days in the capital bickering over seniority. Skeene was keen to depart first, believing that if he arrived at Angostura before the others, Bolívar would grant him overall command. Hippisley, however, felt the role was his by right as he had more military experience and had been the first to be commissioned. Wilson and Gillmore harboured similar ambitions, claiming prior experience in the New World made them the most suitable candidates. These squabbles were never settled and would blight the expedition all the way to Venezuela and beyond. From that moment on, Hippisley noted, it was a case of 'each for himself, independent, and alone'.[6]

As preparations to leave were finally coming to a close, several farewell feasts were given. Besides the senior officers, the merchants financing their operations and Mendéz and Walton were all present. Speeches were made and toasts drunk to the success of their venture. On board the *Emerald*, as the guests crowded round a table in the main cabin, the regimental standard of the 1st Venezuelan Hussars was unfurled. It featured the motto 'Union, Constancia y Valor' ('Unity, Constancy and Valour'), lofty sentiments which many present would fail to uphold.[7] Just before the ships departed, several men had a change of heart. Sneaking away from their sleeping comrades they deserted the cause, leaving their unpaid debts behind them.

Between mid- and late 1817, the ships weighed anchor and set sail, heading down the Thames amidst flocks of wheeling sea birds. Once past the Downs and on the south coast, unfavourable winds caused further delays. The captains turned into port and were forced to drop anchor for several weeks until the weather changed. Most of the volunteers took the opportunity to go ashore and by the end of 1817, the streets of Portsmouth were 'crowded by ... adventurers'.[8] James H. Robinson, a surgeon sailing on the *Dowson* with Campbell's Black Rifles, was amongst them. Unlike several self-styled surgeons who would sail to South America, Robinson was highly qualified. After graduating in medicine at Edinburgh University, he had served for ten years with the Royal Navy and had published three works on disease and infection.[9] Whilst waiting for the winds to change, he spent a month in Portsmouth, where several of his comrades visited the city's infamous 'Love Acre'. One night a practical joker decided to have some fun at their expense. Running up and down outside the brothels, he yelled out that the *Dowson* was ready to sail. Robinson was clearly amused by the spectacle that followed. Red-faced, the men spilled out onto the streets, struggled into their clothes and raced half-dressed to the quayside, only then realizing their mistake.[10]

Not all the volunteers enjoyed the delays. Although a full five months ahead of the other colonels, Donald MacDonald, the commander of the 1st Venezuelan Lancers, was still not quick enough to escape his creditors and was arrested in Portsmouth over a £30 debt. Fearing he would lose all his passengers if the colonel did not sail, the captain of the *Two Friends*, Cornelius Ryan, lent him the money to buy his freedom. As they left Portsmouth harbour, Ryan was already beginning to regret his generosity. Arguments between the two men would punctuate the remainder of the voyage.[11]

Another cause of anxiety amongst those stranded on the south coast in late 1817 was the rumour of their imminent detention for breaking the Prince Regent's proclamation. One memoirist heard that the government intended 'to stop all vessels with arms and troops on board for South America', but others insisted the story was merely the fabrication of Spanish agents employed by the Duc de San Carlos to dissuade them from embarking.[12] If so, it seems to have had some success as several more deserted at this stage, slipping ashore and disappearing into the night. The only volunteers to actually experience any government interference were those on board the *Grace*. At 1.00am on 9 December 1817, after drinking 'sufficient [wine] to lose the steady control of his mind' in the Dolphin Tavern on the Isle of Wight, Lieutenant Sutton accused his fellow passenger, Major Lockyer, of joining the patriot cause merely to escape his debts.[13] Lockyer took immediate offence. Sending his second, Captain Redesdale, to whisper a challenge in Sutton's ear, he returned to the *Grace* to get his duelling pistols. At dawn, the two protagonists, their seconds and the unit's doctor met in a secluded spot to settle the matter. Shivering and hungover, Sutton offered his apologies and insisted that he would not return fire. Nevertheless, Lockyer took careful aim and, when the 'signal was given by the dropping of a handkerchief', coolly shot his opponent through the chest. Sutton died instantly.[14] According to the coroner's report, 'the ball entered by the right breast, penetrated both ventricles of the heart, and burrowed itself in the integuments of the left side.'[15] Whilst Lockyer made good his escape and would eventually reach South America, both seconds were arrested and the *Grace* impounded by customs agents in Cowes. To the disgust of the Duc de San Carlos, however, no charges were brought.[16] The ship was released and the volunteers continued to the Caribbean.

In late November 1817 the winds finally changed. The *Prince* and *Emerald* set sail immediately and were soon heading south into the Bay of Biscay, but before the three remaining ships could leave, 'a most tremendous storm of wind, rain, hail, thunder and lightning' that was 'not … equalled … for fifty years' swept the south coast.[17] The *Dowson* and *Britannia* were caught in open ocean and the *Indian* was forced to anchor off Spithead to avoid being blown onto shore. That night, Lieutenant Hackett, aboard the *Britannia*, was given his first taste of the fury of a storm at sea:

> The waves broke over the vessel in masses of white foam … through the darkness … [they] produced the grandest effect I ever beheld. For security from the … breakers I was obliged to lodge myself … between the mizzen-mast and the round-house, as … it would be impossible for me to keep my legs, when even the sailors … were washed from side to side… Having … gone to report to … [Colonel Gillmore] I found him making a precipitate retreat from the state room, dripping wet, the sea having forced itself through the scuttle, and inundated his bed.[18]

On 2 December, conditions temporarily improved. The *Dowson* and *Britannia* took advantage of the lull to return to shore. The *Indian*, on the other hand, would have no such respite. That afternoon a boat rowed out from the beach with orders from Colonel Skeene's financial backers in London. Worried that the ship might be impounded, they urged the captain, Mr James Davidson, to 'proceed to sea, be the wind and weather as they might.'[19] Although reports that later surfaced in *The Courier* stated that the *Indian* was not seaworthy, Davidson had little choice but to comply.[20] Until the 6th he made some progress. Then the weather turned again and the ship was buffeted by hurricane-strength winds. For six days and nights the ship rode the storm but on the 13th it was dashed against the rocks 30 miles to the west of Ushant, an island just off the Brittany coast notorious for its 'reefs and half submerged islets … strong tidal streams, fierce currents and frequent fog'.[21] The initial impact would have thrown those on board sprawling across the deck. Caught between the rocks and the raging gale, the ship began to break up a quarter of a mile from the beach.[22] The rigging snapped, the sails tore and the oak beams groaned, splintered and split. The entire bow section was shorn off. Several men dived into the sea and struck out for shore, leaving the women and children to their fate.[23] Drowned or smashed against the rocks, the battered bodies of those they had abandoned were later seen floating amidst the wreckage.

The next morning local fishermen found the beach littered with corpses, and amongst them they discovered shirts marked with the names of captains Mead and Whittam. A small boat had also been washed ashore. Inside were two pigs, thought to be 'the only living creatures' to have survived.[24] The initial reports that all 193 men, women and children had perished proved premature, however. A month later, *The Times* revealed that 11 men had managed to escape in 'an open boat'.[25] After enduring two days at sea, they were picked up and taken to Ireland. One of the survivors was John Johnstone, a Napoleonic veteran who had volunteered for Wilson's 2nd Hussars. Such was his 'ardent desire' to join the patriots that he was not dissuaded by his brush with death.[26] He signed up with a later expedition and would go on to distinguish himself in the war.

In late December, newspaper reports of the tragedy reached the picturesque Cornish village of Fowey, where Colonel Campbell's Rifles had been forced to take shelter earlier in the month. Afraid of returning to sea, several officers resigned and the men rose up in 'daily riot and mutiny'.[27] Campbell was forced to act decisively. Singling out two NCOs by the names of Cobbett and Hunt, he dismissed them from the regiment and had them put ashore in irons. With the ringleaders dealt with, several days of rest and dances soon restored morale. When the winds abated on the morning of 2 January 1818, the Black Rifles boarded the *Dowson* and prepared to depart. Amongst the green-jacketed officers standing on deck was 'little' Lieutenant Thomas Wright.[28] At 19, he was one of the youngest, but also one of the most experienced on board. In 1810, when just 11, he had been sent to Portsmouth to join the Royal Navy. Two years later he set sail for the United States in HMS *Newcastle*, a brand new 60-gun ship of the line. After seeing action under Admiral Borlase Warren in the War of 1812, Wright had been home on leave when he heard the Black Rifles were recruiting. He would survive the war and go on to write his memoirs as an old man living in Ecuador. The book opens with the *Dowson* slipping out of Fowey harbour. Whilst local ladies ran along the cliff tops waving their handkerchiefs to their new-found sweethearts on board, the regimental band struck up the tune 'The Girl I Left Behind Me'.[29] Only a handful of those on the ship would ever see their homeland again.

The Girl I Left Behind Me

I'm lonesome since I crossed the hill,
And o'er the moor and valley,
Such grievous thoughts my heart do fill,
Since parting with my Sally.
I seek no more the fine or gay,
For each does but remind me,
How swift the hours did pass away,
With the girl I left behind me.

Oh, ne'er shall I forget the night
The stars were bright above me,
And gently lent their silvery light,
When first she vowed to love me.
But now I'm bound to Brighton Camp
Kind heaven, then, pray guide me,
And send me safely back again
To the girl I left behind me.[30]

Once underway on the open ocean, the voyage was a tedious affair. Waves lapped against the hull and canvas snapped, suddenly drawn taut by a gust of wind; an all-pervading reek of tar and pitch and the malodorous stench emanating from the livestock in the hold were ever present. Whilst the majority passed the time drinking, gambling or picking fights with their peers, Daniel O'Leary, a highly motivated young man who held the rank of coronet in Wilson's Red Hussars, used the idle hours more productively. Born in Cork in 1802, O'Leary was the eighth of ten children. During the Napoleonic Wars, his father had prospered by supplying the Royal Navy with butter and groceries, but peace and the subsequent recession had ruined him. Looking for a way out of penury, O'Leary had travelled to London in 1817 to join the patriot cause. A rosy-cheeked 5ft 6in tall 16-year old with a mess of curly hair and ruddy complexion, O'Leary was extraordinarily focused for his age. He passed the days aboard the *Prince* buried in Spanish literature and grammar books, determined to master the language before he reached South America.

Whilst the young Irish coronet locked himself away in his cabin and studied, all hell broke loose on deck. Listing dangerously 'to one side like a drunkard', the *Prince* was barely seaworthy and constantly took on water as she limped across the Atlantic.[31] The Hussars were called upon to work the bilge pumps day and night and on more than one occasion, the leaky corvette nearly joined the *Indian* at the bottom of the ocean. Colonel Wilson's 'violent' conduct only exacerbated the situation.[32] Notorious for an explosive temper, he would frequently fly into a rage and lash out at his subordinates at the slightest provocation. By the time they sighted the West Indies, the situation had deteriorated so badly that Captain Nightingale considered diverting from his course 'in search of British legal protection'.[33]

By contrast, the voyage of the 1st Hussars was a well-ordered affair. Very much a believer in doing things by the book, Colonel Hippisley established a regimented daily routine on board the *Emerald*. His memoirs, which were later used by Lord Byron as a soporific, have preserved the minutiae of life aboard ship. 'Reveillé was to sound at daybreak', whereupon 'all the men and women will be turned up on deck.' None were 'to remain below under pretence of sickness' unless their names appeared 'in the surgeon's report'.[34] Breakfast was served at eight and 'dinner' at noon. Smoking was prohibited between decks and 'all lights in the men's berths' had 'to be extinguished at eight o'clock'.[35] Religious services were compulsory and Hippisley's missives regarding cleanliness were equally strict. All had 'to wash their feet … twice a week' and 'the quartermaster-serjeant' was to carry out rigorous inspections of the men's trunks every morning and evening to ensure that 'no dirt or filth' was 'concealed under or behind them'.[36] The colonel also found time to lead his men in drill, prepare them for inter-ship fighting and encourage his officers to practise their sabre skills.

On the *Britannia*, Gillmore's gunners were given target practice with the cannon twice a day, and the men engaged in musket and pistol drill.[37] In the Bay of Biscay they further honed their marksmanship, firing at a 20ft great white shark which followed the ship for two days. After trying and failing to hook the 'monster', the volunteers resorted to their rifles 'whenever he presented his head above water' and although 'the balls … frequently struck him', they had little effect.[38] On the *Dowson*, Campbell's Rifles sighted a sperm whale. Others encountered shoals of flying fish, which 'proved excellent' eating, and one volunteer even landed a 35lb barracuda.[39]

In early August 1817, the *Two Friends* arrived at Funchal Bay, Madeira. Colonel MacDonald's men lowered the boats and headed for shore. Fearing they might be pirates, a shore battery fired a cannon ball across their bows, sending the volunteers racing back to the ship. Customs agents were then sent out to establish their identity. Reassured that they merely wanted to buy provisions, the Lancers were eventually allowed to disembark. As soon as they reached shore the first of many drunken duels commenced. A tall Irish veteran of the 60th Foot squared up to the master's mate. The men paced out the allotted distance in the sand, turned and fired. Both missed and were persuaded to halt before any blood was shed. The men then continued into town and hired mules to tour the interior of the island. According to one observer, the spectacle of these gloriously uniformed cavalrymen winding their way up the hillside mounted on such beasts could not have been 'exceeded in ridiculousness'.[40] Deeply unimpressed by the monasteries, the sightseers later returned to Funchal, where they 'rehearse[d] the dreadful charges they were to make among the enemies of liberty in South America'.[41] Too much drink had dulled their skills in the saddle, however, and farce ensued. Rushing 'down the steep streets at full speed, and suddenly checking their rozinantes, [they] were precipitated from their saddles to the ground, and rose … the objects of derision and contempt, to the astonished population'.[42] Not content with such antics, the volunteers began brawling in the streets and the town guard was deployed to separate them. It was only through the intervention of the resident British consul that the offenders avoided jail. Realizing his men had already overstayed their welcome, MacDonald gave the order to leave. As they sailed out of the bay, one of those on board prophesised 'the islanders of Madeira will long remember the turbulent passengers in the *Two Friends*'.[43] He was later proved correct, to the detriment of those following behind.

Perhaps as he had risen from the ranks, MacDonald seems to have commanded little respect from his officers. To make matters worse, six had stocked up on spirits whilst in Funchal, buying an astonishing 180 gallons between them. For the remainder of the voyage, their 'daily, nay hourly drinking' only added to the chaos on board.[44] Alcohol abuse was the blight of the armed forces throughout the Georgian era. One observer noted that 'no officer was supposed to be fit to command … that was not able to consume three bottles of port or more during dinner'.[45] Both Wellington's soldiers and Nelson's sailors had received regular rations of spirits and the men serving under the six colonels were no exception. Daily allowances of grog varied from a half to a full pint from ship to ship. The ration for officers was even more generous. Those on the *Emerald* enjoyed 'a pint of wine … at dinner, a gill of spirits at supper time and a bottle of porter per diem'.[46] Although some saw drinking as the major social issue of the day, many believed its supposed health benefits outweighed any problems it might cause.[47] Water was often contaminated and spirits were thought to ward off disease as well as having powerful restorative effects. One officer in a later expedition took such beliefs to extremes. He 'laid down a certain regime for himself' which he claimed would keep him fit and healthy:

> At five in the morning [he had] a glass of sling, a glass of grog after, some Toddy at 11 o'clock, Solomon grundy at one, dinner at three o'clock, two tumblers of grog after, a smoke at 5 o'clock, tea at 7, a nip at 8, and a smoke at nine, and then … upon the meeting of the club … four additional tumblers … and yet he swore he would out live us all.[48]

The storm that had sunk the *Indian* caught up with Hippisley's 1st Hussars in the Bay of Biscay, stretching out their voyage to 15 days. Giant waves rolled over the *Emerald*, soaking the seasick passengers and decimating their livestock. Pigs and chickens were drowned below deck or washed overboard. With the winds howling outside, Colonel Hippisley and his officers enjoyed one last drunken feast in the roundhouse:

> We ... sat down to a most excellent dinner; our last pig which had been drowned some days previous ... looked amazingly well on the table, and the whole of the feathered tribe remaining lent their assistance... Our wine was good, and we regaled ourselves with a pint of sherry among three at dinner, and a bottle between two, after.[49]

As well as needing to resupply, Hippisley had a second reason for calling at Madeira. The *Emerald* was carrying a paying passenger, Mr Thomas Cowie, who intended to winter with his aunt who lived on the island. When they arrived at Funchal Bay in early 1818, however, the Portuguese authorities had no intention of allowing them to land. With the exploits of MacDonald's Lancers in mind, the governor ordered his shore batteries to fire a warning shot to dissuade Captain Weatherly from approaching. The cannon ball 'passed between the heads of Major [James Towers] English and the French officer', very nearly bringing the former's role in South American history to a premature close.[50] Despite repeated threats and protests, the Portuguese refused to reconsider their decision. A merchant, who was later allowed to row out with fresh supplies, informed them that the 'dreadful disturbances that took place' five months previously had prompted the prohibition.[51] Cowie was left with no choice but to accompany the Hussars all the way to the West Indies.

Two of Hippisley's officers were promoted after the *Emerald* left the island. Having recovered from his close call with the cannon ball, Major English was made lieutenant-colonel for being 'active and zealous on all occasions' and Captain Trewen was awarded a majority.[52] Not all the officers pleased their colonel, however. One, who remained anonymous in Hippisley's narrative, was tried for theft during the voyage and would later be dismissed from the regiment upon landing. His peers presiding over the court martial begged the colonel not to report the incident to the Venezuelans. Hippisley acceded and the offender went on to join another regiment on arrival. The troop sergeant-major of the Hussars was punished much more severely after being convicted of the same crime. Hippisley had him stripped to the waist, tied to the mast and flogged, a decision which would later return to haunt him.

British officers of the era used flogging to punish a variety of offences, from drunkenness and insubordination to failure to meet required standards on parade.

The severity of the crime was reflected in the number of blows, which could range from 50 to 500. Offenders frequently passed out from the pain and, on occasion, had the flesh flayed from their backs until their ribs were visible. The punishment was so feared that it was not unknown for those convicted to commit suicide. Despite its apparent barbarity, flogging enjoyed widespread support. One captain who had been promoted from the ranks even admitted that he 'was never worth a damn until [he] got 300 lashes'.[53]

After leaving Madeira, the ships entered the open ocean. Cabin fever soon set in and seemingly insignificant quarrels would develop into bitter feuds, occasionally terminating in a duel. One contest, which took place on the *Two Friends* midway across the ocean, was a farcical affair. The protagonists fired a total of six shots with no apparent effect. Unknown to one, their pistols had been loaded with cork pellets rather than lead shot. When the subterfuge was revealed, the victim meekly retired below decks, his ears ringing with the laughter of his comrades. Other duels had far more serious consequences, however, as the account below, relating to a later expedition, testifies:

> A quarrel ensued … which led to a duel … fought on the forecastle … [the loser] received a ball in the chin at the Symphysis, which fractured the jaw; on our arrival … [the duellists] were dismissed [from] the service.[54]

The commander of the expedition was clearly not prepared to tolerate duelling, but many in the military and civil courts alike habitually turned a blind eye to the practice. Although technically against the law, if gentlemen followed the well-established etiquette and there was no suggestion of foul play, they were unlikely to be found guilty. Of 172 duels reported during the 60-year reign of George III, only 18 resulted in trials. The majority of the defendants were acquitted. Seven were found guilty of manslaughter, whilst three were convicted of murder. Of these one later received a royal pardon. Just two were executed.[55]

Midway across the Atlantic, as the ships neared the Equator, their crews performed the Ceremony of Shaving. This initiation rite, which was forced upon those who had never sailed into the southern seas, supposedly bestowed Neptune's protection. In reality, however, it was little more than an excuse for the sailors to extort bribes from wealthy passengers. The ceremony began the night before crossing the line, when a booming voice, purported to be that of Neptune, emanated from the hold:

'What Ship Ahoy?'
The captain replied, whereupon a second question was asked:
'How many children are aboard?'

The number of those to undergo the ritual was given and Neptune then bade them goodnight, warning that he would be back in the morning. On the *Britannia*, his return to the deep was represented by a tarred hog's head which was set on fire and dropped into the brine. Lieutenant Hackett was entranced by the performance. Leaning on the stern rail, he watched the barrel disappear into the night. 'Its flaming appearance, as it occasionally rose upon the bosom of the waves, had a very curious and pleasing effect.'[56]

The next day at noon to a flourish of trumpets, Neptune returned, emerging from the forecastle 'seated … upon a gun-carriage [and] surrounded by a numerous train of Nereides'.[57] Beside him sat Amphitrite his bride, 'most delicately personated by another Jack tar [and] attired with all the elegance that oakum and sailcloth could bestow'.[58] The sailors then demanded their levy. One volunteer escaped 'by paying his godship two quarts of Brandy'. Those who refused were pinned down and roughly shaved with 'an iron hoop hacked like a saw'.[59] On the *Britannia*, the entire ceremony was allegedly performed 'without the slightest deviation from good humour and harmony'.[60] Several officers on the *Dowson*, on the other hand, 'had the skin nearly rasped from their chin'.[61] Matters were even more acrimonious on board the *Two Friends*. When members of the ship's crew advanced across the deck, MacDonald's Lancers drew their pistols and threatened to open fire. Muttering warnings of Neptune's wrath, the sailors were forced to retreat. It would not be long before they had an opportunity to get their revenge.

After a voyage of between 40 and 60 days, the lookouts sighted the Windward Islands of the Caribbean. The *Two Friends* was the first ship to arrive, reaching Saint Thomas's on 24 September 1817. The following year, on 15 January, the *Emerald* passed Antigua and on the 22nd, the *Britannia* sighted Barbuda. The *Prince* was next and the arrival of the *Dowson* on 18 February completed the first wave of volunteers. It would still be several months before they reached Bolívar's forces in the Venezuelan interior, however. In the interim, hundreds would desert, resign or perish. Only the strongest and most resolute would reach the republican capital alive.

Chapter 3

'A FEW BANDS OF ITINERANT FREEBOOTERS'

Leaving the trials of the Atlantic Ocean behind them, the volunteers crossed into the eastern Caribbean, one of the most beautiful stretches of water in the world, studded with a 500-mile chain of picturesque islands, ranging from Puerto Rico in the far north to Trinidad, the largest of the group, lying just ten miles north-east of the Venezuelan mainland. Framed by bountiful reefs and beaches, these verdant gems rose from the sea, their forested slopes crowned by volcanic peaks. Amongst this beauty, a low-level, largely political conflict driven by spies and propaganda had been smouldering throughout the region since the formation of Miranda's First Republic in 1810. This cold war was regularly ignited by savage attacks on shipping by the Spanish or republican navies, or the swarms of privateers that plagued the area. The Spanish fleet was based between Puerto Cabello and Cumaná, fortified ports to the west and east of Caracas; Güiria, a secondary naval base on the Gulf of Paria that guarded the entrance of the Orinoco; and the island ports of Havana in Cuba and Santa Cruz in Puerto Rico. By 1817, however, Spain's once great navy was a shadow of its former self, and as most of the armed vessels were busy protecting merchant shipping, the royalists were rarely able to take the offensive. By contrast, the patriot commander Admiral Luis Brion had fewer merchantmen to protect and was better able to concentrate his fleet for attack.

'A creole … rather advanced in years, of a commanding and stern deportment, dark penetrating eyes, and remarkably long black mustachios',[1] Brion was a veteran of both land and sea actions, and had fought on two continents. Born in 1782 on the Dutch controlled island of Curaçao, he had been sent to Holland at the age of 12 to complete his education, and became involved in the Franco-Dutch War against the British and

Russian fleets. Captured by the British shortly after the outbreak of hostilities, he remained in custody until the end of the war. Upon his return to Curaçao, the British were threatening to occupy the island as part of an ongoing Caribbean expansion, which saw them acquire Trinidad in 1797. Brion took up arms, fighting in several engagements before Curaçao finally capitulated in 1807. Forced to flee, he settled on the island of Saint Thomas's, where he set up a lucrative trading company prior to joining the republican cause in Venezuela in 1813. An experienced entrepreneur, he negotiated a deal with Bolívar that allowed him to keep the lion's share of any prizes he captured, providing he financed the fleet himself. Motivated by plunder rather than ideals, Brion was considered by many, including the British authorities, as little more than a legalized pirate. His ships regularly prowled the Spanish Main (the Caribbean coastline of South America) for merchantmen and any royalists they captured would be put to the sword. Brion's primary role, however, was to hold open the trade route from the British islands in the Caribbean up the Orinoco to Angostura. Without this lifeline, the Third Republic would be unable to survive.

Although supposedly under patriot command, the swarms of privateers (based out of lawless backwaters such as the Island of Amelia, off the east coast of Florida, and San Andres, near Panama) were in reality a law unto themselves and posed a threat to all merchant shipping. Crewed by a myriad of nations, including British deserters from the Royal Navy, the privateers sailed between neutral ports, flying whichever flag would lull their chosen prey into a false sense of security. As they opened fire, the republican banners of Venezuela, Mexico and Buenos Aires were unfurled to add a veneer of legality to their depredations. The strongest naval power in the Caribbean in the 19th century was the Royal Navy. Several armed frigates, schooners and sloops operated out of Jamaica, Trinidad and Grenada. Although he had no sanction to interfere in the war between Spain and her breakaway colonies, the British commander, Admiral Sir Home Popham, often acted as if his role was to police the entire region. Similarly, Sir Ralph Woodford, the belligerent governor of Trinidad, ensured that the rule of law applied to His Majesty's subjects regardless of their political persuasion.

Seeking news of the situation in Venezuela and nervous of landing at a British colony following Westminster's edicts, the five remaining colonels (Hippisley, Campbell, MacDonald, Wilson and Gillmore) had arranged to rendezvous at either the Danish-controlled island of Saint Thomas's, or Saint Bartholomew's (Saint Bart's), the sole Swedish possession in the Caribbean. As both were neutral, the colonels had assumed that they would provide safe haven whilst they recovered from the voyage and considered their next move. The *Two Friends*, carrying Donald MacDonald and the 1st Venezuelan Lancers, sailed into Saint Thomas's at noon on 24 September 1817.

Built upon the flanks of three conical hills whose summits were topped with fortresses, Charlotte Amalie was a bustling free port. The cobbled streets were alive with traders hawking goods and the horseshoe-shaped harbour was crowded with shipping. As few crops were grown in the arid soil, the governor was reliant on the nearby Spanish colony of San Juan on Puerto Rico for provisions. This dependence interfered with his purported neutrality, as MacDonald was about to discover.

Although the colonels had agreed to maintain a low profile, in his excitement MacDonald threw caution to the wind. The Lancers landed in full uniform. Sweating furiously in the midday sun, they attracted considerable attention. After settling in at a local tavern, MacDonald began boasting of his command. Passers-by stopped to listen to the booming Scot, who claimed his expedition had the official backing of the British government. Word of their arrival spread quickly. Soon the Danish governor requested an audience with MacDonald and asked to see evidence of Westminster's consent. When the Scot was unable to produce any documentation, the governor, caught between his country's official neutrality and his desire not to upset his suppliers, dispatched a schooner to San Juan for instructions on how to proceed.

Ignorant of the governor's decision, the Lancers sought out reports of the situation in Venezuela. What they were told did little to inspire confidence. As the official newspaper of the republic, the *Orinoco Gazette*, would not be launched for another year, the only source of information was the Spanish press on nearby Puerto Rico and the propaganda spread by royalist agents in town. The latter claimed that the independence movement consisted solely of 'a few bands of itinerant freebooters'[2] and that its leaders ruled over their impoverished troops with the 'authority of despots'.[3] These sentiments were echoed in reports heard by colonels Hippisley, Wilson, Gillmore and Campbell when they arrived at Saint Bartholomew's in early 1818. Surgeon Robinson wrote of 'dreadful accounts' emanating from the Main.[4] Lieutenant Hackett was told of the 'indiscriminate massacre of prisoners' and Mr Ritchie, the supercargo on board the *Britannia*, was informed that the patriot troops subsisted on mule flesh and fruit and were herded into battle armed only with clubs and knives.[5]

In fact the royalist propaganda was surprisingly accurate. Although the patriots were firmly established along the Orinoco and controlled the island of Margarita, their territory provided little in the way of profit or provisions. The royalists, on the other hand, held neighbouring New Granada, by far the wealthiest of their possessions in northern South America, and also controlled the most densely populated and economically important areas of Venezuela. Studded with plantations, the Caribbean coastline and the fertile valleys of Aragua produced most of the country's food and boasted lucrative harvests of sugar cane, tobacco and chocolate. The cities provided plenty of recruits for the army and the cash crops filled their coffers with coin. To the south of the loyalist Caribbean coastline and to the west of the patriot-held stretches of the mid and lower Orinoco, lay the vast inland plains of Los Llanos, a hotly contested buffer zone. Whilst the royalists controlled many of the region's sparsely spread towns and villages, the countryside belonged to patriot guerrillas. Although these light troops were highly effective at skirmishing and ambush, it was poorly equipped conscripts who formed the bulk of Bolívar's army. They were rarely paid and often lacked rations. In contrast, their opponents enjoyed better leadership and were superior in both training and arms. To make matters worse, the conquest of Angostura had not been as profitable as The Liberator had hoped. As the five colonels arrived in the Caribbean, the Third Republic was close to collapse.

Despite these reports, many of the British volunteers initially enjoyed their time on Saint Bartholomew's and got on well with their Swedish hosts. Hippisley's officers, the first to arrive, were honoured with a reception at the governor's house and a tour of the island's fortifications. Two weeks later, after Wilson's *Prince* and Gillmore's *Britannia* had dropped anchor, Governor Rosenvard invited them to celebrate the Crown Prince of Sweden's birthday at Government House. As a band played 'God Save the King', Gillmore and Wilson entered, their uniforms festooned with glittering medals, which Hippisley sarcastically noted must have been 'received … from some unknown Prince or Monarch since their departure from England'.[6] Afterwards 'a very elegant supper was [then] displayed, composed of the richest and most delicate produce of the West Indies'.[7] Following the meal, Rosenvard offered a toast to the King of England. In return, Colonel Wilson 'proposed the memory of Charles the Twelfth, the recollection of which [was] particularly flattering to the vanity of a Swede'.[8] Dancing and more drinking followed. The governor partnered Maria Graham, the beautiful young major's wife who had turned heads on the *Prince*. The revellers did not retire until 3.00am.

During their time on the islands, the volunteers began to explore. Trudging inland through dense tropical rainforest, they came across the sugar plantations that made the colonies so profitable. For many this was their first encounter with slavery, an issue that split public opinion in Britain in the early 19th century. Although the practice would not be outlawed throughout the Empire until 1833, Granville Sharpe and William Wilberforce, pioneers of London's fashionable abolition movement, had already achieved a notable victory when, in 1807, trading in slaves had been banned. Influenced by such enlightened figures, many volunteers were appalled. Lieutenant Hackett, for one, thought the practice 'abhorrent to nature and humanity'.[9] Although sympathetic to their plight, it is also important to note that the volunteers, perhaps without exception, regarded the blacks as inferior. After stumbling across a 'Negro dance' one Sunday, the Black Rifles' surgeon, James Robinson, recorded their traditional chants in his journal in terms that a modern-day natural historian might use to describe an animal's mating call. Their singing, although 'far from … unpleasant', had a 'wild air' and was accompanied by a 'general howl set up by the women'.[10] This ability to profess disgust at the way the blacks were treated, whilst at the same time viewing them as somehow subhuman, was typical of the double standards of Georgian Britain and would be mirrored when the volunteers encountered indigenous Americans on the Spanish Main.

After several idle weeks on the islands, with the dispiriting rumours about Venezuela continuing to circulate, the volunteers' morale went into decline. Many sought consolation from the bottle. Duels invariably followed, the officers' aim now much improved with their feet firmly planted on dry land. On Saint Thomas's, several 'trifling misunderstandings' resulted in challenges, one of which ended with the death of the 1st Lancers' 'best' officer, a Napoleonic naval captain who had spent several years as a prisoner of war in Verdun.[11] To make matters worse, the victor, along with both seconds, 'found it expedient to leave the island speedily and secretly' when the Danish governor hinted that otherwise 'he should be obliged to take serious notice of the occurrence'.[12] On Saint Bartholomew's, the situation was not helped by continued squabbling amongst the colonels. Lieutenant Hackett thought them 'influenced solely by an anxiety for personal precedency' and Colonel Gillmore himself admitted that their 'misconduct … was, in a great measure, the cause of many officers' disillusionment'.[13] The worst offender was Colonel Wilson, whose increasingly volatile behaviour plumbed new depths of absurdity with the arrival of a Spanish merchantman in Gustavia Bay.

Richly laden with a cargo of wine, brandy, oil and spices bound for Cádiz, the merchantman made a tempting target for the many privateers in town, one of whom approached Wilson with a proposition. His ego flattered, the colonel agreed to seize the ship with a few other volunteers. All went well until the night before the raid, when they were overheard discussing their plan in a local tavern. The news soon reached the governor and the would-be boarding party were arrested en route to the docks, heavily armed and with their faces blacked out with soot. Although they were soon released, Wilson's actions proved the final straw for many of his officers. Along with several others, his long-suffering second, Major Graham, transferred into Campbell's Rifles. Others gave up on the idea of serving the patriots altogether.

This fragmentation occurred throughout the volunteer units. As the smallest, Colonel Gillmore's artillery regiment was the worst affected and, within a few weeks of arrival at Saint Bartholomew's, it had virtually ceased to exist. Believing his command would no longer function as a fighting unit, Gillmore disbanded those that remained. The colonel, along with Lieutenant Charles Brown and 19 others, transferred to Campbell's Rifles. The rest either joined British Army regiments in the Caribbean or sailed to North America to start new lives. The 1st Lancers split due to the actions of their supercargo and ship's captain, Cornelius Ryan, whose sole concern was to sell the goods he had brought out from London. Having been contracted to take the Lancers to either Margarita or Angostura, Ryan reneged on the agreement shortly after their arrival at Saint Thomas's. As Colonel MacDonald, Lieutenant Vowell and 22 others were enjoying a regular morning walk around the hills overlooking Charlotte Amalie Bay, the captain upped anchor and stole off, taking 30 of the Lancers with him. Vowell was despondent as he watched the ship sail away.[14] Having harboured a grudge against MacDonald ever since loaning him money back in Portsmouth, Ryan had finally got his revenge. Steering due south he made for the island of Margarita, a patriot stronghold just off the Venezuelan mainland, where he hoped to sell his cargo before returning home.

When the *Two Friends* arrived at Margarita, the island was in turmoil. The stores were nearly empty and 'salt fish and plantains' were all that could be spared.[15] To make matters worse, the governor, General Arismendi, refused to honour the Lancers' contracts as he already had more officers than he needed. Impatient as ever, Ryan did not wait for matters to improve. Boarding a ship bound for Angostura, where he hoped to sell the cargo he had brought out from England, once more he abandoned his companions to their fate. Many resigned their commissions and 'dispersed themselves amongst the different islands, and in the United States'.[16] Those that remained rapidly grew disenchanted with the service. After they had committed various, and no doubt alcohol-fuelled 'excesses', Arismendi had them thrown into jail, then proceeded to strip the *Two Friends* of her cannon and take the supplies on board for his own men.[17] Led by Captain Thomas Dundas, a veteran of the British Army who had served in Sicily, France, Spain and the United States, the remaining Lancers broke out of jail, crept aboard the *Two Friends* and fled the island, hurried on their way by cannon fire from the shore batteries.[18] After sailing to Santo Domingo, Dundas eventually found his way back to London. Surprisingly, he would later re-enlist with Mendéz and return to the Main.[19]

Meanwhile back on Saint Thomas's, the governor's schooner had returned from Santa Cruz. The Danes' Spanish suppliers had made it clear that they were jeopardizing their arrangement by harbouring the volunteers and the governor ordered MacDonald to leave. Borrowing from Vowell, whose £2,000 inheritance was rapidly dwindling, the colonel brought passage for his 22 men on board the *Mary*, an American schooner heading north to Amelia, a small island off the east coast of Florida which was under patriot control. There they hoped to join a unit led by Gregor MacGregor, a Scottish adventurer who held the rank of brigadier general in the patriot army. A veteran of the Napoleonic Wars, MacGregor had joined the cause in 1811 and had seen action in both New Granada and Venezuela before an argument with a senior officer (General Manuel Piar) had led to his disillusionment with Bolívar's men. In 1817 he had sailed to the United States to raise troops, and captured Amelia from the Spanish after an audacious surprise attack. Whilst in London, Colonel MacDonald had been given a letter of introduction to MacGregor and decided that the journey to Amelia would be less perilous than that to Angostura. Nevertheless, the voyage proved a difficult one. Extremely short on rations, the Lancers survived by eating dolphin and sharks caught en route. After a passage of nine days, they arrived on 25 October 1817.[20]

All was confusion on Amelia. The day before MacDonald's arrival, MacGregor had returned to Britain to recruit men for a raid on the New Granadan coastline, leaving his deputy, Commodore Aury, in command.[21] A French-born buccaneer who lacked his chief's charisma, Aury was struggling to control the privateer crews stationed on the island. With MacGregor away in Europe, they spent their days drunk on the proceeds of their 'liberated' booty. Vowell noted that 'almost every second building ... was a liquor shop and dancing house; and the excessive cheapness of wine, and spirits of all kinds ... kept the place in one continued uproar'.[22] Having missed MacGregor, the Lancers were directionless once more. Morale suffered and resignations followed. Seeing his command continue to crumble, MacDonald was left with just one option, to head for Angostura without delay. Once again he was reliant on Vowell's diminishing fortune to finance the journey.[23] After striking a deal with a ship's captain, the 18 volunteers endured a treacherous passage south to Grenada. There they boarded a patriot barque, *La Felicité*, whose French captain was glad to have protection for the voyage ahead. A fast ship, *La Felicité* made rapid progress and the Lancers reached the mouth of the Orinoco in January 1818.

Meanwhile, a few hundred miles to the north-west, the warm welcome the rest of the volunteers had been enjoying on Saint Bartholomew's was also beginning to turn sour. Following Wilson's laughable attempt at piracy, Governor Rosenvard 'prohibited several ... officers from ... proceeding on shore' and posted 'sentries upon the beach ... [to enforce] his commands'.[24] With their privileges removed, the colonels determined to push on for the Spanish Main without delay.[25] Hippisley's Hussars were the first to leave, heading for Grenada at the end of January 1818. The 58 officers and

NCOs remaining with Colonel Wilson followed shortly after in the *Prince*, and on 21 February the remainder under colonels Campbell and Gillmore left on the *Dowson*.[26] The officers that had resigned remained behind. Those who could afford it bought passage back to England. Others were stranded in the Caribbean for several months. They were soon reduced to selling their clothes and possessions in exchange for food and lodging. After these funds had dried up, they took to 'walking about the streets', sleeping rough and begging in order to survive.[27] Several died of the illnesses that scoured the region. Some eventually found work as slave drivers or pickers on local plantations, while others bought passage to the United States (which was considerably cheaper than sailing to England) or joined the many privateers that were constantly seeking replacement crew.

The *Emerald*, carrying Hippisley's 1st Hussars, reached Saint George's, the capital of Grenada, in February 1818. Upon landing, the colonel ordered his men to maintain a low profile. His plans for anonymity were scuppered, however, when their arrival was announced in the *Grenada Gazette*. On discovering their intentions, the governor informed the volunteers that as their expedition was outside the boundaries of British law, they were under no compulsion to remain with the regiment; they were free to leave, with the legal cancellation of any debts they might have incurred. The officers were offered free passage home on British ships and the NCOs were told they could find work on the island. Although Hippisley and several patriot agents in Saint George's urged them not to, five officers and 40 NCOs accepted the offer.[28] To make matters worse, on the morning of 10 February 1818, a duel took place involving Captain Gustavus Butler Hippisley, the colonel's eldest son. Two nights before, he had drunkenly quarrelled with a fellow officer, Lieutenant Braybrooke, over the alleged theft of the latter's cloak. Waking the next morning, the protagonists seemed to realize the absurdity of the situation. Hippisley sought out Braybrooke to apologize and his would-be adversary 'accepted [his] extended hand'.[29] Thinking the matter closed, the captain was shocked to receive a note from Braybrooke later that day demanding satisfaction. As Hippisley's honour would not permit a second apology, the duel took place in a secluded spot the next morning. Watched by their seconds and the unit's surgeons, the two men paced out the distance and fired. Their first shots missed. The guns were reloaded and the men took aim once more. On the second fire, Braybrooke was hit and he died shortly afterwards.[30] When the governor heard of the killing, he put a bounty of £100 on Hippisley's head, forcing him to remain in hiding for the duration of the Hussars' stay on the island.[31] During daylight hours he rowed offshore, waiting in the blistering sun until dark, before returning to sleep in a squalid slave hut on the outskirts of town.

As Captain Weatherly refused to take the *Emerald* any further, Hippisley divided the remaining men between two chartered schooners, whose shallow berths would allow them to proceed up the Orinoco. The first contingent, comprising two lieutenants and 18 NCOs under Lieutenant-Colonel English, would travel with the heavy baggage on the *Liberty*. Hippisley and the rest would follow on the *Republican*. Just as the *Liberty* was about to depart, however, George G. Munro, the chief judge on Grenada, ordered Hippisley's arrest on two charges: firstly, for breaching the Prince Regent's proclamation and, secondly, for his illegal use of the lash on the passage out.[32] The case never got to court, however. The charges were dropped and Lieutenant-Colonel English's detachment set sail shortly afterwards.

The volunteers under Wilson and Campbell received similar treatment from the authorities on Grenada. The *Prince* was seized under 'some pretence or other' and the men were offered incentives to resign.[33] An editorial published in *The Times* later that year revealed that British ships suspected of carrying gunpowder or recruits were also detained in Saint Kitt's. It seems that a coordinated policy was in place throughout the region.[34] Although several British governors, particularly Sir Ralph Woodford in Trinidad, were highly zealous in enforcing this policy, all seizures were eventually overruled by London.[35] Despite the government's official stance, it was clear that powerful figures in Westminster were determined that the volunteers and their belligerent cargoes would reach their destination intact.

The majority of the volunteers who had not resigned or succumbed to disease eventually ended up in Port of Spain, Trinidad. Situated on a sweeping, sandy bay, backed by palm trees, the town made a convenient jumping off point for the Venezuelan mainland, which was clearly visible just ten miles away across the Gulf of Paria. Since 1808, when fire had devastated the town, it had been extensively rebuilt by the British governor, Sir Ralph Woodford, and was now one of the most impressive colonies in the British Caribbean. The wealth that had paid for the wide streets, public buildings and whitewashed houses had been reaped from a lucrative but illegal trade with Venezuela. Since 1817, when Bolívar had established his base of operations in Angostura, the business had reached new heights. Smugglers from the island and nearby Grenada supplied the patriots with arms and ammunition in exchange for mules and cattle, which fetched excellent prices in the colonies. This trade had not escaped the attention of the Spanish authorities and their privateers and gunboats regularly patrolled the gulf, boarding any ships they considered suspicious. The most infamous gunboat commander was a Creole named Captain Gabozo. Renowned for his 'savage and inhuman barbarity', Gabozo harboured a particularly vehement hatred of the British.[36]

Throughout 1818, letters appeared in the English and Irish press detailing the volunteers' attempts to slip past the blockade with varying degrees of success. Some were blissfully unaware of the danger and sailed across the gulf without incident. Others were intercepted but managed to escape with their lives. One report, written in Trinidad on 20 June 1818, claimed that two out of three boats to sail for Angostura that week were pursued. Forced to run the ships aground, the crews took cover in the jungle. The royalists followed brandishing cutlasses but, having already secured the prizes, were discouraged from further pursuit by a few scattered shots. Other volunteers were even less fortunate. Lieutenants Harris and Watson, for example, were captured by Cipriani Oroco, one of Gabozo's colleagues, whilst sailing up a small estuary near the Orinoco.[37] After forcing them to strip, Oroco bound their hands, 'drew his knife and stabbed them'. Still alive, they fell into the water. 'While struggling therein … [Oroco] took his lance, and run them through the body.'[38] Despite their fearsome reputation, the Spanish gunboats mounted only one or two cannon and therefore only posed a threat to civilian shipping or small groups of lightly armed men. Most of the volunteer detachments were not even threatened whilst sailing across the gulf. MacDonald and the 23 volunteers on *La Felicité*, John Needham's 11 men, English's advance guard, and Wilson and Hippisley's Hussars all crossed without incident, reaching the mouth of the Orinoco between December 1817 and March the following year.

The only significant group of volunteers remaining in the Caribbean by mid-1818 were those commanded by colonels Campbell and Gillmore. Roughly numbering 150, they had returned to Saint Bartholomew's after reaching Grenada, where they met Luis Brion, Admiral of the Venezuelan fleet, on 14 April 1818. After persuading the colonels to join him with fictitious reports of the capture of Caracas, Brion negotiated the purchase of the supplies their supercargoes had brought out from England.[39] As the republic's coffers were empty, he gave them credit notes which he promised would be reimbursed by January 1819.[40] With the only alternative being to return to England empty handed, the supercargoes had little choice but to accept. Having secured the arms, powder and uniforms so desperately needed, Brion and the volunteers set sail on a tour of the southern Caribbean to round up any stragglers before making for Angostura.

The patriot fleet comprised eight armed ships, ranging from the six-gun, 50-man *Guerrière* to the 24-gun flagship, the *Victoria*. Formerly known as the *Emerald*, this was the same ship that had carried the 1st Hussars to the New World. Her supercargo, James Mackintosh, had met Brion at the mouth of the Orinoco and arranged the sale. As the fleet set sail from Saint Bartholomew's, the *Victoria* was commanded by Captain

Cowie, the passenger who had sailed out with Hippisley's 1st Hussars intending to spend the winter on Madeira with his aunt. The majority of Brion's captains and crew were also British, many of them veterans who had served in the Royal Navy during the recent war against France.

The time the volunteers spent with the fleet was anything but uneventful. Cruising the Caribbean, they stopped at Mona Island amongst others, collecting supplies and picking up volunteers who had previously been left behind. Later, the fleet was in Margarita at the same time as the North American ambassador, John Baptist Irvine, who was on a mission to establish diplomatic relations with the new republic. On arriving at the port of Juan Griego, the Americans were greeted by a large crowd, including Governor Arismendi, Admiral Brion and several British volunteers. To the delight of the travelling dignitaries, the Black Rifles' band immediately struck up 'Yankie Doodle' whilst 'a salute was fired from the batteries' around the bay.[41] On another occasion, when passing Barbados, the fleet was pursued by the *Brazen*, a British sloop of war, whose captain had been ordered to detain the volunteers for breaking the Prince Regent's proclamation. Brion threatened to open fire and although the British had privately agreed not to fight their own countrymen, the *Brazen*'s captain, Mr Stirling, dared not call his bluff. After a four-hour standoff, the fleet was allowed to continue on its way. A few days later they were chased by the Spanish. Finding himself out-gunned, with 87 cannon to the royalists' 144, Brion ordered his crews to put on all sail. To the relief of everyone on board, they eventually lost their pursuers. Later still, after the fleet had left the Five Islands, a plot led by nine British sailors to murder Brion and his officers and surrender the ships in a royalist port was uncovered. On hearing of the plan, Captain Cowie 'piped all hands upon deck, and began to single out the suspected mutineers, two of whom … rushed through the guard of marines, and throwing themselves overboard were drowned'.[42] The rest were sentenced to hang. But as the nooses were placed round their necks, Brion reduced their punishment to 'condemnation to the gunboats in the Orinoco for two years', a sentence which Lieutenant Brown thought 'infinitely worse than death'.[43] Following the attempted mutiny, yellow fever broke out. Duncan Campbell, the eldest son of the founder of the Black Rifles, was one of the first taken ill. In deference to Colonel Campbell, Brion anchored off the island of San Martín and allowed the lad to be taken ashore in the hope that he would recover. Despite the best attentions of the Black Rifles' doctor, however, the 18-year old passed away on 23 June and was buried at the church in the Great Bay.[44] His death proved the final straw for his father, who resigned his commission and returned to England with his surviving son. Now led by Lieutenant-Colonel Piggot with Captain Sandes as second in command, the remaining Rifles and artillerymen reached the mouth of the Orinoco towards the end of August 1818.

Of the 800 volunteers who had embarked from London and Brussels, only 300 remained. A total of 182 had drowned off Ushant. Fever, resignations and desertions accounted for the rest.[45] On the final leg of their journey to Angostura, disease, alligator attacks and Indian raids would reduce their numbers even further. Only a quarter of those who had set out would reach the capital alive.

PART TWO

INTO THE HEART OF DARKNESS
1818–1819

… we crawled very slow[ly upriver]. The reaches opened before us and closed behind, as if the forest had stepped leisurely across the water to bar the way for our return. We penetrated deeper and deeper into the heart of darkness… We were wanderers on a prehistoric earth, on an earth that wore the aspect of an unknown planet. We could have fancied ourselves the first of men.

Joseph Conrad – Heart of Darkness

Chapter 4

'THE VAST HOWLING WILDERNESS'

A t 1,500 miles long, the Orinoco is South America's second largest river. Rising in the rugged mountains of the Serra Parima on the border with Brazil, it cascades down to the grasslands of Los Llanos. Slowing and swelling, the river snakes through this featureless landscape for over 1,000 miles, then enters rolling, wooded country, framed by distant mountain peaks. After passing the city of Angostura, the land flattens and the woods give way to impenetrable rainforest. Some 300 miles later, along twisting, overgrown waterways lies a maze of channels and lakes that forms the Amacuro Delta, from where the Orinoco spills its muddy waters into the Gulf of Paria and the Caribbean Sea beyond.

When still 20 miles offshore, and before the low-lying land was even visible, the volunteers encountered a huge sand bar crested by a wave that stretched to the horizon. Built by fluvial deposits over the millennia, the bar formed a giant arc around the Amacuro Delta, denying access to ships that drew more than 16ft of water. When the *Tiger* carrying Hippisley's Hussars arrived in March 1818, the wind was against them. For a week they were held in position. The sensation of surfing on the swell was 'most sickening' and the colonel was delighted when the winds changed and carried them over the bar.[1] At first only a shimmering heat vapour rising from the rainforest indicated the land ahead, but gradually a vast green panorama emerged.[2]

The Amacuro Delta is labyrinthine. As many channels are unnavigable and others are dead ends, the volunteers who arrived unguided spent several days finding the correct entrance. Most, however, carried local pilots who soon steered them towards the yawning, five-mile-wide mouth. Lieutenant Alexander thought it a spectacular sight:

> The breadth of the river, the stately trees that grow on its banks, down to the water's edge,
> even dipping their branches in the stream, and the beautiful little islands that stud its surface

here and there, are all on a scale for which we look in vain in European latitudes. Monkeys, birds and beasts abound upon its banks, while the unwieldy alligator at times rears his scaly tree like form.[3]

Navigating into the mouth was a treacherous business. Giant boulders carried downstream amidst the boiling outflow could hole a ship's hull and there was also a strong tidal current. On *La Felicité*, Vowell noted that the water, dark with 'thick oozy mud', was flowing against them at 4mph.[4] Some captains ordered the volunteers to tie ropes to the trees and bodily haul the ships onwards. Others anchored and waited for the wind to turn. The first landmark they saw was Pilot Island, where a resident Indian would offer to lead travellers up-river for a silver peso.[5] When Hippisley's Hussars passed, his hut was empty, leaving them no choice but to proceed unguided. The *Tiger*'s captain, Mr Hill, was most put out and vented his anger 'by firing a four-pounder shot through the side of the hut as … [they] sailed along'.[6]

Brion's fleet reached Pilot Island three months later in July. Forced to abandon their ships due to the shallowness of the river, the admiral and his sailors continued on two gunboats that had been awaiting their arrival. A second party, under Lieutenant-Colonel Piggot, made up from the remnants of the Rifle regiment and bolstered by some of Gillmore's artillery brigade, followed on two small brigs, the *Spartan* and the *Favourite*. As not all could fit on board, several volunteers (including those who were sick) were left behind to guard the ships until Brion's return. After setting up the cannon in defensive positions onshore, they built temporary huts then grounded the smaller boats to scrub their hulls clean.

Yellow fever, commonly known as the 'black vomit', claimed several victims as the volunteers continued up-river.[7] Major Graham was one of the first to die. His body was unceremoniously dumped overboard, leaving his 'lovely' wife Maria widowed before they had even seen the enemy.[8] A British sailor on the *Spartan*, also with Brion's flotilla, was lost under more unusual circumstances. Whilst fishing off the bow, he hooked 'a monster' and was pulled into the water. Standing nearby, Lieutenant-Colonel Piggot raised the alarm, but although 'his hat and pocket-book floated on the surface in about three minutes … no traces were to be seen of his body'.[9] The ship's captain, a seasoned traveller on the river, hypothesized that he had been taken by a giant crocodile.

As the sun sank beneath the trees, the boats anchored close in to the bank for their first night on the river. After dark the jungle came alive. 'The hissing of the water-serpent … the howling of the beasts [and] the splashing … from the alligators' rendered sleep nigh on impossible.[10] Huddled together on deck, the volunteers chain-smoked cigars to ward off the clouds of mosquitoes that plagued them. After knocking back some 'execrably bad gin', Surgeon Robinson was one of the few who managed to doze off.[11] Awaking later with a fuzzy head, he found himself covered in a 'mass of small blisters, from the millions of bites ... [he] had received during the night'.[12] Nevertheless, first light brought a tremendous sense of relief. Lieutenant Brown recalled that 'never was a reprieve more welcome to a poor wretch at the gallows, than the return of day to us'.[13]

The climate was equally oppressive. The smaller boats afforded little shade, the sun was unrelenting and the humidity intense. At midday, the skies would unleash a downpour, leaving the volunteers shivering and vulnerable to fever. Also common, particularly in the rainy season, were violent storms that turned the normally placid waters into 'an agitated sea'.[14] Whipped up by fierce gales, waves crashed over the gunnels and threatened to overturn the boats. Other days were still and stifling. The strength of the current and lack of wind meant progress up-river was painfully slow. Not allowing for such delays, some captains had not taken enough food. Many volunteers survived on nothing more than biscuits and beef, which they hung from the masts to dry. As the days passed, the meat became infested and maggots rained down on deck. Unsurprisingly, the majority of the British officers loathed the region. For Major Milligan it was 'a swampy forest ... with a huge muddy drain running through the middle ... full of snakes, jaguars, and alligators' and inhabited by 'a sprinkling of wretched human savages, who think ant paste a luxury'.[15] Others, however, could overlook the hardships and were entranced by the exotic wildlife, none more so than Lieutenant Richard Vowell. The Englishman recorded all he saw in great detail. 'Huge water snakes ... lurk[ed] in the swamps', while 'monkeys follow[ed] the vessel, springing from tree to tree' and 'parrots and macaws ... tucans and other birds of beautiful plumage' completed the 'splendid picture'.[16] Those less disposed to natural history hunted the animals to supplement their meagre rations. Surgeon Robinson, for example, was delighted to bag 'a large red monkey', weighing 'about 20 or 25 pounds'. After boiling it for dinner, he shared the meat with his companions.[17]

After a few days on the river, the volunteers encountered the local Indians. Known as *Warao* (boat people), these hunter-gatherers had dominated the delta long before the arrival of the Spanish in the 16th century, but had since been subjected to a virtual serfdom by the Creole elite of Caracas. Living in riverside huts on stilts to avoid the seasonal flooding, they hunted fish and turtles from dugout canoes. Initial meetings with the volunteers were tense affairs. When MacDonald's 1st Lancers saw a flotilla of canoes paddling towards them 'out of the neighbouring creeks ... [they] were at first apprehensive, but soon found their visitors were merely attracted by curiosity'.[18] Encounters usually led to mutually beneficial trade. In exchange for clothes or coins, the volunteers bought fish, maize and fruit. Each group was equally fascinated by the other.

Robinson noted that some were 'painted all over … with a sort of red nut'. Others 'had their heads decorated with a rude garland, formed of parrot feathers'.[19] The enlightened Vowell thought them 'fine looking, tall' and 'muscular', whilst Lieutenant Brown observed with contempt that both sexes were 'entirely naked'.[20] Many had 'their arms and legs … bound round with string made of the fibres of the cocoa tree', a custom which caused the limbs to swell and produced 'a very singular appearance'.[21]

Continuing up-river, the volunteers came to Sacópano and Barancas, former Catholic missions surrounded by forested hills, which reminded one homesick major of County Wicklow.[22] Each had 'about two hundred [Indian] inhabitants', living in crude huts 'covered with the plantain and cocoa leaf'.[23] Several Creole merchants were also resident. Engaged in a lively trade smuggling goods to Trinidad and Grenada, they enjoyed a far higher standard of living. Some even possessed 'comfortable furniture, and domestic appliances'.[24] After reprovisioning, the British troops embarked and eventually reached Old Guyana (Ciudad Guayana) having spent between four and 21 days on the river.

Built on raised ground at a bend in the river, the town had been captured by the patriots shortly before MacDonald's Lancers arrived in January 1818. All 300 defenders had been slaughtered. To Lieutenant Vowell's disgust, their putrefying remains were still scattered around town.[25] In the centre were 40 thatched, red houses belonging to the richer Creole residents, and several small stores where 'rum, poor claret, bad Madeira, chocolate, coffee' and tobacco were available.[26] Further inland stood a warehouse used for drying beef, the stench of which was all-pervading. Together with a prison and barracks, it was built around the main square. On the outskirts were 200 simple wooden huts inhabited by *Warao* Indians. To the north-west, on a hill overlooking the river and only accessible by ladder, stood Fort Raphael, its stone walls mounted by six 12-pdrs. A second battery protected by earthen ramparts was situated on a neighbouring summit. Although they approved of the defensive strength of the position, the volunteers were less impressed with the town's 200-strong garrison. The majority were only '13 or 14 years of age, and tottering under the weight of their muskets'. Lieutenant Brown noted that 'principally blacks', many had 'only a piece of linen round the loins'.[27] Others wore uniforms brought out from London on the *Hunter*, bearing the same motto of 'Vencer o Morir' as used by the British volunteers. Brown thought it not 'at all well calculated for such a wretched looking set of beings'.[28]

Several volunteers noted that for an ostensibly Catholic country, there were surprisingly few priests in Old Guyana. As Lieutenant Brown surmised, this was due to an unofficial patriot policy of extermination. In the early years of the war, the clergy had preached of Ferdinand VII's divine right to rule. This had undermined support for the patriots and so angered their commanders that they 'indiscriminately massacred' the clergy 'wherever they were to be found'.[29] In the towns and villages of Los Llanos, the priests fled to the royalist strongholds in the north and organized religion ceased to be a part of daily life. Children as old as seven had not been baptized and no-one had heard confession for years. The priests living along the banks of the Orinoco had suffered a crueller fate. Of the 41 who had worked in the Catholic missions when the republicans had seized the area in early 1817, seven had fled, 14 had died in captivity and 20 had been executed. Patriot troops had hacked them to death with machetes and lances, then burnt the bodies where they fell.[30]

On their first night in Old Guyana, MacDonald's Lancers were given a hero's welcome and the governor put on a dance in their honour. They excited considerable curiosity amongst the locals and each was 'compelled to form … the centre of a gazing and exclaiming circle of Guayanezes', who questioned them about their motives for joining the cause and their homeland across the Atlantic.[31] As very few of the volunteers could speak Spanish, communication was difficult and many experienced culture shock, not least when 'treated' to the efforts of the local troubadours, which as Vowell explained, they struggled to appreciate:

> The music – if it merits the name – consisted of several vihuèlas, (a small kind of guitars) and harps, in time to which half a dozen professed singers screamed some unintelligible couplets at the top of their voices. These minstrels … were accompanied by rattles, made of hollow calabashes, containing some grains of maize; with short handles by which they were shaken; also by several women … seated round a table, [who] vied with each other in … beating time with their … hands.[32]

Aquardiente, a powerful local spirit, was served in abundance and the officers soon overcame their shyness. Several were even persuaded to join in regional dances 'such as the *Bambùco*, *Zajudìna* and *Marri-Marri*'.[33] One volunteer performed a succession of drunken pirouettes, as the locals yelled '*viven los ingleses!*' in encouragement. A dinner of roast beef, cheese and honey was then brought out. Local women with cigars clamped between their lips served the meat with long forks, placing it directly into the volunteers' mouths. After dinner the drinking, smoking and dancing continued long into the night.

When Hippisley and the 1st Hussars arrived at Old Guyana three months later, they were met by Brion's fleet, which was heading down-river en route to a rendezvous with the volunteers led by colonels Campbell and Gillmore. Hippisley was impressed by the admiral, who was finely dressed in 'a dark blue jacket, [with] red cuffs and collar … and ribbed with gold lace'.[34] With typical pomposity the colonel ordered a 13-gun salute, which Brion did not return as he was saving his powder for the enemy. The admiral then inspected the volunteers, who paraded on the deck of the *Tiger* in full regimental dress. The next morning, Hippisley enjoyed a fine breakfast at Brion's table, which included 'several dainties; meats hot and cold, chocolate, coffee and some good French wines'.[35] After they had finished eating, Hippisley's less troublesome son Charles, who had served in the Royal Marines for five years, was transferred to Admiral Brion's fleet as 4th lieutenant on the *Colombia*, a brig commanded by yet another Briton, Captain Hill. After bidding him farewell, the Hussars pushed on up-river.

Shortly after their encounter with the fleet, the Hussars lost Sergeant-Major Higgins, 'a meritorious ... old soldier' and long-term companion of Hippisley, to a sudden illness.[36] The colonel ordered a full regimental funeral. A firing party of 13 blasted three volleys over the water 'as a mark of respect', before his body was committed to the river. Others who died were not afforded such dignity, as Surgeon Robinson learnt when he stumbled across a desecrated grave on the banks of the Orinoco. Discovering the remnants of a letter written in English, he deduced it had contained the remains of a British volunteer.[37] Although Robinson believed scavenging beasts were to blame, many volunteers' graves were dug up by desperate locals, driven by the value of the uniforms they were buried in.

Beyond Old Guyana the Orinoco became unsuitable for larger boats, so the volunteers boarded large, open canoes known as *flecheras*. As they had 'a standing mast', 'a spacious square sail' and oars for when the breeze slackened, the men were soon making better progress.[38] As they advanced the landscape changed. Hills flanked the riverbanks and mountains became visible on the horizon. The trees thinned and the humidity slackened. The wildlife, on the other hand, remained abundant. 'Sportive' river dolphins played around the boats in 'multitudes' and fish, prawns and turtles of up to 30lb in weight provided the men with fresh meat.[39] Hippisley particularly enjoyed the crayfish, which he claimed were 'as delicious as those found in ... Southampton river'.[40] Another volunteer wrote of 'a species of river monster' that Vowell identified as the manatee, prized by the Indians 'for the sake of its oil'.[41] The Englishman was also surprised by the abilities of the electric eel, writing that 'it has the power of communicating a severe shock; so much so, that it is impossible to hold it in the hand, or to tread on it'.[42]

Roughly four days and 60 miles beyond Old Guyana, the volunteers reached Bolívar's capital of Angostura. Situated on the side of a hill on the north bank of the river, the city could be seen from a distance of eight miles by approaching ships. The first building to emerge from the tree tops was a large tower strongly mounted with cannon. Opposite appeared the hamlet of Soledad, where the capital's elite had country retreats. A ferry linking the two sites left every half hour to a signal blown through a conch shell, gathered from Angostura's natural harbour. Year round the port was alive with merchant ships flying the flags of England, France, Holland and the United States. Sailors ran back and forth unloading arms and ammunition, whilst wild mules and cattle were herded aboard for the return leg. Despite the crocodiles and rapid current, townsfolk could be seen bathing in the river, its lukewarm waters providing some respite from the heat and humidity.

After dropping anchor, the volunteers disembarked to take in the sights. Near the shore was a riverside battery, beyond which lay the main street. Roughly one mile in length, it ran parallel to the Orinoco some 100 paces back from the high-water mark, and was lined with the grandest houses in town. Mainly of one storey and built with whitewashed bricks of straw and lime, the houses had flat roofs where the owners could enjoy the breeze that blew off the river in the evenings. The finest of these residences, boasting a central courtyard and balcony, was owned by Admiral Brion. As he spent most of his time cruising the Caribbean, however, he had rented it to the Scottish-born merchant, James Hamilton, in his absence.

One of a growing number of foreign investors, Hamilton had been supplying the republic with arms, ammunition and uniforms since his arrival in early 1818. As Bolívar could rarely afford to pay upfront, Hamilton accepted trade and credit notes and stood to profit handsomely if the war was won. By 1820 the government owed him '£30,000' and he had become so influential that 'there is no proceeding of moment in the state, in which he is not consulted'.[43] A flamboyant figure, the Scot habitually took to the streets in full highland dress, where he was often seen with another well-known British resident, Doctor Kirby. The doctor, who also lived on the riverside row, made his living treating leading Creoles, merchants and 'the crews of foreign vessels'.[44] Sharing a 'spacious house' with his Cambridgeshire wife, he kept 'riding mules' as well as 'a plentiful stock of poultry and other substantial comforts'.[45] Other luxurious houses owned by European traders or local dignitaries, the town jail, custom house and an 'excellent' tavern completed the principal avenue. The tavern had a 'spacious and superbly fitted up' interior, filled with 'billiard and hazard tables' and carried on a roaring trade at all hours of the day and night.[46] None of the surviving sources mention prostitution in Angostura, but brothels certainly existed and no doubt enjoyed a boom in trade with the arrival of the foreign volunteers.

Fronting the main street was a shady, tree-lined *Alameda*, with 'a spacious carriage-road' and 'neat foot-pavement' where the people would promenade in the evenings.[47] Side roads lined with stone-built houses intersected the main street at right angles. Paved with jagged pieces of flint, rock and limestone, which made walking 'an exercise in agony', they were rank with refuse picked over by 'muscovy cocks and hens' that would occasionally find their way into the volunteers' cooking pots.[48] Minor thoroughfares ran parallel, creating a series of blocks that staggered up the hillside, with cannon sited at the major intersections. One road ran upwards to the main square, situated a quarter of a mile from the river. To the east of the two-acre plaza stood the cathedral. This huge gothic construction was unfinished as work had been put on hold when the patriot siege had begun in 1816. Lacking a roof, the building was exposed to the elements and rapidly falling into decay. The Governor's Palace, a one-storey brick building, stood opposite. Lieutenant Vowell thought it very badly constructed. Not helped by the sloping ground on which the square was sited, it was on the verge of collapse. A cavernous military prison, filled with 300 royalists captured after the city's capitulation in mid-1817, formed the third side of the square. A chapel, barracks and various private houses completed it. Mixed among the piles of rubble from the unfinished cathedral lay heaps of human remains. Some had fallen during the siege, others had been killed in the wave of executions that followed.[49]

On the outer reaches of the capital, Lieutenant Brown came across a killing field. It was clear 'from the marks … upon … the skulls', the Englishman later noted, 'that they had been dispatched by their conquerors in cold blood'. The corpses had then been left unburied 'to feed the wild beasts'.[50] Surgeon Robinson made a similarly grisly discovery. The morning after putting up his hammock in his newly acquired lodgings, he found that one of the 'hooks had been used … for scragging the old Spaniards' and 'the blood, &c. about it, left no room for doubt'.[51] Stumbling outside, he found yet more evidence of the massacres that had occurred. 'Hundreds of skulls and other bones lay' scattered about, and 'a good-looking hammock' hidden behind vegetation 'contained the body of some human being about half decayed'.[52]

The memoirs of several early volunteers mention a small chair that stood against the cathedral wall on the east side of the plaza, its purpose to advertise the fate of those who dared turn against Bolívar. On 16 October 1817 the patriot general, Manuel Piar, the only mixed-race member of an otherwise all white supreme command, had been tied to the chair and executed by firing squad.[53] Lieutenant Brown later heard that he had died with great dignity. Refusing the offer of a blindfold, he signalled the soldiers to open fire with a casual wave of his hand. Seven balls had 'lodged … in different parts of his body, two of them passing through his stomach into the wall behind'.[54] The volley had echoed across the square to the palace where The Liberator was lurking, lacking the courage to watch the sentence carried out. The incident would go down as one of the darkest in the history of the republic and remains controversial to this day. Despite considerable military success, Piar's championing of the mulatto cause had made him powerful enemies, some of whom had accused him of plotting the slaughter of the white elite and planning to form a black republic. It is now believed that these charges were overblown and in fact he was merely lobbying for improved rights for those of mixed race who were severely discriminated against under Spanish law. Knowing that the rapid suppression of any threat of race war was sure to gain him approval from the nervous white elite in

Caracas, Bolívar pretended to believe the accusation. As well as gaining him support in the capital, sanctioning the execution also sent a clear warning to any other generals considering a challenge for command. Although the truth behind Piar's demise may never be fully revealed, the story serves to illustrate the deeply divided nature of the patriot forces. Far from being a single united body, the republican army was actually made up of loosely organized bands led by local chieftains, constantly struggling for dominance and only held together by the force of Bolívar's will. The Liberator had little choice but to react ruthlessly when faced with any threats to his authority. Otherwise he risked seeing his fragile army fragment and the dream of independence disappear forever.

By early 1818, despite its limited population of a mere 5,000–10,000, Angostura was one of the world's most cosmopolitan cities. European and North American merchants rubbed shoulders with free blacks, Indian conscripts, slaves and Creoles. Over the coming months, this melting pot would be further enriched by successive waves of British volunteers. MacDonald's and Needham's men were the first to arrive. Few in number, they were received with hospitality. When the 1st and 2nd Hussars landed in April, however, the situation had changed. Food supplies and lodgings were scarce and the 200 new arrivals were seen as little more than competition. To make matters worse, the Hussars drank the town dry and emergency rations of locally produced *aquardiente* had to be shipped in to meet their needs.[55] The rank and file were quartered in barracks near the main square, whilst the colonel and his officers stayed in private houses. Typically, senior commanders like Hippisley enjoyed luxurious residences on the river front. The lower commissioned ranks, on the other hand, were forced to make do with more Spartan arrangements. A later volunteer, Captain William Adam of the Irish Legion, painted a vivid picture of the quarters he shared with two others in the capital in late 1819:

> The house was situated in the centre of the town, and was only one storey high: It was separated into two apartments, the larger of which occupied the front, facing the street; the other was in the rere ... both were floored with tile. In one corner of the front room was a hammock, and, in another a table, the frame of which was unplaned, and the leaf covered with a hide drawn tight, and nailed down on every side.[56]

Colonel Hippisley spent his time in Angostura trying to secure the payment Mendéz had promised his men. His attempts were frustrated, however, and he soon discovered that the republic was virtually penniless. The supplies that Bolívar had hoped to capture had been evacuated at the last minute and, following several recent catastrophic reverses on the battlefield, the enemy had captured the army's pay chest, baggage, and large amounts of arms and ammunition. What little cash remained was needed for replacing these losses and the patriot paymasters were certainly not keen to mete out bounty to recently arrived volunteers. After Hippisley's exasperated troops had threatened to mutiny, a token payment of ten pesos per officer and three pesos per NCO was scraped together by taxing the local inhabitants, turning many of them further against the volunteers. This sum, which amounted to a mere twentieth of what they had been promised, only served to briefly supplement the meagre rations provided and did little to placate the men. Despite their frequent complaints, however, the British were actually considerably better off than the majority of Bolívar's troops. Many of the native soldiers had either been forcibly enlisted or had joined up to avoid starving to death. They neither expected nor received more than food, clothing and the occasional opportunity to plunder.

Ignorant of their comparatively privileged position and depressed by the gulf between Mendéz's promises and the reality on the ground, the volunteers' morale sank to new lows. The contrast between the war many had recently fought in Europe and the grim struggle they were currently embroiled in only made matters worse. These differences were neatly encapsulated by a scene that Robinson observed as he looked out over the river one evening:

> An Aide-de-camp is generally a high fellow in Britain, and so is a Colonel; but here, where I now write this, I observe the first swimming in the river, washing his mule; while the other, a little farther on, is busy washing his shirt: I do not place this word in the *plural* as he very likely has only *one*. [57]

To raise his officers' spirits, Colonel Hippisley organized a ball. Three hundred guests arrived, including many of the eligible ladies in town. Predictably the party was riotous. 'The refreshment rooms were broken into *sans ceremonie*, in order to attack the porter, wine, and spirits, and the whole was drunk off, without rule or decorum.'[58] The guests did not leave until three the next morning. In February the *Hunter* arrived from London. As well as muskets and 'condemned' Royal Marine coats and jackets for Bolívar's infantry, the ship also brought out the Red Hussars' scarlet and gold uniforms. The *Hunter*'s North American supercargo, John Princep, was an associate of James Hamilton who along with several other British and North American merchants was plying a lucrative, if highly risky trade running guns across the Caribbean. Those that eluded the royalist blockade in the Gulf of Paria swapped the munitions for mules and oxen which were then tightly packed into the hold for the return leg.[59] Abundant in Los Llanos, the animals could be bought at Angostura for as little as 40 silver pesos and ten silver pesos respectively. Commanding three times the price in the West Indies, they made Hamilton and his peers rich men.[60]

At the bottom of the hill to the west of Angostura were stinking slums, and a stagnant lake into which the poor slung their dead, contributing to the ill-health that the city was famed for. Vowell claimed that 'no place in the world could be more admirably calculated to foster [yellow fever]', and another volunteer noted how as many as 20 residents succumbed daily.[61] Unaccustomed to the climate and with no natural resistance, the British suffered disproportionately. Lieutenant Plunkett of the 1st Hussars was amongst those who died. The morning after his arrival, Hippisley attended the young officer's funeral service, given in Spanish in the chapel on the main square. Being a protestant, and therefore a heretic, Plunkett was not permitted burial in hallowed ground. Instead, his body was interred beside the walls of the fort on the outskirts of Angostura, an area that soon became the unofficial British cemetery.

The volunteers who survived the first few days of the disease were taken to convalesce in a former convent on the edge of the town.[62] The British doctors believed the fresh air would aid recovery, but, as their only remedies were bleeding, purging and the use of emetics, their patients deteriorated at an alarming rate. Those considered contagious or untreatable were taken to a 'cold and gloomy ... subterranean chamber' where they were left to die.[63] Some expired in a state of delirium, oblivious to their suffering. Others remained lucid until the end, vomiting blood and in terrible pain. Several volunteers became unfit for service through accident or self-abuse. Lieutenant Charles Smith was shot 'whilst playing with some old muskets in a storehouse'. Half his hip was blown away by the 'shot, slugs, and wadding'. Amazingly, he went on to make a full recovery.[64] Captain Dudley, on the other hand, 'rendered himself useless, by his constant adherence to an excess of spirit drinking' and was dismissed from the service.[65] Resignations further weakened the British units. Lieutenants Pritt and Lamb of the 1st Hussars, for example, left on the *Rabbit* in April 1818. Their boat capsized a few miles down-river and both were drowned. Adding to the volunteers' problems was Colonel Wilson's ever more unpredictable behaviour. One afternoon, when Hippisley's master tailor dared to ask for 'the payment of a small bill due for work', the colonel lashed out with his riding crop.[66] The blow 'cut open ... [his] head and ... dreadfully disfigured ... [his] face'.[67] Hippisley complained to the authorities but before they could act, Wilson gathered the 42 remaining Red Hussars and pushed on up-river.[68] Eventually, all the dwindling bands would head for Los Llanos where the main body of Bolívar's army was campaigning. In January, Vowell and MacDonald's 14 remaining 1st Lancers were the first to sail. Five months later, after leaving some of their women and children in Angostura to look after the heavy baggage, they were followed by the 150 men of the 1st and 2nd Hussars.[69]

Up-river from Angostura, the volunteers encountered scorpions, tarantulas and leeches, stinging fish and mockingbirds, 10ft snakes and 8in centipedes. Far more common were the crocodiles, which were even larger and more aggressive than those they had previously seen. Although the low-velocity musket rounds often failed to penetrate their toughened hides, shooting at the reptiles became a favourite distraction. Hippisley witnessed one successful hunt when several of his officers surprised a sleeping giant. Even though caught unawares, it 'was sometime before they could overpower it' by thrusting their sabres into its eyes and mouth.[70] More feared than the crocodiles were the panthers and jaguars that prowled the forests. Whilst hunting birds when his boat had anchored close in to the bank for the night, Surgeon Robinson was horrifed when one of the predators burst from the bushes and chased him back to camp. Luckily for the surgeon, his pursuer was frightened by the noise and light and retreated into the woods. The cat was later tracked down and shot. Lieutenant Alexander also had a close encounter. Whilst relaxing in his hammock, he 'heard a slight stirring in the leaves as of feet approaching'. The boat captain, no doubt aware of what was about to happen, 'fired his fowling piece' into the bushes. Immediately 'it was answered by the growl of a tiger, heavy and long, but evidently in retreat'.[71] Not all those stalked by the big cats lived to tell the tale. An NCO in the 1st Hussars named Cookson foolishly wandered off alone one afternoon while his companions were cooking. He was attacked, dragged deeper into the jungle and devoured. His remains were never found.

Local Indians also claimed some victims. Those that had made their homes on the riverbank had suffered terribly during the war. Both sides had forcibly recruited in the area and, as the women and children followed when their men were dragged off in chains, whole villages had become depopulated. By 1818, hundreds had deserted and made their way home. Poverty and the threat of starvation drove them to prey on passing boats.[72] With their fine uniforms and the latest arms and equipment, the British volunteers proved too tempting to resist. The highest-profile victim was Colonel MacDonald, killed up-river from Angostura in March 1818. Having become separated from the remaining Lancers, he was only accompanied by his servant boy and Coronet Langtree at the time of his death. After going ashore in all his finery to purchase food, the Indians had 'marked him out as prey'.[73] At dawn, 50 canoes sallied out to where the colonel's party lay at anchor in mid-river. Unsure of their intentions, the master of the vessel advised MacDonald to fire a warning shot into the water. The Scot obliged, but rather than retreating, the Indians 'quickly paddled up to the flechero, and ... discharged a flight of arrows, which wounded several people'. Seeing they were about to be boarded, 'MacDonald drew his sword and ... the havoc commenced'. According to one source, the colonel 'killed eight, while ... [Langtree] destroyed six', before they were pressed into a corner, 'overpowered and ... cut to pieces'.[74] Everyone on board was then murdered, 'with the exception of ... [MacDonald's servant] boy.' As the Indians finished off the wounded, he escaped by diving overboard and swimming for the far bank, followed by volleys of arrows. By the time he pulled himself from the water, 'four … [were] sticking in his body, which he broke off short and afterwards got extracted'.[75] After hiding in the woods for several days, the boy was picked up by a passing boat and the incident was reported to General Páez, one of Bolívar's most celebrated commanders. Weeks later the killers were caught red-handed, clutching a sable fur belonging to the colonel that was marked with the stamp of Gil and Company. Páez's retribution was swift and brutal. Perhaps on the volunteers' suggestion, the prisoners were strapped to the muzzles of 18-pdr cannon in the fort of San Fernando, in imitation of an old Mughal military punishment. The port fires were then lit and the men blown to pieces. Following Skeene's drowning and Campbell's resignation, just three of the six colonels remained.

After passing the village of Cuicara, the volunteers came to the confluence of the Orinoco and Apure rivers. Hippisley noticed 'a very marked distinction … between … [their] appearance'.[76] Whilst the Apure was 'as serpentine in its meanderings as the Orinoco', it was 'on a much smaller scale', in many stretches merely half a mile across.[77] Just like the larger river, however, it teemed with life. Crocodiles lined the banks, basking in the sun 'with their jaws wide open at right angles'. Manatee and 'noisy and impetuous' dolphins swam through the waters and tightly packed flocks of birds flashed overhead like 'black cloud[s]'.[78] After several days on the Apure, Vowell and the 12 remaining Lancers disembarked at Caujaral, a small village on the edge of the plains. In a matter of days, these pioneers would be the first British group to join Bolívar's army. It was to prove an inauspicious beginning. The vast majority would be cut down on the battlefield or executed by the enemy in the forthcoming campaign.

Chapter 5

'CAPTAIN GRANT'S PRIZE CLARIONET'

Covering approximately 173,750 square miles, Los Llanos comprises extensive savannahs stretching from the western chain of the Andes in New Granada to the rainforests of eastern Venezuela. The plains never exceed a height of 650ft, are perfectly flat and are crisscrossed by a series of rivers feeding into the Orinoco. During the wet season from December to April, the rivers burst their banks and the savannahs erupt into a sea of billowing grasses, dotted with areas of woodland and thickets of bamboo. For the rest of the year, a scorching sun in a cloudless sky transforms the landscape. 'The grass dries out and turns to dust; the ground cracks' and wildfires sweep across the plains, leaving a feast of roasted rodents for the buzzard-like *zamoras* following in their wake.[1]

By the early 19th century, herds of cattle and horses (introduced by the Conquistadores) had become so numerous that when armies marched through the region, cavalry outriders had to clear a path through the animals for the infantry to pass.[2] Feral dogs roamed in packs. Alligators, panthers, jaguars and 30ft anacondas, known as *camendi*, lurked in the forests and swampland, preying on deer and giant rodents. The latter, known as *capybara*, grazed 'in herds of fifty to sixty' on the edges 'of lagoons, and small streams' amongst flocks of feeding waterfowl.[3] Vowell observed that they were excellent swimmers, 'capable of remaining as long under water as a seal'.[4]

Before the arrival of the Spanish, the *Uahibo* and *Guahibo* tribes had dominated the region, but the balance of power had since shifted. The plains were now home to their mixed race descendants, the Llaneros (who made up 41 per cent of the population), and to roving bands of escaped slaves and deserters. The Llaneros were toughened ranchers and master horsemen; Venezuela's version of the Texan cowboy or Argentinean gaucho. Living in family groups, they ran isolated farms. Often separated by a full day's ride, these communities spotted the area like islands on an inland sea. Well-armed and mounted on swift-footed ponies, the Llaneros could ride rings round European cavalry and subsist off the land indefinitely. At the start of the war they had fought for the royalists under José Boves, a psychopathic tyrant whose forces had in large part led to the downfall of Bolívar's Second Republic. In 1814 Boves had been killed when a patriot lance ripped open his stomach, and by 1818 the majority of the Llaneros had sided with the republicans under a charismatic new leader, José Antonio Páez. Ambushing supply trains and making lightning raids on royalist outposts, they killed every Spaniard they caught and melted away before the survivors could react. Although the royalists held several towns in the region, the miles of empty grassland between belonged to Páez.

In January 1818, Vowell and the 1st Venezuelan Lancers disembarked at Caujaral, a Llanero town on the Arauca River occupied by a handful of patriot soldiers. On learning that Bolívar's army had passed through two weeks earlier, the British immediately set off in pursuit. Led northwards to San Juan de Payara, they passed through a strip of dense woodland, which thinned out to reveal a landscape of grassland and scattered copses. A large open village with a 'well built'[5] church, San Juan had wide, dusty streets flanked by thatched mud houses of 'a ruinous appearance', with hung cow hides serving as doors.[6] The inhabitants were 'a wretchedly poor set of beings', whom Vowell referred to as the *Guagívis*.[7] Noting that the women pierced their lower lips with 'long thorns', the Englishman 'gave one of the squaws' a few pins that he happened to have in his possession:

> She immediately called ... a girl of about twelve years old, (apparently her daughter) ... pierced her lip, with ... indifference and dexterity, with ... an alligators tooth; and placed the pins in the orifice. The poor girl bore this operation with great patience; and appeared to be perfectly consoled, by the possession of her new ornament. She ran directly ... to display it to her companions; considering, no doubt, that pins were much more fashionable than thorns.[8]

In the first week of February, the volunteers entered 'the infinite monotony' of the plains.[9] One British officer observed that the landscape seemed to ripple when the grasses were 'agitated by the winds', giving the savannah 'the appearance of an ocean, with gently undulating waves'.[10] At the end of the first day's ride, they camped by the banks of a stream and witnessed the awesome beauty of the sun setting over the interminable horizon of the plains. Whilst the weather held, the evenings in Los Llanos passed pleasantly. The men gambled or played *vihuelas* and sung the 'Hymn of Liberty' with 'wild enthusiasm'.[11] Dinner was freshly slaughtered beef, skewered and roasted over the fire. No crockery, cutlery, bread or condiments were available to accompany the crude meal. The wealthier British veterans, who had grown accustomed to campaigning in the Napoleonic Wars with a full dinner service, struggled to adapt to the new lifestyle, where the only luxury was the occasional cigar. Sleeping arrangements were equally Spartan. As the temperature plummeted at night, the men huddled together in blankets on the bare ground, warmed by a line of roaring camp fires.

The next morning, the Lancers arrived at the town of San Fernando. Positioned on a crossroads of strategic importance, it was well protected by 'deep ditches ... thick stockades' and several cannon which dominated the Apure River meandering round its walls.[12] Although San Fernando was a few miles behind patriot lines, the Spanish flag fluttered defiantly from the battlements. Bolívar had left a detachment of cavalry to encircle the town and intercept any royalist convoys attempting to supply the garrison. After swimming their horses across the Apure, the British crossed the plains in front of the city prompting the weary defenders to loose 'a shot or two' from extreme range that failed to find their targets.[13] They then rode northwards to Calabozo, steadily closing the gap on Bolívar's troops.

The patriot army which the Lancers were pursuing had begun its 400-mile march six weeks previously in Angostura. Some of the 4,000 troops had sailed up the Orinoco and Arauca rivers. The rest had marched along the banks. After a month, a quarter had been lost to desertion or sickness, but had been replaced when Bolívar was joined by General Páez and 1,000 cavalry at Cañafistola. It was the first time the two men had met. Although serious disagreements would blight their future relationship, the initial meeting was a good-humoured one. After embracing warmly, the wealthy, well-educated urbanite and the crude-mannered, illiterate Llanero stepped back to get the measure of each other. A moment's silence followed. They then burst into laughter at the differences between them. The following morning, their combined forces set out north for Calabozo, where the Spanish Army was encamped.

In mid-February, the volunteers caught up with the army. Resplendent in their bright green uniforms, 'with silver lace ... gold cord' and scarlet facings, the contrast between the Lancers and their new comrades could not have been more pronounced.[14] Bolívar's troops were a ragtag collection of Creoles, Indians and blacks, whose only concession to uniformity was a white feather or scrap of cloth worn in their caps to distinguish friend from foe. At the centre of the army, the infantry were formed in two columns. Some were armed with smoothbore Spanish muskets. Others had rifles, fowling-pieces or carbines. Several had no firearms at all, marching to war with only a lance, machete or bayonet. The veterans were dressed in an assortment of captured Spanish uniforms or the blue and red jackets of the British marines which had recently been sent out from London. New recruits wore loose pantaloons and ponchos weaved from coarse cloth, with straw hats or white handkerchiefs to protect them from the sun. Some marched barefoot, others wore crudely made espadrilles. Boys of 13 walked alongside bearded men in their forties. In the rear, conscripted Indians guarded the baggage train. Armed with bows and arrows, they were naked except for twists of blue cloth round their loins.[15]

The cavalry troops were divided into four sections: the vanguard, the rearguard and two flanking columns. Some were mounted on horses, others had mules. The majority rode bareback, with the reins in their left hands and iron-tipped bamboo lances, 12–14ft in length, in their right. Sabres or small swords hung from their belts by leather thongs alongside pistols, carbines or muskets, sawn-off to make them more manageable on horseback. In pride of place at the head of the army, Páez's elite guard boasted plundered brass helmets and silver-hilted sabres. Bringing up the rear was a bedraggled military band, carrying 'a few old cracked drums' which, Lieutenant Vowell caustically wrote, were 'anything but spirit-stirring'.[16]

Keen to meet the man they had read so much about in the London papers, the volunteers rode to the head of the column, where they found The Liberator surrounded by 'a motley group of staff officers', as diverse and colourful as the troops they led.[17] Rushing up with 'a shrill shout of welcome' and 'a profusion of embraces', Bolívar's staff overwhelmed the reserved British officers with their enthusiasm. However, The Liberator could only manage a melancholy smile.[18] As Vowell noted, the trials of five years campaigning had clearly taken their toll:

> [Although] about thirty five … [Bolívar] looked upwards of forty; in stature [he was] short, perhaps five feet five or six, but well proportioned and remarkably active. His countenance … was thin, and evidently care-worn, with an expression of patient endurance under adversity… His manners not only appeared to [be] elegant, surrounded as he was by men far his inferiors in birth and education, but must have been intrinsically so… The dress which was worn by him and his suite, corresponded perfectly with the scanty resources of the patriot army. His helmet was such as was then usually worn by a private light dragoon… [He also wore] a plain round jacket of blue cloth, with red cuffs … coarse blue trowsers; and … sandals … in his hand [was] a light lance, with a small black banner … embroidered on it a white skull and crossed bones, with the motto 'Muerte ó Libertád!'[19]

Conspicuous amongst the staff officers was the Anglo-Irish Colonel James Rooke, 'a huge, handsome, blue eyed blonde' who had joined the patriots in 1817 and now commanded Bolívar's guard of honour.[20] Born in Dublin in 1772 into an upper-class family of considerable military pedigree, Rooke was a man of rare experience amongst the young officers of the republican army. With 15 relatives commissioned and three, including his father, having reached the rank of general, there had never been any doubt as to his choice of profession. After joining up at the age of 19, Rooke had been swiftly promoted and was bloodied as a captain with the 8th Foot in the Duke of York's disastrous Flanders campaign of 1793. His regiment was then posted to Trincomalee in Ceylon but whether or not Rooke accompanied them is unclear. Nevertheless, three years later he was back in England purchasing a majority in the Queen's Light Dragoons. Later Rooke married Mary Rigge and moved into Rangers' Lodge, his in-laws' opulent family home in Oxfordshire. There he began living beyond his means and mixed with such illustrious company as the Prince of Wales. After three years in Oxfordshire, Mary had given birth to a son and daughter, but the major's high living was beginning to catch up with him. In desperation he took to gambling and by 1801 was virtually bankrupt. Having sold his hunting and racing horses to raise funds, he fled to Paris to escape his creditors. The phoney peace of Amiens, which briefly postponed hostilities with the French, was not to last and when the Napoleonic Wars broke out two years later, Rooke was arrested and sent to a military prison camp in Verdun. After ten years in captivity, with the Peninsular War reaching its climax, he managed to escape. Eager for a taste of the action, he made his way south through enemy territory and eventually reached Wellington's headquarters in Frenada, where he joined a newly formed cavalry regiment. The war was all but over, however, and after the French surrender in 1814, Rooke returned to London. His reunion with Mary was not to last for in November 1814 she died from an unspecified illness at Chalk Hill. Now an unemployed widower in his mid-forties, Rooke's prospects seemed bleak, but Napoleon's dramatic resurgence afforded him one last hurrah on the battlefields of Europe. Serving as an aide-de-camp to the Prince of Orange with the rank of major, Rooke fought at Waterloo and was amongst the 10,200 British soldiers wounded. After the battle he decided to start a new life in the colonies. Leaving his children with relatives, Rooke sailed for Saint Kitt's in 1816 to visit his sister, the wife of the British governor, Colonel Probyn. There he was introduced to Anna Tucker, a 'fascinating and elegant' mulatta of just 16 years of age, who had recently returned from a trip to England to finish her education.[21] Despite the 30-year age difference, the couple were soon married. Rooke was a man who craved excitement and he quickly grew tired of island life. Hearing that the patriots were offering commissions to European veterans, the couple left Saint Kitt's with Anna's slave girl, Jeanette, and sailed south arriving in Angostura in mid-1817.[22] Bolívar immediately took to the vivacious veteran and appointed him to his personal staff.

Despite being twice the age of most of his contemporaries, Rooke was still in his physical prime. Blessed with an iron constitution that protected him from the diseases that would see off so many of his peers, and a sound knowledge of Spanish gained in the Peninsular War, Rooke would prove to be the best of Bolívar's British recruits. Easy-going and optimistic, he retained his admirable good humour throughout the battles, forced marches and retreats which were to follow, a trait which endeared him not only to his general, but to all those he encountered.

After meeting Rooke, the British Lancers were taken on a tour of the army. The troops barraged them with questions about their homeland and motivations for travelling so far. Although most seemed to have no notion of Britain, many devised their own theories as to why the volunteers had joined them. One thought that poverty or starvation had driven them to enlist, whilst another opined that their animosity towards the Spanish, dating back to the days of the Armada, had inspired them.[23] Later, Bolívar sent word that he wanted to speak to the new arrivals. They found him in a shaded copse, swinging in his hammock. After greeting them with the courtesy 'of a man who has seen the world', Bolívar apologized for the lack of luxury and 'expressed his joy at seeing, at last, Europeans in his army, that would be capable of disciplining his troops, and assisting the native officers by their instruction and example'.[24] That night, spent camped by the ford at Los Tres Moriches on the north bank of the Orituco River, was a joyous occasion. Lances and 'capital' horses were presented to the British and they were congratulated on their perfect timing. The next day would see an advance on the Spanish cantonment at Calabozo, ten miles to the north. With surprise on their side, the men were confident of victory.

Before dawn the army broke camp. Fires were stamped out, blankets rolled and the men formed into columns. Leading the formation was General Páez. Barefoot and dressed in loose trousers and an open-necked shirt, at first sight he was indistinguishable from the cavalry that milled about him.[25] However on closer inspection, the well-muscled 27-year old exuded an aura of power and commanded respect. Having grown up on the plains uneducated and illiterate, he was the polar opposite of Bolívar and enjoyed a bond with his troops that his erudite and aloof compatriot could never hope to attain. The Liberator 'waltzed beautifully', rarely drank and enjoyed perusing his campaign library of history and philosophy during rare moments of solitude, Páez (the Caudillo) revelled in blood sports, raised fighting cocks and loved drinking *aquardiente*.[26] Fearless, immensely strong and an exceptional rider, he excelled on the battlefield. Since joining the patriots in 1810, he had slaughtered hundreds, earning him the *nom de guerre* 'The Centaur of the Plains'.[27] The Liberator's martial ineptitude, on the other hand, forced his staff to seek cover whenever he drew his pistols.[28] The long-term aims of the leaders were equally disparate. Whilst Páez's ambition was limited to Los Llanos, Bolívar's vision encompassed the entire continent.

At sunrise the column reached the Mesa of Calabozo, a three-mile square savannah, closed on three sides by the Guarico River. A narrow strip of woodland clinging to the riverbank and a few thickets of scrub were all that broke the monotony of the plain. Situated to the east of the river, the town of Calabozo formed one point of a triangle of habitations, with the hamlet of Misión de Abajo two miles to the south and Misión de Arriba three miles to the east. Before war tore through the region, Calabozo had been the centre of the booming cattle trade in Los Llanos. Its 'large and roomy' houses reflected the prosperity that the population of 7,000 had enjoyed.[29] Surrounding the town centre were earthen ramparts, built 100 years before to provide protection from the Indian attacks which had plagued the settlement's early history. Further fortifications had since been added, including a fort with sturdy redoubts, and a stone strong house dominating the central plaza.

The Spanish troops at Calabozo were commanded by General Pablo Morillo. The senior royalist officer in Venezuela, Morillo was an imposing figure. Tall and 'of large proportions', he was renowned for his fierce temper, although his 'full face, and features' could occasionally 'betoken ... some benevolence'.[30] A veteran of over 40 battles, his

THE BATTLE OF CALABOZO

To Rastro

Guarico

To El Sombrero

Calabozo

Misión de Arriba

Páez

Bolívar

Cedeño

Copse

UNITS

① 1st Bt. Navarra
② 2nd Bt. Navarra
③ La Unión
④ Cavalry Scouts
⑤ Castilla
⑥ Light Company of Navarra
⑦ Queen's Hussars

ⓐ Paez's Guard of honour

ılı Royalist cannon

KEY

Patriot infantry
Patriot cavalry
Royalist infantry
Royalist cavalry
==== Track
River
Ford
Trees/scrub
Town

Misión de Abajo

To San Fernando

0   1
Miles

experience spanned the Napoleonic Wars. Just eight years after being wounded by the British at Trafalgar (whilst a sergeant in the Spanish marines) he had been present at Vitoria as a field marshal in Wellington's army. The battle was his finest hour. At the head of 4,000 of his countrymen he broke the French under Joseph Bonaparte, Napoleon's brother and puppet King of Spain. By 1814, Morillo was a national hero and his appointment as commander of King Ferdinand's South American expedition was met with widespread approval. As well as acquiring fluent English, the general had also learnt much about infantry tactics during his time under Wellington.[31] Troops under his command showed a 'smartness and efficiency' which would have done the best of the British units proud.[32] Daniel O'Leary, the coronet from Wilson's Red Hussars who had spent the voyage from England improving his Spanish, thought him 'of the mould' of 'such men of iron' as 'Pizarro and Cortez'.[33] In common with these cruel predecessors, the general's methods were often brutal. He had left a trail of destruction in his wake ever since arriving at Margarita in 1815, and was feared and loathed by the patriots in equal measure. Despite sightings of 'insurgent' scouts at the nearby Orituco River, Morillo had slept soundly on the night of 11 February and awoke convinced that Bolívar's army was still three days march to the south besieging San Fernando. Accordingly his 2,500 troops were divided into four detachments and spread out across the plains. The main body of three Spanish infantry battalions, two of the Navarra Regiment and one of La Unión, 100 cavalry scouts and a small detachment of artillery, was safe in Calabozo. The other three, on the other hand, were outside the walls and dangerously isolated.

Páez's guard of honour was the first patriot unit to appear before the city. Its sudden arrival surprised a band of 70 Spanish Hussars who had been rounding up wild cattle on the plain. Having finished their work, the Hussars were relaxing in the shade by the river when the Llaneros appeared. Unprepared, unarmed and dismounted, they were easy prey. The din of galloping hooves and the yells of the riders were the first they knew of the approaching peril. Two men reacted quickly enough to escape. Leaping onto their horses, they raced back to town to raise the alarm. Of the rest, only three were spared. The others were run through with lances or shot in the back as they fled. As the dust settled over the dead, the bulk of the 3,500-strong patriot army marched onto the plain. Bolívar formed his men into a thin semicircular line, approximately 1,100 yards in length, that curved round Calabozo, thus cutting off the two remaining Spanish units that were still outside town. Páez's riders were on the right, their flank protected by a large thicket. The infantry held the centre and a second cavalry unit, under General Manuel Cedeño, took the far left of the line. With Bolívar's guard of honour in the centre, Vowell, Rooke and the 22 other British volunteers watched as Páez's guard dismounted and looted the dead Hussars. The Llaneros then formed a loose skirmish screen ahead of the curving patriot line.

Advancing, they opened fire on the edge of town. It was 8.00am. The battle of Calabozo had begun.

Still convinced that the patriot army was miles away, Morillo presumed the shots signalled nothing more than a minor skirmish. Nevertheless, he decided to investigate and gathering his staff and 200 infantry, he led them out through the gates. Leaving the foot soldiers in a fold of dead ground, he cantered out onto the plains to assess the situation. Meanwhile, two bodies of Spanish troops were cut off in the outlying hamlets. As the volume of musketry increased, they realized the precariousness of their situation and set off for the safety of the town. The 450 men of the Castilla Regiment used the available cover well, cutting through the scrub that skirted the Guarico River. The 100-strong light company of Navarra and the 250 men of the Queen's Hussars based two miles to the south, on the other hand, marched across the open plains. They would pay dearly for their mistake.

When Páez noticed Morillo advancing onto the savannah, he swiftly manoeuvred his riders to within striking distance. The Spanish general, meanwhile, had finally accepted the reality of the situation: the patriots had made a lightning advance and caught him at a disadvantage. His troops in Misión de Arriba and Misión de Abajo would have to look after themselves. Turning his horse, he ordered his staff back to town. This was the moment Páez had been waiting for. As soon as the Spaniards' backs were turned he ordered the charge. By the time the royalists realized they were being pursued, the Llaneros were nearly upon them. Morillo cut back with his spurs, but at the crucial moment his horse stumbled, allowing one of Páez's lieutenants to close in. As he was about to strike, a Spanish staff officer rode between them, selflessly taking the lance blow intended for his general; thrown from his horse, he fell to the dust mortally wounded. Colonel Navas, the commander of the Spanish Hussars, and another royalist officer were also killed in the scramble. The rest drew their sabres and cut their way through. Racing back to the walls, they passed their infantry who opened fire as their pursuers poured into the dead ground. The volley proved enough to deter them. Morillo galloped through the gates to safety and Páez's men were forced to turn back and pass the waiting Spanish infantry a second time. Another volley was fired. Several more Llaneros were knocked from their saddles. The rest returned to patriot lines.

On the far right of Bolívar's position, the 450 men of the regiment of Castilla were also making good progress. Cutting through the *sauso* shrubs, trees and brushwood that lined the banks of the Guarico, they went unnoticed by Páez's scouts until they were close to Calabozo.[34] Calling the alarm, the patriots set off to intercept them. As the dust cloud approached, the royalists closed ranks and continued their withdrawal, knowing that whilst they maintained formation in the scrub, the Llaneros had little hope of success. After exchanging a few scattered shots and leaving a handful of dead and wounded behind them, the patriots lost interest. The infantry were presenting an unwavering line of bayonets and, besides, an easier target had already presented itself. Exhausted, but grateful for their good fortune, the men of Castilla were allowed to stagger back to the safety of town.

To the right of the plain were the Spanish Hussars and the light company of Navarra. Despite being continuously harried by small units of skirmishing patriot cavalry, they had also been making some progress until Bolívar sent Colonel Lara's horsemen to engage them. Seeing their approach, the Spanish lost their composure and split into two. The blue and white uniformed cavalry formed line on the open plain, whilst the infantry ran to a small copse, took up firing positions behind the trees and began to pick off the advancing horsemen. Lara halted his men. Aware of the futility of charging riflemen in cover, he sent an aide galloping back to Bolívar, requesting infantry support to drive them into the open. The Liberator ordered 300 men of the regiment of Barcelona forward. Sweating under the rising sun, they positioned themselves between the royalists and the town, cutting off the only line of retreat. They then wheeled towards the copse, drawing the royalists' fire away from their cavalry. The sergeants yelled orders to close up as the musketry plucked men from the formation, but the advance continued. Outnumbered three to one, the Spaniards could not hold them off for long. After a patriot volley, they were flushed out of the copse by a bayonet charge. The Queen's Hussars also found themselves in an increasingly precarious situation. Not only were they threatened by Lara's cavalry, but also by those of generals Manuel Cedeño and José Tadeo Monagas, who had ridden up to join in the impending slaughter. All three now urged their men forward. Lowering their lances, they approached at a canter, then broke into a gallop, ducking behind their horses' necks as they closed to present a smaller profile.

The British, safe in the centre of the patriot line, looked on as the Lancers cut through the thin row of Spanish horsemen. Several were run through, punched from the saddle and hurled to the ground. The Llaneros then spun their mounts round to attack for a second time. The Hussars had already suffered enough. Losing all semblance of order, they retreated, leaving the ground behind them carpeted with their dead. Some sought cover in the copse to which their infantry had fled, but it served them no better than it had their comrades. Vowell later compared what ensued to a 'day's hunt'. Chasing their panicked foes in scattered groups through the trees, the patriot riders killed with lance thrusts or shot the Spaniards down 'like hares'.[35] Of 250 riders who had set out from the hamlet that morning, only 50 reached Calabozo alive. A handful were taken prisoner and 100 others were killed. The remainder scattered across the savannah, only daring to rein in their horses when the din of battle was far behind. Lost and alone in a hostile landscape, many would fall prey to roving bands of patriot guerrillas in the coming weeks.

Even the fate of the Hussars was preferable to that of the light company of Navarra. Finding themselves cut off after being flushed from the copse, the 100 Spaniards formed square and bravely awaited the onslaught. Páez threw his riders against them in waves. The horsemen emerged through smoke that belched from the Spanish muskets, to stab down with their lances or fire their carbines from the saddle. Small fires broke out, ignited by smouldering paper cartridges, adding to the confusion. Despite the odds, the Spaniards held their nerve. Behind an unwavering line of bayonets they fended off six charges. Seeing his tactics were not working, Páez ordered several men to dismount. Although advantageous when faced with cavalry, the square formed an inviting target for infantry fire and the carbines and pistols of the Llaneros took a heavy toll. With their enemies dropping in increasing numbers, the riders were able to close in on them, adding to the carnage with their lances. To Páez's admiration, the Spaniards maintained their formation until the bitter end. Not a single man survived.[36]

Although the majority of the British had spent the morning observing from afar, Captain Peter Grant, a 23-year old Scottish veteran of the 79th Foot, was determined to get closer to the action. A giant, both 'tall' and 'stout', and a 'specimen of eccentricity', Grant had joined the patriots earlier that year, after being laid off as a slave driver on a plantation in Demerara.[37] Alexander Alexander, a future British recruit and former colleague, thought him a 'rogue' and 'a villain' and alleged that he had deserted his regiment before sailing for the Caribbean.[38] Bored with merely watching, Grant slunk off into the woods that swept round the edge of the battlefield on a one-man reconnaissance patrol. Creeping through the undergrowth, he surprised a Spanish straggler leading a mule loaded with wine-skins. Yelling, the Scot barrelled through the scrub with his sword drawn. The Spaniard fell to his knees and begged for mercy. As he tried to explain that he was only a musician and deserved to be spared, the mule made a break for freedom. The tempestuous Scot now faced a quandary. Torn between guarding his captive and chasing after the mule, he was suddenly struck with inspiration. Tying the Spaniard to a tree, he used mime to instruct him to play his clarinet until his return, reasoning that it would be impossible for him to loosen his bonds at the same time. The plan paid off. Flushed with success, Grant returned to his countrymen leading his prisoner with one hand and the booze-laden mule with the other. The Scot's antics amused the volunteers and Creoles alike. The latter went on to dub him 'Pedro Grande' and the story even caused the habitually sombre Bolívar to enjoy 'one of the few hearty laughs … [the British] ever saw him indulge in'.[39]

As Grant's farce was playing out in the woods, the battle was entering its final stages. Hoping to provide a rallying point for the survivors of the units decimated in the plains, Morillo had formed his army on the outskirts of town into three columns. Two light cannon faced to the front and a swarm of light troops had been thrown out to cover the centre and flanks. With their rear well protected by the city walls, the royalists were willing to stand and fight. Yet Bolívar was too canny to attack when they were ready for him. Although Páez's cavalry enjoyed a significant advantage over their counterparts, the patriot infantry were undoubtedly inferior to Morillo's veterans. Knowing he would come off second best in a pitched battle, The Liberator 'contented himself with permitting the Llanéros, to … try the patience of the Spanish artillery men'.[40] Darting up and down between the lines, Páez's riders taunted the enemy by firing their carbines and prompted some wasteful cannon fire. Bolívar soon tired of the standoff, however. The patriots fell back to the river to quench their thirst and the Spanish retreated inside Calabozo, bringing the battle to a close at midday. Silence once more blanketed the plain, broken only by an occasional pistol shot fired by patriot troops picking their way between the corpses to loot the dead and finish off the wounded. Later, large 'dingy black' buzzards, known as *zamoras*, swooped down to pluck out their eyes.[41]

At dusk, Bolívar sent an officer and trumpeter to the walls to demand the Spanish surrender. Regardless of how presumptuous this may have seemed to Morillo, it was a positive development. Previously there had been little communication and the practice of slaughtering prisoners was widespread. As a sign of goodwill, Bolívar also returned 12 officers and 20 soldiers who had been taken prisoner during the battle and promised quarter to all those who laid down their arms. Morillo, however, was in no mood to bargain with the 'insurgents'. In reply, he appeared at the gate and ordered a volley from his troops lining the walls, killing the officer who had delivered the message and wounding the trumpeter. No doubt Morillo's reaction was partly prompted by wounded pride, for 250 of his troops had been killed, 50 taken prisoner and over 100 were missing. They had lost a colonel, a captain and at least two other officers. Even more worryingly, after the destruction of the Queen's Hussars, they no longer had an effective cavalry force that was so essential for rounding up wild cattle on the plains. With limited rations and now no hope of fresh supplies, Morillo had little option but to withdraw over 65 miles north to Sombrero. The town was close to his power base along the Carribbean coast and the broken ground which lay beyond it would afford his infantry the upper hand. The move would take days, however, and Páez's cavalry could turn the march across the open plains into a blood bath.

In contrast, patriot casualties had been light. Whilst the official bulletin admitted just 20 losses, it is likely that at least double that number fell. Nevertheless, the campaign had been only a partial success. Whilst the march from Angostura had been brilliantly executed and had caught the Spanish unawares, the battle had been inconclusive. Bolívar knew he now had to push home his advantage. With 2,000 royalists trapped in Calabozo, it was The Liberator's task to ensure that not a single soldier escaped alive.

Chapter 6

A NAMELESS GRAVE

T he royalist army in Calabozo was caught in a trap. With his supply lines to the coastal cities blocked, Morillo only had provisions left for eight days. All Bolívar had to do, as Páez counselled, was to surround the city and starve his enemy out. The royalists would eventually be forced to leave Calabozo and could then be destroyed piecemeal by the patriot cavalry on the 50-mile march north. The Liberator had other plans, however. With Morillo's army temporarily out of the picture, he envisioned a lightning advance on a lightly defended Caracas and a swift end to the war. Accordingly, the following day the patriots broke camp. Leaving Colonel Guillermo Iribarren with a single squadron of cavalry to watch Morillo, Bolívar led his men nine miles north to Rastro, where he called a meeting with Páez to propose his plan. The Caudillo thought the idea strategically unsound. Firstly, there was the danger of leaving Morillo at their backs. Secondly, as a second enemy army, under General Miguel de La Torre, lay between the patriots and the capital, any move north would inevitably risk encirclement. Páez also warned that the advantage enjoyed by his cavalry on the plains would be lost as they entered the mountainous terrain to the north, where conversely, the veteran royalist infantry would dominate. He urged The Liberator to put his plan on hold and destroy Morillo whilst he was at his mercy. Although Páez's proposal would consolidate the patriot hold over Los Llanos and suited the Caudillo's limited territorial ambition, it lacked Bolívar's vision. The argument raged all night and as dawn rose on 14 February, a consensus was still to be met. Unknown to the protagonists, the royalists had already slipped through Iribarren's net and were well on their way to the safety of the mountains.

Rather than make camp outside the city, Iribarren's Hussars had retired two miles to the south to the comparative comfort of Misión de Abajo, thereby leaving the northern road unguarded. At first Morillo couldn't believe his luck, but after watching the Hussars return to the Misión for a second night (from the vantage point of Calabozo's church tower), he decided to act. As the last of the light seeped from the day, he took a party of horsemen out through the gates to check for any cavalry pickets that he might have missed. The mission was a resounding success. There was no sign of the enemy to the north, and the riders even managed to round up some wild cattle from the prairie for the gruelling march that lay ahead. Knowing that time was of the essence, Morillo galloped back to the plaza to set his plan in motion. After marking the site for future retrieval, the cannon were buried, hundreds of captured muskets were destroyed and troops were ordered to dispose of the excess gunpowder by mixing it into the soil around town. In their haste it ignited. The explosion killed two and wounded six. More worryingly, the sound carried through the night to Iribarren's sentries. To Morillo's delight and disbelief they merely put it down to a false alarm and returned to their slumber.

On the eve of the Spaniards' departure, the local royalists began to voice fears of patriot reprisals should they remain behind. Accordingly Morillo offered them the protection of his army. After hurriedly packing a few possessions, many abandoned their homes. At midnight the evacuation got under way. Marching 'silently and in good order', they left town in three columns that regrouped once they reached the open plains.[1] The civilians, sick and wounded were then placed in the centre of a huge, mobile, infantry square, along with a small number of prisoners taken in the recent action, whilst the handful of remaining cavalry formed a skirmishing screen to cover their rear. Lending their horses to carry the wounded, the general and his officers took the unusual measure of joining their infantry on foot. As the most direct road passed too close to Bolívar's troops at Rastro, Morillo angled his march north-east. The route had the added advantage of skirting the Guarico River. The thickets that grew alongside its banks would offer valuable cover should enemy cavalry appear.

When news of the royalists' flight reached the patriot camp, it prompted fresh argument between Bolívar and Páez. Guessing that Morillo would head for Sombrero, the Caudillo wanted to cut across the meadows to the east to block him. Once more Bolívar had the last word, however, insisting on returning to Calabozo rather than risk losing the royalists' trail on the open plains. The decision made, they set off. After reaching the city at noon, a small garrison was left to guard the baggage, wounded and prisoners before the army continued the pursuit. Morillo was already 12 hours ahead, but The Liberator was finally acting with the urgency that the situation required. Setting a brutal pace, he drove his men on. A few miles later, a grisly discovery brought the column to a halt. Numerically mirroring Bolívar's offer of a prisoner exchange, 12 captured patriot officers and 20 soldiers had been 'cruelly butchered' and their bodies 'ranged in order across the road'.[2] Vowell was not the only one appalled by Morillo's cruelty and soon the army was clamouring for revenge. Fearing mutiny, Bolívar sent a messenger to Calabozo ordering the commander of the garrison to execute all prisoners. British protests were ignored, and only after a rider returned confirming the fate of the prisoners, did the army agree to move on.

Although atrocities were committed in the Napoleonic Wars, especially during the Grand Armée's Russian debacle of 1812, the experience of most British officers had been somewhat different. Wellington's campaigns, fought on the Iberian Peninsula as well as in France and Flanders, had generally seen a code of honour maintained. Aside from the brutal low-level warfare fought between the Spanish guerrillas and the French, and the terrible revenge taken when a city was forced after siege, the slaughter of prisoners in cold blood was rare. Captured officers were allowed to keep their swords and given considerable freedom provided they gave their parole, and battlefield truces to collect the wounded and remove the dead were commonplace. Even though the Creole elite and Morillo's Spanish officers would have been aware of such conventions, they were rarely applied in South America and the vast majority of combatants would have considered them ridiculous. This was the cruel legacy of Bolívar's 'War to the Death', a proclamation he had issued in 1814, stating that anyone who did not actively support his cause would be considered an enemy combatant and treated as such. Many British volunteers struggled to adjust to such callous disregard for human life. It was beyond their experience and broke the code of honour that they held so dear.

Until dawn on the 15th, Morillo's square made good progress, but as the sun rose over the arid plains its pace began to slow. Choking on the dust thrown up by their advance and hampered by the sick and wounded, the suffering increased as the temperature soared. Several civilians and soldiers were unable to keep up. Collapsing by the roadside, they were later captured by patriot cavalry scouts. Most were put to death on the spot. At midday, after a 12-hour forced march, the royalists reached the stream of Uriosa where Morillo called a halt. The men threw down their packs and rushed into the water to slake their thirsts, startling flocks of waterfowl. At 4.00pm, Páez's guard of honour appeared to the south. The Spanish Hussars formed line to receive them whilst their infantry formed up and continued north. As soon as they had closed on the enemy riders, the Llaneros charged. A number of Hussars were killed or wounded in the initial clash. Injured horses tumbled to the dust and men cried out for mercy. After their momentum had carried them through the enemy line, Páez's riders enveloped the survivors. The briefest of melees ensued before the Hussars broke, galloping after their infantry with the whooping Llaneros close behind. Knowing that panic was contagious, Morillo ordered the rear face of the square to halt, turn about and load. The men of La Unión levelled their muskets as the confused mass bore down on them. When the thundering hooves were within a few dozen yards, Morillo gave the order to fire. A ragged volley ripped out. Seven Hussars fell dead and a mass of horses went tumbling. As the smoke cleared, it revealed that the sacrifice had been worthwhile for the patriot riders had withdrawn. Shortly afterwards, the units of Cedeño and Monagas arrived, putting 2,000 cavalry at Páez's disposal. Without giving the Spaniards a chance to catch their breath, he threw them against the square in successive waves. Morillo's rearguard maintained discipline, and the men's steady fire as they edged backwards kept the horsemen at bay. After nightfall the attacks became less frequent, finally coming to an end at 2am. The patriot cavalry were too exhausted to continue, yet still the Spanish trudged on.

At dawn, the rising sun revealed the Ford of Samán over the river Guarico. Ahead lay the town of Sombrero and a series of wooded hills that represented the royalists' salvation. Having marched for one day and two nights, the last under constant attack, the troops were exhausted; yet Morillo knew that he could still not afford to relax his guard. Taking up defensive positions in the thicket on the north bank of the river, he ordered his men to cover the main ford. Once in place, the troops ate their remaining rations and waited for the republicans to make their move. Knowing it would be folly to send his riders against the royalists now that they were under cover, Páez restricted them to sniping from a distance whilst awaiting Bolívar's infantry, who eventually limped into view late that afternoon. Their march had been even more arduous than that of their enemy and impressed even Morillo, but they had paid a heavy price for their determination.[3] Their feet blistered and bloody, the men collapsed to the ground in exhaustion. Nevertheless, Bolívar decided to attack without delay. It was to be his third major error of judgement in three days.

The town of Sombrero was built on the summit of a wooded rise, which sloped gently north-westward from the Guarico. As the battle took place in the middle of the dry season, the river was fordable at several points. The track the two armies had been following led directly to the main crossing, the Ford of Sáman, before climbing the rise and passing through the centre of town. Both banks were covered in woodland, rendering Páez's cavalry useless in the forthcoming fight. Unlike Calabozo, the battle of Sombrero would be decided by infantry.

Even though a Spanish deserter had told Páez of an unguarded ford up-river, Bolívar choose to assault the Spanish position head-on. With the 24 British volunteers amongst them, the guard of honour, commanded by Lieutenant-Colonel Anzoátegui, was to lead the attack. Despite their exhaustion, Vowell noted that the men were keen to fight, animated by the memory of the atrocity they had passed on the road. Advancing into the shade of the woods, they came under ferocious fire from the 800 men of the 1st Navarra Battalion whom Morillo had ordered to hold the ford. However, Anzoátegui's men pushed on, taking casualties as they picked their way forward with the musket balls whipping through the trees. When they reached the far bank, the men formed line and a brief but bloody firefight ensued.

Infantry tactics of the era revolved around the limitations of the muzzle-fed, smoothbore musket. Reloading was a multi-stage process, drilled into recruits until they could fire two or three shots per minute. Firstly, a paper cartridge which held gunpowder and a single lead ball was bitten open. After adding a pinch to the musket's flash pan, the powder was poured down the barrel. The lead ball and cartridge scrap were then thrown in and rammed home. After cocking the hammer, which held a flint tightly gripped in its jaws, the musket was brought up to the shoulder and fired. On striking the flash pan, the flint sparked and the powder ignited, setting off the main charge. The ball was then sent hurtling down the 40in barrel towards its target. This, at least, was the theory. In practice, misfires were common, barrels were prone to splitting, the flints frequently shattered and the powder in the pan often failed.[4] Bad weather could also play havoc with the guns. Rainfall soaked the powder and made reloading impossible. Although a rag could be wrapped around the workings to keep it dry for the first shot, afterwards it became useless as a firearm. Even when they fired, muskets were shockingly inaccurate and most models did not even have sights.

THE BATTLE OF SOMBRERO

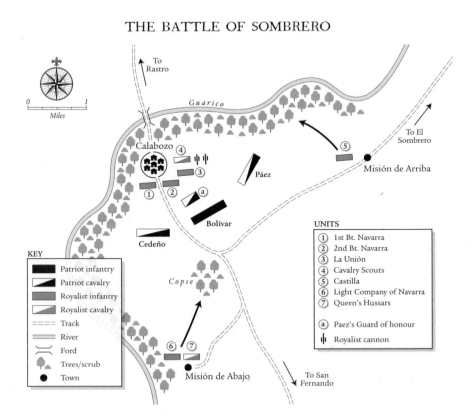

Contemporary studies indicate that at its effective range of 80 yards, less than 20 per cent of shots hit their target.[5] Training reflected these issues. Unlike the modern soldier who is taught to aim for specific targets, the Napoleonic infantryman of the line had to concentrate on reloading as swiftly as possible and maintain a rolling wave of fire in the general direction of the enemy. The limitations of the musket encouraged many commanders to prefer the 16in steel bayonet, the effectiveness of which was largely psychological. If troops could be made to rush at their enemy through the storm of shot fired against them, then their foes would invariably flee before the steel-tipped line crashed home. When the enemy was well disciplined or aided by difficult terrain, the success of such an attack was more doubtful, however, as the men of Bolívar's guard of honour were about to discover.

After firing a few volleys, Anzoátegui ordered his men to fix bayonets and charge across the river. Splashing through the shallow water, they scrambled up the far bank, but were driven back by a hail of musketry. Three times Anzoátegui re-formed the survivors and attacked, but to no avail. Scores were shot and died in the muddy water. One of the first to fall was an Italian staff officer, Colonel Passoni, who presented a fine target as he rode up and down the line urging the men forward. On the third attack, Anzoátegui himself was hit and stretchered from the field.

With the guard of honour close to breaking point, Bolívar tried to change the focus of the battle, throwing the battalions of Barlovento and Apure against the royalists' right. Morillo countered by reinforcing the position with his reserve. Again the patriots were held back by ordered Spanish volleys. Sensing Bolívar's exhausted troops were close to collapse, Morillo committed the last of his reserves, dispatching Brigadier Pascal Real and the 2nd Navarra Battalion to make a flanking attack against the patriot right. Real crossed the Guarico by another ford and caught Anzoátegui's men by surprise. Fully occupied with the firefight to their front, they failed to notice the new threat until it was too late. The Spanish infantry came crashing through the woods, a powder-blackened face behind every bayonet. Assailed on two sides, the guard of honour broke and fled. Two companies of the Castilla Battalion joined in the pursuit and the retreat became general. Whilst the battalions of Barlovento and Apure maintained their formation as they pulled back to the plains, the panic-stricken men of the guard scattered into the woods in ones and twos, only to be hunted down and bayoneted. No doubt remembering their butchered comrades on the plain outside Calabozo, Morillo's troops wreaked a terrible revenge. By the time the killing was done, the woods were 'seeded with dead'.[6] Such was the scale of the guard of honour's destruction that a Spanish private, Martín de la Chica, captured its standard – the pride of any regiment that was often defended to the last man.

Thirsty and exhausted, the patriot survivors sought refuge under the protection of their cavalry on the open plain. Unwilling to reveal themselves, the royalists remained in the cover of the woods, ending the bloody infantry clash just 15 minutes after it had begun. With his foot soldiers defeated, Bolívar belatedly consented to Páez's plan. At the head of his cavalry, the Caudillo galloped round the royalist positions in a sweeping flanking manoeuvre, crossing the Guarico at the unprotected ford up-river. From the high ground on the far bank, Morillo gauged Páez's intention, however, and withdrew his forces into the hills to the north, preventing any possible cavalry pursuit and bringing the encounter to a conclusion.

Over 100 patriots had died. Many more were wounded. The toll amongst the officers was particularly heavy. Besides Passoni and Anzoátegui there were 19 other commissioned casualties, including several British volunteers. Most lost their lives in the woods following the rout and were later buried in 'a nameless grave'.[7] After the battle, the divergent interests of Bolívar and Páez once again threatened to tear the army apart. Despite the defeat, The Liberator still wanted to move on to Caracas, but the Llanero was equally vehement that they return to Calabozo. Several motives drove Bolívar to push his policy. Aside from the symbolic, political and financial importance of the capital itself, the fertile valleys of Aragua that lay to its south-west produced rich crops of tobacco, coffee and cocoa, the revenues of which helped finance the royalists' war effort. Bolívar, who had grown up on a ranch in the area, knew its capture would aid his cause whilst proving equally detrimental to the enemy. A final consideration was that he would also be on home ground. There was little sense of national identity in Venezuela and outside the Spanish power base along the coast, regional or even local politics prevailed. Bolívar knew that Páez was the true master of the plains, and that his command of any army raised there could only continue with the Caudillo's support. Once he reached the valleys of Aragua and the countryside surrounding Caracas, on the other hand, his authority would be secure.

In the end, fear that his army would disintegrate if he continued to defy Páez momentarily overcame Bolívar's desire to attack the capital, and on 21 February, the army returned to Calabozo where a recruitment drive began. Still largely oblivious to the battle of wills dictating the army's destiny, the British survivors, now numbering fewer than a dozen, enjoyed the pick of the accommodation in the city, a luxury they appreciated following the hardships of the campaign.[8] Following the defeat morale was low amongst the conscripts, and men were deserting the cause as fast as new recruits could be found. On one night alone, an entire cavalry brigade slipped away never to return. Knowing that whilst the army was inactive and in friendly territory the temptation to desert was too strong for many to resist, Bolívar began to regret moving to Calabozo and his thoughts returned to his original plan. This time, however, to avoid an irrevocable split with his ally, he compromised. Páez and his guard of honour were allowed to ride due south to renew the siege of San Fernando, whilst The Liberator would restart his floundering campaign by taking the remaining troops north to threaten Caracas.

On 3 March, Bolívar's troops set off. Two days later at the village of San Pablo, they were reinforced by a regiment of cavalry led by generals José Monagas and Rafael Urdaneta. Accompanying them were Lieutenant-Colonel John Needham, Captain John Ferrier and the nine other officers and NCOs who had sailed from Belgium. Having joined Urdaneta at Angostura, they brought the total number of British with Bolívar to 17.[9] On the 7th, the army arrived at Ortiz. The town lay between the plains and the high cultivated valleys of Aragua, beyond which were Caracas and the coast. As the mountain road was unsuitable for cannon, Bolívar sent his artillery back to Calabozo. The army then wound its way into the wooded foothills. Whilst the infantry toiled up the slopes, the cavalry divided into two units under generals Monagas and Pedro Zaraza, and moved ahead to scout the route.

Many years later, Vowell would recall the journey through the high country in some detail. As they climbed, they passed the deserted, war-torn towns of Flores, Parapara and San Juan de los Morros, the latter famed for the mighty rock formations that rose beyond it to the north. After the sterility of the plains, the natural abundance of the Aragua Valley seemed paradisiacal. On the upper slopes 'European fruits and vegetables flourished', whilst the higher humidity of the valley floor suited the 'varied products of the tropics'.[10] Sick of the monotonous diet of unseasoned beef dished out in Los Llanos, the volunteers were delighted with the fresh produce. Vowell particularly enjoyed the cocoa that prior to the onset of war had fetched a high price on the European market. On 11 March the army arrived at Villa de Cura, 'a considerable town', where 'many of the houses were inhabited, and provisions of every kind were ... plentiful'.[11] The volunteers were quartered in a magnificent building in the main square, the royalist owner of which had fled the rebels' advance.[12] On the march the next morning, they enjoyed views across the valleys 'beautiful beyond description'.[13] At midday, Bolívar called a halt at the ranch of San Mateo, his childhood home. Most of the 1,000 slaves who used to work the land had long since fled or been conscripted, but a few old women still remained. Vowell was moved by their reaction upon seeing 'their old master'. They 'appeared quite delighted ... surrounding him, embracing his knees, and rejoicing at his return'.[14]

Amongst the slaves Vowell saw that afternoon may well have been Hipolíta, Bolívar's beloved former nanny. No doubt influenced by this formative relationship, The Liberator was sincere in his desire for universal emancipation, a belief which was reflected in the policies he pursued throughout his career. In 1810 Bolívar and Miranda had banned the trading of slaves as it directly contravened the beliefs of the Enlightenment upon which the revolution had been founded. Six years later, when he landed near Barcelona to establish the Third Republic, Bolívar had issued a proclamation offering all slaves who joined his army their freedom, thus repaying his debt to Alexandre Pétion of Haiti who had made the pledge a precondition for providing the expedition with arms and supplies. In 1821 a policy of enforced manumission would be introduced, but would prove so unpopular amongst the country's elite that it would become impossible to impose. Although Bolívar immediately freed the few slaves remaining on his own estates, the practice continued largely unchecked amongst his aristocratic peers. They argued that their vast ranches faced economic collapse without free labour and feared a repeat of the Haitian-inspired slave revolt of May 1795 which had terrified the inhabitants of the city of Coro in north-west Venezuela. Although badly organized and brutally crushed, the memory of Chirino and González's uprising still haunted the ruling classes. Undeterred, Bolívar continued to write abolition into law but his moves were blocked at every turn, and the practice would not be entirely outlawed in Venezuela until 1854.

On the morning of 13 March, the army was welcomed into the city of La Victoria, whose people were 'well known … for their patriotic principles'.[15] Now just 20 miles from the capital, the sense of excitement was palpable. The locals 'raised triumphal arches across the streets … [and] vied … with each other in their demonstrations of rejoicing'.[16] General Urdaneta was named governor of the city and preparations began for a ball in honour of the occasion. Believing he had his enemy on the back foot, Bolívar had no time for such frivolities, so he pushed on without delay to Caracas.

Unknown to The Liberator, General Morillo was a mere matter of miles away. The Spaniard had been busy since Sombrero. Touring the cities and towns to the west of Caracas, he had gathered considerable reinforcements and was now ready to go on the offensive. Planning to encircle the republican army, he had divided his forces into two. Morillo himself was in command of the largest contingent. Consisting of 5,000 infantry, cavalry and a few guns, it was based several miles to the west of the patriots. A second army of 900 men under General Miguel de La Torre was to the east, on the approaches to Caracas. As Urdaneta was preparing for the ball, Morillo was closing on the enemy rear whilst the patriot troops, in their turn, were advancing to attack La Torre. So intent was Bolívar on seizing the capital that he didn't realize he was falling into a trap.

On 14 March, the patriot vanguard arrived at Cocuizas on the outskirts of Caracas, where it encountered La Torre's men. The first shots were ringing out between the opposing pickets when Bolívar received disastrous news. The cavalry outposts of Monagas and Zaraza, which he had sent to Maracay and La Cabrera to guard his rear, had been routed by Morillo's vanguard under General Tomás Morales and were now fleeing in the face of the Spanish advance. Bolívar now had La Torre ahead of him and Morillo behind. To be caught between the two would be catastrophic. He had little choice but to retreat and hope that he could reach the crossroads at La Victoria before Morillo sealed the trap.

That night a storm broke out. Rain lashed down on the retreating column and the mountain track was churned into a morass. When the patriots reached the outskirts of La Victoria, La Torre's vanguard suddenly appeared behind them. Colonel Vásquez formed his cavalry in line across the road to buy enough time for the rest of the army to escape. In the city centre, where the locals had been enjoying Urdaneta's ball, news of the patriot withdrawal was met with panic. Fearful of being caught by the Spanish advance, the revellers spilled out onto the streets to join the army. Hard pressed by La Torre's troops and realizing that Morillo's 5,000 would also soon appear, Bolívar gave them just five minutes to evacuate. As the firing from the skirmish in their rear drew ever closer, Vowell witnessed the panic increase to a crescendo:

> … the condition of the unfortunate emigrants was wretched beyond description. Husbands, who had no time to take leave of their wives and families; and delicate females, some with infants at the breast, ignorant of the fate of their husbands and fathers and without a friend to assist them, were mingled promiscuously with the troops and baggage mules, on mountain roads in many places knee deep in mud. Several had rushed out of the ball room, on the first alarm, and had joined the retreat, without the possibility of obtaining shoes or clothing better suited to such weather… Although most officers belonging to the army, who were possessed of a horse or a mule – especially the British volunteers – gave it up readily to these unfortunate females, yet numbers were obliged to hurry along on foot, without shoes or sufficient covering. Many dropped during the night, through fatigue and exhaustion, and either perished from the inclemency of the weather, or still worse, fell into the hands of the merciless Spaniards, from whom they could only expect the most brutal treatment.[17]

Later that night Vowell saw Bolívar riding alone; although his face was muffled in the folds of his cloak, the Englishman still noted his despair. At dawn on 15 March the patriots reached Villa de Cura, where they were joined by Zaraza's cavalry. Now safe from the risk of encirclement a halt was called, allowing the ravenous troops to bolt some rations or snatch a few moments of sleep on the muddy ground whilst Bolívar held a council of war. After a heated debate, the patriot generals decided to face the Spanish at La Puerta, a high valley a few miles to the south-west, rather then risk being overtaken and surrounded in the mountains. At 2.00am on the 16th, at the village of Bocachica, Morales's cavalry burst upon them again. Two companies of infantry from the regiment of Barcelona were added to Vásquez's rearguard and together they conducted a fighting withdrawal. At 4.00am the main body of the army arrived at La Puerta. After sending the civilians, wounded and baggage on to San Juan de los Morros, The Liberator deployed his men into line of battle and awaited the Spanish onslaught.

Chapter 7

'A LOCK OF ... AUBURN HAIR'

L a Puerta was an inauspicious choice of battlefield for the patriots. In February 1814, the valley had witnessed the defeat of over 3,000 men led by Campo Elías. Four months later, with the debris of the previous encounter still littering the field, the victorious royalist general, José Boves, had repeated the feat, destroying a second patriot army under Bolívar himself.[1] The battles led to the downfall of the Second Republic and forced The Liberator's flight to New Granada. Although the memory may well have haunted Bolívar four years later, it seems not to have influenced his decision to stand and fight.

The battlefield was made up of undulating land divided by a steep-banked mountain brook, known as the Quebrada del Semen. So precipitous was the descent into the water that aside from a solitary ford, it formed an impassable barrier to cavalry. On either side of the stream the land sloped steeply upwards. A series of low wooded hills rose to the east and the valley was surrounded by rocky, scrub-covered heights. The road which the armies had followed from Villa de Cura entered the plain from the north-west. After fording the stream beside a small house, it left through a narrow ravine leading to the town of San Juan de los Morros, the patriots' only line of retreat.

Before dawn, Bolívar formed his 1,500 infantry in line along the south bank of the stream. Colonel Valdés, an inveterate gambler who would come to be loathed by the volunteers, commanded the left wing, comprising the battalions of Barlovento and Barcelona. The centre was held by the Valeroso Regiment, formed in column and commanded by General Urdaneta. Bolívar's guard of honour, without Anzoátegui (who was still recovering from the wound he had suffered at Sombrero) was on the right. Aside from Lieutenant-Colonel Rooke, who stayed by The Liberator's side throughout the battle as his aide-de-camp, the 17 British volunteers were spread throughout the infantry regiments in twos and threes.[2] The patriot cavalry were kept in reserve in three columns. Following heavy losses at Maracay in the build-up to the battle, both riders and horses were exhausted. They would only play a minor role in the coming fight.

For the first time since the retreat had begun, The Liberator was looking particularly animated. Wearing a distinctive leopard skin cap, he rode up and down the line encouraging his 'tatterdemalion bands'.[3] Shivering in the chill night air, they listened to the crackle of approaching musketry as Vásquez's cavalry inched backwards in the face of the Spanish vanguard. At first light the riders galloped into sight. Splashing across the ford, they headed to the rear to join the reserve. Minutes later the royalists appeared. Well-armed and resplendent in their new uniforms, La Torre's men marched out of the rising sun down the road from Villa de Cura, crashed to a halt and formed line a few hundred yards from the far bank of the stream.

At first, neither side was willing to engage the other. The patriots had only halted their retreat as a stand-up fight was preferable to being overtaken and surrounded in the mountains. La Torre was also happy to delay. Unknown to his enemies, the 1,500 troops he had deployed were merely the vanguard of a much larger force under Morillo, still

THE BATTLE OF SEMEN

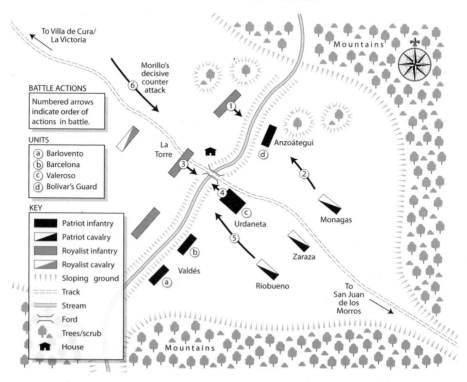

several miles away. If La Torre could hold the patriots for long enough, the arrival of Morillo's troops would surely seal their victory.

Even the bravest of veterans were besieged by doubt in the moments before a battle. A British officer serving in Wellington's Peninsular campaign left an insightful account which would no doubt have struck a cord with the volunteers at Semen:

> ... time appears to move upon leaden wings; every minute seems an hour, and every hour a day. Then a strange commingling of levity and seriousness within ... [each man] – a levity which prompts him to laugh, he scarce knows why; and a seriousness which urges him ... to lift up a mental prayer to the Throne of Grace. On such occasions, little or no conversation passes. The privates generally lean upon their firelocks – the officers upon their swords; and few words, except monosyllables ... are wasted ... the faces of the bravest often change colour, and the limbs of the most resolute tremble, not with fear, but with anxiety... On the whole, it is a situation of higher excitement, and darker and deeper agitation, than any other in human life; nor can he be said to have felt all which man is capable of feeling, who has not filled it.[4]

When the fighting began, it started slowly. Several small-scale skirmishes broke out, with neither side committing itself fully. The first was initiated by La Torre. Ordering his left flank to deploy light troops, he hoped to capture the heights dominating the east of the battlefield.

Light troops were the Napoleonic general's most frequently deployed 'weapon'. Thrown ahead of their parent formations, the skirmishers formed a loose screen between the lines, where they conducted their own private struggle against the light troops of the enemy. Unlike the majority of foot soldiers, who fought shoulder to shoulder in fixed formations, skirmishers were trained to use their initiative and had a comparatively high degree of autonomy. Commonly working in pairs, they advanced in small rushes. One provided cover, crouched behind a rock or bush, whilst his partner dashed forward. Once within range, they fired at their own pace, taking deliberate aim at specific targets, their goal to drive the enemy skirmishers back towards their lines. Only then could the victors move forward and begin picking off enemy officers. One historian has compared Napoleonic skirmishers to a swarm of midges: 'giving way in the face of any determined ... advance but quickly returning if the enemy halted, and constantly biting.'[5] Although effective in softening up opposing formations, light troops were not without weaknesses. They lacked the destructive, demoralizing punch of volley fire required to win set piece battles and their fluidity could leave them exposed to enemy cavalry. Training manuals of the day provided scant instruction for those caught in the open. One unhelpfully advised they feign death in the hope that the cavalry thunder past, leaving them unmolested.

The first Spanish attempt to win the heights on the patriots' right was repulsed by the light troops of Bolívar's guard of honour, but further skirmishes broke out as the royalists continued to probe for weaknesses. Bolívar cantered up and down the line all morning, accompanied by Rooke and his other aides, whom he periodically dispatched with orders to counter each Spanish thrust. At 10.00am, La Torre threw his heaviest skirmisher attack yet against Bolívar's right. Outnumbered, the republican light troops fell back to their main line, allowing the royalist sharpshooters to move in and pick their targets. Their musketry dropped several officers and the whole line began to cede ground. Seeing the danger, Bolívar ordered his cavalry reserve into action. The riders swept round from the rear, wheeled and charged. Cheering, they drove the enemy skirmishers before them. Many were ridden down and lanced from behind. The rest scurried back to the safety of their lines.

As the tempo of the battle built throughout the morning, the latest British recruit to join Bolívar's army was nearing the field. Having left Angostura in late February, Lieutenant-Colonel James English, commander of Colonel Hippisley's advance party, had travelled up the Orinoco and Apure rivers to San Fernando. He had then continued on horseback to Calabozo, where Lieutenant Thomas Smith and the two NCOs who had been accompanying him (now too weakened by illness to go on) were left behind. The lieutenant-colonel had then made the final leg of his journey alone. As he neared La Puerta towards mid-morning, English heard musketry ahead and spurring his horse up a rise, he was rewarded with a panoramic view of the battlefield. Riding down to the patriot lines, he reported to Bolívar. Amongst the gaggle of staff officers surrounding the general, English recognized Lieutenant-Colonel Rooke, an 'old acquaintance' from his days in the British Army.[6] After welcoming the new arrival, Bolívar sent him into action with Captain Grant (of the prize clarinet) to scout the extreme right wing and ensure no royalists were able to outflank them. Riding out to the edge of a steep ravine, the 36-year old former army clerk came under fire for the first time when Spanish 'sharpshooters' opened up from the far side of the ridge.[7] English was hit 'on the left shoulder'. Luckily, 'the chain strap' of his uniform bore the brunt of the impact and the bullet caused only 'momentary pain' and 'a slight contusion'.[8] Seeing the ravine was impassable and the flank secure, the two British officers turned back. With rifle fire kicking up spouts of dust behind them, they galloped down into the valley to report to Bolívar.

At midday, La Torre threw an infantry column against the patriot centre to divert attention from his failing left flank. The screen of skirmishers lining the riverbank barely slowed their momentum. Bolívar ordered General Urdaneta to take the regiments of Valeroso, Barcelona and his guard of honour and throw them back. The lines met and began exchanging volleys over the stream. Sergeants yelled out firing commands with relentless rhythm. *MAKE READY! ... PRESENT! ... FIRE!* Their faces blackened by powder smoke and stung by shards of flying flint, the men reloaded. Biting open the paper cartridges, they spat the ball down the barrel, put a pinch of powder in the pan and rammed the charge home. The lines were so close that men in the front ranks could make out individuals facing them. When the smoke was lifted by the breeze, glances were exchanged and insults traded. Volley followed volley. The patriot standards were set ablaze by scorched wadding spat from the royalists' muskets. Dozens of men fell as the balls bit home, thudding into flesh, clattering off belt buckles and ringing off bayonets. For 15 minutes the volleys crashed out, echoing down the valley to Morillo's advancing division. Throwing down their packs, the royalist reinforcements raced forward. Despite having marched through the night, they were desperate to reach the field on time.

Back at the heart of the action, Bolívar seemed to 'lose his senses'.[9] Forcing his way through the ranks, The Liberator grabbed one of the burning banners and advanced to the riverbank. With complete disregard for his own safety, he flung the flag into the enemy line, exhorting his men to rush forward and retrieve it. With a cheer the patriots swarmed down the bank, a number of British officers amongst them. A final volley cut several down. The rest splashed across the stream, now running red and filled with corpses, and plunged into the Spanish ranks. Their line buckled but did not break. Vicious hand-to-hand fighting broke out. Men bayoneted, stabbed, clawed and clubbed one another to death.

Peering through the smoke from his position behind the patriot centre, Urdaneta ordered Commander Riobueno to lead his cavalry down the riverbank and hit the Spanish column in the flank. The assault proved too much for the royalists, who began to edge backwards, but the advantage had been gained at a heavy cost. Several patriot officers had fallen in the final charges and General Urdaneta himself had been hit as he was ordering Riobueno into the attack. Streaming forwards over the bodies of their own dead, the patriot masses were now largely leaderless. The attack began to lose cohesion and the battle swung in the balance once more.

With perfect timing, Morillo entered the fray. Having grown increasingly anxious on his approach though the valley, the general and his staff had spurred their horses into the gallop and arrived on the field ahead of their infantry. When composing his memoirs several years later, Morillo recalled how he tried to rally the men, but neither his 'voice nor the efforts of the commanders or officers ... could ... control the general disorder'.[10] Moments later his infantry arrived. The first to take the field was the battalion of La Unión. Forming column on a small rise just behind the front line, the soldiers opened fire onto the patriot centre. Immediately the leaderless troops began to inch back. A royalist Creole battalion from Valencia then formed up to the right of La Unión and fired further volleys into the retreating mass. In the patriot rear, the cavalry reserve sensed their infantry's mounting panic and took off down the road to San Juan before it was too late. Left alone to their fate, the republican infantry faced disaster.

Seeing his chance to finish the patriot centre, Morillo took command of a squad of horse artillery that had just gained the field and led the riders in a thunderous charge. Men were crushed under hoof and a Scottish captain named Noble MacMullin was knocked unconscious in the crush. The charge's momentum carried the horse artillery deep into the patriot centre and the lines were now utterly confused. For a few desperate moments the hand-to-hand fighting reached new depths of brutality. Captain José Ortega of the horse artillery was dragged from his saddle and killed by a bayonet thrust to the chest. One of his troopers, Manuel Mengibar, intent on avenging Ortega's death, cut his way into a knot of patriots, seized a battalion standard and carried it proudly to the rear. A while later, Morillo himself was nearly killed. Having seen the general and his staff riding towards him, a patriot soldier had hidden behind a tree. Leaping out as he passed, he wounded the general with his lance, before being hacked to pieces.[11] Despite the blood pouring down his side Morillo remained in the saddle. Grabbing the banner seized moments before by Mengibar, he cut back with his spurs and urged his troops to victory.

On the far right of the patriot line, lieutenants Vowell and Braithwaite were leading the 90-strong Grenadier Company of the Barloventos, tasked with dislodging a detachment of skirmishers from a small wood to their front. Despite Vowell's urgings, the Grenadiers refused to take cover. They faced the royalists standing shoulder to shoulder, blindly firing volleys into a growing sea of smoke. The royalists, on the other hand, used their training well. Having taken positions 'behind every rock and tree' they poured on a murderous fire, cutting the Grenadiers to ribbons.[12] Soon only the British officers and 15 men were left standing. Seeing the rest of the patriot line to their left buckle and rout, the survivors dropped their weapons and fled into the hills.

In the centre, Bolívar tried to rally his men, but in vain. Caught up in the human tide, he was swept through the ravine towards San Juan de los Morros. The last vestiges of patriot resistance then collapsed. Dropping their guns, the entire line turned on its heels. The Spaniards were merciless in victory, cutting into the knot of men as they struggled through the narrow pass. Those who fell were bayoneted as they begged for mercy. Others were crushed underfoot. Back by the stream, Captain MacMullin came to, only to find himself surrounded by the enemy. Fortunately for the Scot, just as one royalist was poised to deliver the *coup de grâce*, he was recognized as a foreigner and taken captive instead. Whilst being marched to the rear, he overheard a discussion of Morillo's wound and decided upon a ploy that undoubtedly saved his life. Praying he would remember the little medical training he had received, he announced he was a doctor and offered to treat the general on condition his life was spared. The Spaniards swallowed the story and MacMullin was taken to a small hut where Morillo was being treated. At first sight, the general's wound was horrific. Having pierced his left side between hip and stomach, the lance had passed through his body ripping a 3in wide exit hole through his back.[13] Luckily for MacMullin, however, it had missed all the vital organs and after successfully binding the wound, he was thanked and led to the rear. His good fortune was completed shortly afterwards when he managed to escape in the confusion that very night. After eventually rejoining his astonished comrades, MacMullin gained considerable celebrity as the tale of his ruse and subsequent flight over the mountains spread.

Regardless of such tales of individual good fortune, the battle of La Puerta was a crippling defeat for the patriots. Bolívar's infantry had virtually ceased to exist. As many as 800 died on the field, the majority cut down in the ravine or along the road to San Juan de los Morros following the rout. An eye witness report printed in *The Times* claimed 'that for five leagues ... nothing was seen but dead bodies'.[14] Amongst the dead were 40 patriot officers, including eight British volunteers. Others escaped the battlefield, but were later captured and killed in cold blood. One report printed in *The Courier* claimed that the royalists put 500 prisoners 'to the sword'.[15] Hundreds more were wounded, but managed to escape. Adding to his scars from Waterloo, Lieutenant-Colonel Rooke was hit twice as he followed Bolívar round the field. Coronet Brown was also badly wounded. Both men escaped the field and were sent back to Angostura to recover. Besides the casualties, the patriots also lost vast quantities of arms, ammunition, horses and supplies. Bolívar's personal papers fell into enemy hands and three captured standards, including that taken by Mengibar, were sent to Caracas and paraded triumphantly through the streets.

With hindsight, the patriot defeat was unsurprising. The broken terrain determined that Semen was a battle decided by infantry and the Spanish foot soldiers were better armed, equipped, clothed and disciplined than their foes, who, with the timely arrival of Morillo's troops, had also been outnumbered. Bolívar had led his men bravely and although he cannot be blamed for the defeat, the massacre that followed was largely precipitated by his choice of battlefield. Perhaps the most crucial consideration when positioning troops was the ease with which the field could be abandoned. At Semen the only line of retreat was through a bottleneck ravine. Even though this seems like a gross error, it may well have been part of Bolívar's deliberate design. In later battles, notably Pantano de Vargas, he would also place his troops in positions which offered little hope of escape. His enemies believed these sites were chosen as he had little faith that his troops would hold firm.[16] In choosing to put his men, quite literally, with their backs against the wall, Bolívar ensured they would fight.

Even though the patriots had suffered terribly, they would eventually replace their losses. The royalists, on the other hand, would never fight so well again. Perhaps the most significant long-term consequence of the battle was Morillo's inability to recover from his wound. This would prove far more costly for the royalists than the 400 casualties they had suffered. The general endured crippling pain down his left side for the remainder of his life, limiting his role in subsequent campaigns. The lance blow also left deep scars in his psyche. Prior to Semen, Morillo had shown a verve and commitment which had kept the royalists in the fight; yet following the battle he had lost much of his drive. On 18 March, just two days after the victory, he begged the king to be relieved of command. Ferdinand VII knew his worth, however, and refused the request. Morillo would remain in South America for three more years, but the single-minded, ruthless determination which had characterized his leadership would never return.

Now led by La Torre, the royalists chased the patriots ten miles along the track to San Juan de los Morros before exhaustion forced them to abandon the pursuit. The patriot retreat then continued southwards, halting momentarily in Caño del Caiman, where Bolívar met Commander Blanca, who had ridden to offer his aid after hearing of the disaster. After ordering Blanca to wait and rally any stragglers, Bolívar continued south to Rastro. Four days later, Blanca's force was attacked by Colonel López and 500 cavalry. The patriot commander was cut down and his troops killed or dispersed. Having taken to the field at Semen with a complement of 2,500, by the time Bolívar's army reached Rastro, it was reduced to an exhausted rabble of just 300 men.

Small groups of survivors were still scattered throughout the hills to the south and east of the battlefield several days after the defeat. Some were captured and executed. Others melted away and returned to their families, but a loyal few managed to rejoin the army. One of the latter was Lieutenant Richard Vowell. Heavily encumbered by their kit, Vowell and Braithwaite had been left behind when their troops were routed. Braithwaite was captured and subsequently executed by firing squad, but Vowell had managed to hide. Crawling through the undergrowth, he emerged onto a flat rock overlooking the battlefield. Beneath him the valley 'was thickly spotted over with bodies, especially in the defile leading to Los Morros, where men and horses were lying in heaps'.[17] To one side, on 'a small eminence', a group of enemy officers interrogated prisoners who were then shot.[18] As night approached, La Torre set up camp on the field and sent patrols into the surrounding area to search for fugitives. Vowell spent the evening hiding in the scrub, before creeping out 'towards midnight' to make his escape. Keeping to the low ground, he passed by the stream, careful not to disturb 'the vultures and wild dogs [that] had already commenced their banquet'. He then 'proceeded cautiously up the bed of the river … concealed by … bushes on the banks'.[19]

Glad to leave the carnage behind, Vowell rested in a thick copse near a sugar cane patch where he was looked after by a sympathetic local farmer and his daughters. After a few days, having recovered his strength, he resolved to push on. The family bid him farewell 'with many embraces and kind wishes' and gave him food, a tinderbox, a pipe and tobacco.[20] Vowell then travelled south-west through thick forest, followed by '*araquato*' monkeys swinging through the treetops in troops 40-strong.[21] At night he slept in the open, listening to prowling panthers and snakes slithering past. Beginning to despair of ever seeing his comrades again, the gregarious Englishman even considered handing himself in to the enemy. But then just as his spirits were hitting their lowest ebb, he came across a fellow fugitive, 2nd Lieutenant Bicente Artaóna. Driven together through desperation, the unlikely couple soon became firm friends. Jumping over boulders flanking cascading streams, they descended from the mountains. Later, on the wooded hills north of the plains, they were nearly caught by a detachment of royalist cavalry under Colonel López. Less vigilant were some snoozing sentries at San Juan de Parapara. Arriving at Ortiz, they were given provisions by Don Cayetano, a local priest and patriot sympathizer. Vowell gladly accepted his offer of a change of clothes as his uniform, purchased for £200 in London just a few months previously, was now worn to rags.[22]

After leaving Ortiz, Vowell and Artaóna entered a thick palm forest, where they were woken one morning by a band of patriot guerrillas. The 80 riders greeted them warmly and slaughtered a young bullock to feed them. Having eaten his fill, Vowell sat back to observe his new companions. 'Their clothing, although not uniform, was very good of its kind, and had evidently been obtained by plunder; to which they were also ... indebted for their silver-mounted bridles. They were all well-armed with carbines, lances and sabres; and had dragoons' valises behind their saddles.'[23] The guerrillas 'appeared to be on a perfect equality with each other, except that they all paid deference to a tall powerful negro'. This was the infamous Bicentico Hurtádo, whose facial scars and missing fingers attested to a history of violence.

Vowell soon grew to despise the guerrillas, who spent their days feasting, drinking and fighting with knives. In the evenings they set up ambushes on the roads outside Ortiz. Any men taken prisoner were killed immediately. Women were held for ransom or for pleasure. One afternoon, whilst riding through a guava wood, 'the men discovered ... a very large water-snake ... which they resolved to kill'. Vowell was fascinated by the encounter. On 'being disturbed', the snake 'raised its head out of the marsh, to the full height of a man, and appeared ready to dart on the first person that should venture within its reach'. The men, 'advancing cautiously, threw a lazo round its throat'. Having attached the other end to the tail of a horse, they dragged it 'along the plain about half a league, until it was so far rendered incapable of resistance, that one of the men dismounted, and cut off its head at several blows with a *machete*'. Vowell then examined the beast. It was 'full twenty-five feet in length, and thick in proportion'. As its 'belly appear[ed] ... preternaturally distended', the guerrillas 'opened [it] out of curiosity, and found it to contain a young calf, which did not appear to have been long swallowed'.[24] Several days later, after an abortive, alcohol-fuelled raid on Ortiz, the bandits were driven from the region by a Spanish cavalry patrol. Heading south into patriot territory, Vowell finally rejoined the army at San Fernando in early May, six weeks after his adventure had begun.

Bolívar couldn't believe his eyes when Vowell was shown into his quarters. A string of oaths and curses escaped his lips before he regained his composure.[25] Whilst Vowell ate, Bolívar questioned him about the areas he had passed through and the enemy units he had seen. After his recent privations, Vowell was delighted with his meal at the general's table, especially the wine, which was 'no where else to be met with'.[26] Later, he rejoined his few remaining comrades and was told of what had happened since the battle. On 24 March, eight days after Semen, Bolívar's 300 survivors had been reinforced by 2,500 cavalry under Páez. The Caudillo had also brought good news. Having finally starved the royalist garrison out of San Fernando, killing or capturing the majority as they fled, he had consolidated patriot control over the southern plains. Reinvigorated by the report and fresh troops, Bolívar decided to go back on the offensive. Lacking foot soldiers, he threw together a makeshift infantry regiment composed entirely of officers. The new unit, named *Sagrado* (sacred), was led by The Liberator himself. Anzoátegui, having now recovered from the wounds sustained at Sombrero, was given the post of sergeant-major. Amongst the ranks was Lieutenant-Colonel English, one of the few British officers remaining with the army. Despite having worn the same shirt for eight days, the former clerk remained remarkably upbeat. In a hastily scribbled note to Colonel Hippisley (then in Angostura with the 1st Hussars) he predicted that 'the next battle will, without doubt, decide the fortune of Venezuela', adding that 'all are confident [of victory], because general Paez with his Llaneros, are under arms'.[27]

Bolívar attacked the royalists at Ortiz on 26 March. Although The Liberator's cautious advance afforded him the advantage of surprise, General La Torre had placed his 1,000 men in an excellent position. High up above the plain, the royalists held a narrow, rocky ravine which protected both their flanks whilst also negating the patriots' cavalry advantage. At 11.30am, the battle commenced. The officers of the newly formed *Sagrado* unit were the first to advance. In intense heat, they closed with the outlying Spanish picket under Captain Urquiza. Despite being vastly outnumbered, Urquiza's troops maintained discipline, falling back slowly over the broken ground, occasionally stopping to give their attackers a volley. The delay allowed La Torre to reinforce them with the

1st Company of Castilla. The patriots still outnumbered them by four to one, however, and continued to inch forward up the slope. Seeing that he risked being pushed from the high ground, La Torre ordered the American loyalist regiment of Valencia to join the fray. Charging downhill with fixed bayonets, the men swept the patriots before them. Scurrying down the slope, several were bayoneted in the back. Others were overtaken and captured.

Meanwhile, on the right of the Spanish lines, 200 patriot cavalry led by Genaro Vásquez dismounted, loaded their carbines and attempted to outflank the enemy. As they neared the summit of a neighbouring ridge, they were spotted. A brief exchange of gunfire ensued, before they were also sent tumbling down to the plain by another determined royalist charge. Vásquez was wounded three times in the encounter and died that night. Whilst the Llanero Lancers lurked menacingly on the plains below, La Torre was afraid to follow up these partial victories, allowing Bolívar to rally his men and launch them uphill in a final attack. Picking their way up the slope between the dead and wounded, they closed with the enemy. Once more, the royalists held firm. Their accurate fire opened bloody gaps in the patriot line. Hit in the stomach, men doubled up in agony, cradling their spilled guts; others fell with shattered limbs; those shot through the head died instantly. Soon the patriots were showing signs of breaking. Amidst the gun smoke, English noticed General Carlos Soublette, one of Bolívar's staff officers. More used to writing dispatches than firing a musket in the line, Soublette was 'seeking shelter' from the hail of lead 'behind a tree'.[28] English had no time to berate him. The patriots were now rapidly ceding ground. With each shot they took a pace or two backwards. Men in the front ranks tried to burrow into the heart of the formation whilst those in the rear and on the flanks peeled away. Seeing the enemy line splinter, La Torre ordered his men to charge. Not waiting for the bayonets to reach them, the patriots fled. Whooping, the royalists pursued them. A massacre was only prevented by a series of furious covering charges driven home by Páez's Lancers once they had reached the plains. Several Spaniards were killed and the rest pushed back up the slope where the Llaneros were unable to follow. This proved to be the final action of the day. The men, having fought for six hours in intense heat, were exhausted. Nevertheless, the battle proved indecisive. Neither side could fairly claim to have gained a strategic advantage, but the patriots' losses had been far heavier. Roughly 300 had been killed or wounded, compared to 121 royalists.

After the battle the patriots retired to the river. The men washed the powder residue from their mouths after hours of loading and firing. As the dust settled, James English encountered Páez lying 'on the ground foaming at the mouth'. The general was in the grip of one of his habitual epileptic fits, brought on by battle rage. Undaunted, English 'went up to [him] … and having sprinkled some water in his face, and forced a little down his throat, he speedily recovered'.[39] The Caudillo, who had killed '39 enemy that day', presented the 'bloody lance' by his side to English, 'as a memento of his friendship and affection'.[30] The colonel, who had been promoted by Bolívar for his bravery on the field, was so proud of his gory souvenir that he would later have it included in a portrait he commissioned on his return to England.[31]

The next morning the patriots retreated towards San Fernando. En route, Bolívar paused in a village recently abandoned by the royalists. After hearing 'loud lamentations … near the door of a cottage', he entered, only to return ashen faced to the officers waiting outside. Amongst them was Colonel English. Bolívar prophesized that if he went in, he would remain a patriot until his dying day. Taking up the challenge, he went in.

> An old man and woman, and their daughter, a beautiful girl, aged 16, [were] lying on the ground, weltering in their blood, with their throats cut from ear to ear. The crime of this aged couple was, that they had two sons employed in General Bolívar's army. Colonel E. before he left … cut a lock of … long, auburn hair from the youthful victim.[32]

As Bolívar had predicted, the encounter proved profound. English pledged his future to the cause and after returning to Angostura, he signed a lucrative contract with Antonio Zea, Bolívar's vice-president, to return to London to enlist a further 1,500 volunteers. His first-hand knowledge of the hardship and disappointment that would await them in Venezuela did not prevent him from accepting the position.

Chapter 8

'GENERAL WILSON FOR EVER!'

By May 1818, the remnants of the patriot army had gathered in San Fernando. Heading up-river to join them, Hippisley's and Wilson's Hussars would swell the British presence in Los Llanos to some 200 men. As their boats approached the town along the Apure, Hippisley ordered his men to put on their full dress uniforms. Soon, however, there were signs that such ostentation would be sorely out of place. A succession of corpses came floating towards them from the patriot lines. At first the bodies were those of mules and horses but then they saw that butchered human remains were caught up amongst the animals. Some of their heads had been nearly severed and 'others [had] ... a large gash across the neck'. As Hippisley was to discover, these were 'some of the unfortunate prisoners whom ... [Bolívar] had ... put to death.'[1]

On the quay at San Fernando, Hippisley was met by Colonel Wilson, who had arrived a few hours before. Wilson then led him through the streets to meet Bolívar. The town was crowded with soldiers and in a great state of agitation. Following the string of recent reverses, a mutiny was brewing which had the potential to tear the army apart. After pushing his way through the crowds, Hippisley was greeted by a group of English officers standing on the steps of the general's headquarters. Amongst them was Lieutenant-Colonel Needham, who ushered him inside. Bolívar was waiting in a small room off the hall. The recent defeats had clearly taken their toll on the general. 'Though but thirty eight', Bolívar seemed 50 years old and was 'marked with every symptom of anxiety, care, and ... despondency'.[2] To add to his woes, he was suffering terribly from saddle sores. After months on horseback traversing the plains, one of the boils had burst, leaving a pus-filled wound that left him unable to sit down comfortably, far less ride.[3]

With Captain Beix of Needham's unit interpreting, Bolívar updated Hippisley on the strategic situation. Since the battle of Ortiz, the patriots had endured two further defeats.

At Rincon de los Toros, when his camp was raided by a royalist assassination party, The Liberator had barely escaped with his life. Forced to flee after the Spanish cavalry had routed his troops, he had ridden off on a mule half-dressed and alone, leaving 300 of his men dead on the field. A month later the remains of his infantry had been annihilated in the hills around Laguna de los Patos. Amongst the casualties was the Irish Surgeon, Daniel Hely, a friend of Vowell's from the 1st Lancers, who had been captured when his comrades had fled. Taken to the square at Calabozo, he was tied to a bench where only weeks before he and Vowell had jokingly staged their own executions. Hely was then shot dead by firing squad.[4] Logistically, the situation was equally desperate. Food supplies were dangerously low and the army was reduced to 1,200 muskets and just six cartridges per man. After the interview, Hippisley was ordered to prepare his men for inspection the following day. Outside, 'all was confusion, terror and dismay'.[5] On his way back to the river, he stumbled across a temporary hospital, inside which 150 wounded were crammed together. Some 'held up a stump of an arm, shattered by a ball, or lopped off with a sword' while others 'lay bleeding to death' and several had 'lost the scalp or upper part of the skull', exposing 'the action of the ... brain to view'.[6]

The next morning, the British woke to find that hordes of soldiers were gathering in the plaza. The army's morale was at rock bottom and the troops were close to open revolt. Following the crowds to the square, Vowell saw that General Cedeño, a patriot cavalry commander, had become the focus of their wrath. Many blamed him for the costly defeat at Laguna de los Patos and some still bore a grudge for his perceived role in Piar's execution in 1817. As Vowell looked on, the crowd hissed their disapproval and began shoving Cedeño around the square. Just when it seemed he was about to be lynched, his mounted bodyguard arrived. Forcing their way through the rioters, they surrounded Cedeño and a skirmish commenced.[7] Bolívar, meanwhile, was nowhere to be seen. Fearing for his life, he had 'shut himself up in his quarters' and was unable or unwilling to take control. Amongst the wild Llaneros, only the presence of Páez could restore order. Dressed 'in a green ill-cut jacket ... white jean pantaloons ... and shoes with silver spurs', he rode into the square.[8] Immediately, the mob fell silent:

> [Páez] took Zedeño by the hand, and led him trembling, pale, and agitated through the midst of the infuriated rioters, who ... dared not raise a finger... [Páez] ordered ... officers of both parties ... to be set in the stocks ... they subjected without a murmur ... [he] then provided Zedeño with a gun-boat and advised him to retire ... and order was restored.[9]

With passions cooled, Bolívar reappeared and the inspection took place. After reviewing the British Hussars stood stiffly to attention in the main square, The Liberator praised

Hippisley on their appearance. He then informed the colonel that he would be heading down-river to Angostura. The rainy season was fast approaching and Los Llanos would soon flood, bringing the campaigning season to a close. The army would then take winter quarters and Bolívar left Hippisley and Wilson with a choice as to whether they would return to the capital with him or stay with Páez at San Fernando. The four remaining 1st Lancers, a handful of survivors from Needham's Belgian contingent and Wilson's 50 Red Hussars were unanimous in their desire to remain. Having come this far, Wilson would not countenance 'returning … [to Angostura] without having … heard a shot fired' in anger.[10] The 1st Hussars, on the other hand, failed to reach a consensus. Unnerved by the anarchy in San Fernando, Hippisley and a few loyal supporters were determined to leave. The majority of his officers and NCOs disagreed.

On 23 May these tensions came to a head. That afternoon, the dissenters found a large supply of alcohol and by the time darkness fell, nearly all were roaring drunk. Hippisley found them gathered round a bonfire, drinking, dancing and yelling seditious cries of 'General Wilson for ever!'[11] Unwilling to stand such insubordination, Hippisley ordered them to fall in. When they refused, he 'drew [his] pistol … and threatened to shoot the first man who dared to name any officer to their command but [himself]'.[12] Recognizing the empty threat for what it was they ignored him, leaving the colonel and about 30 NCOs and officers who had remained loyal to slink off to the boats with the regiment's baggage.[13] When the mutineers tried to stop them, a brawl broke out on the riverbank. Fearing they would be overwhelmed, Hippisley and his followers boarded their *flechera*. As they pushed off from the bank, the mutineers launched a fresh attack. After 'a few cuts with the sabre were exchanged', Hippisley 'was obliged to call aloud, that … [he] would fire a volley of musketry amongst them'.[14] The loaded guns dissuaded the attackers and the colonel was allowed to slip away, the calls of 'long live General Wilson!' ringing in his ears as the current swept them down-river.

Why was Hippisley rejected by his men? Surgeon James Robinson, who later met two of the mutineers, believed that his 'insolent and tyrannical conduct' and 'politic, sneaking and deceitful' behaviour were to blame. Furthermore, staying with Páez promised the opportunity to plunder, a powerful incentive when pay was only rarely received, yet it was something that Hippisley's code of conduct would never have allowed him to countenance. Other volunteers, complaining of Hippisley's 'moral reputation' and lack of 'professional honour and skill', blamed Mendéz for recruiting him in the first place.[15] Also significant was the influence asserted by Colonel Wilson. Convinced he was destined for greatness, Wilson had long dreamt of a leading role in the republican army. Now that Hippisley, previously the senior British figure in the army, was out of the picture, he was ready to put his plan into practice.

In his newly acquired role as commander of all the British troops at San Fernando, Wilson was invited to join Páez and several other senior commanders for lunch on 28 May.[16] Seated at a long table in a barn not far from the Red Hussars' quarters, the two men 'drank a good deal of wine and spirits' and were soon 'in a very good humour'.[17] Wilson's Irish coronet, Daniel O'Leary, was also present. Unlike the vast majority of the volunteers who were in awe of Páez, O'Leary thought little of the crude-mannered Caudillo. Seated near his colonel, he noted that 'Wilson flattered … [Páez] in a most fulsome way' and the Caudillo 'accepted … [the compliments] as genuine praise which he was truly entitled to'.[18] Throughout the banquet various toasts were proposed and soon it was Wilson's turn to take centre stage. He would later claim that it was his ignorance of Páez's precise rank that led him to commit the fateful *faux pas* that followed. Struggling to his feet, he proposed in flawed Spanish that the company should drink to their host, 'Captain General Páez'. It wasn't until later that Wilson learnt of his mistake. Unaware of the complexities of Spanish military hierarchy, the colonel had inadvertently raised Páez several ranks above the post of general that he actually held. Although seemingly innocuous, Wilson's mistake had planted a seed of discontent in the Caudillo's mind. He was soon convinced that he had been unfairly treated by Bolívar and deserved the recognition that the higher position would afford.[19] Wilson was not about to dissuade his host from his new-found conviction, and by the end of the meal, the colonel's continued flattery had also persuaded the Llanero that Bolívar's time was past and that he should replace him as commander-in-chief. His ego was flattered by the attention of the elegant Englishman, who held similar ambitions to his own. Without fully grasping the consequences of their seditious plot, the two men had agreed on a virtual *coup d'état* and it was decided that Páez's new status should be announced at a parade the following week. In the days that followed, Wilson unwittingly became more and more embroiled in the matter; firstly, he was asked to explain the situation to a gathering of junior officers; then later, he was pressured into adding his signature at the head of a list of those who approved of Páez's promotion.[20]

Contemporary observers put forward various explanations for Wilson's behaviour. Some believed he was a Spanish spy, paid to bring down the republic from within. The allegation was printed in both the *Dublin Evening Post* and London's *Morning Chronicle*.[21] Many of those who knew Wilson personally, however, including Vowell and Hippisley, remained unconvinced by such reports. After he had returned to England, Hippisley met the *Morning Chronicle*'s William Walton at Mendéz's offices. He listened incredulously as the columnist informed him that he could 'prove the payment of two bills drawn by … [Wilson], even on his passage out, which were accepted and paid by the Spanish ambassador'. Hippisley later dismissed these claims in his narrative, writing that he 'had never harboured the most distant idea that ... [Wilson] was a traitor ... or that he would have bartered his honour ... for Spanish gold'.[22]

Far from being a royalist agent, the most plausible explanation for Wilson's actions is much more down to earth. The only charges that can perhaps be fairly levelled against him are those of arrogance, megalomania and an inflated sense of his own worth. Having graduated from Oxford University in his teens, Wilson had grown up believing he was destined for great things, but had failed to live up to his early potential. After four years service in the British Army, he had retired with the relatively lowly rank of lieutenant. His subsequent dabblings in publishing had proved equally fruitless. With Hippisley's disgrace and The Liberator's temporary absence, Wilson had sensed an opportunity to follow in Páez's wake and achieve the greatness he felt he deserved. Envisaging a future as second in command to Páez, he dreamed of raising an army of 10,000 veterans which he would lead to victory as the 'all conquering General Wilson'. In a letter to 'a lady in London', that later came to light in the *Dublin Evening Post*, he boasted: 'I laugh at the power to-day, which I may wield *myself* to-morrow, but with a more determined hand.'[23] He had sorely underestimated The Liberator's will to cling to power, however, and his naivety would be his downfall.

A week after the lunch, the day of Páez's parade dawned. From his place on the right of the line, O'Leary observed proceedings:

> Several chiefs ... assembled, bringing with them as many *llaneros* as they could muster. A motley group it was, to be sure. Some seven or eight hundred men on horseback, all badly clad and some almost in a perfect state of nudity, formed in anything but an orderly style in a plain to the east of town. Our corps [the Red Hussars] formed to the right of the whole – an honour meant to our splendid uniforms, I suppose. When the farce was ready to commence, Paez, accompanied by some thirty [or] forty field officers and aids de camp [appeared]. The gen[eral] was hailed by loud vivas and, as soon as these had ceased, an *acta* was read naming him Capt[ain] Gen[eral]. Another volley of vivas followed and then some of the most expert horsemen were ordered to show off. The field business over, the chiefs assembled to sign the *acta* ... the day had scarcely closed when someone whispered in his [Páez's] ear that he was doing wrong.[24]

Perhaps reminded of Piar's fate, Páez finally realized the danger he was courting and decided to sacrifice his British accomplice to save his own skin. The next night he sent a message to Bolívar portraying himself as an innocent bystander caught up in Wilson's plot.

In June, when the rainy season began in earnest, the army moved to Achaguas, a small town on the banks of the Apurito, which became an island as the flood waters rose.

Wilson, for his part, returned to Angostura, planning to sail to London and raise his army of 10,000. Within 24 hours of his arrival in the capital his dreams were shattered. The would-be general was arrested and confined to quarters by order of Bolívar himself. Whilst Páez would escape with a warning, Wilson's punishment would be far more severe. Many volunteers thought that he would be shot in the main square, but Bolívar had other plans. Wilson was offered the opportunity to defend himself at a court martial, but was warned that if he insisted on a trial, Bolívar would be forced to demand the highest possible punishment. Unsurprisingly he declined, and, on 4 August, was sent down-river to be imprisoned in Fort San Francisco in Old Guyana.

Wilson spent 'upwards of four months' in a 12ft by 8ft windowless cell. Six weeks in he became seriously ill. In a letter to Bolívar begging for 'clemency', he claimed that William Walton (the columnist of the *Morning Chronicle* who would later betray him) would vouch for his commitment to the republican cause.[25] The Liberator made no reply. When the colonel was eventually released ten weeks later, it was only on the condition that he left the country immediately. Accepting the terms, he made his way to Trinidad 'in a mighty rage', informing any who would listen that he intended to join the royalists and 'bring a ship from England … [to] take everything in the going to, or coming from the Oronoco'.[26] His threats turned out to be no more than hot air. After sailing back to London on the brig *Byron*, he was ridiculed by the British press and would never set foot in the New World again. The six colonels were now reduced to just two. Skeene had drowned off Ushant, Campbell had resigned and MacDonald had been murdered by river pirates. Only Gillmore and Hippisley remained.

Back in Achaguas, Daniel O'Leary was growing increasingly disillusioned with the Llaneros' methods. The final straw came when witnessing the slaughter of several prisoners, a scene he captured in his memoirs:

> Prisoners were frequently brought in, for the most part American[s who] … had probably been compelled to serve with the Spaniards. Groups of ten and twelve were … put to death … the patriots were economic of gunpowder … and the wretched were doomed to have their sufferings augmented and prolonged by the sword of the executioner… I have often seen the head severed from the trunk at the first blow. Whenever this occurred a loud laugh from the creole spectators expressed their satisfaction.[27]

Sickened by the brutality, O'Leary asked for permission to return to the capital and sailed up-river in June.

The volunteers that remained in Achaguas witnessed the changes that occurred during the rainy season. The arid plains were transformed into a sea of swamps and swollen rivers and the streets became clogged with knee-deep mud. The handful who had survived the battles of early 1818 were amused by the attempts of their newly arrived countrymen to traverse town in their glittering uniforms, and soon decided that being dressed in rags under such circumstances was no real disadvantage.[28] Some spent the long evenings visiting the refugees who had been swept along with the army during its retreat. The house of Don Manuel Quadras, a priest from Guasdualito and 'a man of superior education and talents', was a particular favourite. As well as Quadras's conversation, Vowell and his peers also enjoyed the company of his sister and two young nieces, who 'were always ready to enliven the dull hours' with their singing and guitars.[29] Others passed the time gambling. For Rooke, whose addiction had already led to bankruptcy, the frequent opportunities to indulge must have been impossible to resist. The taverns had gaming tables where crowds gathered to watch huge sums wagered on the turn of a single card. Other impromptu sessions broke out in the men's quarters or around the camp fire at night. Whilst 'Veng et un' and 'hazard' were favoured by the foreigners, the Creoles preferred gambling with dice and playing a card game called 'monte'.[30] Marathon sessions were common, with participants playing for 'whole days and nights'.[31] Predictably, alcohol was ever present. The players drank and the tables became awash with silver pesos and doubloons. After emptying their purses, they would 'stake their horses, equipments, and every article belonging to them, in order to continue'.[32]

Páez grew 'uncommonly fond' of the volunteers and 'did everything in his power to make … [them] as comfortable as possible'.[33] As well as providing 'a corral full of milch-cows' for their exclusive use, he also addressed the lack of pay.[34] In a room on the town square, the Caudillo's men melted down captured silver. 'Stirrups, sword scabbards … various other ornaments … and church plate' were all used.[35] The metal was mixed 'with one fourth of copper', stamped and cut into irregular polygons to produce crude coins which were then distributed to the troops.[36] As a consequence of their respect for Páez, the locals gladly accepted the currency, even though the government in Angostura declared it worthless outside the plains.[37] With a little spending money in their pockets the volunteers were able 'to purchase … any little comforts available', and their lot began to improve.[38]

Whenever Páez could lay his hands on sufficient *aquardiente*, a party would be held. Everyone in town was invited. The alcohol flowed and dancing followed. Páez 'was considered, by the ladies of Achaguas, the best dancer' in town.[39] At other times the British watched the Llaneros drive herds of wild horses into the square, where they would break them in for their own amusement. The volunteers were amazed by their skill. After lassoing their chosen target, two or three men would hold the rope until the horse exhausted itself and fell into the mud. They would then surround it, put a hood over its head and tie its legs. If the horse continued to fight, it was bashed about the head with cudgels. Before it could recover, the Llaneros threw a saddle over its back. The battle of wills then began:

When the rider has mounted ... the horse appears, at first, so confused and astonished, as to be incapable of motion; but is soon roused by the shouts and blows of the rider's companions ... the exertions that he [then] makes to get rid of his burthen are wonderful... The technical term, which the Llanéros apply to the wild horse's first struggles, is *corcovear*, from the manner in which the animal arches its back, and springs forth in a succession of bounds; striking the ground with all four feet at the same time... As long as the horse continues to plunge in this way the rider makes frequent use of the cudgel... This ... soon breaks the animal's spirit; and, in a day or two, he begins to move in a slow unwilling trot, which is considered as a certain symptom of his commencing to be tamed.[40]

Early in the morning of 24 June, the Llaneros celebrated Saint John the Baptist's Day. Páez and his staff, dressed in just 'shirts and drawers', paraded on their horses through the flooded streets, playing *vihuèlas* and calling for everybody, 'especially the foreigners', to join them.[41] Any who refused were dragged from their beds. The procession then degenerated into a mud fight and soon 'the natural colours of both horses and men were ... completely indistinguishable'. After tiring of the game, the general led them towards the Apurito, where they spurred their horses into the water to wash themselves clean, before returning to town for a spectacular feast. 'What this *dejeunè à la fourchette* wanted in elegance,' Vowell thought, 'was amply compensated by ... [its] variety':

There were ribs, *zezínas*, and *rayas* of beef, wild hogs from Mericúri, and venison from the neighbouring woods of Gamarra. Of poultry, there were wild ducks, *pauxís*, and *guacharacas*... Plenty of fish from the Apuríto [and] maíz bread, in *arépas*, *bolos*, and *roscas*, with cheese and *guarápo*, crowned the banquet.[42]

After the celebrations, Páez selected six British officers to accompany him on a tour of Los Llanos. The men were chosen by two criteria: the strength of their Spanish and their ability to swim. Vowell was delighted to pass both. They spent several weeks in the waterlogged savannahs, going days without seeing another person, but regularly passing 1000-strong herds of wild cattle and horses. Vowell found the stallions' curiosity remarkable. Surrounding the men, they would 'gallop round in compact masses ... apparently for the purpose of reconnoitring the strangers'.[43] Although the majority of the *hatos* (ranches) that they passed had been abandoned during the war, Páez would invariably guide them to one that remained inhabited as night fell, using occasional clumps of trees, each of which was individually named, to navigate the seemingly featureless savannah. Upon arrival, a calf was slaughtered. After the meal, the volunteers slept on bullock-hide beds.

Occasionally they passed fields of sugar cane. The *trapiches* (mills) produced a sweet juice which was made into a potent hooch named *guarápo*. Plantains also grew well in the plains. The small fields attracted hummingbirds and venomous snakes. Some ranchers grew tobacco for personal use. As well as smoking the weed, they used it in a way Vowell had never seen before. After boiling the roots and leaves with 'red peppers and other strong ingredients', the liquid was strained and 'evaporated to a consistence something thinner than Spanish liquorice'.[44] Men and women alike chewed on it continuously. Ever keen to experiment, Vowell soon learnt that the drug was considerably more potent when taken in this manner.[45]

Chapter 9

MR DEWEY'S FATAL PREMONITION

While Wilson and Páez were plotting in Los Llanos, Colonel Hippisley was heading down-river to Angostura.[1] The journey was a nightmare. As well as being exposed to the elements, his *flechera* was dreadfully overcrowded. Packed into the open boat were 31 volunteers, 50 wounded soldiers and 10 women. On 26 May they caught up with Bolívar, who had set off from San Fernando the day before them. Knowing that Hippisley would demand repayment for the expenses he had incurred in London, The Liberator was keen to avoid him. A farcical chase ensued, with The Liberator's boat managing to stay just out of Hippisley's reach. Nevertheless, the time was not completely wasted, as the 48-year old colonel was delighted with the company of 'a bouncing half-cast girl of sixteen'.[2]

As the rains poured down, the river rose by 15ft. The sandbanks that had impeded the volunteers' progress when heading up-river were now submerged. In several places the river had burst its banks, flooding the surrounding plains. Where previously mighty trees had lined the banks, now only the uppermost branches were visible. On the tenth day they came to La Boca del Infierno (Hell's Mouth), a series of whirlpools, rapids and waterfalls close to the spot where MacDonald had been killed. One month before the area had presented few problems, but in the rainy season it proved a terrifying experience for the volunteers, the majority of whom were unable to swim. Hippisley later remembered one particularly close encounter:

> ... in descending one of the falls, [we] came so close ... [to] a large ... rock, that even the captain of the flechera grew pale, and trembled. The boat was then sucked into a whirlpool, which roared with a most terrific noise ... having performed three or four very quick circular motions, she was thrown forth again to run with the stream.[3]

On the night of 6 June a storm began. 'The lightning continued visible for seven seconds ... sometimes traversing the whole horizon, and forming an immense circle of liquid fire. The very rain that fell was hot.'[4] The following day they arrived in Angostura, where Hippisley endured a series of fruitless interviews with Bolívar. James Rooke, who had been promoted to the rank of colonel, interpreted his demands. Seeing that he was getting nowhere, Hippisley eventually decided to take up his grievances directly with Mendéz in the British courts. After nominating Rooke as his replacement, he left the capital at the beginning of July and sailed down-river to Trinidad. There he found passage back to England and arrived in Scarborough in August 1818. One of Hippisley's fellow passengers was Captain George Elsom. Originally part of Skeene's ill-fated corps, Elsom had escaped the *Indian* disaster when left behind on the Isle of Wight. After finding passage out to South America with 30 others, Elsom had finally arrived in the capital in April 1818 and had been contracted by Antonio Zea, Bolívar's vice-president, to return to London to recruit more troops for the patriot cause.

Back in Angostura all was in chaos. Provisions were running low and competition for what remained was growing increasingly fierce as yet more volunteers arrived. Disgusted with the situation, many only lasted a matter of days. One group that was met by Bolívar himself did not even stay that long. Amongst them was a French veteran, who asked for permission to leave as soon as he had stepped off the boat:

> 'What does this mean?' asked the chief; 'Do you wish for your passport the moment you enter the country? ... for what reason?' The French officer, shrugging ... his shoulders, very coolly replied, that he had perceived so many native colonels walking around the garrison bare-footed, with only pieces of blankets to cover them, that he dreaded what his fate must soon be ... he therefore requested his passport and was presented it.[5]

Realizing that forcing foreign officers to serve would be counterproductive, Bolívar issued a proclamation in August 1818 announcing that any who were dissatisfied were free to leave. Several took advantage of the offer. Others applied for leave of absence to travel to the British colonies, where they hoped to restore their health, which had been shattered by tropical disease.[6] On the positive side, the republicans were now producing their own newspaper. *El Correo del Orinoco* had been set up in June by Andrew Roderick, a professional printer who had brought a press from England and may well have arrived in the capital with Hippisley's or Wilson's Hussars. The paper was a mixture of local advertisements, government proclamations, reports from the front line and stories of pertinent developments in Europe and North America. Roderick's contribution to the war effort was vital. The paper helped to neutralize royalist propaganda, gave the patriots a voice and added a sense of permanency to the fledgling republic.

In mid-July, Admiral Brion, Piggot's Rifles and the remains of Gillmore's artillery corps reached the capital bringing gunpowder, lead ball and 10,000 muskets. Their arrival boosted flagging spirits and prompted The Liberator to begin planning the following season's campaign. His first move was to send a unit to reinforce the overland approaches to the north-west of the capital. General Monagas, who was holding the area, was under severe pressure from the enemy which was being supplied by nearby bases on the Caribbean coast. Having recovered from his wounds, Colonel Rooke was chosen to lead the reinforcements. By early September he had organized a unit of 300 horse, including 100 British volunteers. Amongst them was Richard Vowell, who had recently returned from Los Llanos.

In August Admiral Brion left the capital. Supplied with gunpowder and arms brought out on the *Dowson*, he was determined to deal with Gabozo's troublesome gunboats once and for all. Güiria, Gabozo's base, was a 'small town' built on a narrow spit of land jutting out eastwards into the Gulf of Paria.[7] A spine of jagged peaks covered by impenetrable jungle ran the length of the peninsula. Separating the forest from the sea was a strip of golden sand. Inaccessible by land, the town boasted a fort dominating the sea approaches, garrisoned by 350 Creoles, blacks and Indians under Josef Guerrero. An additional battery of 12 cannon was dug in on the beach. Beyond was the royalists' first line of defence, a moored flotilla of eight gunboats. When not required for the depredations of Gabozo, Oroco and other privateers, these boats were anchored in a line offshore. Each was 20–35ft in length, 4–6ft broad, armed with one or two light cannon and manned by up to 30 sailors.

On the morning of 23 August, the *Scamander*, a 36-gun frigate of the Royal Navy's Caribbean fleet, dropped anchor in the shallows off Güiria. Sir Ralph Woodford, the governor of Trinidad, had ordered the captain, Mr Elliot, to demand the return of a British merchant sloop, which had been captured by the royalists 'some months previously' and had been grounded on the beach outside the fort ever since. Guerrero flatly refused. 'Beat[ing] to quarters', Elliot 'hoisted the signal for battle'.[8] Just then Brion's ships appeared, approaching out of the rising sun. Elliot decided to sit back and see if the patriots could do his job for him.

Two days earlier, the patriot flotilla of four ships had gathered outside Port of Spain, Trinidad. Two of the four captains and many of the crew were British volunteers, the majority Royal Navy veterans. The admiral's flagship, the 24-gun frigate *Victoria*, was commanded by Captain Cowie; eight of the 275 crew members, including the second in command, Captain Thomas, were British. The brig *Colombia*, mounting two 12-pdr carronades and a deadly 'long eighteen' on a pivot on the poop deck, was commanded by Captain Hill (the same officer who had taken the 1st Hussars up the Orinoco on the

Tiger in March); Hill's crew included 4th Lieutenant Charles Hippisley, the colonel's younger son, and Surgeon Dewey, another who had previously served with the 1st Hussars. The other ships were the 12-gun schooner *Spartan*, whose 95 crew members were led by Captain Favelo, and the *Favourite*, with 70 men under Captain Bernard.

The fleet moved on Güiria early in the morning of the 23rd. At 9.00am it was seen simultaneously by lookouts on the *Scamander* and the royalists in the fort. Cannon were fired to raise the alarm and sailors swam out to man the gunboats offshore. The patriots advanced in line. Hill's *Colombia* led the attack, closely followed by the *Favourite*, with the *Victoria* and the *Spartan* bringing up the rear. A little over half a mile from the fort the leading ships dropped anchor. Brion was lying a quarter of a mile further out and the *Spartan* was still manoeuvring when, at 11.30am, the royalists opened fire.

Both sides initially used round shot, iron balls of 6–24lb in weight and 3½–5in diameter. Hits could punch through an enemy's hull, rifle across deck cutting through the seamen servicing their cannon, or slice through the rigging or rudder. Often the most horrific injuries were caused by shards of wood sent flying along the deck as shots splintered timber. At 500 yards, crews would switch to canister or grape, metal cans packed with musket balls. Bursting apart after leaving the barrel, they sprayed their load in a lethal arc.[9]

Unlike the best crews of the age, who held their fire as long as they dared, both sides at Güiria began shooting at 1,000 yards. Neither the patriots nor the royalists did much damage at first. Then, after 20 minutes, a dead calm descended, rendering Brion's ships immobile. Seeing his opportunity, the royalist commander ordered four gunboats to row out and seize the *Colombia*. Both sides kept up a steady fire as the boats pulled closer. By the time they were within 'pistol range', men were cut down with every shot. Hopelessly outnumbered, Hill knew his crew were doomed if they remained on board. After cutting a bloody swathe with an 18-pdr loaded with canister, he gave the order to abandon ship.

'Unmanageable' in the calm, the *Colombia* had been drifting slowly to stern during the firefight, and was now close to crashing into the the *Favourite*.[10] 'At the very moment the royalists' gun-boats boarded her on the bow', they collided, allowing Captain Hill and the survivors to leap across to Favelo's ship. With side-arms and cannon fire, the combined crews managed to hold off their attackers.[11] Only when their safety was assured did Hill realize that one of his officers was missing. When the rest of the crew had crossed over, Surgeon Dewey had remained behind on the *Colombia*, hidden below deck.

Two days prior to the attack, Dewey had a fateful premonition. In his dream, he had hidden 'under a *tasso* cask, just as ... [the royalists] were boarding, and thus preserved his life'. Hill and the others 'had laughed at him' at the time, but outside Güiria, the dream took on new significance.[12] As the boats drifted apart, the royalists searched the *Colombia*'s hold for plunder and the surgeon was soon found. 'Dragged … on deck by his hair, and aft to the tafferil rail … [he was held] up so as to be seen … [by his comrades on *The Favourite* and] mortally wounded by several sabre cuts to the head.'[13] The royalists then towed their prize into shore. After running her aground on the beach, they threw 'the wretched surgeon … on the sand … in a burning sun, and there he remained', bleeding to death, whilst the battle of Güiria raged about him.[14]

After the action, Brion sent boats to the *Favourite* to transport Hill and his crew to the *Victoria*. When the Englishman reached the flagship, she was exchanging fire with both the royalist gunboats and the battery in the fort:

> On ascending the deck … everything appeared in confusion: a shot from the battery had just struck the main-mast as we were going up her side. The first thing which presented itself to my view were three buckets of stiff grog, one before each of the masts[,] to which the officers and men had free access. The admiral was dressed in uniform, a brace of pistols in his girdle, a dagger in his bosom, and his sabre by his side; stuck fast between the mizzen-mast and the wheel, from whence he was loudly vociferating to the officers not to come near him, for fear of drawing the enemies' attention, which might cause them to point a shot at the place where he stood.[15]

At 12.50pm, three more royalist gunboats rowed out from the shore. As well as the battery in the fort, the patriots were now facing the close-range fire of seven adversaries. As a hail of shot cut over the waves, the *Victoria*'s spring was shot away, making her difficult to control. With his flagship crippled and knowing reinforcements would soon arrive, Brion signalled the retreat and the flotilla sailed out of range. At 5.00pm, with the ships of the fleet at anchor far out in the gulf, Commodore Diaz joined them with seven gunboats. On board, led by General Bermúdez, were 70 boy soldiers, 'the oldest not exceeding fifteen years'.[16] In conference with Brion and Diaz, the general came up with a plan for the following day: he would attack by land whilst the fleet bombarded the enemy from the water. Before the plan could be put into effect, however, a further tragedy occurred. Concerned that the royalist gunboats would attack under cover of darkness, the patriots anchored their ships in a protective huddle and Brion instructed his crew to reposition one of the *Victoria*'s 18-pdr cannon to enable an all-round field of fire:

> Just as … [the cannon] was brought abreast of the capstan, the gun … did by some unfortunate accident go off, and blew away nine men, who were hauling on the tackles. The carronade had been loaded with round, grape and langridge shot. Two Englishmen were unfortunately among the number who fell.[17]

Of the nine casualties, seven 'were literally blown to pieces'. The others 'lost their arms and legs' and endured their final 'hour in the most excruciating torture'.[18]

Despite the setback, Brion attacked early the next morning. By 5.30am, Bermúdez's infantry had landed on the beach three miles east of town. Their route across the sands was occasionally blocked by huge rocks, forcing the men to cut their way inland through dense jungle. Progress was torturously slow. When the royalist sentries finally caught sight of them at midday, the batteries fired their cannon to raise the alarm, prompting the townsfolk to run inside the fort for protection. At 1.20pm Diaz's gunboats, one of which had been commandeered by Hill and his crew, began to cut across the gulf towards town. Meanwhile, Bermúdez's boy soldiers became bogged down in a running skirmish fought through the thick undergrowth. As the temperatures soared, the dull reports of their musketry carried across the water to Hill's crew. Eager to support their comrades, the rowers pulled harder, driving their gunboats inshore.

At 4.45pm the combined patriot fleet dropped anchor half a mile from the fort and opened fire. Despite the royalists' best efforts to drive them off, the ships edged ever closer as the afternoon progressed. As they closed in, the patriots loaded a combination of grapeshot and round. Looking on from the *Scamander*, Captain Elliot noted that at 5.00pm precisely, the *Spartan* unleashed a fearsome double-shotted 'broadside ... with devastating effect'.[19] Meanwhile, in the woods half a mile to the east of town, Bermúdez's troops were engaged in an increasingly desperate firefight. Royalist resistance escalated as they pushed closer to the fort and Bermúdez was forced to sound the retreat 'to hide the fewness of their numbers'.[20] The patriot fleet, on the other hand, was beginning to win its side of the battle. At 6.00pm, one of the magazines on a royalist gunboat caught fire and then exploded. 'Dreadfully burnt', the crew were left thrashing about in the water as the boat sank beneath the waves.[21]

The loss of the gunboat panicked the remaining royalist sailors. Abandoning their boats, they dived into the water and swam for shore. Keeping up 'a heavy fire', the patriots 'killed a great number of them'.[22] The survivors hauled themselves up the beach and into the fort, pulling up the drawbridge behind them. Seeing their comrades routed, the infantry facing Bermúdez in the woods also fell back. By 6.30pm, as the last of the light was seeping from the day, the patriot foot soldiers took the town, forcing the remaining defenders to take refuge in the fort. During the firefight, three houses caught alight, throwing flickering shadows across the town as the battle entered its final stages.

Sailing into shore, the *Favourite* and *Victoria* fired volleys of grape at the defenders in the fort with their 18- and 24-pdrs. The close-range fire did 'great execution' and by midnight the royalists had suffered enough. Leaping over the rear wall, the survivors fled into the forest, 'leaving behind their arms, ammunition and ... even ... their cegars'.[23]

Bermúdez's men flooded into the fort in their wake. No quarter was shown to the wounded. Hunted down in the dark, they were killed with bayonets. The royalists lost over 130 men in the two-day battle and 30 corpses were found heaped in the redoubt alone. Brion's losses were comparatively light. Just 20 had been killed and wounded, including the nine that had perished in the accident on the first night. Amongst the dead was Surgeon Dewey. His mutilated body was found the morning after the battle. According to Captain Hill, it was 'in a most mangled state; upwards of twenty-four stabs [were] about his body, his arm [was] cut off, and his head nearly severed from the shoulders'.[24]

A few weeks before the battle of Güiria, the Black Rifles had arrived in Angostura led by the 34-year old Lieutenant-Colonel Robert Piggot, an Irish veteran of considerable experience. Having enlisted as an ensign in the 54th Foot in 1804, he went on to purchase his captaincy and saw action in the Peninsular War before retiring on half pay after Waterloo. Piggot was perhaps the most professional, if not the most successful of all of Bolívar's British officers. A 'rigid commander, on parade, and in the field', he also had the personal touch that so endeared him to his men. Once duty was over, 'he was the brother, the friend, [and] the companion of his officers, and the father' of his men.[25] A consummate professional, Piggot was far from impressed with the state of affairs in Angostura. Poor rations combined with a rapid spread of disease lowered morale. To make matters worse, the money the volunteers had been promised was nowhere to be seen. 'Indignant' at the perceived slight, several officers threatened to resign.[26] Unwilling to call their bluff, the town council granted them 15 pesos per head whilst the men were awarded five pesos each. Bolívar gave his personal reassurance that all would be paid in full as soon as funds became available. Their anger appeased, the Rifles were 'induced' to remain.[27] Despite these issues, Captain Jamie Phelan, a native of Thomastown in Ireland (who had served with the British Artillery for 11 years), undoubtedly enjoyed his stay in the capital. Billeted in a private house, Phelan fell in love with the owner's daughter, 'a young, rich, and amiable Spanish lady, who spoke the English language fluently'.[28] Their courtship was cut short, however, when the Rifles were dispatched down-river to recruit and train local Indians to make up the rank and file.

Founded in the early colonial period by Capuchin and Franciscan friars, the Indian missions were a series of 30 collectivized settlements spread along the lower Orinoco.[29] Each had a central square dominated by a church. Adjacent were the padre's quarters and a large storehouse. The *Guarauno* converts lived on the outskirts in 'neat cottages built of bamboo … thatched with the leaves of the *morichi* palm'.[30] Prior to the commencement of hostilities, the missions had been extremely successful, producing a surplus of fruit and vegetables which were sold up-river. Since 1810, however, the inhabitants had been ruthlessly exploited by both sides. Forced recruitment was commonplace. When the men were dragged away in chains, the women and children followed them to the front, leaving the villages virtual ghost towns.

Throughout its colonial history, Latin American society had been dominated by a deep-rooted class system, based on racist divisions, which continued largely unchanged as the continent staggered towards independence. All political power, wealth, land and influence rested in the hands of whites of Spanish descent, who made up a mere ½ per cent of the population. Bolívar had been born into this aristocracy and although he would attempt to break down these divisions, as a product of the elite he shared many of their prejudices. Beneath the ruling class was a second tier of whites. As immigrants from the Canary Islands as opposed to mainland Spain, the *Canarios*, who accounted for 25 per cent of the population, were considered socially inferior. Nevertheless, they enjoyed a higher standard of living than the 400,000 *pardos* (people of mixed race) who made up a third class accounting for nearly 50 per cent of residents. The fourth class was made up of 70,000 blacks, including slaves, fugitives and freed men. On the bottom of the heap, and exploited by all those above them, were the Indians (*Guaraunos*). In pre-colonial times Venezuela had supported several hundred thousand indigenous inhabitants. Reduced by centuries of disease and abuse, by 1810 they made up just 15 per cent of the population.[31]

A total of 400 *Guaraunos*, aged from 14 to 54, were forced to join the Black Rifles and taken up-river to Upata, a 'beautifully situated' town surrounded by 'an amphitheatre of hills' 80 miles to the east of Angostura.[32] Training commenced on 16 September. Infantry instruction was a well-established science, the basic tenets of which had remained unchanged since the 17th century. Commanders employed a series of complex formations on the battlefield, which were drilled into recruits until they became second nature. Foot soldiers were required to form square, line or column at a moment's notice. Some manoeuvres, with the square being the most notorious, were particularly difficult to master and several weeks of practice were normally needed before proficiency was acquired. Recruits also underwent weapons training. The various stages involved in firing and loading their side-arms were drilled into them through endless repetition. Once satisfied with their performance, commanders would move on to live-fire exercises and target practice. Three modes of marching were also learnt. 'Ordinary' consisted of 90 paces per minute, 'quick step' was 105 and 'double quick' required 120. Such a repertoire of skills was not easily mastered. William Napier, a vastly experienced Peninsular War veteran and authority on Wellington's campaigns, estimated that it took three years to instil perfect discipline in a recruit.[33] Colonel Piggot had four weeks.

After their basic training, Bolívar ordered the Black Rifles to return to Angostura, from where they would sail up-river to join Páez's army at San Fernando for the next campaign. During their time at Upata, yellow fever had broken out. Two officers and several NCOs had to be left behind, leaving just 20 of the original regiment remaining. Although most eventually recovered, Captain Poole, who had joined as a lieutenant, was buried in Upata on 8 November 1818.[34] His possessions were itemized and documented. Along with several unpaid IOUs addressed to his fellow officers, three pairs of trousers, nine shirts, several jackets, a silver watch, a hammock and a sword were listed.[35]

When the Rifles passed through Angostura in October, they were seen by Lieutenant Brown. Of the original 400 Indian recruits, as many as 130 'had already deserted', despite the use of both firing squad and flogging to terrify them into obedience.[36] Those remaining were shackled together on the quay whilst they waited to embark. Brown thought the men 'of very low stature' and considered 'the [naked] women that followed them ... most disgusting objects'.[37] He predicted they would fare poorly in the coming campaign.[38] Whilst in the capital, the troops were given dark green uniforms, similar to those worn by the rifle regiments that had fought under Wellington in Spain and Flanders. More used to wearing loincloths, the Indians struggled with their new clothes, much to the amusement of another British officer who witnessed the scene:

> Never did the infant survey with more astonishment and satisfaction, the trappings of its doll, than did these individuals contemplate the mighty alteration about to be made to their persons... Some put their legs in the arms of the coat, and brought the skirts up, and buttoned them round their loins. Others ... tied the legs of the pantaloons ... allowing the upper part ... to hang before like the skirts of the coat... It was also attempted to make them wear shoes; but this was soon abandoned, as they could not walk a step in them.[39]

On 21 October, Bolívar inspected the regiment. Afterwards, he awarded the 25-year old Captain Sandes a majority and professed that he was 'much pleased' with the troops. That night, at a dinner given for the leading Creole officers, he commented on Piggot's success and said he hoped that General Anzoátegui and the volunteers' other detractors 'would now confess that there was, at least, ONE Officer amongst the Foreigners'.[40] Unlike Lieutenant Brown's disparaging remarks, Bolívar's initial assessment of the Rifles would prove remarkably prescient. After some initial setbacks, they would become one of the most renowned units in the patriot army and would win battles from the Caribbean coast to the highlands of Peru.

Chapter 10

THE SECOND WAVE

I n late 1818, the trickle of British volunteers turned into a flood. In total, three new regiments were raised, the first by James Towers English, the charismatic amateur who had served with Hippisley's 1st Hussars. Having ingratiated himself with his commanding officer, English had bluffed his way to lieutenant-colonel by the time he reached Angostura in early 1818 and had received a further promotion from Bolívar himself after his heroics at Ortiz. On his return to the capital after the battle, he was contracted by Antonio Zea, The Liberator's vice-president, to sail to London and recruit 1,000 infantry. Unlike previously raised units, English was to form his entirely with British troops from the rank and file up. In return, Zea had promised him the rank of general and £50 for every man enlisted.[1] Although the former clerk's prime motivation seems to have been financial, the chance of securing the fame, power and glory that had so far eluded him was also a major factor.

English arrived in London on 7 September 1818.[2] After contacting López Mendéz, he rented a property near the Strand and began advertising for recruits. Posters were pinned up in prominent places, promising bounties of 200 pesos and promotions for those who had previously served in the British Army. Taking advantage of the republicans' popularity, English made several public appearances. At fashionable parties the self-styled 'hero of Ortiz' would boast of his heroics to swooning ladies and impressionable young men. Often he spoke of the murdered girl he had seen after the battle, finishing his performance by producing the lock of her auburn hair to gasps of shock and delight.[3] Reported in the press, his antics attracted the attention not only of potential recruits, but also of the republic's enemies.

The Duc de San Carlos, the Spanish ambassador in London, sent a series of letters to the Foreign Office, finally forcing Lord Castlereagh to intervene. He warned López

Mendéz that he faced deportation if he persisted, but his tentative actions did little to stem the flow of volunteers. Undeterred, the Venezuelan continued to send Bolívar reinforcements and Castlereagh failed to follow through with his threat. In a seemingly uncoordinated move, Lord Sidmouth of the Home Office dispatched agents to spy on the goings-on at Grafton Street in September 1818. The names and backgrounds of those involved, the ships they chartered and the times and venues of meetings held were all recorded. In one file marked 'top secret', an agent noted that an American schooner chartered to transport recruits had her cannon 'secreted in the ballast, to mount immediately after their clearance from the English Coast'.[4] The report concluded: 'Should it be judged necessary to detect this Shipment after its final Clearance from the River' then 'the informant could be engaged to execute the same'.[5] It appears that Sidmouth did not take up the offer, however, and the schooner was allowed to depart unmolested.

One of English's recruits was George Laval Chesterton, a half pay officer in the Royal Artillery. Strolling down the Strand one day, he came across 'numerous large placards' advertising the cause, 'boastfully lauded in the accustomed broad type'.[6] With few prospects in England, Chesterton decided to take up the challenge. Following a reference on the poster, he walked to 'Solomon and Co., army clothiers, at Charing Cross', where the tailor directed him to English's residence in Norfolk Street.[7] Upon arrival, he 'was instantly ushered' in and interviewed.[8] According to Chesterton, English cut an impressive figure. 'A man of medium stature, with a swarthy complexion, black hair, whiskers, and mustachios', he 'could assume either a most forbidding or inviting demeanour'.[9] English asked Chesterton for references, a precaution which the would-be recruit thought 'bore the stamp of honourable caution'.[10] When Chesterton's experience had been 'established', he was commissioned as a lieutenant in the light company of the regiment, which was named the British Legion.[11]

Although recruitment was highly successful, English's lack of expertise would cost his troops dear on campaign. A 'generous and open hearted' man and connoisseur of fine art, he was eminently unsuited to the life of a soldier. The former clerk's entire military experience had been garnered under Hippisley's command and although he had seen action at Semen and Ortiz, he had never before commanded men in battle. Despite his lack of experience, English was a charismatic and likeable character and by 1819 was well practised in the art of deception. He clearly impressed Hippisley, who promoted him over the heads of more experienced veterans; and Bolívar, although admittedly in a desperate situation following the string of defeats in early 1818, also appears to have fallen under his spell.

The merchant Charles Herring was another who was taken in by this smooth-talking charlatan. With his business partners, messrs Salisbury and Richardson, Herring was persuaded to back the Legion's expedition to the tune of £73,710. Eight ships, ranging in size from the 189-berth *Francis and Eliza* to the *Henrietta*, a cargo sloop which could only carry 70 souls, were chartered for the voyage. The merchants also paid for a bewildering range of supplies, including 1,000 plain felt caps, 90 red and blue dress jackets, 1,370 knapsacks worth 2s 5d a piece, 570 'canteens with straps' and 400 4lb cannon balls.[12]

The 1,200 men of the British Legion were divided into three squadrons. The first, commanded by Major John Blosset, English's experienced second in command, consisted of three ships and left in January 1819. The second detachment, led by English himself, sailed in late February. The last to depart, the *Henrietta*, carrying the Legion's arms and uniforms, left from Hamburg in March in an attempt to allay the suspicions of the British authorities. Of the voyages of the first and third detachments little is known, but as Chesterton sailed with the second, some details of the journey survive.

After the stores were loaded in London, the four ships that made up the squadron sailed down the Thames, cutting south through the Channel before anchoring off Lymington, where English had arranged to meet some late arrivals. As his uniform had been delayed, Chesterton embarked there, having endured a stagecoach journey southwards from the capital through driving rain. The bad weather then continued, delaying the ships' departure. Despite the postponement, the volunteers spent 'a most agreeable week' at anchor in the bay.[13] The rank and file represented a cross section of working class Britain. Amongst them were John Blanton, a weaver from Bradford; the Dublin watchmaker, Private Middleton; and Sergeant John Williams, a labourer from Wrexham.[14] Crammed into the hold, they passed the time drinking, swapping stories and discussing what the future would bring. Meanwhile, the officers attended parties and after-dinner dances accompanied by the Legion's fine band. Such was 'the wild enthusiasm in favour of the cause' that Chesterton was inspired to write a poem, which was later chosen as the Legion's official anthem.[15] Sung to the tune of 'Ye Gentlemen of England', it was 'adopted by the men, and was sung by them incessantly, and under every variety of circumstance':[16]

> Behold with pride you hallowed Isle
> Where freedom's root has thriven
> Your march is sanctioned by her smile,
> And cheer'd by that of heaven
> To plant the tree
> Of liberty
> Is ever hail'd on high:
> Then falter none,
> But sally on
> To conquer or to die.[17]

Despite such promising beginnings, the volunteers would encounter serious problems before they even arrived in South America, and their initial enthusiasm for the cause would soon fade.

The second of the three regiments raised in 1818 was recruited by Captain George Elsom. One of several brothers from Hatton Gardens in London, Elsom had done well in the family lumber business as a young man, but when rewarded with increased responsibility, his subsequent mismanagement led the company to bankruptcy. His father was forced to take work selling coal and his mother became a washerwoman. Undeterred, Elsom returned to the lumber industry. Yet again the project failed, as did a string of short-lived ventures established throughout the city centre. When 'Elsom and Adams' wire merchants went under, he only managed to avoid debtors' prison through contacts in the local constabulary.

After a brief sojourn on the continent, he gained a captain's commission with Colonel Skeene after claiming prior service as an ensign in a volunteer regiment. Fortunately, he was left ashore when the *Indian* sailed and was wrecked off the French coast. Despite his narrow escape, he persevered and later found passage to South America on board the *Sarah*, arriving in Angostura on 13 June 1818. Five days later he began negotiations with Zea, and within a week was sailing back to London to recruit a volunteer regiment.[18] A combination of Elsom's business experience and the republic's desperation resulted in Zea promising him 300 pesos for each man he signed up.[19]

After arriving in London in August, Elsom secured the financial backing of John Ditton Powles, an associate of Charles Herring, the merchant who backed English's venture. Other merchants also signed up, eager to have a share in the emerging South American market, and Elsom swiftly accumulated the funds he required. With his finances secured, he needed a partner with military experience. John Uslar, the man he chose, was one of the most professional volunteers to fight in South America and his experience and expertise at selecting recruits would make Elsom's regiment the most celebrated of all the British units.

Uslar had served as a lieutenant in the 2nd Dragoons of the King's German Legion, an elite regiment recruited from Hanover that fought with distinction under Wellington in the Peninsular War and performed heroic deeds at Waterloo. With Uslar's capability, Elsom's enlistment proceeded rapidly. By the end of 1818 they had raised 900 hand-picked infantry, the vast majority of which were veterans of the recent wars. The troops embarked in four detachments, the first sailing in December 1818. The final ship, carrying Elsom himself, followed six months later.

Amongst the recruits was Lieutenant Charles Minchin, a doctor's son from Dublin. After studying until the age of 19, he was sent to Europe to complete his education.

There he learnt that troops were being raised in London to support the republican cause. 'Drunk on the ideals of glory and liberty', the 21-year old immediately signed up and even managed to talk his brother William into joining. Although neither had military experience, influential family contacts including a former navy captain secured commissions for them in Elsom's regiment, and the brothers boarded the *Hero* in March 1819. According to Minchin's later recollections, the voyage across the Atlantic was a dangerous one, 'in which they were many times on the point of shipwreck'.[20] Nevertheless, the *Hero* reached Angostura safely in April 1819.

Whilst English and Elsom were raising regiments for Venezuela, a third expedition destined for the coast of neighbouring New Granada was being assembled by 'Sir' Gregor MacGregor. An unprincipled, 35-year old adventurer 'somewhat inclined to corpulency', the Scot had already enjoyed a colourful career and was well known to the British press.[21] After a short stint in the navy, he had served in both the British and Portuguese armies in the Peninsular War before sailing to the New World in 1811 to become one of Bolívar's first British volunteers. During the voyage he adopted the epithet 'sir', allegedly derived from a distant ancestor who had married 'a native princess' whilst on a short-lived expedition to colonize modern-day Panama.[22] Regardless of the veracity of such claims, the title no doubt impressed his new employers. Joining the patriots shortly after the foundation of the First Republic, he served initially as Miranda's aide and then as a cavalry commander, later cementing his position by marrying Bolívar's niece, Josefa Govera. After the collapse of the First Republic, he remained loyal to Bolívar and went on to play a vital role in the capture of Santafé de Bogotá, the capital of New Granada, in 1813. Three years later, having accompanied The Liberator on his Haitian odyssey, MacGregor returned to Venezuela. Although his forces were defeated as part of the collapse of the Second Republic, the Scot masterminded a superb fighting withdrawal, saving his army with several masterful rearguard actions. During the campaign his relationship with the republicans seems to have soured, however, and after a heated argument with General Piar, he took an extended leave of absence and travelled north to the United States.

In late 1816, after visiting Philadelphia and Washington, MacGregor decided to break from the Venezuelan republicans for good and began to raise his own personal army to capture the island of Fernandina off the east coast of Florida. Although officially ruled by Madrid, the province was a largely forgotten backwater inhabited only by outlaws, adventurers and Seminole Indians. It proved the ideal recruiting ground. With 57 desperate men signed up, he made his attack. More through bluff and swagger than military expertise, the island fell with little resistance. Under MacGregor's mandate, it became a short-lived haven for privateers sailing under patriot colours. Unable to control the ill-disciplined rogues purportedly under his command, and realizing that a showdown with the ever-expanding United States was imminent, MacGregor abandoned the island after only 64 days. Leaving the French buccaneer Commodore Aury in command, he returned to England, arriving on 21 September 1818.

In London he approached Colonel Maceroni, an Italian veteran who had served in the French Army, with a plan to raise troops for South America. Together they propositioned Don José Maria del Real, the patriot representative of New Granada, with a plan to capture a royalist-held town on the coast and establish a new republic. Del Real accepted, and through a combination of MacGregor's celebrity and Maceroni's financial resources, 1,696 men were recruited. The commanders were less than discerning in their selection and few of the troops were veterans. Although all the men and many of the officers were British, others were recruited from the remnants of a variety of European armies. Some did not speak English, and others had little regard for those who up until 1815 had been their bitter enemies. This lack of unity and the poor quality of the men recruited would lead to disaster once the expedition reached the New World.

Simón Bolívar (1783–1830) and Francisco de Paula Santander (1792–1840). The painting depicts
The Liberator leading his army towards Santafé de Bogotá in the aftermath of the rout of the Spanish
3rd Division at Boyacá, 10 August 1829. (Bridgeman Art Library)

The Battle of Carabobo. This is a detail of a mural which covers the domed ceiling of the Salón Elíptico
in the Presidential Palace in Caracas. The British Legion are shown advancing. (South American Pictures)

Engraving of Simón Bolívar. The Liberator of six countries, Bolívar remains South America's greatest hero.

Jose Antonio Páez. The 'Centaur of Los Llanos', General Páez was greatly respected by the British volunteers.

Portsmouth Point by Thomas Rowlandson, (c.1811). Many of the British volunteers left for South America from Portsmouth amongst similar scenes of debauchery. (National Maritime Museum, Greenwich)

The Peterloo Massacre *by George Cruikshank, (c.1819). The euphoria following Waterloo would not last. In the aftermath of the conflict, Britain's economy went into decline. The civil unrest which followed culminated in this infamous massacre in August 1819. (Topfoto)*

Vue de la Magdalena. *Colombia's largest river was the main transport link between the Andean highlands and the Caribbean coast. Many of the volunteers travelled along it and some would fall prey to the crocodiles basking on its banks. (Image courtesy of The Latin American Library, Tulane University, New Orleans)*

Lying two hundred miles up the Orinoco, Angostura was the capital of Bolívar's Third Republic and a major point of entry for the British volunteers. (Image courtesy of The Latin American Library, Tulane University, New Orleans)

Old Guyana. *Halfway up the Orinoco to Angostura, Old Guyana was the first Venezuelan settlement seen by many of the volunteers. (© British Library Board)*

The perils of South America were numerous: as well as the enemy, the volunteers had to cope with tropical disease, the ravages of the extreme climate and wild animal attacks, such as the tiger depicted here. (© British Library Board)

General Páez's Llanero lancers, formerly cattle ranchers from Venezuela's vast inland plains, proved more than a match for the Spanish cavalry. (© British Library Board)

This page: The Point of Honour *by George Cruikshank, 1825. A common punishment among the volunteers, flogging was first employed by Colonel Hippisley of the 1st Venezuelan Hussars to punish a troop sergeant major charged with theft during the voyage across the Atlantic. (National Maritime Museum, Greenwich)*

Opposite, bottom: The Soldier and his Rabona. *This watercolour is thought to depict a soldier of the Black Rifles. Whilst the officers were originally all British, the rank and file of the unit was raised in South America.*

Above left: *General James Towers English, 1818. English had this painting commissioned on his return to England to raise the British Legion. The lance was presented to him by General Páez. The Llanero had used it to kill 40 royalists at the battle of Ortiz.*

Above right: The Author in the Travelling Costume of the Country. *Charles Cochrane was the author of an 1825 memoir which detailed his travels through Colombia. Cochrane met many of the volunteers and recorded several of their stories. (© British Library Board)*

Vuelvan Cara! *by Arturo Michelina. The painting shows Páez commanding his Llaneros to turn about and attack the royalist forces pursuing them. The ensuing victory is still celebrated in Venezuela today.* (*The Granger Collection / Topfoto*)

La Boca del Infierno. *These rapids on the upper reaches of the Orinoco presented a serious challenge to any travellers passing by in the rainy season.* (© *British Library Board*)

Chapter 11

'PRISONER TO A HORDE OF BARBARIANS'

At the beginning of January 1819, as the rains subsided in Los Llanos, the royalists and patriots alike were busy preparing for the new campaign. Under the command of the foul-tempered General Anzoátegui, 1,000 infantry were in San Juan de Payara, a small Llanero town on the banks of the Arauca. With them were 200 British volunteers. Amongst the officers was Colonel Ferrier. A dark-haired doctor's son from Manchester with a piercing gaze, Ferrier had served with the 43rd Foot before sailing to South America. At San Juan he was in charge of a unit of eight cannon.[1] The officers and NCOs of Piggot's Black Rifles were also there, as was Daniel O'Leary. After leaving the Hussars in August 1818 at Achaguas, O'Leary had been appointed Anzoátegui's aide-de-camp. Páez, meanwhile, was 20 miles north in San Fernando with 3,000 cavalry. Besides his guard of honour, the Caudillo commanded Colonel Antonio Rangel's Rangers, yet another unit of irregular Llanero horse, and would soon be joined by a British cavalry detachment of 50 men. Led by Colonel James Rooke, the unit included Richard Vowell and the remnants of Wilson's and Hippisley's Hussars.[2]

Rooke's men had spent the second half of the rainy season helping General Monagas guard the overland approaches to the north of Angostura from a royalist advance. 'Having received [British Army] clothing and proper sadlery', they had sailed up-river on the brig *La Bombarda*, enduring a 'tedious passage', before disembarking at Bocas del Pao.[3] As the rain poured down, they rode 'through a disagreeable swampy country' fording several swollen rivers before reaching the headquarters of Monagas.[4] They were then involved in a comprehensive victory near the town of Cantaura, after which the royalist commander restricted his operations to 'occasional skirmishing', an intensely fatiguing form of warfare, much to Vowell's distaste.[5] On outpost duty, isolated far out in the wilderness, the volunteers had 'suffered considerably'. They spent the whole time 'in bivouacs, without once sleeping under a roof' and 'were harassed [by the enemy], day and night, with little intermission'.[6] Whilst Vowell's 'robust frame' and sturdy constitution saved him from sickness, many of his comrades were not so fortunate.[7] Just 50 remained when they set off to join Páez at San Fernando in December. By 1819, they were nearly indistinguishable in appearance to the native troops some had looked upon with scorn the previous year. But with the infectiously optimistic Rooke at their head, spirits remained high. The memoirist Surgeon Robinson recorded meeting them as they moved up-river:

> Scarcely could we muster one pair of shoes among us ... we were thus obliged to walk on the burning sand till our feet were ... blistered, and swollen to a prodigious size. Some of Rooke's officers still preserved two legs to their *once* gold-laced pantaloons; while others were fully as ragged as Octavian in the play of the Mountaineers. When we assembled together to cook our beef, every one, in tolerably good humour, cracked his joke on our ragged appearance.[8]

Meanwhile, the royalists were also preparing for the new campaign. Although still suffering from the lance wound he had received at Semen, General Morillo rejoined the royalist army at its winter headquarters in Calabozo in early January. With 5,000 infantry, 1,000 cavalry and a small contingent of horse-drawn artillery, the Spanish had a significant numerical advantage. Morillo was determined to crown the successes he had enjoyed in 1818 by pushing right through the plains and taking Angostura.

By the middle of the month, news of the arrival of further British volunteers at the mouth of the Orinoco reached the patriots in San Juan. It was rumoured that 4,500 troops had been seen, but the report was wildly exaggerated. In reality, they were merely the first wave of Captain Elsom's expedition and amounted to no more than 300 men. Nevertheless, the news caused considerable excitement. Colonel Ferrier celebrated by firing a few volleys from his cannon and Bolívar set off down-river to rendezvous with the new arrivals at Angostura. His plan for the campaign, as outlined in a letter to William White, was 'to occupy ... [the royalists] with cavalry skirmishes between' the Apure and Arauca 'until the reinforcements ... from England arrive' at the front.[9] Before leaving, he sent strict instructions to Páez not to engage the enemy in strength until he returned. For once, the Caudillo obeyed. San Fernando was put to the torch to deny shelter to Morillo's men and the Llaneros retreated across the Apure.[10] After a half-hearted defence of the line of the river, the withdrawal continued. The royalists took the south bank on 24 January and pushed deeper into the plains. As Morillo's ponderous column advanced, bands of patriot horsemen shadowed them, picking off any stragglers that lagged behind.

Traumatized by the slaughter inflicted on their comrades at Calabozo in 1818, the Spanish cavalry dared not leave the protection of their infantry to disperse them.

Two days ride to the south at San Juan, a black market had sprung up to support the patriot infantry's appetites. Travelling merchants, such as the Frenchmen Monsieur Bonjean and Pierre Robinet, sold 'tobacco and aguardiente for the men' and 'handkerchiefs, millinery, and ornaments of all descriptions, for the female' camp followers.[11] Enjoying an absolute monopoly, the merchants charged 'shamefully exorbitant prices'.[12] They were not the only ones profiteering, however. When 'a small quantity of tobacco' reached camp 'a General officer bought it [all] up' to sell on in small quantities 'at a considerable profit'.[13] Such was the demand for the weed that 'the greatest test of friendship at this time was to be allowed one or two whiffs of a comrade's pipe'.[14] As Vowell later remembered, those without money or obliging friends were forced to take desperate measures:

> One of Paëz's *guardia de honor*, an active resolute Zambo, resolved to endure this privation no longer. He swam the Araüco by night; penetrated, in disguise, through the Spanish out-posts, at the risk of being hung for a spy, as far as Obizpos, where he had relations; and returned in triumph with three pounds of tobacco... Two of the small rolls he sold immediately, at a doubloon and a half each; but the third he would neither sell nor give to anyone, saying, that he had hazarded his life for it, and was determined to enjoy it.[15]

According to a letter written by a Spanish officer, there was also a lively trade in servant boys. 'More than 500 ... of 8 to 9 years of age' had been 'torn crying from the arms of their mothers' and sold to the patriot troops. The British officers were the chief customers. For those lacking cash, 'a colourful shirt' was sufficient to purchase their services.[16] Some customers were soon disappointed, however. One later complained that his 'servant deserted to the Spaniards, and took with him fourteen pieces of ... linen'.[17]

San Juan had little in the way of entertainment. By January the officers of the Black Rifles were glad of any distraction. The most popular were the regular Llanero rodeos using wild cattle corralled on the outskirts of town. Amongst the spectators one night was Lieutenant Alexander:

> It consisted in turning a bullock out of the pen, and goading him forward. When he begins to run, numbers follow him on horseback. One pursued the animal until he seized him by the tail, and gave him a sudden jerk, which seldom failed to throw the poor animal on his back or side. It was then allowed to rise, when another began the pursuit, and so on until ... they were satisfied with the cruel sport. Some of the English joined in ... but only got laughed at, for they were not expert enough to throw the animal.[18]

Not to be outdone by their hosts, the Rifle officers showed off their mascot, the 'fine bull bitch' which they had brought out from England.[19] 'She was one evening set at a bull, which she seized ... by the nose and held down, while the agonized animal roared aloud to the surprise and admiration of the Creoles. We told them, that in England men did not contend with brutes at play, but let [them contend with each other].'[20]

Occasionally, alternative entertainment was to be had with the arrival of the *Chinganáros* (travelling performers), likened by Vowell to gypsies, who roamed the country 'fantastically dressed and painted', dancing and dazzling their audiences with astounding acrobatic feats.[21] As well as busking in the towns they passed, they also performed in both the patriots' and royalists' encampments. As the young English officer explained, they enjoyed a unique neutrality in the conflict:

> These people are held in utter contempt ... by all ... and not even the meanest tribes ... will hold any intercourse with the Chinganéros, whom they consider degraded by their buffoonery to the level of monkeys. Their agility and humour, nevertheless, rendered their occasional visits always welcome to the light-hearted Criollos; and even the supercilious Spaniards deigned at times to relax from their haughty gravity, and to smile at their unpolished gambols. At the hottest periods of the *guerra á la muerte* the Chinganéros were considered as privileged exceptions to the general rule, which [otherwise] admitted of no sort of neutrality... As they belonged to no party, so they could scarcely be looked on as spies; and, although they had not the least scruple in conveying such intelligence as lay in their way, or even occasionally becoming bearers of private messages from one side to the other, still they atoned for this conduct ... by the perfect impartiality of their communications. In a word, they were considered too despicable and insignificant a race for anger, or even for serious attention.[22]

In the final days of January, as Morillo's army bore down on San Juan, the playful atmosphere changed dramatically. Senior officers were to be seen galloping through the streets requisitioning horses and mules to carry the army's ammunition, leaving the panicked locals with no means of transporting their possessions out of town. To buy them some time to disperse, Páez decided to make a stand in the nearby town of Caujaral on the far bank of the Arauca. As the men fell back to their positions, a mass exodus began:

> The town, and road to the Araüco, were crowded with old men, women and children, flying from their homes into the woods, very few ... had time to save a single article of their property. The shop-keepers were running around in despair; offering any sum of money for horses or mules to save their goods... At last, heavy firing ... announced the advance of

Morillo … all the shops were … abandoned; and … the rear-guard, were directed to destroy whatever they could not carry off.[23]

As the royalists advanced, the Rifles set up camp in the plains behind Caujaral. Huddled together in their blankets, they shivered as the temperature plummeted at night.[24] Having been allocated a hut near the river, Surgeon Robinson was more fortunate than most. Nevertheless, he often lay awake till dawn, swinging in his hammock and listening to the army around him:

> The wild howl of the Indian song … from upwards of twenty different groups, all assembled round their fires, the lowing of thousands of bullocks, the neighing of as many horses, the braying of mules … and the watch-word passing along the various parties of soldiers, on their stations, gave to the natural gloominess of the scene.[25]

When the Spanish vanguard drew near to Caujaral, cavalry skirmishes broke out on the far bank of the Arauca. On 26 January, two enemy scouts were captured and placed under the Rifles' guard. One was a young cavalry sergeant, 'a native of old Spain', the other a Venezuelan private 'of a very dark complexion'.[26] Although both were executed after interrogation, it was the different manner of their deaths that caused Lieutenant Alexander to record the scene:

> On the Sunday evening the sergeant was brought out and shot … his execution was according to military form, and he had a priest with him to the last; but the poor Creole was taken next morning to the open field, and shot with a single musket, without priest or any form, and his head haggled off.[27]

With Morillo's attack imminent, the patriots threw up temporary 'ramparts of mud and branches of trees' and dug trenches along the far bank of the river.[28] After giving Piggot three cheers, the Rifles advanced to the front. 'A part of the bush was cleared away … and the few houses … were knocked down and burned' to improve their field of fire.[29] Elsewhere along the line, two batteries were constructed, defended by rough barricades 'of casks of sugar, salt' and other abandoned goods.[30] Colonel Ferrier's cannon, four 8-pdrs and four 12-pdrs, were dragged into position and loaded with round shot in anticipation of the Spanish advance.

On the morning of 2 February, with the main column of Morillo's troops just hours away, the patriot cavalry who had been holding back their advance began to cross the river. The riders spurred their horses down the far bank and into the water. Kicking with their legs and pulling with one arm whilst the other grasped the horse's tail, they swam to the south bank. The main body of Llaneros came first, dressed in ponchos, 'loose cotton pantaloons' and 'old straw' hats to protect them from the morning sun.[31] Páez's guard of honour, which now counted some British officers including Captain Peter Grant amongst its number, was the last to cross. Wearing the red jackets and blue pantaloons brought out from London the previous year, the 300 members of the corps 'assumed a different aspect' to their comrades.[32]

As the last man splashed up out of the river, an eerie silence descended. The only sounds were the crackling of the burning houses to the Rifles' front and the 'howling' of stray dogs wandering the streets. Word was passed down the line that it was time to 'do or die' and that the troops were 'to stand to the last man'.[33] At 2.00pm the Spanish infantry appeared. 'All dressed in white', they opened fire from a mile out, advancing until they were lining the bushes on the far bank, in some places as close as 300 yards from the patriots' positions.[34] Slowly at first the shooting spread and soon became general. Colonel Ferrier then ordered his artillery to open fire, sending round shot screaming across the Arauca. Crashing through the undergrowth on the far bank, the heavy iron balls plucked men bloodily from the Spanish line.

Typically, field pieces had a crew of four to five men. The first commanded the team and aimed the gun. The second, known as the spongeman, stood to right of the barrel and forced a damp piece of cloth on a wooden staff down the muzzle after each shot to extinguish any smouldering debris left behind. The third man, or loader, stood to the left. After placing the powder charge in the barrel, he loaded a round shot or a tin of canister or grape. The spongeman then reversed his staff and rammed the charge home, while the fourth crew member, the ventsman, blocked the touch-hole with his leather thumb pad to prevent a rush of air which could ignite any smouldering scraps of powder that might have been left behind. The ventsman then pricked the charge bag and inserted a powder-filled quill into the touch-hole. Finally, as the rest stood well back, the fifth crew member ignited the charge with a match attached to a wooden handle, known as a linstock. The quill burnt down to the main charge which exploded, sending the shot hurtling towards the enemy, whilst the gun leapt back several feet.

As the firing across the river intensified, Páez walked his 'dark iron-grey charger' behind the line, encouraging the troops.[35] The officers shook their fists and swords and shouted insults at the enemy, 'calling them ... dogs' and yelling 'Long live the Republic!'[36] With 'the balls ... whizzing' around his head 'like insects', Lieutenant Alexander passed the time 'laughing and joking ... at any circumstance that raised ... [his] mirth'.[37] Luckily for the Englishman and his comrades in the Rifles, the royalists 'levelled far too high'.[38] Mostly their shots tore harmlessly into the branches overhead and only a handful of men were wounded. When hit, they fell from the fire-step and were dragged back to a line of bushes in the rear to await the attentions of Doctor Thomas Foley. A 'Kerry man', Foley had originally sailed with Wilson's Red Hussars and was now the chief physician in Páez's army.[39] On the second day the Spanish firing slackened, leading Lieutenant Alexander to think the move 'more like a feint' than a full blown attack.[40] His supposition was remarkably astute. At that very moment, unbeknown to the patriots, a second party of royalists were preparing to cross the Arauca 17 miles down-river at Marrereño.

By the time Páez realized he had been outflanked, a Spanish infantry company had already established a bridgehead on the far side of the river and was slowly being reinforced by the rest of the battalion. Some paddled across in canoes dragged from San Fernando. Others crossed on rafts, constructed of driftwood and bamboo and lashed together with rawhide. Some even swam. Despite repeated charges from the Llaneros, the men of the light company proved impossible to dislodge. By the end of the day the rest of Morillo's troops had joined them. Seeing that his position upstream at Caujaral was untenable, Páez ordered Ferrier to heave the eight cannon into the river so they would not fall into enemy hands, and once more his army fell back across the plains.

Despite this setback, everything was actually going according to plan for the patriots. It was Páez's intention to draw the royalists deep into the savannah, whilst employing a scorched earth policy to deny them the resources they required. The patriot cavalry rounded up the cattle and burnt the villages, farms, crops and grassland they rode through, so forcing the Spanish to use up their provisions and preventing their cavalry from foraging for food. Surgeon Robinson described the apocalyptic scenes as the army retreated. 'The excessive heat ... was extremely distressing' and the clouds of ashes which filled the air rendered the men 'as black as African negroes'.[41] To further hinder Morillo's advance, Páez sent Colonel Antonio Rangel and 500 horse behind the Spanish troops to cut their line of supply. Having witnessed his father hanged by the royalists whilst still a boy, Rangel was utterly ruthless and ensured that none slipped through the net. In his novel set during the campaign, Vowell later described one of the colonel's ambushes, sprung in a thick wood on the track between San Juan and San Fernando:

When the [royalist] advanced guard reached the farther end of the glade, the officer in command gave the order to halt... Rangèl chose this moment ... [to] signal ... his men, by a few piercing notes on a small bugle ... and they instantly opened ... fire... Several of the escort fell ... at the first volley; and the mules increased the confusion by galloping about in alarm... The carbineers loaded ... and before the Spaniards even had time to unbuckle their lock-covers, another volley was poured among them ... the sergeants ... took upon them the command, as all the commissioned officers had been killed; and the royalists commenced firing, with the ... celerity that distinguished disciplined soldiers, although ... the smoke, which rolled in white clouds among the trees, prevented them from taking … exact aim. Meanwhile the carbineers, each sheltered by a tree, continued their galling fire, whenever the breeze allowed them to distinguish their enemies … until those few of the escort who were as yet unhurt … endeavoured to make good their retreat… [The surviving royalists] made no attempt at a parley, but pressed onward … exchanging shots occasionally … with their almost invisible enemies in the wood; who hung on their rear with deadly, unrelenting purpose, until the last of the fugitives fell.[42]

Morillo's march through the plains was torturously slow. His army was hindered by its baggage and the artillery had to be dragged across ditches and floated over streams. As the troops advanced, their provisions dwindled and rations were cut. To make matters worse, they were constantly harassed by the bands of hostile horsemen that hovered round them, picking off any stragglers at the rear. When the Spanish cavalry gathered in strength to drive them off, the Llaneros disappeared into the labyrinthine swamplands around the lake of Cunaviche. Whilst the patriots knew the area intimately, it was a death trap for the Spanish. Blundering into quicksand or becoming bogged down in the marsh, they fell easy prey to the patriots' lances. Adding to their woes, their horses, which had enjoyed a rich diet of maize and sugar cane during the rainy season, struggled to subsist on the coarse grasses of the prairie, rendering pursuit even more problematic. Even after dark the Spanish were allowed no rest. Using the high grasses to shield his approach, Páez launched midnight raids. Despite these difficulties, Morillo pushed on ever deeper into the plains, hoping to be rewarded with a decisive showdown with the enemy.

Forced to march day and night to keep one step ahead of the Spanish, the patriot infantry under Anzoátegui also began to suffer. As Lieutenant Alexander's horse had been shot when the Rifles abandoned their positions at Caujaral, he walked alongside the rank and file. On the first day of the retreat, the column marched 'until the moon was down at two o'clock in the morning'. When 'Halto' was finally called, Alexander 'crept into a bush, coiled [himself] … up like a squirrel, and instantly fell asleep'.[43] The next morning, having procured a new horse, he found himself riding alongside the baggage and camp followers. Everywhere the young lieutenant turned were 'mules and asses … pigs, poultry … children tied in cows' skins … [and] horses [with] … two and three people on their back[s]'. The civilians were 'of all ages, sexes and colours' and the wives of several soldiers were also 'riding and walking amongst the men'.[44] Aside from the Black Rifles, who were 'regularly dressed in green', the rest of the division were clothed in apparel just as varied as Vowell had seen in 1818, whilst the addition of numerous second-hand British uniforms added a kaleidoscope of colour.[45] 'Men in artillery and cavalry clothing, both red and blue, [were] marching with the infantry.' The staff of the general officers 'were often dressed as privates' and 'cavalry [wore] … infantry and marine uniforms.'[46]

The rations doled out on the retreat were invariably poor. Each man was given 'three pounds of beef' per day, which was 'without a grain of salt, a bit of bread, or anything in the shape of … [a] vegetable'. To drink, the men had 'as much water as they chose to be at the trouble of fetching'.[47] Several volunteers began to suffer from stomach cramps or 'bowel-complaints' as their digestive systems struggled to cope.[48] Dysentery was widespread and some became too ill to continue. After being assessed by Doctor Foley, the sick were sent to the capital to recover or die. Even the veterans of the 1818 campaign were not immune as Captain Grant, the giant Scot of captured clarinet fame, attested.[49] As he told Surgeon Robinson when the two fell in together on the march: 'For the first fifteen days … after I came into this country … I lived well enough; but ever since, my stomach and bowels have been in the devil's own uproar, and I believe were I to swallow the whole riot act, it would not quiet them.'[50] Their exclusively carnivorous diet became so unpalatable, that on observing some monkeys feeding on 'a running slender plant', Robinson decided to make a soup out of it. Although 'a bitter morsel', it provided him with 'great benefit' and the surgeon struggled on.[51]

Despite the hardships, Colonel Rooke's optimism remained undimmed. He was 'content with everybody and everything' and professed that 'he had never had a better time … than during the Arauca campaign'.[52] When asked his opinion of the climate in the plains, which swung between bitterly cold nights and the desiccating sun of mid-afternoon, he replied that it 'was mild, healthy and superior to any other'.[53]

As the column neared the Orinoco, the landscape began to change. Leaving the grassland behind them, the troops came to a desert of 'burning sand and dust'.[54] Water supplies ran low and they suffered 'the indescribably horrid sensation of extreme thirst'.[55] With his 'throat and mouth, foul and parched', Robinson became so desperate he traded his shirt for 'two table spoons' of sugar cane spirit.[56] Occasionally, the route was punctuated by oases. The men discarded their muskets, rushed forward and dropped to their knees to drink. Although 'thick with mud and vermin', the waterholes brought some relief, but as they were also used by wild animals an unexpected element of danger was added, which caught some of the volunteers by surprise.[57] One memoirist noted that 'it was not … uncommon … to see two or three soldiers lying dead at the edge of the small pools … filled with alligators and snakes, of which they had drunk too incautiously'.[58]

With the trials of the retreat, the relationship between the British and South American troops grew fraught. Whilst still in Angostura, several Venezuelan officers had addressed a petition to Bolívar bemoaning 'the great numbers of foreign officers who were commissioned'.[59] The Liberator, who remained a staunch supporter of the volunteers, had 'soon put a stop to their murmurs', but in his absence the problem resurfaced.[60] British complaints and their propensity towards sickness worsened the situation and many Creole officers grew to 'detest' them.[61] Anzoátegui in particular was 'destitute of either pity or remorse', and one afternoon Lieutenant Alexander saw an officer calling the British troops 'dogs' and 'brutes' as he 'struck them with the flat sides of his sword'.[62] Such prejudices soon spread through the ranks. Before long the quartermasters were skimping on the rations they meted out to the volunteers, claiming that feeding them was a waste of meat, and even the Creole privates became very 'saucy'.[63]

Theft was rife throughout the army, with the volunteers particularly vulnerable. They soon found they could not trust their new comrades, who were even 'known to steal the very shoes from off the feet of the British while asleep'.[64] One night, Colonel Rooke had all his baggage taken and was left with nothing but the clothes on his back. Another British officer lost 'two very valuable chargers', despite the elaborate precautions he had taken:

> … having reason to apprehend that … [the horses] would be stolen, as several of his brother officers had met with similar losses, he … tied their halters, which were made of strongly twisted hide, to … his … legs, leaving the animals sufficient room to graze, and laid himself down under a tree to sleep. When he awoke he found, to his dismay, that the horses were both gone, and his legs so firmly fastened to the tree with the halters, that he was obliged to use his sword to release himself.[65]

Throughout the retreat, 'scarce one day passed that there were not three or four' men executed for desertion.[66] The majority were Indian conscripts with little understanding of the patriot cause. Generally, they absconded in droves, 'during the night … to regain their native woods'.[67] Those who were caught were taken 'a little out of the way … and shot with one ball to save ammunition… The muzzles of the guns often being so near as to set fire to the shirts of the victims.' An officer then 'haggled off their heads' with his sword and the bodies were left unburied where they fell.[68]

Throughout the retreat, Vowell served as a dispatch rider for Colonel Rangel. On one occasion he and two brothers were ordered to take a message to Páez. Whilst swimming their horses across the lagoon of Cunaviche, disaster struck. Although Vowell and one brother made it safely to the far side, the other was attacked by an alligator:

> When he was nearly half across, we saw a large *caÿmàn* … issuing from under the mangrove trees. We instantly warned our companion of his danger; but it was too late for him to turn back. When the alligator was … on the point of seizing him, he threw his saddle to it. The ravenous animal immediately caught the whole bundle in its jaws, and disappeared for a few moments; but soon discovered its mistake, and rose in front of the horse, which … reared and threw its rider. He was an excellent swimmer, and had nearly escaped by diving towards the bank; but, on rising for breath, his pursuer also rose, and seized him by the

middle … the alligator, having previously drowned the unfortunate man, [later] appear[ed] on the opposite sand bank with the body, and [stood] there devouring it.[69]

On 12 February, Anzoátegui's infantry reached Urbana, an island formed by the confluence of the Orinoco and Arauca rivers, which Páez had previously stocked with cattle and other provisions. As the Spanish had no boats, the patriots were safe on the island and relaxed in the shade of the extensive foliage. Although conditions improved, the volunteers continued to suffer as a result of their diet. Debilitating 'bowel-complaints, accompanied with discharges of blood became dreadfully extensive' and boatloads of British officers and NCOs were sent down-river to recover.[70] Amongst those affected was Lieutenant Alexander. After 'being questioned by Dr. Foley', he was deemed sufficiently ill for a place on the boats and arrived at the capital on 31 March 1819.[71]

Deprived of provisions by Páez's scorched earth policy, the royalists meanwhile were reduced to butchering their horses and pack animals to survive. With no mules to drag them, the infantry now had the back-breaking task of hauling the cannon through the 'soft marshy soil of the savannas', with 30 men to a gun.[72] One patriot report on their situation stated that 'all Morillo's energy goes into avoiding death by starvation and collecting cattle … which is … most difficult, as all … assure me his cavalry now march by foot'.[73] By 14 February, less than two weeks after the armies had first clashed at Caujaral, Morillo admitted defeat. With his troops weakening with each passing day and continually harassed by swarms of hostile horsemen, he realized he would never bring the patriot infantry to battle and called the retreat. Abandoning their baggage and excess ammunition, the exhausted troops recrossed the Arauca under intense pressure from Páez's cavalry. At first the discipline of the royalists held. Covered by two cannon set up on the far bank, most of the army crossed safely. But as the final soldiers of the rearguard prepared to join them, the patriots attacked and panic swept through the ranks. Vowell witnessed the slaughter:

Those … who were nearest the river threw themselves, or were precipitated by the press, over the steep banks … most of them perished in the stream. The remainder were either lanced as they stood crowded together, or in vain attempted to shelter themselves, by scattering through the wood, where they fell, one by one, by the carbines of Rangèl's corps.[74]

The survivors returned to San Fernando, where Morillo left a strong garrison to rebuild the gutted town's fortifications. Believing the campaigning season was all but over, he then continued westwards, establishing his headquarters at Achaguas on 8 March 1819. Bolívar had other plans, however. Before the end of the year the course of the conflict would be changed forever.

Chapter 12

THE BLACK RIFLES' BAPTISM OF FIRE

Whilst Anzoátegui's men were keeping one step ahead of the royalists in Los Llanos, the first detachment of Colonel Elsom's expedition arrived in Angostura. Once in the capital, Major John Mackintosh took command. The brother of one of the merchants who had financed the six colonels' expeditions, the London-born major had originally been an officer in the Red Hussars. After resigning from the unit following Wilson's antics in the Caribbean, he had spent several months on Grenada managing the family business before heading up the Orinoco for Angostura.[1] There is no record of the 23-year old having any military experience and it would seem he was awarded his rank solely in lieu of the republic's debt to his brother.[2] Nevertheless, he would prove an excellent commander. He was fearless on the battlefield and one of those to serve under him later wrote that he was 'as good a man as ever breathed'.[3]

The first detachment of 275 men that Mackintosh would command had been divided into two companies before leaving London. One sailed on board the *Tartar*, the other on the *Perseverance*. After crossing the Atlantic, they endured a ten-day passage up the Orinoco before dropping anchor at Angostura on 17 January 1819. Initially the new recruits were welcomed with open arms. The officers were invited to parties and 'other jollifications' and a *Te Deum* was held in the square. Captain Thomas Manby, the commander of the 1st Company, was put up by 'Messers Hamilton and Princep', the city's leading merchants, in Brion's old mansion by the riverside.[4] His hosts were 'perfect Gentlemen'. After a day's hunting in the countryside, they feasted on 'bread, sugar … coffee … fish … [and] game', followed by 'cegars'.[5] An 18-year old libertine who 'dearly love[d] women … and wine', Manby was in his element and no doubt the entertainment continued late into the night in the taverns and brothels downtown.[6]

A veteran of three years, Manby had joined the East Suffolk Militia as an ensign and went on to serve in the regular British Army, reaching the rank of lieutenant before retiring on half pay in March 1817.[7] An even more experienced volunteer under his command was the 42-year old Private Francis Fuge. Despite having served for 24 years, Fuge had been dismissed from the British Army in Mauritius in 1816 as 'unfit for further service' due to a long history of 'strictures and chronic rheumatism'.[8] Nevertheless, both men would serve the patriots well.

After a few weeks in Angostura, Manby fell out with the commander of the 2nd Company, Captain John Johnstone, over who had seniority. Although the former insisted his commission pre-dated his rival's, Major Mackintosh favoured his peer and Manby's pleas were ignored. Disgusted, Manby petitioned the government for a transfer to the Black Rifles or to Bolívar's staff. Both were denied. The captain stayed with the regiment and the ill-feeling remained.[9] On 29 January the situation took a turn for the worse. Having discovered that their bounty of 80 pesos was unforthcoming, Fuge and his fellow rank and file 'turned out in the streets' to protest. Several gathered in the square 'to shout like fools about their rights', whilst 'a sergeant and some companions went to the magazine to arm themselves'.[10] After their demand for '66 cartridges' was refused, a scuffle broke out. The British knocked down several opponents before a Creole officer, named Horcha, intervened. Despite being struck several times with a hand saw, he grabbed a rifle and shot the British sergeant through the shoulder.[11] Back in the square 'the militia and inhabitants had … turn[ed] out to quell' the rising. After some jostling, the former opened fire. One volunteer was killed and several wounded before order was restored.[12] In spite of their protests, the men would not be paid until they set sail for the front. Long before then, many were reduced to selling their possessions to survive.[13]

In mid-February, Elsom's 3rd Company arrived on board the *George Canning*. Mackintosh's unit strength was now up to 427 men. With so many Europeans in residence, Don Feliciano Pérez, a land owner from Los Llanos who was visiting Angostura, thought it seemed more like 'a foreign colony' than a Venezuelan town.[14] So pronounced was the British population that local merchants began to import a dizzying variety of goods for their use including such luxuries as 'Scented Soap … Coat-Brushes; ready made Duck Trowsers of the best quality … and good [British] Porter'. All were available for sale 'at No.76' on the riverside promenade.[15]

Preferring the comparative comforts of the city to the deprivations of the plains, several officers from earlier expeditions were beginning to find their way back to town. These malingerers did little but 'skulk … walk the streets, draw their rations, and quarrel with each other'.[16] Such arguments often led to duels. Finding himself in the city due to poor health, Lieutenant Alexander was challenged by Captain Gustavus Butler Hippisley (the colonel's troublesome son, who seemed to have acquired an appetite for duelling after the affair on Grenada). Although on this occasion the lieutenant's illness would not allow him to fight, many duels did take place. Some were well attended by the locals, prompting one volunteer to liken the riverside contests to 'a Roman exhibition of gladiators'.[17] Unofficially the republican government turned a blind eye. Having lived amongst London's elite in 1810 whilst attempting to rally support for the First Republic, Bolívar understood the role duelling played in upper class society. As it was not common in the Hispanic world, however, 'any American who fought was shot for the offence'.[18]

Another malingerer in the capital was Lieutenant Thomas Smith. A 'silly puppy', Smith was the son of a fabulously wealthy mine owner from England, a background which had done little to prepare him for the realities of campaigning in Venezuela.[19] After sailing with the 1st Hussars on the *Emerald*, he had joined Colonel English's advance guard and arrived in Angostura in mid-February 1818. He later fell in with Colonel Wilson at San Fernando and was arrested as an accessory when the pair returned to the capital. Smith was soon released, however, and appears to have remained in the city ever since. It is not known when he first laid covetous eyes on Anna Rooke, the colonel's wife, but shortly after her husband left the capital for Bocas del Pao in September 1818, the two embarked upon a passionate love affair. When rumours of their relationship reached the flamboyant Scottish merchant, James Hamilton, he wrote to the colonel but the letter would not reach the front line for several months.

Although Anna had some affection for her 'dearest Rooke', the 30-year age disparity and the colonel's lengthy absences were exacerbated by his embarrassing inability to support his wife financially.[20] Like many others, the colonel had hoped that his debts would disappear after joining the republicans. But when his 200 peso bounty had failed to materialize, he had been forced to rely on Anna's father for funds.[21] The situation had since deteriorated, with Rooke adding Colonel Hippisley to his list of creditors, so sinking the couple further into debt.[22] By contrast, Lieutenant Smith was young and wealthy and soon 'acquired so much influence over the unfortunate' Anna, 'as to be permitted to … [spend] the greatest part of the night not only in the house, but in her bed chamber'.[23] Upon hearing of such 'horrid faults', Hamilton arranged for her to be sent to her father's house in Saint Kitt's.[24] But her lover was not to be denied. After appealing to the authorities, Smith was granted leave and sailed down the Orinoco to join her.[25]

In April 1819, Major Joseph Farrar was appointed British commandant for Angostura, a post created by Creole administrators sick of dealing with the foreigners' frequent complaints. In an official communiqué, Vice-President Antonio Zea informed Farrar of his new duties: 'All returns and applications for pay, rations, leave of absence, quarters etc. and everything relating to the British troops … must now come through you or no attention will be paid to them.' Farrar's job was anything but easy and he was largely ignored by Captain Hippisley and his fellow hell raisers. To counter their claims of illness, he insisted on signed certification from the head doctor in town, Edward Kirby, but his authority was constantly undermined by senior officers. Rooke's quartermaster, for example, escaped punishment on charges of drunkenness, embezzlement and abuse after Bolívar sent word that all soldiers should be sent back to their units for the start of the campaign.[26] Farrar's position was further complicated by a lack of support from those who coveted his 'easy' posting. In an open letter to *The Times*, written a few months after his appointment, he wrote of some of the difficulties he had encountered:

> … you can form no conception what a set of scoundrels I have had to deal with … fellows with forged commissions from the British service, and guilty of such acts of blackguardism, that even the soldiers under their command are far superior to them. I have, however, determined to bring everyone of them to a public trial.[27]

Eventually, in June 1819 Farrar's persistence yielded results and he brought his nemesis to trial. On the day of his arrest, Captain Hippisley had attended the funeral of a fellow volunteer who had died of fever. After the ceremony, he repaired to a tavern with some British NCOs. In time the wake grew rowdy and a brawl began. Farrar later charged the captain on two counts; firstly, for striking a fellow volunteer; and secondly, for 'unofficerlike conduct'. The latter was brought as it was 'inconsistent in every respect with the character of an officer and a gentleman' to socialize with non-commissioned ranks.[28] Although the verdict was not recorded, it appears that Farrar's efforts may have had some effect. Hippisley would return to England in 1820, but before his departure the troubled young captain would have one final role to play.

Understandably, considering their duels, drunkenness and ostentation, some locals began to resent the British presence. Matters came to a head in December 1818, when a Venezuelan soldier, Sergeant José Herrera, had a heated argument with a merchant by the name of Samuel Forsyth in the latter's riverside abode. After Herrera had accused Forsyth and 'all the English' of being 'thieving rogues who steal from the Republic', he was bundled out of the property. He then hurried home to fetch a knife but by the time he returned, several friends had gathered to protect the merchant.[29] Nevertheless, Herrera forced his way in. The foreigners then threw him out of a window and beat him so badly with sticks that he was 'left … useless for armed service'.[30] At the subsequent trial the court sided with Forsyth. The judge deemed that Herrera's beating was sufficient punishment and the case was dismissed without further action.

On 15 February 1819, Bolívar gave what many consider his greatest speech – the Angostura Address. In front of a prestigious company of politicians, merchants and soldiers gathered in the Governor's Palace, he outlined his dream of uniting Venezuela, New Granada and Ecuador to form Gran Colombia, a single independent superstate. He envisaged a democracy born from the ideals of the age of Enlightenment which would abolish 'distinction, nobility … and privileges', whilst promoting 'the rights of man and freedom of action, thought, speech and press'.[31] Ever the Anglophile, he recommended adopting certain elements of the British approach to government, though rejecting any concept of monarchy. He envisioned a government based around two chambers: 'one a house of elected representatives, the other a hereditary senate' which, like the House of Lords, would temper excessively progressive proposals, whilst also serving as 'a bulwark of liberty' to counteract the ambitions of overly powerful individuals.[32] Bolívar was not a believer in pure democracy, reasoning that after so many years of Spanish rule the peoples of Latin America were not yet ready to govern themselves. Instead, a strong autocratic president was required. Throughout the speech, The Liberator's passion was tangible. His audience were moved to tears and rapturous applause broke out when he finally reclaimed his seat.

By late February Bolívar, and Mackintosh's regiment, were preparing to leave for the front. In the days before their departure, several volunteers absconded and hid themselves in town, prompting the government to threaten to fine or imprison any locals who failed to hand over men concealed on their property.[33] The move was effective, and after the majority had returned, the regiment embarked. The men were paid as they reached the quayside.[34] A disgruntled Private John Evans thought it little more than a transparent attempt to encourage them onto the boats. In place of the 80 pesos they had been promised, the rank and file received two pesos per month, whilst each officer was paid just ten of the 200 pesos originally agreed. Bidding a regretful 'goodbye to all the comforts of … life', Evans climbed aboard.[35] The sails were unfurled and the men headed up-river.

On 10 March they arrived at Anzoátegui's new divisional headquarters in Araguaquen. During the voyage, one man had been lost whilst trying to get his boat off a sandbank; another had deserted at the town of Pao; and a few dozen had fallen sick and been sent back to the capital to recover. At Araguaquen they were joined by the survivors from the six colonels' expedition, bringing the unit's strength back up to 300 men. With the army's morale boosted by the new arrivals, The Liberator was keen to take on the Spanish. Marching out in pursuit of Morillo, they retook the towns abandoned by the royalists during their retreat and besieged those where a garrison had been left. At Cunaviche on 16 March, Páez's cavalry joined the army. After crossing the Arauca River at Caujaral, the combined forces turned west, marching towards the Spanish headquarters at Achaguas.

Whilst riding through San Juan de Payara, a town that the patriots had occupied only a few weeks previously, Vowell was appalled by the destruction he witnessed. Most of the wooden houses had been burnt to the ground. 'Along the street were strewed fragments ... of furniture', whilst 'clothes and bedding ... lay trampled in the sand.'[36] Even the church had been ransacked and books from the library of the local priest had been piled up in the street and burnt. Aware that British troops were serving in the patriot army, Morillo had left 'placards ... sticking on the doors of the houses ... [written] in English, French and Spanish'. They offered any who deserted commissions in the royalist army, or alternatively, safe passage back to Europe.[37]

In mid-March, Páez's scouts reported the presence of an enemy outpost at the sugar mill of Gamarra, a huddle of straw farm buildings in a clearing on the south bank of the Apurito River. On the morning of the 27th, Bolívar decided to attack. Three infantry regiments totalling 800 men, supported by 200 cavalry led by Páez, were sent to deal with the royalists, whilst the rest of the army waited a few miles to the rear. Guided by several locals, Colonel Piggot and Lieutenant O'Leary spearheaded the advance. Walking their horses at the head of the Black Rifles, they approached the mill down a track through the woods. The Barcelona Regiment led by Colonel Ambrosio Plaza followed behind in support, whilst the Barlovento Battalion circled round to the right in a bid to outflank the enemy. Crashing through the undergrowth, the Rifles' vanguard soon came up against outlying royalist pickets. After firing one shot, the Spanish ran back to the mill. Startled by the shooting, Piggot's scouts deserted, leaving the colonel with little idea of which direction to take.

With only 226 infantry and 98 cavalry under Colonel Narcizo López, the Spanish commander, Colonel José Pereira, was outnumbered three to one. Nevertheless, when he heard the first patriot shots echoing through the woods, he formed up his men behind a chain of barricades to meet them. With no guides, Piggot's advance had been slow. By the time the Rifles appeared in the tree line, Pereira's men were ready for them. As the patriots closed, the difference in quality between their Indian conscripts and the veteran Spanish troops facing them became clear.[38] Whilst the royalists maintained their line and kept up a steady fire, Piggot's men soon began to show signs of breaking. For every royalist plucked backwards from the barricades, several patriots fell. Others started to peel off the sides of the formation and edge away from the fight. To make matters worse, the Baker rifles they were issued with were desperately slow to reload and the Barlovento Battalion ordered to support them was still manoeuvring in the woods. Trying to force his men onwards, Piggot had his horse shot from under him. As he struggled to regain his feet, his men fell back to the woods. Picking himself up, the colonel eventually rallied them. Twice more they advanced, but each time were forced back by the ordered volleys of the royalists. Fifteen minutes into the fight, and after the green coated riflemen had retreated for a third time, Pereira ordered his men to fix bayonets. With the 16in steel blades locked into place, the Spaniards charged. Caught by surprise by the sudden counter-attack, the Rifles broke and fled. Dozens were captured. Others were killed in the woods by royalist bayonets. Meanwhile some of the survivors took advantage of the confusion to desert; after sneaking through patriot lines, they slowly made their way back to their villages on the Orinoco.

With the patriot centre broken and the Barlovento Battalion still manoeuvring in the woods, only a few infantry on the left wing remained. Maintaining the royalists' momentum, Colonel López's cavalry charged. Riding through scattered fire, the 98 horsemen killed several with their sabres before the rest ran. Herded before the horsemen, many foolishly fled north towards the Apurito. Trapped between the bloody blades and the swollen river, several dived in; some thrashed their way to the far bank, but the majority were swept down-river and drowned. Although the royalists had inflicted heavy casualties so far, the patriot officers still managed to rally enough men in the woods to regain control of the situation. Knowing they could not beat the Spanish infantry in a musketry duel, they sent small squads forward with burning brands to set fire to the farm instead, and the wooden buildings were soon ablaze. Desperate to escape, the Spaniards streamed out in disorder straight past Páez's cavalry who had been waiting to intercept them. Just as the horsemen were about to charge, however, the Caudillo suffered an epileptic fit. Unwilling to go into action without their chief, the cavalry stalled, giving Pereira time to get his entire force, including the wounded, down to the river and into some waiting canoes. By the time Páez had recovered, the Spaniards were safe on the far bank.

The action at Gamarra had been costly for the patriots, with 300 killed, wounded or dispersed. To make matters worse, Bolívar had now lost the element of surprise. Another consequence of the encounter was that the trademark firearms of the Black Rifles were replaced. Although praised by some for its accuracy, the Baker rifle's slow rate of fire provoked criticism from others. Following Gamarra, Bolívar lost faith in the weapon and decided that the regiment should carry muskets into battle instead. The defeat also affected the army's morale and desertion reached new heights. On one day in March, for example, two of Anzoátegui's officers fled with 28 of their men. To prevent more abandoning the army, Bolívar used the few units he could rely on, such as the British veterans of the 1818 campaign and Páez's guard of honour, as unofficial military police.

The day after the battle the patriots continued their advance. After crossing the Apurito, they turned north, marching to the banks of the Arauca where they camped for the night. That evening Bolívar wrote to Antonio Zea in Angostura, urging him to send special rations which would be more palatable for the British troops:

The quality of the provisions … has caused some illness, especially in the english battalion, that I fear will be destroyed if it continues the campaign without a variation in diet. It is, therefore, necessary that you send me the cargo that the *Hunter* has brought, particularly the flour and rum, as soon as possible.[39]

Amongst those taken ill was Colonel Piggot. Suffering from chronic dysentery, he was forced to concede command to his second, Major Arthur Sandes, and return to the capital to recover his strength.

Born in 1793 in Glenfield, County Kerry, Arthur Sandes was the second of six sons. He had joined the British Army during the Napoleonic Wars and saw action at the battle of Waterloo. Having joined Colonel Campbell's Rifles in 1817 as a lieutenant, Sandes had risen to the rank of captain by the time the regiment reached the Orinoco and was later made a major by Bolívar himself following the inspection at Angostura in October 1818.[40] Fresh faced, with a shock of dark hair and high forehead, at 26 he was a good looking young man in his prime. For Sandes, life was an adventure to be enjoyed and his style of command was similar to that of his soulmate and fellow volunteer, Colonel Rooke. Both had great charisma and led by force of personality rather than by punctiliously sticking to the word of the law. They also shared a love of gambling. Utterly dedicated to those who served under him and fearless on the battlefield, Sandes was loved and respected by his men and officers alike, whilst his ability and good nature would make him 'a great favourite' of The Liberator.[41] In time, the Irishman would reach the rank of general, but a cavalier disregard for his own safety would see him wounded several times. Sandes was also fortunate in his second, Captain William Peacock. From Garry Owen, County Limerick, Peacock was a fine soldier, and said to be 'the handsomest man in the west of Ireland'.[42]

On 1 April 1819, several British soldiers deserted. Complaining that they had been deceived and unable to cope with 'the burning climate and … lack of provisions', three sergeants and two privates of Mackintosh's Rifles stole across the Arauca, hiked through the night to Achaguas and gave themselves up to the royalists.[43] Several other volunteers, including some of the newly arrived officers, had also suffered enough. When one asked for permission to return to Britain, Bolívar had him arrested. The officer later wrote a letter home, detailing his plight:

It is beyond description bad. I am dying by inches… I am under close arrest for demanding my passport, and expressing my sentiments fully to the supreme chief of the wretched treatment we are compelled to suffer, marching all day and night exposed to such heat as I never before experienced, and frequently from 30 to 40 hours without breaking our fast …

the Englishmen drop on the road by dozens ... and are threatened to be shot unless they proceed... I know not what will be the result of this campaign, but if I do not die one way I must another ... for God's sake let me know what is going on in England. I am writing on the root of a tree, it is the only shelter I have had for many weeks.[44]

On 2 April, the patriots caught sight of Morillo's encampment on the far side of the Arauca River. As ever, Páez was desperate to attack and eventually Bolívar allowed him to take 150 hand-picked riders across. Presuming they were the vanguard of the entire patriot army, Morillo sent out a mixed column of infantry and cavalry to deal with the approaching threat. Páez then employed one of his favourite tactics. Halting his men 'within hailing distance', he taunted the enemy troops until they took the bait and charged.[45] The Llaneros then retreated, leaving a cloud of dust in their wake. The sight of their chief tormentors flying before them proved too much for the royalists to resist. Abandoning all order, the Spanish Dragoons galloped after them, leaving their infantry support far behind. This was the moment Páez had been waiting for. As soon as they were too far away from their main army for Morillo to intervene, he waved his black fringed banner in a prearranged signal. All 150 reined in their mounts and charged back the way they had come.

Within a second the situation had changed dramatically for the Spaniards. One moment they were pursuing a routed foe and the next they were desperately trying to turn their horses back to their own lines. The royalists were not quick enough and Páez's men were soon amongst them, killing several in the initial clash. Then the Llaneros wheeled round and plunged back into their ranks. The slaughter that followed was 'prodigious'.[46] By the time the dust had settled, 400 had been killed or wounded. Páez was 'reported to have lanced nine with his own hand', whilst Captain Grant 'killed five'.[47] Horrified by what they had witnessed, the infantry of Morillo's advance column formed a defensive square. Approaching within range, the Llaneros loosed their carbines at the formation, but as night fell they were eventually driven off by cannon fire. Swimming their horses back across the river, they 'rejoined their army in triumph'.[48] None of the Llaneros had been killed and just five were wounded.

Páez was roundly championed for his success, and the battle, which came to be known as *Queseras del Medio*, would go down as one of the patriots' greatest victories. Significantly, its immediate consequence was to bring the campaign to an end. With the rainy season once again drawing near, Morillo retired to his headquarters at the town of Mantecal. Surrounded by heavily forested land where Páez's cavalry could not operate effectively, the fortified town proved impregnable and no actions of consequence occurred for the remainder of the season. Shortly afterwards, news arrived from Madrid that the Spanish economy was in free fall. Starving peasants plagued the country roads, making unescorted travel impossible and severing communications between the major cities. Even more significantly for Morillo, the Spanish people's initial enthusiasm for the war in South America had faded. Stories of the horrific conditions on campaign had filtered back to the Old World, and the contradictory propaganda published in the state-controlled press had been widely discredited. The army was sick of fighting what was seen as an unjust and unwinnable war, and was close to open revolt. One body of recruits intended to bolster royalist forces in Argentina had risen up against their officers on arrival in Buenos Aires, and deserted en masse to the enemy. When news of their mutiny reached Spanish shores, another fleet of reinforcements refused to depart. The situation had become so desperate that reports of a conspiracy to assassinate Ferdinand VII were quickly gaining credibility. All of this left Morillo increasingly isolated. He now knew he could expect little help from home.

Back in Los Llanos, meanwhile, the patriot cavalry continued to mount patrols around the outskirts of the royalist base at Mantecal. When they came across enemy foraging parties, minor skirmishes ensued. Vowell witnessed such an encounter:

> [Páez] had surrounded a detachment of the royalist army, consisting entirely of infantry ... within less than a league of Mantecal, but as his own force ... had but few firearms with them, he could make no impression upon the enemy, which had formed a solid square. The Spaniards ... did not dare to deploy, for the purpose of gaining the edge of the wood; for they held the lancers in great dread, and could not keep them at a sufficient distance to hazard any manoeuvre, on account of the shelter the high grass afforded them... Paëz suddenly thought of firing the dry grass, which was immediately done in several places, to windward of the enemy's position. The flames, of course, effectively dislodged the unfortunate Spaniards; and those who were not suffocated by the smoke, and blown up by their own cartridges, fell an easy prey to ... the lancers.[49]

This cruel massacre was one of the final actions of the campaign. Secure in the knowledge that Bolívar's troops would not be causing any further problems once the rainy season began, Morillo withdrew from Los Llanos entirely. Breaking camp at Mantecal, he crossed the Apure on 1 May and took up winter quarters in the valleys of Aragua. Awaiting his arrival were reports of yet another British expedition that had entered the conflict a few hundred miles to the north-west, on the shores of the Caribbean.

Chapter 13

FIASCO AT PORTOBELO

Accompanied by his wife, her servants and a handful of officers, General MacGregor sailed from the Downs in November 1818. After 'a tedious passage of fifty days', the 18-gun *Hero* anchored at Isle de la Vache, an uninhabited island just off the port of Aux Cayes (Cayes) in Haiti.[1] The *Hero* was soon joined by the *Monarch*, *Onyx* and *Petersburgh Packet*, and by the end of February the Scot was in command of 400 men. The force was divided into five regiments: the Rifles, the Lancers, the Hussars, an infantry unit named Hibernian and a small artillery contingent. Compared to previous expeditions, there were fewer veterans amongst the rank and file. In fact 'nearly two-thirds ... [were] unacquainted with the use of a musket' and the only regiment boasting any real experience was the Rifles under MacGregor's second in command, Colonel Rafter, many of whom arrived 'with ... Waterloo medals' pinned to their chests.[2] A veteran of 12 years, Rafter had served with the British Army in Holland, the West Indies, Spain and Portugal before resigning his captaincy in 1817. His men and a handful of others who had fought with the British Army were 'dressed in the clothing of their former regiments'.[3] Sporting an assortment of civilian garb, the rest of those disembarking onto the beach were unrecognisable as soldiers.

As well as being the least experienced, MacGregor's expedition was also the most multinational of all those sent to South America. Although nearly all the rank and file were British, the officers also included 'French ... Germans, Poles and Prussians'.[4] Two New Granadan priests and their fellow countryman, Don Juan Elias López, a member of the provisional republican government, were also present. All three were former acquaintances of MacGregor's who had narrowly escaped when Morillo's troops had captured Cartegena in 1816. In return for a loan of 12,000 pesos, the Scot had promised to make López the 'governor of the first city he should capture'.[5]

Situated in 'an extensive and beautiful' bay a few miles to the east of the port of Aux Cayes, Isle de la Vache would be MacGregor's base for the next four weeks whilst he gathered supplies and allowed his men to acclimatize.[6] Blanketed by 'close thickets' of 'lofty ... beautiful trees' and boasting several large clearings, the island reminded some of MacGregor's officers of 'gentlemen's parks in England'.[7] From their base, the volunteers could see Aux Cayes across the bay. Its houses were 'coated with white plaster' and 'two squares with rows of lofty coconut trees' could be made out.[8] In one of the plazas stood a pillar commemorating the slave uprising of 1791. Led by Toussaint L'Ouverture, the blacks had turned on their former masters and seized control of the island. Napoleon then sent troops to quell the rebellion, but his forces were defeated in 1804. Within two years of independence, however, Haiti had torn itself apart. Its president was murdered and two new states were born. When the volunteers arrived, the town still bore the scars of warfare. 'Entire streets ... [were] overgrown with grass, and several public buildings reduced to ruins.'[9] Alexandre Pétion, the new leader of the southern republic, was a friend of all those seeking independence and had aided Bolívar in 1816. In keeping with this policy, the population of 5,000 'blacks and mulattos, with a few English, French and Spanish merchants' received the volunteers with open arms.[10] Colonel Rafter was amongst the first to benefit from their hospitality, being delighted when he obtained permission to camp on the beach outside town. He thought it 'a great luxury' and infinitely preferable to sleeping on board the ships. When other volunteers crossed the bay to visit, they attracted considerable attention from the locals, much to Rafter's amusement:

> You cannot imagine the gay crowd we have on these occasions, as almost every Inhabitant of the town has walked out to see us. The General of the Native Troops, a polite little Black man, quite the Parisian in manners, has taken his claret and segars with me on two evenings.[11]

Despite the hospitality, MacGregor's expedition had been plagued by problems from the start. When Major Bezant, the senior officer on the *Monarch*, was rowed to the mainland for a meeting with MacGregor one night, his men, believing themselves abandoned, 'hung up red jackets from the yard arm' in a well known signal of mutiny and besieged the remaining officers in the main cabin.[12] Luckily for MacGregor, Colonel Rafter prevented the rebellion from spreading. Lining the deck of the *Petersburgh Packet* with riflemen, he sailed alongside the *Monarch* and threatened to open fire. Somewhat cowed, the mutineers suspended their siege. The next morning Bezant returned on board to 'unanimous shouts of joy'. The men put down their weapons, the officers regained control and two ringleaders were flogged.[13]

A few days later, the fleet was joined by the *Iphigenia*, a Royal Navy frigate. Sent from Port Royal, Jamaica, by Admiral Sir Home Popham, the frigate's captain had orders to spy on MacGregor's men. In contrast to the treatment of the five colonels the previous year, the *Iphigenia*'s officers were perfectly pleasant to the volunteers. Rafter, Bezant and Captain Heath were invited on board and, according to the expedition's surgeon, Mr Weatherhead, their host later spoke of their visit 'in a most handsome manner'.[14] For the rest of the officers, entertainment was provided by Captain Acton and his performing poodle, Leo. An officer in Rafter's Rifles, Acton had formerly served with the 60th Regiment in the Napoleonic Wars. Leo had drawn crowds in the Peninsular War and remained a favourite amongst the men, who would gather by the beach to applaud his waterside acrobatics.[15]

After a few days on the island, it became apparent that MacGregor had no way of paying the 80 pesos bounty he had promised his men. Consequently, several deserted. Some fled into the interior, planning to survive on wild fruit, scavenging and hunting game. A further 30 men, who had worked in Britain as 'artizans', were induced to settle in Aux Cayes by wealthy local residents.[16] Morale was not helped by poor rations and a lack of clothing and arms. The troops had 'scarcely a musket' between them 'and, neither powder nor ball'. Just when it seemed the expedition was doomed, MacGregor secured a loan of 300 muskets, 50 casks of gunpowder, provisions and a schooner named the *Harriet*, all donated by some South American merchants resident in town. Now clothed, equipped, enjoying 'fresh meat … twice a week' and kept busy with regular firearms drill, morale picked up significantly.

On 9 March the ships set sail. Surgeon Weatherhead recalled that it was 'a fine moonlight night'. Standing at the bow, he watched 'the land receding from … view', until it 'was gradually lost amidst the clouds'. To toast their expedition, MacGregor handed out 'a present of wine, hollands, and porter … for the … officers', whilst the men received a double allowance of rum. 'Music and dancing' followed, accompanied by the bagpipes of the men of Hibernian.[17] At noon the next day, the *Harriet*, MacGregor's schooner, sailed due west for Port Royal, Jamaica, where he hoped to raise more recruits from the York Chasseurs, a recently disbanded British regiment. As well as the Scot, several officers' wives were also on board, believing Port Royal would provide comfortable lodgings until it was safe for them to rejoin their husbands. The rest of the fleet headed 600 miles to the south-west, their destination the island of San Andres, where they were to await MacGregor's return.[18] The voyage was uneventful and the ships arrived between 19 and 22 March. Surgeon Weatherhead was delighted with his new home. 'Beautifully varied by hills and valleys', the island was 'covered with wood, sugar and cotton plantations'.[19] The beef and pork were 'very superior', fowl were to be found 'in abundance' and a variety of crops grew 'round the picturesque houses and cottages'.[20] Originally a Spanish possession, control of San Andres had since passed to the patriot privateers who now used it as a base for their depredations in the region.

With the ships anchored in a deep natural cove the men explored, cooled by 'delightful sea breezes'.[21] Colonel Rafter, who had been left in charge by MacGregor, had the *Hero*'s cannon unloaded and a shore battery constructed to defend the bay. In the days that followed the men felled trees to build a barracks and hospital, whilst the officers took to the countryside for 'pleasant rambles, and shooting excursions'.[22] The good times were not to last. On the 28th, the last of the rum was drunk and the men began to grow restless. As the days passed with no sign of MacGregor's return, discontent threatened to turn to mutiny, prompting Rafter to act before matters got out of control. Choosing two men noted for their 'riotous conduct', he organized a court martial, which sentenced them both to a flogging. The volunteers formed a hollow square and the condemned were marched into the middle. Before the sentence could be carried out, however, the troops broke ranks and threatened their commander. Remaining calm, Rafter 'produced a brace of pistols'. Raising his voice to be heard above the uproar, he addressed the men: 'I have been entrusted by General MacGregor with the command of his troops, and I am determined, at all hazards, to have my orders obeyed... I pledge my honour that, however instant my own death may be, I will shoot the first man who presumes to interrupt.'[23] Faced with such conviction, the men backed down. The prisoners were then stripped to the waist and whipped.

Despite, or perhaps because of, Rafter's efforts, discontent continued to bubble beneath the surface and on 29 March the senior officers held a council of war. Knowing that sooner or later the men would turn on them, they decided that if MacGregor failed to arrive by 5 April, they would proceed to the Spanish Main without him. On the 2nd, Rafter purchased 'a pipe of Gin' from a passing traveller, momentarily quietening the men.[24] Then, just two days before the deadline expired, MacGregor appeared with supplies from Jamaica. Heartfelt 'huzzas' echoed round the cove as he dropped anchor. All was harmonious once more.

That night, MacGregor spoke of his trip. According to the Scot, 'the officers and men' of His Majesty's fleet in Jamaica had given him 'three cheers' as his schooner had sailed into Kingston Bay.[25] From then on, however, the situation had deteriorated. His plans to recruit on the island were blocked by Admiral Popham, the *Harriet* was detained under the Prince Regent's proclamation and MacGregor was 'obliged to remain ... incognito' through fear of arrest.[26] Fortunately, assistance appeared in the form of Mr Hyslop, a resident merchant and long-term supporter of the republican cause. As well as putting up the officers' wives, he provided MacGregor with the *Pit*, a well-stocked sloop.[27]

Under cover of darkness, the Scot slipped out of port on 26 March. During the voyage to San Andres, the expedition suffered its first casualty when Captain Leigh died of yellow fever. His body was tossed overboard and the sloop sailed on.

On 4 April, MacGregor and López marked the formal possession of San Andres by the republican government of New Granada. 'The patriot colours … were hoisted … and a salute of 21 guns … fired by the Hero.'[28] After the ceremony, a dinner was given by López and all the principal officers swore an oath of fealty to the flag. Some 'looked sad when they renounced their allegiance' to Britian, but their spirits rose as the alcohol flowed and the party finished with a rousing rendition of General Woolf's song which was 'sung with all … [the] enthusiasm … the occasion naturally inspired'[29]:

Why Soldier Why?

How stands the glass around?
For shame ye take no care, my boys!
How stands the glass around?
Let wine and mirth abound.
The trumpet sounds.
The colors, they are flying boys
To fight, kill, or wound
May we still be found
Content with our hard fare, my boys,
On the cold, cold ground.
Why, soldiers, why,
Should we be melancholy boys?
Why, soldiers, why,
Whose business 'tis to die?
What sighing, fie!
Damn fear, drink on be jolly boys.
'Tis he, you, or I,
Cold, hot, wet, or dry
We're always bound to follow boys
And scorn to fly.
'Tis but in vain,
I mean not to upbraid, ye, boys,
'Tis but in vain,
For soldiers to complain.

Should next campaign,
Send us to Him that made us, boys,
We're free from pain,
But should we remain.
A bottle and kind land lady
Cures all again.

The next morning the fleet set sail. En route, MacGregor revealed his objective to be the town of Portobelo, a fortified Spanish stronghold on the coast of modern-day Panama. On 7 April land was sighted. They had arrived off the port of Chagres, 45 miles from their intended destination. In the harbour was the *Parthian*, a British brig of war commanded by the marvellously monikered Captain Bigland. As MacGregor's ships tacked westwards down the coast, Bigland followed. Mid-voyage the *Parthian* overtook them and sailed ahead to warn the Spanish garrison of their arrival. On 9 April at 11.00am, the fleet dropped anchor three miles to the leeward of Portobelo in Buenaventura Bay and the troops prepared to disembark.

When he had discovered the area at the beginning of the 16th century, Columbus had been struck by its beauty. Although the site was frequented by passing mariners in the following years, Portobelo was not built until 1584, when the need to defend the shipments of silver and gold mined in Peru prompted the Spanish to build fortified towns along the route taken by their treasure fleets. The cargoes were unloaded at Panama and dragged overland across the isthmus to Portobelo, where they were then loaded onto the Atlantic fleet for the trip to Cádiz. By the 19th century, production had faded and the town had gone into decline.

Situated to the right of the bay, Portobelo was built on a narrow strip of land that fanned out away from the harbour and was surrounded by steep, forested hills. Three forts were sited nearby. One was built on a hill to the east, another faced it across the bay, whilst the third was situated between the two, so close to the sea that the waves lapped against its walls at high tide. All three were of a modern design, their low walls bristling with 114 cannon. The central fort was overlooked by Government House and the mayor's residence, the principal buildings in town, both of which boasted two storeys and were situated on the upper square. A second plaza, closer to the bay, was also surrounded by stone buildings, although the total number of such dwellings did not exceed 150. As well as a few Creole and European dignitaries, 3,000 'Indians, Mulattoes and Negroes' were resident, the vast majority living in 'ill built' huts constructed of 'canes, and thatched with the leaves of the coconut tree'.[30] The main road led eastwards off the lower square and headed into the mountains en route to the Pacific coast and the town of Panama.

Inside the walls, the Spanish governor, Don Juan van Herch, was preparing to repel the invaders. Even before their arrival, he had suffered his fair share of problems. Three-quarters of his garrison of 450 had been laid low with fever. Some had since died and the rest were in hospital. Nevertheless, he decided to take the initative, sending the 100 who remained in good health to oppose the landing. Taking up positions 'behind cocoa nut and orange trees' just back from the beach, they loaded their muskets and waited, whilst the sick who were capable of leaving their beds garrisoned the forts.[31]

At 11.00am a flotilla of small boats was launched from the fleet. Pulling hard at the oars, the sailors drove the landing party towards the beach. As they got closer they could see the enemy, 'under the cover of the bushes ... waving the blood red flag of no quarter'.[32] On board the *Hero*, Major Bezant, MacGregor's artillery commander, gave the order to open fire. Nine 32-pdrs leapt backwards on their cradles. As the grape ripped through the foliage, the bulk of the royalists retreated out of range. On the deck of one of the landing boats, Colonel Rafter 'determined the bearings of Fort St. Juan ... with a pocket compass' to facilitate the jungle march that lay ahead.[33] Just as the sun reached its zenith, Major Baldwin of the Lancers splashed ashore and thrust the colours into the sand. The sight of MacGregor's black cross prompted three cheers from the men crowding the *Hero*'s railings. Then Baldwin formed his company into line and advanced, with musketry kicking up puffs of sand at his feet. When the troops had closed, he gave the order to fire. The volley thundered across the beach.[34] Before the smoke had cleared, they fixed bayonets and charged. With the British screaming towards them, the royalists 'took to their heels' and fled.[35]

By 1.30pm, all 300 men of the storming party were formed up in two columns on the beach. Rafter then led them into the rainforest, guided by a Frenchman hired in Aux Cayes. The plan was to march round the hills and attack the forts from the rear, thereby negating much of their fire power which was aimed towards the sea. As they climbed 'detachments of ... royalists kept up a sharp fire' from the undergrowth and the terrain and humidity made progress torturously slow.[36] The volunteers had to scramble over 'huge rocks' and force their way through 'close-woven thickets of prickly pear ... and brambles'. Steep-banked ravines and fast-flowing streams also had to be crossed. One volunteer later complained that the five-hour march was 'one of the most arduous and fatiguing ... that could be accomplished'.[37] Assigned the unenviable task of lugging Surgeon Weatherhead's equipment uphill, privates Reed and Mutcheson fell behind and were captured. Under interrogation, they convinced the Spanish that they faced 1,000 men. They were then marched across the isthmus and imprisoned in Panama. Rafter, meanwhile, found himself back at the beach where he had landed. The guide had betrayed him; absconding mid-march, he had fled through the woods to Portobelo.

Undeterred, the columns set off along the beach as the shadows lengthened. Guiding them was Colonel Woodbine, a British veteran who had gained considerable experience of bush fighting during the 1812 war against the United States.[38] Although progress was initially good, they soon found their path blocked. Ahead of them, 100 of the enemy had taken up positions behind a large rock. Captain Charles Ross of the Rifles, a veteran of the 60th Foot who had 'fought bravely' at the bloody sieges of Ciudad Rodriguez and Badajoz in the Peninsular War, deployed his company in line.[39] After advancing into 'scattered and ineffectual' musketry, Ross halted and ordered his men to open fire.[40] 'Three ... were laid dead' by the volley.[41] The rest fled across the sands to town.

Continuing their advance, the men came under fire from batteries on both sides of the harbour. At first, the round shot bounding along the beach could be easily avoided. As cannon were low-velocity weapons, the flight of the ball could be traced as a narrow, grey, pencil streak arcing through the air. Rafter's men simply opened ranks and the round shot flew past them. As they advanced, the *Hero* sailed into the harbour to engage the forts' guns. Once within range, Major Bezant proved his gunnery skills yet again, 'firing two shots for their one'.[42] With round shot screaming into the eastern fort, the return fire slackened. All the while MacGregor stood 'with a glass in his hand' directing 'the Major in pointing the guns'.[43] He nearly paid a heavy price for his bravery. As Surgeon Weatherhead looked on, 'a ball passed [just] over [the Scot's] ... head and [tore] through the mainsail'.[44]

As the Rifles got closer to town, the round shot became more and more difficult to avoid, forcing Rafter to take his men into the jungle. With Woodbine at their head, they hacked their way inland and emerged opposite the upper battery. Any plans of a daylight attack were soon discouraged, as the forts swung their fire away from the *Hero* to counter the new threat. The cannon tore up the earth around them, throwing bushes, earth and roots into the air. One man fell badly wounded. The rest returned to the woods to struggle further uphill, taking new positions behind the uppermost fort. As they crested the heights, the sun dipped beneath the horizon. The gruelling march on empty stomachs had taken its toll and the men collapsed with exhaustion. Despite the protestations of the impetuous Colonel Woodbine, Rafter, who was the senior officer by order of MacGregor, pulled rank and postponed the attack until the following morning.

Having believed that they would clinch victory by nightfall, the men had not taken food or blankets on the march. Consequently they passed the night cold, hungry and miserable. So close were they to the forts that they could hear the sentries talking on the battlements. Around midnight, 'a general uproar [was heard] throughout the whole Town', then the heavens opened and a 'most tremendous rain' fell. Unable to sleep in the downpour, the volunteers were left alone with their thoughts, anticipating the task that lay ahead. Back in the bay, their comrades began to fear they had been captured. Worried that the enemy might try to board them during the night, Captain Hudson took the ships out to sea. The men crowded the decks and waited to see what daylight would reveal.

Before dawn Rafter sent a squad to reconnoitre the defences and at 5.00am he ordered the bugler to sound the advance. Weatherhead watched from the hillside as Captain Ross and a company of Rifles swept down towards the forts 'in the most gallant style'.[45] The surgeon followed in their wake, but all too soon realized that something was wrong. 'No enemy appeared, not a shot was fired' and the officers began to fear they were falling into a trap.[46] Nevertheless, Ross 'descended into the ditch and scaled the ramparts'.[47] He was met with silence. Having believed Reed and Mutcheson's misinformation, the Spanish governor had abandoned the town and its outlying forts at midnight. Whilst Ross looked disbelievingly about him, the Spanish were already well on their way to Panama.

Portobelo was eerily silent. 'Two or three old negro-women' were the only souls to be seen. 'The houses were shut up ... trunks and drawers were emptied, old clothes [and] linen ... lay scattered about [and] cooking utensils ... were found overset around the fire-places.' As the search continued, it became apparent how hurried Van Herch's retreat had been. The cannon had been left loaded and the Spaniards had failed to spike them. Cattle, rice, flour and salt beef had all been abandoned. 'Even the royal standard' had been left forlornly flying above the town hall.[48] Although a few stores were broken into in the immediate aftermath of the town's capture, Rafter soon regained control. A parade was held in the main square, the men 'harangued' for looting and guards placed to prevent 'further depredation'.[49] The colonel then divided the men into sections and sent them to occupy the forts, magazine, custom house, treasury and arsenal. A hospital was established for the wounded and a mess house and store room set up.

At 8.00am the *Hero* sailed into harbour, passing the Royal Navy's *Parthian*, which was just leaving. Unknown to MacGregor, Bigland's men had spent the night loading the town's treasury into the *Parthian*'s hold. The loss of this huge sum, some 70,000 pesos, was a serious blow for the Scot. Rafter's caution and the French guide's treachery were blamed. Before landing, MacGregor sent 60 of Bezant's artillery to man the forts in case of counter-attack, and sailors seized the six boats abandoned in the bay. Never one to pass up an opportunity for a dramatic entrance, MacGregor then stepped ashore to the roar of a celebratory broadside. Preceded by a band that played 'See the Conquering Hero Comes', he then installed himself in Government House.[50] As a finale, he tore down the Spanish flag and 'walked over it several times, deriving from this curious and contemptible proceeding, a peculiar and heartfelt gratification'.[51]

Once established in Government House, MacGregor began proclaiming the town's capture to the wider world. Mr Cot, a printer hired whilst the expedition had been in London, was ordered to produce several copies of the victory bulletin. The document, entitled 'The first division of the army of New Granada had covered itself in glory', was later reproduced in several London dailies, including *The Times*, *The Courier* and the *Morning Chronicle*. Copies were also displayed in the surrounding countryside with assurances that the locals would be well treated should they choose to return. Two of the forts were renamed Fort Glory and Fort MacGregor in honour of the victory, and that night a celebratory dinner was given in Government House. All the leading officers and the few civilians who remained were invited. Captain Ross was promoted to major for his heroics, and gold and silver medals were awarded to the officers and rank and file respectively. An edict stipulated that they were 'to be worn at the left breast, suspended by a green ribbon with crimson edges'.[52] That afternoon Señor Innahal, who had served as mayor under the Spanish, presented himself at Government House and declared his friendship 'to the cause of Independence'.[53] Despite the misgivings of several officers, his word appears not to have been doubted by MacGregor. He and a number of companions 'were allowed to retain their respective offices' and given freedom of the town, a decision that the Scot would later regret.[54]

In the first days after the town's capture, MacGregor took several steps to protect his men from attack. A picket was mounted seven miles down the road to Panama on the east bank of the Chagres River, and the general himself led a sweep of the outlying area to make sure it was clear of enemy troops. Although none were encountered that day, they were frequently sighted on the far bank in the coming weeks and even ventured over the river on occasion.[55] On Sunday the 11th, a *Te Deum* and High Mass were performed at one of Portobelo's two churches. Many of the inhabitants, having read MacGregor's proclamation, had by then returned to town 'from the bush, where they had fled'. The service was well attended by civilians and soldiers alike. At noon the forts' 114 cannon were all fired to check they were fully operational. One exploded killing two of Bezant's men. That same afternoon, 100 locals pledged allegiance to the newly founded republic after a speech by MacGregor. The new unit, named 'The Regiment of America Libre', was given to Colonel Johnstone who marched them to the river to join the advance guard.

After this initial burst of activity, MacGregor grew increasingly hedonistic and self-obsessed. Days went by in a blur of 'feasts and ceremonies'. A number of 'Cantanas in verse and prose' praising the 'hero' Sir Gregor MacGregor were composed and performed.[56] Orders of knighthood were established and 'rewards and distinguishing badges for different degrees of merit' were dreamt up. In the afternoons he 'slunk into a lethargic slumber', whilst the nights were 'devoted to festive orgies' held in Government House.[57] MacGregor's laziness was not the ultimate cause of his downfall, however. His most calamitous decision appears to have been to pay his men. The rank and file received four pesos and the officers ten pesos of a counterfeit coin picked up in Jamaica. To their 'general disgust', the locals were obliged to accept the fakes and many people left town in protest. Those who remained began to turn against the volunteers.[58] When two further payments of ten and six pesos to all ranks were made in the course of a week, the men turned to drink. 'Very little duty was done … [and] the greater number … were drunk in the streets, from morning to night.' When their cash had run out, several sold their possessions, such as cartridges and gun-locks, for more alcohol. The officers, meanwhile, 'were indolent or careless … prolonging the pleasures of the mess-table to a late hour … or intriguing at night with the wives and daughters of the worthy inhabitants'. Surgeon Weatherhead wrote that 'in fact … all were as happy and merry as it is possible for any unthinking set of beings to be'.[59]

Amidst the climate of self-indulgence, several volunteers fell ill. Major Ross was seized by fever on the day of his promotion, and on 14 April, Captain Myers of the Lancers was the first to die. He was buried that evening 'in the area of the hospital, with military honours'.[60] After leaving his sickbed and seemingly on the road to recovery, Lieutenant Craig had a relapse and died the next day. Several men were also taken ill. Five succumbed and were buried alongside their officers. When Major Bezant began to feel unwell, he decided to quit the service whilst he was still able and sailed out of town on a captured schooner with two French officers, captains Bombatch and Cambuscade. Another officer slipped out of port with a rumoured 5,000 pesos worth of jewellery and silver plate, said to have been found underneath the altar of the church.[61]

By mid-April, Weatherhead began to observe 'several strangers of suspicious character' wandering freely through town.[62] When confronted, they 'showed passports obtained by' Mayor Innahal, leaving their would-be jailers with little choice but to release them.[63] At the same time, the picket on the Chagres River noted an increased enemy presence and rumours began to spread of an imminent royalist attack. In response, MacGregor instated a 6.00pm curfew, but after two quiet nights he lowered his guard.

Meanwhile, the royalist commander in Panama, Major-General Hore, a native of Dublin who had served with the Spanish Army since the days of the Peninsular War, had been closely monitoring the reports coming in from across the isthmus. On 19 April he decided the time to attack had come. At the head of a mixed force of 500, including Spanish infantry, artillery and 'sharpshooters' as well as two units of militia, he set off on the ten-day march across the mountains.[64] His principal spy in town was none other than the supposedly pro-patriot Mayor Innahal. On hearing of Hore's imminent arrival, the mayor set a plan in motion to ensure a royalist success. On the afternoon of the 29th, he invited MacGregor and his most senior officers to dinner. For reasons that remain unknown the general declined, but several others accepted the offer. With a supply of rum recently arrived from Jamaica, the party was soon in full flow.[65] Later, the officers burst into song in honour of those who were about to betray them. All the while, Innahal 'seemed to listen … with a … feint smile' and, when the drink ran out, he offered to fetch more from his own supplies.[66] The party finally broke up at 2am. Amongst the volunteers staggering home to their quarters that night was Major Baldwin, the officer in charge of replacing the picket at the Chagres River. In his inebriated state, he left the approaches to the city unguarded. When all was quiet, Innahal and his fellow conspirators slipped out of Portobelo to rendezvous with Hore's men, who were waiting in the woods outside town.

On hearing the morning cannon fired from Fort MacGregor at first light, Hore presumed his plan had been uncovered. He was about to abandon the assault when his second in command, Don José Santa Cruz, begged to be allowed to lead the attack home anyway. Reluctantly Hore agreed, so Santa Cruz, accompanied by Corporal Bos, 'a brave but atrocious character', led a party of 20 men towards town.[67] The first to die were Captain Acton and Mr Binstead, the expedition's paymaster, when they were enjoying an early morning bath in a stream on the hillside. Caught with their guard down when the Spaniards burst from the undergrowth, they were quickly overpowered. Bos then ran them through with his bayonet before they could call out a warning to their comrades slumbering in town. Acton's performing poodle, Leo, was killed alongside his master.[68] The Spaniards then dashed down the hill, heading straight for the main square.

Doctor Phythian of the Hussars was in charge of the town guard that morning. Whilst leading the men in drill in the main square, the Spaniards suddenly appeared. After gathering their wits, Phythian's forces 'kept up a smart fire' from 'behind the pillars of the piazza of … government-house', momentarily halting the Spaniards' advance.[69] Having sold most of their cartridges for alcohol, however, they soon ran out of ammunition and were forced to pull back to the lower fort. From the heights above town Hore saw the volunteers fleeing in disarray. Emboldened, he ordered reinforcements to join his men.

Nearby in the hospital, Surgeon Weatherhead was awoken by the musketry. Leaping out of bed, he dressed and dashed into the main hall. He was appalled by the chaos that confronted him. 'The sick were crowding out at the gate, dropping from the windows, and running towards the fort.' After seizing his musket, sword and pistols, he forced his way through the gates and sprinted towards the square. At the church he saw the route ahead was blocked. 'About 12 or 14 men in white uniforms, had been placed on the bridge.' Whilst considering his next move, he was spotted. The Spaniards 'levelled their pieces ... and fired'. One of the balls passed through the rim of his hat, grazing the tip of his ear. Others thumped into the walls behind him.[70] Deciding to head for the fort, he climbed over the side of the bridge and lowered himself into the water. En route, he passed 'the bodies of several men who had been shot' whilst fleeing.[71] After reaching the walls, he climbed in through a cannon embrasure. Inside he was met by a gathering crowd of survivors.[72]

By now the royalists were systematically clearing the houses around the upper square. Terrified by the shooting, Mrs Cot, the printer's wife, cowered in her room, waiting for the royalists to enter. When her time came, 'they fired through the doors, then broke ... in ... [and] stabbed her husband in the arm'. Making signs that they were unarmed, the Cots persuaded the soldiers to spare them.[73] Major Baldwin and the still feverous Major Ross were also captured in their rooms. The New Granadan Don Juan Elias López, on the other hand, was not prepared to surrender so meekly. When the royalists approached his room, he seized his pistols and fired two balls through the door. Instantly returning fire, the royalists forced their way in and 'bayoneted him upon the spot'.[74] Lieutenants Stewart and O'Haggan and 'the brave' Captain Gondon were also killed.[75] Having rushed to the plaza when he first heard the shooting, Gondon had seen some deserters from the America Libre Regiment in the ranks of the enemy and demanded they join him. The traitors replied with a volley. After returning fire with a brace of pistols, Gondon charged brandishing his sword. Although he 'laid three of the militia dead at his feet', there was little he could do in the face of such overwhelming odds.[76] 'Covered with wounds', he eventually fell. His former recruits then 'brutally wreaked their vengeance on his ... body'.[77]

Back at Government House, MacGregor finally put in an appearance. 'Confused and undecided', he stumbled out of his bedroom 'sans hat, coat or breeches' whilst one of his aides-de-camp, Coronet Colclough, held the Spaniards at bay at the head of the stairs.[78] After killing two with his pistols, Colclough 'thrust his sword through the body of a third', but was then wounded by 'a ball through the left hand'.[79] While the Spaniards temporarily withdrew to regroup, Mr Bennet, MacGregor's draughtsman, suggested escaping out of the window. Hurling their blankets before them, they leapt one by one to the square 20ft below. The Spaniards saw Bennet land first and ran over to take him prisoner, but in the chaos that ensued as Colclough, Phythian and MacGregor fell amongst them, all four managed to escape. Despite breaking two ribs in the fall, the general and Colclough sprinted towards the beach, whilst Bennet and Phythian made for the fort. With musket balls kicking up spouts of water around them, MacGregor and Colclough dived into the breakers and struck out for the ships. Once in deep water, MacGregor stripped and threw his clothes to one side to draw the royalists' fire. They then spent an hour treading water before a boat from the *Hero* was sent to collect them.

Bennet and Phythian, meanwhile, had reached the fort, clambering over the embrasures unscathed 'amidst a shower of balls'.[80] Amongst those already inside was Colonel Rafter. Having been woken by the shooting, he had run through the streets half-dressed, pausing only to shoot two Spaniards who had got in his way. Colonel O'Hara, on the other hand, had been hit after the men inside had refused to open the gate for him. The ball had 'passed through his body, from side to side', piercing the lungs 'in two places'.[81] He would die two days later, his last words a lament for his daughter.[82]

The volunteers who had avoided death or capture were now split into three groups. The largest numbering 150 were in the lower fort, 20 Lancers led by Captain Black were holding out in the upper fort, whilst 11, including MacGregor himself, were watching the drama unfold from the safety of the ships. Having secured the town, Hore now turned his attention to dealing with these suvivors. From the battlements of the upper fort, Captain Black could see enemy columns 'marching into the square, and along the street' toward him.[83] Others took up sniping positions on the first floor of Government House and the mayor's residence, overlooking the lower fort. The volunteers manning the guns closest to them came under heavy fire, and were soon 'falling every minute'.[84] Deciding the position was too exposed, two artillery officers 'disgracefully abandoned their duty' leaving Captain Farnham to command the battery alone. 'In the midst of balls for four hours and a half on every part of the bastion', Farnham fought heroically, bringing 'the men forward to the guns' and keeping 'them to their duty'.[85] Despite their efforts, however, the odds were stacked against them – the gun carriages were 'decayed and unwieldy' and the men barely trained.[86] Wildly blazing away at the snipers with round shot, they only succeeded in honeycombing the walls of the mayor's house. In the hail of return fire, a large number of the gunners were killed.[87]

Hore, meanwhile, sent a column of soldiers up the hillside behind town to fire down at Captain Black's Lancers in the upper fort. Watching from the battlements, 'Black allowed the enemy to concentrate', whilst 'charging one of his great guns with canister and grape'. When he lit the fuse, it had 'the very best effect'. The men in the fort 'heard the shrieks of the wounded and dying, and the enemy were observed descending the hill in the greatest confusion and flying towards town'.[88]

Rafter took advantage of the subsequent lull to send a boat out to the *Hero*. It returned with orders from MacGregor to 'defend the fort to the last, spike the guns [and] beware of treachery'.[89] The Scot also promised that the fleet would move in to support them within the hour. In the meantime, Farnham's efforts with the cannon had received an unexpected reward. The mayor's house 'had been so syringed with grape-shot ... that it was no longer tenable' and the Spanish snipers crouching in the windows were forced to abandon it before it collapsed.[90] Buoyed by this success, Farnham swung two guns round to face Government House, from where the remaining sharpshooters continued to torment him. The first shot, 'being levelled rather too high, unroofed one of the [neighbouring] houses'. Although a miss, it showed that the volunteers still had bite. Enthused, a series of 'huzzas' rose up from the volunteers. In reply, a flag of truce was waved by the Spaniards.[91] Rafter ordered his men to cease fire and a nervous silence settled over town.

After a few minutes, two Spanish officers approached the lower fort. To Weatherhead's disgust, they were permitted to enter 'unblindfolded' to parley.[92] Their proposal that the British 'surrender at discretion' was met 'with hisses' from the men and bravado from Rafter, who declared he would sooner blow up the fort whilst they were still inside than surrender to a Spaniard.[93] Subsequently the officers changed their demands. They offered the volunteers the chance to embark freely on the ships, which would be provisioned for a month, if they would lay down their arms and surrender the forts intact. Moreover, the officers would be allowed to retain their swords and baggage and the men to keep their knapsacks. Rafter then held a council of war in the canteen to discuss the terms. Holding to their deep-seated beliefs that a Spaniard should never be trusted, several officers were wary, but the matter was taken out of their hands when a representative of the men came forward and told them they would surrender regardless of any decision. With little choice, Rafter accepted the terms, but not before making a final speech to the men:

> Evidently much affected ... [he] told them what a disgraceful condition their undisciplined and irregular conduct had brought them, [and] that he and every officer present felt it a stain upon their characters to have commanded them... Several of the men felt very much hurt ... and in their rage broke off the butt ends of their muskets and set the wine and spirits in the canteen adrift... We were then marched into the square and ... the enemy's troops surrounded us.[94]

Reasoning that he was dealing with mere pirates, Hore had never had any intention of honouring the deal. The men were divided from the officers and the two groups were marched off to prison in Panama. The Spaniards then manned the forts' cannon and turned them towards the ships in the bay. MacGregor was driven off with a few round shot. Of the 300 volunteers who had captured Portobelo less than a month previously, only 11 escaped alive. Eighty had been killed and over 200 captured. Most of the prisoners would be executed or die of disease in the months ahead.

Back in Los Llanos, even though the dry season had come to an end, Bolívar was about to embark on a new campaign. His audacity would be well rewarded. It would prove to be the turning point of the war.

PART THREE

THE TIPPING POINT
1819–1820

In actual battle, young soldiers are apt to have a feeling (from which many old ones are not exempt) namely, that they are but insignificant characters – only a humble individual out of many thousands, and that his conduct, be it good or bad, can have little influence over the fate of the day. This is a monstrous mistake, which it ought to be the duty of every military writer to endeavour to correct; for in battle, as elsewhere, no man is insignificant unless he chooses to make himself so.

Sir John Kincaid, 95th Rifles

Chapter 14

THE PARAMO OF PISBA

I n May 1819 Morillo withdrew from the plains. Heading north-east to shorten his supply lines to Caracas, he established new headquarters in Calabozo, whilst the patriots moved into his abandoned base at Mantecal. Both armies were relieved to settle down for the winter. Bolívar, however, had other plans. Ever since the string of defeats in early 1818, he had been considering switching the focus of the revolution to neighbouring New Granada. By surprising the Spanish 3rd Division and seizing the capital, Santafé de Bogotá, he could radically alter the course of the war.

Bolívar's motives were not simply strategic. A keen student of the past, he was conscious of his place in history and equally aware of the value of reinforcing his personality cult. Crossing the Andes was a highly symbolic move which would elevate him to an exclusive pantheon of heroes. Just as Hannibal had crossed the Alps to take on the might of the Roman Empire and Napoleon had traversed the Saint Bernard Pass to defeat the Austrians at Marengo, Bolívar would climb the spine of South America to deliver a crushing blow to his enemies.

The groundwork for the campaign had been laid back in August 1818, when General Francisco de Paula Santander had been dispatched to the New Granadan province of Casanare with a cavalry unit to incite rebellion and ascertain if the region was ready to throw off the Spanish yoke. A severe, humourless man with a vindictive side to his personality, the 27-year old was fiercely ambitious and proved the perfect man for the job. Not only did he find New Granada ripe for revolution, he also managed to recruit a regiment of volunteers for the cause. With his army reinforced, Santander moved onto the offensive, intercepting two columns of the 3rd Division, who were marching from New Granada to join their comrades in Venezuela. 'Sick, underpaid and divided', the 3rd Division was an entirely different prospect to Morillo's veterans and its commander, the young and inexperienced General José Maria Barreiro, was soon defeated with 1,000 men lost. In the retreat that followed, the road back over the highlands was strewn with a trail of arms, ammunition and baggage.[1] Upon reading Santander's victory report, Bolívar knew the time to strike had come.

The 300-mile march to New Granada would see the army traverse the flooded plains to the south-east of Achaguas before scaling the Andes and advancing on Santafé. Although the season and terrain were against him, Bolívar believed that the royalists would be caught by surprise and hoped the approaches to the city would be left virtually unguarded. In mid-May 1819, he called a council of war to announce his plans. O'Leary thought the setting suitably apocalyptic:

> [It was held] in the ruins of a cabin in the deserted ... village of Setenta on the right bank of the Apure. There was no table. There were no chairs... A party of royalists, who had bivouacked there some time before, had killed several heads of cattle. The rain and ... sun ... bleached ... skulls ... served as seats on which the destiny of a great country was about to be decided.[2]

Many of the officers present were sceptical and several thought the mission suicidal. The debate was heated and raged throughout the day. Páez was not interested in advancing beyond Los Llanos, and Anzoátegui even considered deposing Bolívar and naming the Caudillo as commander in chief.[3] The plot never came to fruition, however, as Colonel Antonio Rangel refused to take part.[4] Alone amongst those present, Colonel Rooke backed Bolívar unreservedly, declaring that he would follow him to Cape Horn if he so desired it. Perhaps inspired by his example, the dissenters eventually agreed to Bolívar's plan. Nevertheless, Páez's lack of enthusiasm permeated through to his men and on 25 May, the night before they were due to depart, an entire regiment of 200 Hussars deserted.

The next morning the order to break camp was given. As the troops and baggage train filed out of town, the heavens opened and the plains were soon churned into a morass. There would be no let up in the downpour for weeks. The first halt was at Guasdualito, 'a small town ... on the upper plains of Varínas, where the rivers Apúri and Araüco approach ... each other'.[5] Here the army divided into two. Knowing Páez was uncommitted to the plan, Bolívar ordered him to remain in the plains with the majority of the cavalry and 240 of the British volunteers, whilst the rest of the army pushed on.[6] The Caudillo was left with strict instructions to attack Cúcuta, a frontier town 150 miles to the west, to divert attention from the main thrust against Santafé. Once Bolívar's column had departed, however, the Caudillo soon forgot his promise. He thought The Liberator a madman to attempt such a march in the height of the rainy season and was convinced the expedition would end in failure. As a result, he decided to hang back and consolidate his hold on Los Llanos. The British volunteers who remained with him would see little action over the next two years.

The 2,186 men that left Guasdualito were divided into four infantry units and three sections of cavalry. The majority were the same mixture of Indian, black and mixed race conscripts that the patriots had been deploying since 1810, but the army was significantly strengthened by two recent acquisitions: Colonel Rooke's infantry and three squadrons of Llaneros under colonels Carbajal and Rondon. The devastating charges of the Lancers and the organization, determination and discipline of the British veterans would make this remodelled army the finest Bolívar had ever led. Some 180 British volunteers took part in the campaign, the vast majority under Colonel Rooke. Known as the British Legion, his unit was built around the 30 surviving veterans of the six colonels' expedition, reinforced by 120 new arrivals raised by Colonel Elsom. Rooke's second in command was Major Mackintosh. Amongst his officers were Captain John Johnstone and a young Irish lieutenant named Laurence McGuire. With the rank and file was the 42-year old veteran Francis Fuge. Notable by his absence was Lieutenant Richard Vowell, who had been sent to Angostura with dispatches for Vice-President Zea. On arrival he had contracted yellow fever, and was still convalescing in the capital as the army departed from Guasdualito. Some 35 other volunteers were with the vanguard, including Captain O'Leary, who was assigned to Anzoátegui's staff, and doctors Foley and Blair. Also marching with the vanguard were the Black Rifles, in which 30 British officers and NCOs remained. Major Sandes was in command, assisted by Lieutenant Thomas Wright and Major Peacock amongst others.

On 4 June the army reached the river Arauca. Swollen by the heavy rains, it proved impossible to ford. Floats of 'drift-wood' and stretched 'bullock's hides' were built. Then the best swimmers struck out across the torrent with 'long lassos' tied round their middle.[7] The rest were hauled over in small groups, clinging to the rafts loaded with baggage, arms and ammunition. Once the troops had crossed, several floats were lashed together to carry the army's two cannon. Eventually the exhausting ordeal was complete. As Rooke's men rested on the far bank, one officer observed that Captain John Johnstone was the only man amongst them to have preserved his boots. All the others had worn theirs through several weeks before and now marched in crudely made espadrilles. Those boots are 'worth their weight in gold' the officer announced.[8] 'Of this there is no doubt,' Johnstone replied. 'But there's no reason why I shouldn't suffer like my comrades.'[9] With that he hurled them into the river and continued the march barefoot.

The next stage took the army across the plains of Casanare. Countless streams and rivers crisscrossed the region and, with the rains, they had burst their banks and flooded the surrounding land. The men were 'obliged to march … for many hours … up to the middle in water' and frequently became stuck fast in thigh deep mud. Whilst crossing 'one very inconsiderable stream', over 100 men were attacked by piranha. Several had 'one or two pounds of the fleshy part of the thigh or calf' torn away.[10] Others were plagued by flesh-eating ticks. Captain William Harris of the Black Rifles was amongst those forced to drop out of the march and convalesce with local villagers. Nightfall offered the men little respite. They could rarely find a dry spot of ground to rest on and what little sleep they managed was snatched in restless bursts. For once, the situation got the better of Colonel Rooke. Perhaps brooding on the rumours of his wife's infidelity, the colonel finally snapped whilst having an absurd discussion with Doctor Foley. O'Leary overheard them arguing about whether Caracas or Bogotá would make a more suitable capital for Bolívar's visionary state of Gran Colombia. Even though the two men had not seen either city, the discussion grew heated and eventually they had to be dragged apart to prevent them coming to blows.

On 8 June, Bolívar's troops linked up with Santander's division in the town of Tame.[11] The army, now increased to 3,400 men, pressed on in two columns. The van was led by Santander. The rearguard, which included Rooke's Legion, was under the staff officer General Carlos Soublette. At 29, Soublette was older than many of his peers. He had put his loyalty to Bolívar beyond doubt on countless occasions since joining the revolution in 1816. Reserved yet eloquent and with impeccable manners, Soublette was one of the few republican commanders who could match the British officers in conduct and etiquette. The former 'schoolmaster' was also one of Bolívar's ablest administrators, at his best when employed in a logistical role.[12] His fighting prowess, on the other hand, left much to be desired.

As the column approached the Andes in mid-June, the landscape began to change. The ground became uneven and the 'stagnant pools' and 'sluggish muddy rivers' of the lowlands were replaced by 'rapid rivulets' bounding down from the mountains ahead.[13] Plantations and houses were more frequently seen and 'poultry and pigs', rare in Los Llanos, became more common. It grew colder as they climbed, 'especially just before day break, when the wind … [blew] over the snowy ridges of the Cordilléra'.[14] Through the swirling rain the volunteers caught occasional glimpses of the mountains. One later compared them to land sighted after a long voyage. Lieutenant Laurence McGuire of the 3rd Company of Rooke's Legion, was also impressed. In a letter home he informed his family that 'the mountains of Carlingford' were mere foothills by comparison.[15] The Llaneros, on the other hand, were appalled. Stunned 'that a world so different to theirs existed', they insisted that 'only mad men would persist in the attempt'.[16] To make matters worse, traversing the stony roads proved an exercise in agony for their horses. Accustomed as they were to the soft, sandy ground of the plains, many went lame and had to be abandoned. Considering it undignified to continue on foot, the proud plainsmen of Carbajal's corps began to desert in droves every time a halt was called. Soon only the colonel and a few of his officers remained.

As the gradient increased, the two columns separated. Whilst Santander's troops made comparatively good progress, Soublette's column, encumbered by the baggage train, soon lagged three days behind. The mules and bullocks dragging the cannon and ammunition suffered terribly as they inched forward on the slippery tracks. Many drowned when crossing swollen rivers and others expired under the weight of their loads. Bringing up the rear, the men of the British Legion picked their way past the corpses. Five days after leaving the plains, barely an animal remained alive. The troops had to take up their loads and the officers continued on foot. Climbing higher, the columns entered 'immense forests', thickly packed with trees 'of a vast size', whose branches hung over the road, 'nearly excluding the light of day'.[17] Nothing but ivy, moss and lichen grew under the canopy, providing scant sustenance for the handful of pack animals that remained. Torrents of cascading water frequently blocked the path. When no ford was apparent, canoes that had been dragged up from the plains were used to ferry the guns and baggage across. The troops then waded through the rushing waters, aided by an indefatigable Bolívar, who inspired them to 'redouble their efforts' by 'talking of the glory' that lay ahead.[18] At one crossing he 'passed repeatedly across ... carrying soldiers who were weak, and women who were following their husbands'.[19] Despite his efforts, several were swept off their feet and carried downstream. Some emerged from the water spluttering and cold, but others were never seen again.

On 27 June Santander's vanguard reached Paya, a royalist mountain outpost set amongst 'beautiful valleys and glens'. On the outskirts a picket of 50 men opened fire on the head of the patriot column. Hopelessly outnumbered, the Spaniards soon fell back to the bridge over the river Paya, where they were joined by the rest of the town's garrison of 300 men. Entrenched in a 'formidable position' defending the road to Labranza Grande, the Spanish commander now had more than enough men to hold his ground indefinitely.[20] Luckily for Santander's troops, however, he ordered the retreat after four and a half hours. Reasoning that the attack was nothing more than a scouting probe, he believed his withdrawal would have no consequences of note. After destroying the bridge, the royalists retreated down a pass through the mountains, leaving four of their number dead by the river. Not realizing that the troops they had been facing were actually the vanguard of a much larger force, the Spanish commander then sent a misleading report to General Barreiro.

After the skirmish, Bolívar allowed his men a few days' rest in Paya before attempting the final ascent. The people of the cordillera (cerrános) were generous hosts. The soldiers were given food and shelter, whilst The Liberator penned a proclamation which was dispatched across the mountains, calling on the people of New Granada to rise up in rebellion. After being issued with rations of meat and carrots for four days, Santander's vanguard, now accompanied by the Black Rifles and the rest of Anzoátegui's division, set out on 30 June. Two paths left the village for New Granada. The first route was the least difficult, but was defended by the troops that had withdrawn from Paya and who now were expecting them. Bolívar therefore opted for the path less travelled. A torturously circuitous scramble, it wound upwards through dense forest, before crossing the 12,800ft-high pass over the desolate Paramo of Pisba. Believing the route virtually impassable in winter, the Spaniards had left it unguarded.

On 9 July Soublette followed the vanguard with half his troops, leaving the British Legion 'half dead' from exhaustion after its climb, in Paya with the baggage train.[21] As all the pack animals had died, Soublette had been hoping to employ local Indian porters to carry the munitions and baggage. None were willing to help, however, as they feared the wrath of the royalists should Bolívar be defeated. Soublette therefore buried 11 cases of guns and ammunition for future collection, leaving the rest with Rooke, who finally left town on 13 July.

After Paya the march grew increasingly difficult. Inching forwards, the men frequently had to cross ravines whilst the rain pelted down and waterfalls thundered overhead. For the wider chasms *tarabítas* were used. These rickety cable car contraptions were constructed of twisted hide ropes lashed between trees. Suspended beneath was a cradle 'made ... of basket work or hide' which was 'drawn back and forwards' across the abyss. Some gaps were of 'tremendous depth' rendering it 'advisable for those ... [with] weak nerves to close their eyes when crossing'.[22] In other places landslides had strewn boulders across the path, forcing the men to climb up the banks where razor sharp rocks cut their feet to ribbons. Late on the 13th, Rooke's troops emerged from the woods onto the foot of the Paramo, where they stopped for the night. With the wind tearing across the open expanse of the moor, they huddled together in groups on the rocky ground. Unable to light fires in the downpour, they shivered through the night, dressed only in a few threadbare rags that still held together. Several froze to death before dawn.

The next morning a 'wan, sickly light' revealed an alien landscape. Clumps of 'dark coloured lichens' clung to the rocks on the high ground and the hollows were studded with *espeletia*, a shrub with thick, silver, down-covered leaves.[23] When the wind snatched away the blanketing mist, dark, razor edged peaks were revealed. Although Rooke's men no longer had a path to follow, the route was marked by the debris and dead left behind by the vanguard. The 'fragments of sadlery, trunks' and frozen corpses seemed like 'the traces of a routed army'.[24] Major John Mackintosh, Rooke's second in command, 'counted the … bodies of eighty soldiers, and might have enumerated many more, had [he] … not lost [his] … reckoning'.[25] As he passed, the major tried to wrench the dead men's muskets from their hands, but found it impossible 'from the firm manner in which they grasped them'.[26] Many small crosses marked the final resting places of travellers who had died in previous years. For some, the sight brought on 'a sense of extreme … remoteness from the world'.[27] Altitude sickness killed dozens. Those affected, known as *emparamados*, died in two ways. 'In some cases the vital powers' were 'suddenly arrested', leaving 'the body for some time' with 'all the appearance of life'. Others were 'seized with a sort of frenzy, foaming at the mouth, and tearing' themselves 'till exhaustion and torpor terminate[d]' their 'existence'.[28]

On the second day on the Paramo, Daniel O'Leary was resting to one side of the pass when he noticed a group of privates from the Black Rifles approaching. As he watched, they paused to gather round a figure huddled on the rocky ground. Intrigued, the captain went over to find out what was happening. One of the privates told him that 'a pregnant woman … had just had her waters break'. Inspired by her example, the young Irishman got to his feet and stumbled on. Darkness fell before the columns could reach the forest on the far side, forcing the men to spend a second sleepless night on the moor. Once again, the cold and altitude decimated their ranks. Lieutenant Westbrook of the Black Rifles was one of hundreds who died. Despite the dreadful conditions, some found a desolate beauty to the mountains at night. 'The number of the stars was … much increased, and their twinkling … a great deal brighter. The moon was … more prominent … and the dark map, on its surface … plainer to the … eye.'[29] The next morning the vanguard descended into 'the beautiful and fertile valleys of Tunja', 8,200ft above sea level.[30] Zigzagging downwards over the rugged landscape, the soldiers were soon enveloped by thick woods. O'Leary was relieved to catch sight of the woman he had noticed the night before. Clutched in her arms was her new baby 'apparently in the best of health'.[31] Those who had survived the crossing were stronger for the experience. 'Looking back at the cloud covered peaks', they vowed to fight on to the end.[32]

The vanguard reached the village of Socha on 5 July, followed by the first half of Anzoátegui's rearguard on the 6th. Sick of Viceroy Sámano's repressive regime, the locals received them with 'a thousand demonstrations of joy'.[33] As well as presents of 'bread, tobacco and [home brewed] *chica*', they donated their clothes to the soldiers and provided several horses for the officers and cavalry.[34] Bolívar wasted no time in organizing his army. A hospital was established and scouts sent off in all directions to gather horses and supplies. As news of their arrival spread, 'fugitive patriots' who had been hiding in the hills rode into camp to join them.[35] On the 8th, Santander's vanguard advanced down the valley. Later, Colonel Lara was dispatched at the head of a mule train to resupply Soublette's corps and the British Legion who were still struggling over the pass. Buoyed by the aid, they finally limped into Socha on 15 July. Forty men of the British Legion, nearly one-third of total that had set out from Mantecal 51 days earlier, had died. The army as a whole had suffered similar casualties, with 300 in total perishing on the march.

Further down the valley, small-scale skirmishes had already broken out around the villages of Gameza and Corrales. Lieutenant-Colonel Duran's cavalry of Santander's division scored an early victory when they surprised and captured an enemy unit, but on 10 July the royalists tasted success of their own. Two separate patriot columns of infantry and cavalry on reconnaissance missions were attacked. The 200 cavalry of the first column, under Colonel Justo Briceño, fled when they were charged by the light company of the King's 1st Battalion. Pursued through the streets of Corrales, the patriots were forced to drive their horses into the river on the far side of town to escape. Five men were captured, 20 were killed and 70 horses were lost. The patriot infantry column, meanwhile, had been attacked by the Grenadiers of the King's Battalion, with 28 captured and the rest dispersed or killed. Under orders from Viceroy Sámano, the prisoners were tied 'back to back' and run through with bayonets.[36]

Slowly realizing the seriousness of the situation, General Barreiro confined himself to probing attacks whilst gathering his forces on the nearby heights of Topága. On 11 July, six companies of the 2nd Battalion of Numancia caught sight of Santander's 1,000-strong division, led by Bolívar himself, advancing down the road from Gameza. Outnumbered, the royalists fell back to the bridge to the west of the village. In total, Barreiro had 900 infantry and 180 cavalry defending the position. Five of the six companies of Numancia formed line along the bank of the river, whilst their light troops held the bridge. In support on the high ground behind them were the cavalry and a company of the King's 1st Battalion.

Seeing the royalists waiting for him, Bolívar halted in the village to prepare his attack. Sandes's Black Rifles, now 250 strong, took part alongside Santander's 400 light troops of New Granada and 300 men of the Bravos de Páez. After advancing out of town using the cover of folds in the ground, the patriots charged across the bridge into a withering crossfire. Several were shot dead and fell into the water. When the survivors gained the far side, the men of Numancia counter-attacked. Forced to cede ground the patriots broke. Two Spanish companies pursued them to the outskirts of Gameza, bayoneting several before withdrawing. Undaunted, Santander rallied for a second attempt, ordering his men to advance to the river and form line. A ferocious musketry duel followed. In a momentary lull in the fighting, Juan José Reyes, a republican officer, rode onto the bridge to challenge an 'extremely arrogant and well uniformed' Spaniard he had spotted through the smoke. The ensuing single combat took place on the bridge in full view of both sides. For several minutes as the armies looked on, the protagonists thrust, cut and parried with their sabres. Then, seeing his opponent tiring, Reyes gathered his strength and decapitated the Spaniard with a single swing. His head fell to one side of the bridge whilst his body plummeted into the river on the other. The patriots cheered and Reyes returned to the ranks. When the firing resumed, Santander was hit by a spent musket ball. Although lacking killing weight, the shot bruised him severely, forcing him to dismount. A worried Bolívar rode to his side but was soon reassured that Santander would survive. As the battle wore on, the tide began to swing behind the patriots. Fearing his position was about to be overwhelmed, Barreiro brought reinforcements down from Topága. The fresh troops enveloped the enemy flank and poured on a deadly crossfire from the high ground which eventually forced the patriots to retire. After fighting for five hours, they limped back to the village, leaving 200 corpses littering the field.

For the next ten days both generals held back. Bolívar used the time to train the volunteers that continued to flood into his camp. Then, on the 20th, he advanced. Moving to the open plains of Bonza, he set up headquarters behind the walls and ditches of a large building known as The Pantry. The two armies were now within sight of each other and minor skirmishes flared up nightly between the pickets. On the afternoon of the 21st, two companies of infantry and one of cavalry arrived at the royalist camp. The reinforcements strengthened Barreiro's army to over 3,000 troops and convinced him that it would soon be time to attack. The next day, the patriots were also reinforced, when the British Legion finally rejoined Bolívar's army. Upon arrival, Rooke sought out the general to deliver his report. He found him 'seated on a trunk, with … [a] lunch of roasted meat, bread and chocolate spread out in front of him on a crude wooden bench'. Whilst they ate, Rooke assured Bolívar that contrary to reports, the British Legion had not suffered at all in passing the Paramo and was, in fact, in the best of spirits and eager to take on the enemy. Lunch was then interrupted by the foul-tempered Anzoátegui, who contradicted Rooke and spoke of the terrible losses his men had endured. The irrepressibly optimistic colonel's response caused even The Liberator to raise a rare smile:

'I don't deny it' exclaimed Rooke 'but it's equally true that they deserved their fate … they were the worst in my unit and their deaths have only improved it.'[37]

Within a month Rooke would be dead, but before then he had one final battle left to fight. The blonde, blue-eyed veteran would distinguish himself on the field and his deeds would enshrine his name in the annals of New Granadan history forever.

Chapter 15

THE RETURN OF GENERAL ENGLISH

As Bolívar prepared to liberate New Granada, General English's Legion was landing on the Venezuelan island of Margarita 800 miles to the north-east. The troops had sailed to South America in three detachments. On 10 February 1819, the advance party of 500 men under Major John Blosset arrived.[1] English and the second detachment joined them in early April, whilst the *Henrietta*, laden with the regiment's arms and ammunition, did not reach the island until the end of the month.

English's flotilla had run into difficulties before it had even left British shores. Adverse winds caused delays at Lymington, and mid-Atlantic typhus had broken out. On board the *Francis and Eliza*, Doctor Fitzgibbon was soon 'exhausted by his onerous attendance on the sick and dying'.[2] His treatments of bleeding, purging and blistering merely exacerbated his patients' decline, however, and 'many deaths ensued'.[3] On 1 April, Trinidad and Tobago hove into view.[4] A few hours later the ships passed through the Dragon's Mouth, a ten-mile-wide channel separating the British colonies from the South American mainland. Standing on the deck of the *Francis and Eliza*, Lieutenant Chesterton took in the view. High cliffs crowded the ship on both sides. Clinging to the precipices were 'cacti with ... red blossoms, dwarf aloes, and other exotics' and trees grew 'arching over the dark tide below'.[5]

Remembering the reception Colonel Hippisley had received in Trinidad in 1818, English weighed anchor at 'a respectful distance' from Port of Spain.[6] After penning a dispatch to Bolívar, he was taken ashore for a previously arranged rendezvous with a patriot agent. In their absence, British officials rowed out to the fleet and endeavoured to dissuade the volunteers from continuing.[7] Sir Ralph Woodford, the British governor, had been forewarned of the Legion's arrival, and was determined to enforce the Foreign Enlistment Act. When he came face to face with English on the quayside a blazing row ensued, culminating in the governor threatening to use the

18-gun HMS *Fly* to 'dispute' their voyage to Margarita. Furious, English returned to the ships, weighed anchor and set sail. In his haste, he failed to miss the six men who had swum ashore and deserted until he was far out to sea. Although the voyage was hounded by 'strong and baffling currents' the *Fly* failed to make an appearance. Margarita was sighted two days later.

The flotilla arrived off Juan Griego, a small fishing port in the north-west with the 'best harbour' on the island.[8] Deciding 'that due éclat should distinguish [its] … ingress', the general ordered his officers to don full regimental dress whilst two young second lieutenants unfurled the colours.[9] A salute was then fired from the ships' cannon and duly returned by the *Victoria*, the pride of Admiral Brion's fleet riding at anchor in the bay. Watching beside a battery of 32-pdrs on a bluff above the beach was Captain Charles Brown. Originally a lieutenant with Colonel Gillmore's artillery brigade, Brown had sailed to Juan Griego a few months previously when the colonel had been ordered to take command of the shore defences.[10] Whilst he looked on, English's troops boarded the boats and were rowed ashore through flocks of 'pelicans, gulls' and 'cormorants'.[11]

That evening the troops marched three miles to the village of El Norté to meet General Rafael Urdaneta, the commander of the division they were to join. Climbing upwards from the beach, the track wound into forested foothills, abounding in wiry shrubs and wild cactus.[12] Foot-long green and gold lizards scrambled under rocks, while woodpeckers and flocks of 'beautiful parrots [and] parroquets' flew overhead.[13] The men found the birds made 'apt scholars' and were 'quickly taught to imitate the … human voice'.[14] Nearing their destination, they saw an old Spanish roadblock 'made up of hampers filled with sand' dating back to Morillo's invasion of 1816.[15]

El Norté was little more than a hamlet, with 20 'miserable' huts on the outskirts leading to 100 houses clustered round a central square.[16] There were only two buildings of note – Governor Arismendi's quarters, which Brown deemed 'tolerable', and a whitewashed church 'built of stone and brick' that had witnessed Bolívar's declaration of the Third Republic three years earlier.[17] On a rise behind the square was a small fort with a single 24-pdr on a pivot, commanding 'a most delightful prospect' over the surrounding hills.[18] After reviewing the troops, Urdaneta sent them on to Pampatar, a town on the east coast where Major Blosset's advance guard had been stationed for several weeks. The 15-mile slog traversed 'a chain of lofty and stupendous mountains' and took the volunteers past the fortifications where General Arismendi, the republican governor of the island, had held out for months with a few hundred men against Morillo's thousands in 1816.[19] The track then descended into the capital. Once a beautiful city, Ascuncion had been sacked by the royalists and now lay in ruins. Beyond the capital, the track continued to Pampatar, built at the foot of three mountains rising from the sea.

On 14 May the *Henrietta* arrived with the Legion's arms, uniforms and supplies. General English distributed the goods and a parade was held by way of celebration. Joined by the remnants of Gillmore's artillery brigade, the Legion's 1,000 men formed an open square on the outskirts of town. When all was ready, Mrs Mary English, the general's beautiful new bride, rode into the centre on a fine horse presented to her by Urdaneta and gave a spirit-stirring speech intended to boost morale.[20] Afterwards, she dismounted and presented the regimental colours to the Legion, bringing the ceremony to a close.[21]

After the parade, the troops returned to quarters. Some were housed in buildings which had been gutted with fire during Morillo's attacks. The doors had been ripped from their hinges, the rooms were blackened with smoke and 'swarmed with fleas and other vermin'.[22] Others slept in a row of tatty tents on the beach, which had previously belonged to Wellington's troops in the Peninsular War. The officers' quarters were little better. Rations were small and irregularly issued and chiefly consisted of raw sugar cane which the British struggled to digest. Whilst the officers received a small allowance, there was no sign of the bounty the men had been promised and most were soon reduced to selling what little they had to supplement their diet. Other enterprising individuals cut the lead buttons from their jackets to exchange for food.[23] To make matters worse, Blosset's men spoke openly of the dreadful conditions they had endured for the last two months and the sicknesses that had decimated their ranks. Under such circumstances, it is little surprise that the men's thoughts turned to mutiny and even the officers called a meeting to 'address a remonstrance to their commander'.[24] As a result, 36 signed a letter of complaint. On receiving it English was furious, and demanded their arrest. Realizing that such a move would destroy the Legion before it had even begun to fight, Major Blosset intervened. A veteran of the 28th Foot, who had fought the French in Egypt at the turn of the century, it was not the first time the major had faced such difficulties and he soon managed to calm his fellow officers down.[25] The men, on the other hand, would not prove so compliant.

Later that afternoon a parade was called. Although most of the troops reluctantly fell in, those of Lieutenant Chesterton's light company refused. It fell to Major Robinson to take command. Entering their quarters he drew his sword, went up to the first man and asked if he intended to obey. When the soldier growled a negative, Robinson struck him a blow 'that nearly cleft his skull' in two.[26] The next man gave a more satisfactory answer and the company joined the rest of the regiment formed in a hollow square on the sandy marshes outside town. 'Silent as the grave', the men looked on as a drumhead court martial was improvised to punish the 'principal delinquents'.[27] Each was awarded 300 lashes. The men were then stripped, their arms bound and their backs exposed to the bite of the whip. But as the drummer boys readied the lash, Blosset had a change of heart. After pardoning the condemned, he warned the regiment that no such mercy would be shown again. The men fell out and returned to their quarters. All appeared calm, but in fact the problems had only just begun.

After sunset the troops ran amok. Emboldened by the anonymity of the night, they raced through town, drinking, looting and discharging their muskets whilst their officers cowered in their quarters 'for fear of assassination'.[28] With daylight came sore heads. The men were subdued and order restored. A second square was formed and the ringleaders ordered to be flogged, 'without a murmur from the ranks'.[29] This time there would be no last-minute reprieve. Over the coming weeks, dozens of men attempted to desert. Sneaking from the camp at night, they swam into the bay and stowed away on board merchant ships. Some were successful, often in collusion with sympathetic British or American sailors. Others were caught and dragged back in chains by Admiral Brion's marines.

By now, fever had taken hold. Before long the hospital in Pampatar was filled with the sick and dying. Typhus and yellow fever were the main killers. As the nearest fresh water supply was a long trek from the encampment, the sick drank from stagnant ponds, bringing on attacks of dysentery which speeded their demise. By mid-May 200 had died.[30] Amongst the sick was Colonel Joseph Gillmore. A few months later, not having recovered, he resigned his commission and returned to Britain, ending the involvement of all six colonels in the war.

In late May the situation on Margarita began to improve. First the *George Canning* arrived from Angostura with a cargo of cattle. Then, in early June, more ships arrived with rum, flour and salted pork.[31] With a surplus of supplies, General Urdaneta began to plan for the expedition ahead. His mission was to divert attention away from Bolívar's thrust across the Andes, and tie up as many royalist troops as he could by making a series of attacks along the Caribbean coast. His targets, the royalist strongholds of Barcelona and Cumaná, lay 35 miles to the south-east across the Caribbean and could be seen from the hills above Pampatar on a fine day. Taunted by the sight, the troops were desperate to leave but before they could set sail, Brion's fleet was caught in 'a heavy squall' whilst patrolling the coast. The *Victoria* 'lost one of her top masts … and … sprung a leak'.[32] By the time she limped into port, she had 9ft of water in the hold and was listing badly. The rest of the fleet also suffered and 'a thorough refit' was required.[33]

English was philosophical about the delay. Whilst carpenters and sail-makers sawed, sewed and climbed up the masts to lay the new sails, the troops had time to become seasoned to the rigours of the climate and receive training from Blosset and his fellow veterans. Rising at 3.00am, they spent the mornings 'marching, drilling and countermarching'.[34] By the time they left the island, they had 'acquired a perfect knowledge of their duty' and English thought 'every man ... worth three' times what they had been on landing.[35]

After the fleet had been refitted, a struggle for supremacy between the highest ranking Creole commanders on the island caused further delays. Ever since General Urdaneta had arrived in early March, he had faced competition for command of the division from Governor Arismendi. Unaware of The Liberator's plans, Arismendi felt himself unfairly overlooked and his jealousy and suspicion made cooperation impossible. Soon it seemed as though internecine fighting would break out. Ignorant of the political complexies of the situation, the British began to fear for their safety. 'The guards were trebled, and strong parties armed to the teeth nightly patrolled.'[36] Towards the end of May, Urdaneta ordered his second in command, Colonel Manuel Valdés, to stage a *coup d'état* to secure control of the island. After selecting a squad from the British Legion to accompany him, Valdés sailed round the island on a waiting man-of-war and landed under cover of darkness at Juan Griego. 'Long before day-break' the troops had taken up positions surrounding the governor's house.[37] Arismendi had spent the night enjoying a late dinner and had only just retired when Valdés forced his way into his bed chamber. Bleary-eyed, the governor was marched from his room at bayonet point, bundled aboard the man-of-war and taken to Pampatar, before continuing on to Angostura where he would be tried for 'disobedience to the orders of the president'.[38]

Rafael Urdaneta could not have been more different from his rival. Whilst Arismendi was a man of the people, in the mould of Páez, Urdaneta had been born into a wealthy landowning family of Spanish descent. At the age of 12 he had been sent to Santafé de Bogotá to complete his education and was amongst the first to enlist in the patriot army when the city declared its independence in 1810. Beginning his military career as a lieutenant, Urdaneta had seen action in the early campaigns and enjoyed rapid promotion. By 1813 he had attained the rank of general of brigade and was established as one of Bolívar's 'greatest favourites'.[39] The volunteers would not share The Liberator's admiration, however, and soon grew to despise his sloth, indecision and 'complying and intriguing disposition'.[40] The animosity was mutual and would have disastrous results in the forthcoming campaign.[41]

In mid-July the expedition was finally ready to sail. On the 10th, Urdaneta authorized the payment of four pesos per officer and two pesos per man, and ordered the Legion back over the mountains to the harbour at Juan Griego. Locals 'thronged the roads, and *vivas* long and loud' greeted the troops as they crossed the island.[42] By the time they arrived at Juan Griego they were in high spirits. 'Permission was ... [then] accorded to the men to roam at large.'[43] With money in their pockets, 'drunkenness grievously prevailed'.[44] The next morning, 'the scarcely sober force' boarded the boats.[45]

In total, 1,250 troops embarked on five transports. As well as the Legion, now reduced to 800 men through disease and desertion, 300 Venezuelans and a detachment of 150 Hanoverian Rifles under Colonel Uslar also sailed. Uslar, who had originally been recruited by Colonel Elsom, had been destined for Angostura and the Andean campaign, but after being blown off course had been forced to make landfall in Margarita instead. Experienced and well-disciplined, his troops were swiftly incorporated into Urdaneta's task force. The remnants of Gillmore's old artillery brigade also embarked, the crews of their two 6-pdr cannon now led by Lieutenant-Colonel Woodberry. Brion's 15 warships and seven gunboats were to escort the expedition and work in concert with the land forces once they reached the coast. Several of the officers were British. Captain Chitty, 'a brave and intelligent' veteran, commanded the *Liberator*, a 16-gun brig-of-war crewed by 100 sailors 'of all colours and all Nations'; Captain Coates was in charge of a brig named in honour of General English; and Colonel Jackson led the marines.[46] As well as the soldiers and sailors, the ships were crowded with refugees who had lived on the mainland before the royalists had arrived and were keen to return to their homes. Several soldiers' wives and children also embarked, but, due to a persistent illness, English's wife Mary was forced to remain behind. Standing on the shore waving farewell, she cut a forlorn figure as the ships weighed anchor and sailed from the bay.

Early in the evening of the 16th, after an uneventful voyage, the fleet arrived off Pozuelas, a sweeping bay ten miles to the north-east of Barcelona. As the ships approached, enemy pickets raced back to town to raise the alarm.[47] The following morning the cannon were rowed ashore and the men disembarked by companies. Although unopposed, the landing proved 'difficult'.[48] Watching proceedings, Lieutenant Chesterton grew increasingly irritated as the operation dragged on. All the while an enemy telegraph station situated nearby on the fortified peninsula of El Morro was sending communications to the city. After sunset the division was finally assembled onshore. Urdaneta ordered the Legion and a body of 200 Venezuelan troops to march through the night to Barcelona. They were to assault the city before joining Jackson's marines to storm El Morro. Ten miles of flooded marshland crossed by a 'rotten and boggy' track lay between them and their destination.[49] With no horses or mules to aid them, the 6-pdrs were soon 'imbedded' up to their axles in mud.[50] A squad of men was left to guard them. The rest of the column struggled on. With the troops sinking 'knee-deep [in the mud] at every stride', they didn't reach the outskirts of Barcelona until daybreak.[51]

The majority of the royalist garrison had fled to the village of Santo Spirito, 12 leagues (approximately 36 miles) south-east on the road to Caracas. Before leaving, their commander Colonel San Just had sent 300 soldiers to reinforce El Morro and had ordered a squad of men to destroy the wooden bridge over the Neveri River leading into town. Although the central arch was soon pulled down, the supports proved more resilient. The royalists were still struggling to destroy them when the first patriot scouts came within sight. A few shots were enough to disperse San Just's men. After minor repairs, the bridge proved passable and the Legion entered town.

Founded in 1671 by homesick Catalan colonists, Barcelona was a town of 'respectable pretensions'.[52] Its regular, 'well-disposed [but narrow] streets', lined with 'many good houses', led to a spacious central square.[53] To the west stood a magnificent cathedral famous for housing the mummified corpse of a local saint. The northern side was dominated by the scorched ruins of a fort, the site of a patriot last stand when the royalists had taken the town in 1817. Lieutenant-Colonel Chamberlain, one of the earliest English volunteers, had become something of a legend for his 'sublime self-immolation' at the culmination of the siege.[54] A former captain in the British Army, Chamberlain had joined Bolívar in Haiti at the start of the Third Republic. After taking Barcelona, The Liberator had pushed on towards Angostura, leaving Chamberlain with orders to hold out for three days. As soon as Bolívar departed, the royalists counter-attacked and 1,500 soldiers and civilians took refuge in the fort. Lacking cannon to batter a breach, the royalists tried to starve them out. Three months passed with no sign of relief. Giving up hope, the starving garrison opened the gates to the enemy. Chamberlain, whose orders to continue fighting had been ignored, retired to an inner chamber as the royalists raced through the corridors killing every defender they found. Two pistol shots then rang out. When the Spaniards burst into his quarters, they found Chamberlain and his Venezuelan wife dead in each others' arms.

Two years after the massacre, the Legion entered town. The streets were deserted. The only people remaining were some old women found cowering in the cathedral, who would 'fly like hares' whenever the volunteers approached. The Spanish priests had told them the British were 'savages and cannibals, who would … cut the flesh reeking from their bodies … to devour'.[55] They had also been informed that the foreigners had a rather unusual appendage, as one volunteer explained:

> When we first made efforts to establish a friendly understanding with them, many were observed to walk round the men, and cast scrutinizing looks at them, as if searching for something… On being questioned … they informed us that their worthy pastors had assured them, that nature had been so bountiful as to furnish us with tails, like monkeys… They were also led to believe, that our heads were sunk beneath our shoulders, as low as our bosoms … it was some days before they were quite sure that we would not fatten upon them, as a portion of customary and favourite food.[56]

With no sign of the enemy, the troops were dismissed, and 'contrary to all Military precaution', allowed to wander freely around town.[57] Looting broke out, quantities of spirits were found and the men began drinking. Urdaneta and English did little to stop them. After a few hours the alcohol ran out. The men lay insensible in the streets or collapsed in doorways. Urdaneta thought the scene resembled the aftermath of a battle. Meanwhile, in the bay of Pozuelas, Brion had grown tired of waiting for support and decided to attack the 300 royalists on El Morro alone.

Jutting out into the sea alongside the entrance of the Neveri River, El Morro was 'a lofty hill in the exact form of a sugar loaf', crowned by a series of fortifications.[58] At high tide the isthmus connecting it to the mainland was covered by 'more than four or five feet of water' rendering it an island.[59] Seven stone castles and three earthworks, mounting 24 heavy cannon, had been built along the highest ridge. At 9.00am the ships sailed up to the entrance of the river. As they drew level with the forts, they opened up with deafening broadsides. The firing continued for an hour. Round shot crashed into the earthworks, but the defenders held their fire. Then 'a swarm of boats' was lowered and rowed towards shore.[60] Once on the beach, Colonel Jackson formed his storming party into two columns of 100 men and advanced up the slope. The royalists fired two cannon, bringing down a marine officer, who would later die of his wounds, and injuring six others. They then abandoned their positions and fled, most making it to the woods on the mainland. The commander of the garrison and 13 others were less fortunate. Whilst they were crossing the open ground of the isthmus, the *Patriot* and the *Franklin* sailed close in to shore and fired broadsides of grape. All 14 were killed instantly.[61]

The next morning, to the patriots' surprise, the Spanish fleet was lying at anchor in the bay. General English counted 'two large corvettes, a brig, two schooners, and nine gunboats'.[62] Some 400 troops were on board, sent by the governor of nearby Cumaná to reinforce the garrison. With Brion's fleet anchored out of sight behind a bluff and unaware that the patriots were in control of El Morro and Barcelona, the royalists thought they had no cause for alarm. Keeping out of view, Jackson's marines and a company of British volunteers under Lieutenant Chesterton boarded the patriot ships, whilst Colonel Blosset and 300 British troops took up positions in El Morro, hoisting Spanish colours to lure the royalists in. Later that afternoon, as the volunteers watched from behind loaded cannon, the Spanish reinforcements boarded their boats and rowed towards them. Whilst still at long range, Lieutenant-Colonel Harrison of the Legion 'unadvisedly' ordered his men to open fire.[63] The round shot fell short. Great plumes of water rose skyward and the royalist reinforcements rowed back to their ships.

Although the Spanish fleet was out-gunned, disorganized and seemingly at his mercy, Admiral Brion hesitated to attack. Some of the British captains gathered on the *Victoria* believed cowardice prompted the delay. 'Curses ... were vented', some 'not confined to inaudible murmurs' and eventually the admiral gave the order to move out.[64] At first the enemy was 'so far ahead, that the pursuit appeared to be a mockery'. Then the wind changed. As the royalists floundered, the patriots prepared to board. Cutlasses were sharpened, firearms loaded and each man given a 'distinguishing badge' to pin to his shirt.[65] As they closed in, Lieutenant Chesterton noticed Brion at his side. 'Pale and tremulous', he was 'exhibiting all the external symptoms of the coward'. Later, the wind picked up and the royalists got under way again. The threat of imminent combat having passed, the admiral appeared greatly relieved.[66] The pursuit continued all night. At dawn the royalists sailed into the port of Cumaná and anchored close in to the walls. With the enemy ships under the protection of their shore batteries, there was little the patriots could do. After firing a 'salute of twelve guns', to the 'universal derision' of all those on board, Brion gave the order to return to Barcelona.[67]

On shore, the rest of the volunteers were settling into their quarters in town. Whilst his men slept in an abandoned barracks on the far side of the Neveri River, English was staying in 'a comfortable residence' near the square filled with looted furniture.[68] Once installed, he drafted a letter to messrs Herring, Jaffray, Richardson and Salisbury, the Legion's financial backers, informing them of the capture of Barcelona. He reported that £20,000 worth of goods, including rum, cotton, tobacco and hides had been seized as well as the cannon taken on El Morro. When the letter arrived in London on 5 October, the news was met with joy. Mr Herring shook Jaffray 'heartily' by the hand, 'Salisbury was almost dancing and [even] Richardson ... looked gay and sprightly'.[69] General Urdaneta, on the other hand, knew that their troubles had just begun. His most pressing concern was to organize a union with the mounted troops under General Bermúdez, who were operating in the area. As his expedition lacked cavalry, Urdaneta could not round up wild cattle and his men faced starvation once their rations ran out. All dispatches to Bermúdez were intercepted, however, and Urdaneta's plans to move down the coast to Cumaná were delayed for some time.

At night, scattered shots were heard as the patriot pickets sparred with royalist scouts on the outskirts of town. Fearing attack, the officers slept in their boots, 'with their swords ... placed beside them'.[70] English and Urdaneta, however, did little in response. Rather than barricading the numerous access roads into town, the latter passed his time with two mistresses, lounging in his hammock, smoking cigars or gambling with his staff. English, meanwhile, remained locked in his quarters.[71] Aside from a few outlying pickets, their sole concession to defence was to order a unit of sailors and 50 men of the Legion, under Captain Barker, to stand guard in the central square.

A few hours before dawn on 21 July, Colonel San Just set out from Spirito Santo with 30 Lancers to make a raid. Knowing that Bermúdez's cavalry were hourly expected, he had his men put white feathers in their caps in imitation of their enemies. His plan was to kill English and Urdaneta whilst they were still 'in their beds' and disappear before the Legion could react.[72] As the sun rose, the Lancers entered town yelling 'Viva la Patria!' and firing into the air. In the main square, the commander of the sailors was startled awake. Jumping to his feet, a half-smoked cigar firmly clamped between his lips, he formed his men into line as the cavalry clattered to a halt. Remaining 'a few seconds in doubt', they held their fire.[73] Captain Barker demanded the password and received a fatal pistol shot in reply. General English had also been woken by the commotion. Leaping out of his hammock, he rushed into the square as the royalists charged. The guards fired a volley, bringing down several men and horses. Then hand-to-hand fighting broke out. Two volunteers were killed as the cavalry cut and thrust about them.[74] Another fell 'with seven lance wounds' in his body, but survived.[75] The sailors then fired their pistols and rushed into the melee. In the confusion, General English and his staff managed to retreat across the bridge and ordered the rest of the Legion to form column. Hearing the call to arms, San Just ordered his men to retreat before they were overwhelmed. A few patriot stragglers were cut down as they escaped through the narrow streets. Others, seeing the Lancers galloping towards them, threw themselves into the river to escape.[76] Severely shaken by the incident, General English suffered a mental collapse. He slept little in the nights that followed and was later 'compelled to go on board' a brig of war in the bay to recover.[77]

Following San Just's raid, royalist proclamations promising a cash reward to any volunteer who deserted began to circulate through town.[78] Despite the British officers' best efforts, the declarations achieved their desired effect. On the night of 22 July, 40 men slipped past the pickets and made their way eastwards towards royalist lines. Not knowing the terrain, they became confused and split into two bands. One had the misfortune of running into a 'ragged regiment' of mounted patriot guerrillas who patrolled the area, which led to 19 being killed and five captured.[79] The rest made it across country to Cumaná. At noon the next day the prisoners were court-martialled. The outcome was never in doubt. Blosset selected 'two files from each company' to form the firing squad. The 'unhappy culprits' were blindfolded and led into a three-sided square formed by their comrades. As the sentence was read, a murmur of discontent rolled through the ranks. In response, Urdaneta declared that three of the men, to be chosen by lot, would be spared. There would be no reprieve for the others. To an officer's command, the volley echoed out. The men were killed instantly. Much subdued, the troops were marched past the bodies to reflect on their fate.

On 26 July, 'having derived considerable benefit from … [his] short rest', General English returned to town.[80] The same night, royalists began harassing the patriot pickets on the outskirts. Colonel Lowe noted that the skirmishers were mainly Guaquieri Indians, armed with bows and arrows, which they fired 'with incredible certainty'.[81] On the 27th and 28th the attacks increased in ferocity. The sentries were constantly on alert and became exhausted. Peering through the darkness, they tried to spot the enemy attackers who would appear suddenly out of the woods, fire a few arrows then retreat before they could gather to oppose them. On the 29th, Urdaneta abandoned the suburbs and the Legion fell back to some improvised barricades that Lieutenant Oben had built round the central square. General English and his staff were obliged to take up residence in 'a great overgrown mansion, without an atom of furniture' on the far side of the river. The general spent his time in 'a small room upstairs ... perfectly free from intrusion' swinging in his hammock with 'a few old Spanish books' to soothe himself to sleep.[82]

By the 30th the situation had become desperate. Men were continuing to desert, the town was growing increasingly insecure and provisions were running low. With no word from Bermúdez's cavalry, Urdaneta decided to abandon the town. At a meeting of the principal officers, several destinations were put forward. English and Brion proposed they stick to their original intentions and attack Cumaná, whilst Urdaneta counselled marching across country to Angostura via the town of Maturín. Others were keen to return to Margarita.[83] In the end, Brion's support proved decisive. Enticed by the wealth of Cumaná, he backed English's plan.

Before they departed, Barcelona was 'given up to the troops for plunder'.[84] For two days they ran amok, smashing doors, stealing alcohol and looting anything of value. Some even dug pits to hide the booty they were unable to carry, intending to return at a later date.[85] Far from trying to stop them, the officers, both Creole and British, reserved the richest pickings in the cathedral for themselves. Chesterton helped himself to 'some trifling silver relics' and English stole 'an ancient painting' he found fixed in an iron frame above the altar.[86] The general was delighted with his find, noting in his diary that it was 'a battle piece between the Spaniards and the Moors ... by Jose Dias, a[n] ... artist, [considered] great in his day'.[87] Behind the altar, Colonel Blosset found several crowns studded with 'topaz, ruby, emerald, and other stones'.[88] After choosing one as a gift for his wife, he shared out those that remained.[89] The next morning the soldiers forced their way in and finished the job their officers had begun. When the army embarked on Brion's fleet that afternoon, the cathedral was left 'sacked and gutted', the town stripped bare and the locals cursing the day that the Legion had entered their lives.[90]

Chapter 16

THE BATTLE OF VARGAS

The campaign in New Granada, 700 miles to the south-west of Barcelona, was entering a crucial phase. With the arrival of Rooke's Legion at Corrales de Bonza, Bolívar was ready to move onto the offensive. Breaking camp at dawn on 25 July, he advanced down the road to Paipa to outflank the royalist army. The march went well until they reached the river Sogamoso. Swollen with heavy rains, the ford proved impassable. Rafts had to be constructed to ferry the men and baggage to the far bank. During the delay, enemy scouts spotted them from the heights above the river. Informed of Bolívar's movements, at 9.00am Barreiro broke camp at Topága to intercept them. After crossing the Sogamoso up-river, he lined his 3,500 troops along a series of hills, blocking the patriots' advance. It was a formidable position. His best men, 1,000 Spanish veterans of the King's Battalion, held the right flank. A mixed unit of the remnants of the Tambo Battalion, the troops that the patriots had encountered whilst crossing the mountains at Paya, and some companies of the 2nd and 3rd Numancia took up positions in the centre. His cavalry, the King's Dragoons of Granada, and some infantry companies were held in reserve.

Although delighted that Barreiro was offering battle for the first time since the campaign had begun, Bolívar hesistated before committing his men. The enemy's position was one of considerable strength, whilst many of the patriot infantry were untried and his cavalry lacked horses. To withdraw, on the other hand, would be even more problematic. Isolated in enemy territory with little hope of resupply, a protracted campaign would result in the slow disintegration of his army through desertion and sickness. Choosing the lesser of two evils, The Liberator made up his mind. His troops would stand and fight.

THE BATTLE OF VARGAS

The field of Vargas was dominated by a string of wooded hills. Rising steeply from the left rear of the patriot line, they swept round to their front past a prominent hill (now known as Alto de la Guerra), before reaching the ridge where the royalists had taken up position. In the centre, between the two armies, was a gentle slope split by a sunken track. This furrowed its way upwards to Barreiro's lines after passing a farmhouse in the

THE BATTLE OF VARGAS

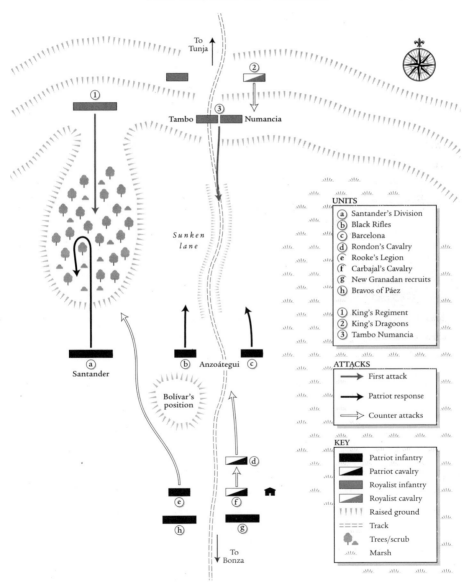

To Tunja

Tambo   Numancia

UNITS
(a) Santander's Division
(b) Black Rifles
(c) Barcelona
(d) Rondon's Cavalry
(e) Rooke's Legion
(f) Carbajal's Cavalry
(g) New Granadan recruits
(h) Bravos of Páez

(1) King's Regiment
(2) King's Dragoons
(3) Tambo Numancia

Sunken lane

(a) Santander

(b) Anzoátegui (c)

Bolívar's position

(d)

(e)

(f)

(h)

(g)

To Bonza

ATTACKS
→ First attack
→ Patriot response
⇒ Counter attacks

KEY
◼ Patriot infantry
◢ Patriot cavalry
◼ Royalist infantry
◢ Royalist cavalry
| | | | Raised ground
==== Track
🌳 Trees/scrub
Marsh

patriot rear. The right of the field was covered by impassable swampland. Outnumbered and outmanoeuvred, Bolívar would have to use his 2,600 troops well. Santander's division was ordered to hold the left flank at the foot of Alto de la Guerra, while Sandes's Rifles and the Barcelona Regiment were positioned in the centre on either side of the track. His best troops, the cavalry and Rooke's Legion, were held in reserve in the farmhouse along with the 400 recently recruited New Granadan infantry. Lacking training and 'armed principally with lances' their role was to give added bulk to the army, guard the baggage and help with the wounded.[1]

From a vantage point on a small rise to the front of his line, Barreiro opened the battle at midday, sending his light troops skirting round the swampland to engage the patriot right. At the same time the King's Battalion under Colonel Nicolas López advanced along the heights towards Alto de la Guerra. The Spanish general's plan was one of pure aggression, moulded by his conviction that no insurgent army could stand up to European troops. By attacking with his best unit to the patriot left in the opening exchanges, he was going straight for the jugular. If López's men broke through, Bolívar's army would be surrounded and cut off from their baggage and reserves. Emboldened by Morillo's victories in Venezuela, Barreiro believed the battle would be decided by his first attack.

With the soldiers of the King's Battalion threatening his left flank, The Liberator ordered Santander's division into the hills to oppose them. Whilst 400 of the 1,000 men were veterans, the rest were conscripted Indians from the plains of Casanare and considered the weakest of all of the front line republican troops. Although they gained the heights in time to block the advance, they buckled under the Spaniards' opening volleys. After half an hour of rolling musketry, López ordered his men to fix bayonets and charge. Before they hit home, Santander's men broke and fled, leaving the route open for the King's Battalion to move round and envelop the patriot rear.[2]

At 2.00pm Barreiro ordered his centre to advance. The lines came together and a musketry duel ensued. The volleys crashed out twice a minute. In the ranks of the Black Rifles and Barcelona Regiment, sergeants yelled out firing orders in an attempt to make themselves heard above the din. Soon the Spanish infantry's superior musketry began to tell. More and more men fell out of the patriot line dead or wounded. Others fled the field or excused themselves from the fight by dragging injured comrades clear. Gaps appeared and the firing became irregular. Fearing defeat, the Black Rifles inched backwards. Sandes tried to hold them using the flat of his sword, but a musket ball came whistling through the smoke and hit him in the foot. By late afternoon the situation looked desperate. The patriot centre was being pushed back, their left flank had fled the field and the King's Battalion was threatening to drive a wedge between the main body and the rearguard. From a rocky rise a little way back from the front, Bolívar decided to throw in the first of his reserves. After dispatching an aide, he unsheathed his sword and charged into the melee with Anzoátegui and O'Leary at his side.

With the sun sinking low in the sky, the general's aide arrived at the farmhouse with orders for Rooke's men to drive López's regiment from the hills. As well as outnumbering the Legion 'nearly six to one' the royalists were ready and waiting on high ground.[3] Even so, Rooke was undeterred. Perhaps dreaming of emulating his forefathers, or deliberately putting himself in harm's way to escape his growing debts and the shame of his wife's infidelity, he led his 92 men on a lung-bursting scramble up the slope. The Spaniards crowning the hill opened fire as soon as they came into range. Rooke was the first to be hit. Two balls entered his right arm above the elbow, shattering the humerus and driving splintered shards of bone through the flesh. He fell to the ground and was soon left behind. Halfway up the slope, the rest of the Legion paused. With musket balls whistling past 'as thick as hailstones', one officer complained that it would be madness to continue.[4] Fearing a rout, Rooke's second, Major Mackintosh, retorted that nothing was impossible for British bayonets.[5] Memories of Flanders, Portugal and Spain rekindled the Legion's fighting spirit. The men rallied and Mackintosh led them on, forbidding them to return fire as they climbed for fear of losing momentum. Several were shot dead or wounded on the approach. The rest ignored their cries and pressed on. Upon reaching the summit, Mackintosh formed line and prepared to fire.

MAKE READY! The men brought their muskets up to the recover and the front rank dropped to one knee. *PRESENT!* The line seemed to make a quarter turn to the right as the guns came up to their shoulders. *FIRE!* The muskets kicked back and the balls hurtled towards the white-coated ranks. At close-range, a musket volley could do horrendous damage. Several of the Spaniards were killed outright. Others were felled with gaping, bloody wounds. Before they could recover, Mackintosh ordered the charge. Faced with a steel-tipped line of powder-blackened faces, the royalists fell back, but the momentum of the attack was broken by the trees crowning the summit and López soon rallied his men. A rolling firefight then broke out, with neither side gaining the advantage. The Peninsular veterans amongst the volunteers later said 'they [had] never experienced so terrible a fire'.[6] An hour into the contest Lieutenant McGuire had a narrow escape 'when a ball passed through ... [his] cap'. The Irishman was then shot through the foot.[7] By this point, the British were down to the last of their 40 cartridges. The volume of musketry was subsiding and López's veterans were starting to gain the upper hand. His position untenable, Mackintosh ordered his men back down the slope to the farmhouse for more ammunition. Watching from the safety of the ridge, Barreiro was delighted with the way his plan was developing. His troops were edging the fight in the centre and the King's Battalion was tantalizingly close to its objective on the right.

He thought that the destruction of the patriots was inevitable and believed 'not a single man would … escape alive'.[8]

The fighting in the centre had been playing back and forth all afternoon. Ceding and retaking the same ground, both sides passed the prostrate forms of their own dead and wounded. The royalists had mounted two bayonet charges, driving the Rifles and Barcelona Regiment before them. Each time, however, Sandes rallied his men and brought them back to the fight. Ignoring the pain in his foot, he rode up and down the line bellowing at his troops to hold firm, whilst the sergeants re-dressed the ranks. Late in the day, Barreiro regained the upper hand by throwing two fresh companies into the attack. Faced with new opponents and seeing Rooke's men retreating down the hill to their rear, the patriots sensed defeat. Just as the tide of battle seemed to be swinging against them, the Spaniards then charged for a third time. Bolívar, however, had one last card to play.

Back at the farmhouse, Colonel Rondon, the son of a slave from the upper plains of Venezuela, was ordered to ride out with his troops in an effort to save the republic. Even though his fellow commander Colonel Carbajal hesitated, Rondon trotted out with just 14 men. O'Leary thought them 'the most skilful lancers of the Llanos'.[9] Wheeling round Sandes and his troops, they charged the royalist centre, their horses' hooves throwing up clods of earth as they raced up the slope. Buoyed by the sight, Sandes led his men alongside them in the attack. Disorganized after their last drive forward, the royalists were unprepared when Rondon's Lancers plunged into their ranks; and when the Black Rifles charged in beside them, throwing themselves against the enemy bayonets 'with fury', the fighting in the centre deteriorated into a confused melee.[10] At the head of his men, Sandes had his horse killed under him and he was later shot through the thigh.[11] Bleeding profusely from two wounds, he became too weak to stand. Even so, he 'could not be prevailed to quit the field'.[12] Leaning against the carcass of his horse, the 25-year old from Kerry vowed to stay with his men until the end.

Whilst the British troops were refilling their ammunition pouches back at the farm, Mackintosh caught sight of General Santander. Ever since his division had been routed at the start of the battle, the general had been sheltering behind a stone wall, handing out cartridges to those who came back from the front. Anzoátegui, who had rarely been out of the fighting, was also present. Turning to Mackintosh, he remarked with his usual bitterness that the motto of 'to conquer or die' was supposed to apply to every one of them.[13] With no time for such bickering, Bolívar ordered Mackintosh and the Legion to re-engage the King's Battalion. Supported by the Bravos de Páez and Commander Joaquin Paris, the only soldier from Santander's division to re-enter the fight, the volunteers raced up the wooded slope for the second time that day.[14] The ensuing firefight was played out amidst lengthening shadows. After 30 minutes it was the royalists' turn to run low on ammunition. Nonetheless, they fought on courageously. Picking their targets through the trees, they made the patriots pay dearly for each inch of ground.

With his plan in tatters, Barreiro tried to order the last of his reserves into the fight, but the momentum had now swung against him. Having witnessed the bloodshed that had gone on all afternoon, four companies of infantry refused to advance, leaving only the Dragoons of Granada to reinforce the centre. Believing the terrain unsuitable for cavalry, Barreiro ordered them to dismount. As they advanced up the sunken lane, the second patriot cavalry unit under Colonel Carbajal charged into them. Crowded into the narrow space, only the front rank of six Dragoons could fire. Their pistols did nothing to slow the charge and their sabres were to prove no match for the reach of the Llaneros' lances. Several Spaniards were crushed under hoof. Others were run through and the whole formation was driven backwards. Two of their standards were taken after the sergeants carrying them were killed. The survivors then broke, pursued by the whooping Llaneros who cut them down as they ran.

As the patriots appeared to be gaining the upper hand, storm clouds scudded overhead and torrential rain fell across the battlefield. With their cartridges soaked, the men resorted to hand-to-hand fighting, clubbing, slashing and stabbing each other with musket butt, sabre, lance and bayonet. Captain O'Leary was in the thick of the fighting, lathered in sweat and the blood of his enemies. As the last of the light seeped out of the day, his opponent's sabre opened up a gash across his forehead that would scar the young Irishman for the rest of his life. Whilst he was taken to the rear to be treated, the battle staggered towards its conclusion. The troops on both sides were exhausted, their powder was useless and in the gathering gloom it was becoming impossible to determine friend from foe. As the survivors drifted away from the fight, many became disorientated. Dozens would not find their camps until morning and hundreds of wounded were left groaning on the field overnight.

Although the battle of Vargas was indecisive, it would have crucial repercussions. For the royalist command, the stalemate was a bitter blow. It shook their confidence and caused many to reconsider their opinions of the insurgents' hopes of final victory. Furthermore, Barreiro had ceded the initiative and was forced into a dispiriting retreat. Tired, hungry and unpaid, the morale of the royalists slumped. Many began to fear republican reprisals should Bolívar win the war and men deserted the King's standard in droves. The patriots, on the other hand, were jubilant. Having so narrowly avoided defeat, the draw felt like victory. The soldiers were confident and the local people were inspired to back them unreservedly. Over the next few days, large numbers of local volunteers would pour into camp and others donated food, horses and supplies.

The night after the battle, as the remnants of the patriot army regrouped at the farmhouse, Bolívar ordered patrols to return to the field to gather abandoned weapons and bring back the wounded. Leading one such patrol was the army's chaplain, Andrés María Gallo. As he neared the foot of Alto de la Guerra, Gallo heard some faint groans carrying towards him through the chill night air. Approaching closer, he saw Colonel Rooke staggering weakly towards him. Supporting the colonel between them, the party returned to the farmhouse, where Rooke was lain down on a simple wooden bench. Only then, in the flickering candlelight, did the chaplain realize the seriousness of his wounds. Rooke was 'as white as marble with all the blood loss he had suffered… The ball[s] that wounded him had blown his left arm to pieces from the elbow up and the veins and arteries had all bled out.'[15] Thinking he would die before morning, Gallo gave the colonel the last rites. Even as he lay 'bathed in blood', Rooke remained focused on the cause.[16] Seeing one of Bolívar's staff officers passing by, he asked if The Liberator had been pleased with his conduct on the field. The officer replied that Bolívar considered him a hero.

Dawn had risen by the time Doctor Foley arrived. As the wound was too complicated to deal with, the only solution was amputation. Although barbaric by modern standards, battlefield surgery in the Napoleonic era was a well-established science. Musket balls were removed with forceps, heavy bleeding was cauterized with boiling pitch and amputation was a common procedure.[17] One contemporary described the process in vivid detail. 'The surgeon cuts through the skin, slices through the muscles, then the nerves, saws right through the bone, severing arteries from which blood spatters the surgeon himself.'[18] Success depended on the speed with which the operation was performed and how far up the limb the incision occurred. Survival statistics from the period are frequently contradictory, but it appears a significant minority went on to test the cheery hypothesis of the pre-eminent French surgeon of the age, Pierre Dionis, who quipped 'it is better to live with three limbs, than to die with four'.[19] The high risk of infection in the tropics, combined with a lack of medical expertise, made a patient's prospects in the wars of independence far less promising, however. Several memoirists expressed low opinions of the foreign surgeons employed by Bolívar and some suggested that being European was the only qualification required. Lieutenant Alexander claimed that 'there was only one surgeon … who … knew more of his profession than I did myself' and another volunteer remarked that in his entire time on the continent, he had only met one man who had survived an amputation.[20]

As Foley prepared his tools, Rooke took one last look at the arm 'he was about to lose forever', reflecting on its 'perfection', before suffering the operation 'with his accustomed good humour'.[21] Foley sliced through the flesh near the shoulder, cut the bone with a saw, then cauterized the stump in the fire. Father Gallo, who had stayed with the colonel during the night, noted that Rooke remained motionless throughout and uttered not one word of complaint. No doubt reeling from alcohol, which was the only anaesthetic available, the colonel then grabbed his severed limb by the wrist. Staggering to his feet, he held it aloft and yelled 'long live the motherland!'[22] When Foley asked whether it was England, Ireland or New Granada he was referring to, Rooke's reply was 'the land where I will be buried'.

Too weak to travel with the army as it moved south-west for the final showdown with Barreiro, the colonel was sent a few miles from the battlefield to convalesce in the Augustine monastery of Belencito. Foley 'left every necessary direction with the friars for the treatment of the patient and dressing the stump'.[23] His instructions were ignored, however, and the friars' muddled, homespun ministrations only speeded his demise. 'Having taken off the bandages [they] stuffed the wound with lint, moistened with oil and wine', a treatment which brought on the 'poor colonel's death' a few days after the battle.[24] It is not known if he died before James Hamilton's letter arrived confirming his suspicions about Anna's infidelity.

Sandes and O'Leary were more fortunate. Both survived their wounds and would return to active service. The major took considerably longer than the captain to recover, but was fortunate to avoid the serious infection that often accompanied musket wounds. The lead balls picked up grease, flecks of wadding and powder as they left the barrel and often drove scraps of clothing into the flesh on impact. Any foreign bodies not removed became infected and could prove fatal. Sabre injuries like O'Leary's, particularly those inflicted with the blade as opposed to the more serious puncture wounds caused by the point, were generally cleaner. Accordingly they had significantly lower mortality rates.[25] Immediately after his wound was washed, bandaged and bound, O'Leary returned to active service and made a full recovery.

Only after the battle did the extent of the 'butcher's bill' become clear. Both sides had suffered 300 dead and wounded. Rooke's Legion, which had entered the combat with 92 men, was reduced to 61 effectives, an extraordinarily high 30 per cent casualty rate.[26] As well as Rooke and McGuire, Lieutenant MacManus and 20 of the rank and file had been wounded. Amongst them was Francis Fuge, the 42-year old veteran who had served in the British Army for 24 years.[27] Besides the wounded, there were those who were killed outright. Mackintosh's aide, Lieutenant Daniel Cazely, and seven soldiers from the Legion got 'their passports for the next world'. The mortality rate was over 8 per cent compared to the 5 per cent that had died under Wellington at Waterloo.[28] The Black Rifles had also suffered considerably and Anzoátegui was forced to admit he had been wrong about the British. Far from not being 'worth the meat they ate', as he had claimed during the Apure campaign, he now conceded that they 'were worth their weight in gold'.[29] The campaign was far from over, however. Barreiro's troops were battered but not beaten and the volunteers would have to endure another battle before final victory was won.

Chapter 17

'A PLACE CALLED BOYACÁ'

When news of the battle of Vargas reached Santafé de Bogotá, 100 miles to the south-west, the people dared to dream that royalist rule was coming to an end. As a warning to those who thought of joining the 'insurgents', Viceroy Sámano erected a gallows in the plaza in front of his palace. Small *banquillos* (wooden seats) were set up along the main streets awaiting traitors who would face a firing squad, and spies were sent out to report any seditious talk. To make the people believe that the 'insurgents' had been defeated, church bells were rung and 'pompous bulletins ... published, announcing great victories obtained by his Catholic Majesty's troops'.[1] The locals were not taken in, however, and word of Bolívar's resistance spread. The days of the viceroy's tyranny were numbered. Santafé's patriots would not have long to wait.

When the sun rose over the swamp of Vargas the morning after the battle, both armies were still in the field. The Spanish had taken up defensive positions facing the farmhouse Bolívar was using as his headquarters, but neither side had the stomach to continue the fight. After burying their dead, the patriots withdrew to Corrales de Bonza, whilst Barreiro retreated six miles to the town of Paipa. On 28 July, Bolívar issued an edict declaring martial law, covering the villages his troops had occupied on their march down from the mountains. All men aged between 15 and 40 were to report to the army. Execution was threatened should any fail to comply. Within days, 800 had been enlisted. Bandaged, but otherwise suffering no ill effects from the sabre wound he had suffered at Vargas, Captain O'Leary was tasked with training them. Their unkempt hair put the young Irishman in mind of pre-shorn Samsons and their scruffy appearance did little to inspire his confidence. Mainly local Indians and peasant farmers, they had no military experience. When firing their muskets, they closed their eyes and turned their heads, 'putting their comrades in more danger than the enemy'.[2] Nevertheless, by the time they had finished basic training, O'Leary was reasonably satisfied with his efforts.[3]

The next stage of the campaign was all about manoeuvre. If Bolívar could get between Barreiro's army and Santafé de Bogotá, he would be at a significant advantage. By cutting his enemy's supply lines, he would force him to give battle at a site of his own choosing and the capital's small garrison, cut off from the army, would most likely flee without a fight. Fully aware of this possibility Barreiro was determined to prevent it, but it was Bolívar who took the initiative, breaking camp on 3 August to march towards Paipa. Not wishing to engage the patriots unless on his own terms, Barreiro abandoned the town and took up positions on the heights overlooking the junction of the Tunja Socorro road. The patriots set up camp opposite, on the far bank of the river Sogamoso. The next day the two armies watched each other until late evening, when Bolívar detached some men to attack the only bridge. Whilst the enemy was distracted, the rest of his army feigned a march to the north as if returning to Bonza, but once out of sight, they wheeled to the south-west. Marching throughout the night at the double, they looped round the royalists' positions, cutting them off from the capital.

At 11.00am, at the head of a vanguard of 300 cavalry, The Liberator rode into Tunja, the main town on the road to Santafé. Earlier that morning the governor, Lieutenant-Colonel Loño, had marched with four companies of infantry, two mortars and a 4-pdr cannon to reinforce Barreiro, leaving the garrison severely under strength. Outnumbered by Bolívar's cavalry, the garrison soon surrendered. When the patriot infantry arrived at 3.00pm, they took up position in the convent on the heights overlooking the town. From the armoury, 600 muskets and thousands of cartridges were taken and distributed amongst O'Leary's new recruits. Having gained the upper hand, Bolívar settled in to await the royalists' next move.

Barreiro did not discover that he had been outmanoeuvred until the morning of the 5th, when refugees fleeing Tunja arrived at his camp. Forming his troops into four sections, he marched towards the patriot army down the main road. At 5.00pm, they were spotted by a patrol of patriot Dragoons. Launching several attacks on the rear of the royalist column, they killed or captured any who fell behind. Meeting up with Loño's reinforcements, Barreiro then pushed on in driving rain that had turned the unpaved track into a quagmire. Struggling forward with the cannon, they finally reached Motavita, a village one and a half hours march from Tunja, on the morning of the 6th. Later that afternoon, Barreiro sent some cavalry scouts to reconnoitre the patriot position. After clashing with Bolívar's cavalry on the outskirts, they reported that the patriots remained encamped around town.

In an attempt to regain the initiative, Barreiro broke camp before dawn. Taking a little-used track over the moors as the rain pelted down, his troops made for the bridge of Boyacá, intending to bypass the patriot position and block their route to the capital. His march was soon spotted by patriot scouts, however, who galloped to Tunja to inform Bolívar. On hearing the news, The Liberator 'effected a lightning march' of his own down the main road to Santafé.[4] A desperate race was now on. With the drummers rattling out a frenetic beat, the patriot vanguard arrived in the vicinity of the bridge just before the royalists. With his troops hidden behind a ridge line to the east of the main road, Bolívar rode up to the heights to observe the enemy approach shortly before 2.00pm. Through the rain, he trained his telescope on the white-coated troops descending from the moors. The royalists were split into two columns, with their vanguard a full two miles ahead of the main body. If Bolívar could drive a wedge between them, victory would be all but assured. Barreiro, meanwhile, was equally confident. Believing he had outmanoeuvred his enemies, he allowed his troops to rest on the hillside whilst the vanguard moved forward to secure the bridge. Little did he realize that the move played straight into Bolívar's hands. The royalists were falling into a trap.

A series of gently undulating hills, concealing several areas of dead ground, formed the field. To the south was the Boyacá River with shrubs and trees growing thickly along its banks. Normally little more than a stream, it had been swollen by the heavy rainfall and, at 6ft deep, was now all but impossible to ford. The Tunja–Santafé road running between the two armies crossed the river over a narrow stone bridge. At the foot of a rise crowned with oak trees, where the track over the moors joined the road, a coaching inn stood with high outlying walls. Controlling the route to the capital, the river crossing had long been of the utmost strategic importance, and had witnessed a momentous battle 300 years earlier when local Indians were heavily defeated by Spanish Conquistadores. This time, however, the roles would be reversed.

With the royalist vanguard nearing the bridge, Bolívar ordered a squadron of scouts to ride up to the crest of the oak-topped hill and lure the enemy into his trap. Leading the vanguard was Colonel Jiménez, a bloodthirsty Spaniard better known as 'El Caricortardo, from a sabre wound he had … received in the face'.[5] As soon as he saw the patriot horsemen appear, Jiménez ordered his men to attack, his impetuosity further stretching the gap between his troops and Barreiro's. Heavily outnumbered, the cavalry scouts fired a few scattered shots and retreated. Then, to Jiménez's horror, Santander's vanguard suddenly appeared in column from the dead ground. At its head, a heavy screen of skirmishers opened fire, driving the royalists back down the hill in confusion. When they reached the coaching inn, Jiménez managed to rally his men. Sheltered by the high stone walls, they loaded their muskets and awaited the onslaught.

The crackle of musketry carried down the valley to Anzoátegui's rearguard. Knowing that the men needed to reach the bridge before the main body of Barreiro's army, Bolívar rode back to goad them on. He told the Americans that the British made fun of them, whilst informing Mackintosh's men that the Rifles had outshone them so far on the campaign. With their pride stung, the men redoubled their efforts and appeared on the field ahead of the Spanish rearguard. Suddenly realizing the danger he was in, Barreiro ordered the 1st King's Battalion to advance at the double and fill the growing gap in his lines.

Protected by the stone wall of the inn, Jiménez's regulars held their position, picking their targets through the rain. With the patriot skirmishers struggling to make an impact, Colonel Paris, second in command of Santander's vanguard, led the Cazadores Battalion to their support. Advancing to close-range, the battalion deployed into line and released a devastating volley. The men then locked their 16in bayonets in place and charged through the smoke. After a bloody hand-to-hand struggle, the Spaniards were driven from the wall, leaving the position carpeted with their dead and wounded.

THE BATTLE OF BOYACÁ

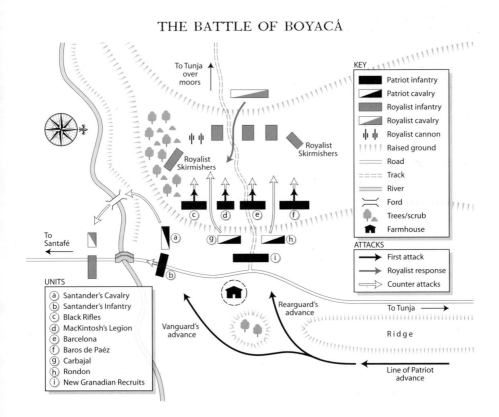

199

Seeing the King's Battalion moving down from the moors to link up with the royalist vanguard, Bolívar ordered the Black Rifles under Major Peacock and Mackintosh's British Legion to block their advance. Propelled into action by their drummers, the troops moved forward in column. Then, as they closed with the enemy, Mackintosh and Peacock gave the order to deploy. The companies moved half-right through a quarter of a circle, all the while facing to the front, to form a thin red line. Still advancing, they closed to musket range and began exchanging volleys with the royalists. With the smoke obscuring their target, the men loaded and fired with clockwork rhythm, priming their flash pans with a pinch of powder before pouring the rest down the barrel. As the musket balls whipped through the air about them, casualties mounted. The drummers put down their instruments and dragged the wounded back from the line. Captain James Byrne, who had been with the Black Rifles since 1817, was amongst the dead, but still the volunteers held their ground. With his army split in two, Barreiro's situation was growing increasingly desperate.

Realizing it was now impossible to link up with Barreiro, Colonel Jiménez ordered his troops to fall back across the bridge. Whilst a company held off Santander's men, the rest took up defensive positions on the far bank. Their job done, the men of the rearguard then ran back across the cobble stones under a hail of fire. In pursuit, Santander's forces were cut down by concentrated Spanish musketry. Unable to push their way over the bridge, the patriots lined the opposite bank and returned fire.

Meanwhile Barreiro had formed his rearguard along the top of a low hill to the north of the road. His infantry were in column in the centre, supported by the artillery Lieutenant-Colonel Loño had brought from Tunja. The two mortars and single 4-pdr were manhandled through the mud ten paces to the front of the line, giving them a lethal field of fire covering the slope down to the main road. The Spanish cavalry stood on a rise to the rear and thick screens of skirmishers held the flanks. His men deployed, Barreiro then moved his light troops on the right a short way forward to occupy a wooded gulley, enfilading the patriot line of advance.

Facing Barreiro's men at the foot of the slope, Anzoátegui's rearguard deployed for battle. The 200-strong Rifles held the left flank. Dressed in rags, dead men's clothes and peasants' garments, Mackintosh's unit stood in column to their right. The regiments of Barcelona and the Bravos de Páez formed up beside them. Rondon's and Carbajal's Lancers made up a second line, whilst the newly raised units from Tunja and Socorro were held in reserve. Lieutenant Thomas Wright of the Black Rifles thought Anzoátegui magnificent on the day of the battle. Riding up and down the line, he encouraged his men, assuring them victory would be theirs. As his aide, Captain O'Leary galloped alongside him and was periodically dispatched to the bridge to maintain contact with Santander.

Preceded by a screen of skirmishers, the patriot line advanced shortly after 2.00pm. Dashing forward in pairs to engage the enemy light troops, the skirmishers fanned out ahead of their parent formations, picking off enemy officers with accurate fire. As the columns toiled up the slope behind them, Anzoátegui dispatched some troops to clear the gully on his left. Unable to resist the bayonet-tipped onslaught, the royalist light troops scrambled out of the ravine and ran back to the safety of their main line. The Spanish cannon then opened fire. After grazing the turf, the cannon balls skipped up and bounded on. Ploughing through the patriot ranks, they knocked men flying through the air like skittles. Fortunately for the patriots, however, the recoil from the fifth shot blew the barrel of the royalists' single cannon off its carriage, rendering it useless for the rest of the battle. After ordering Lieutenant-Colonel Loño to send an infantry company to protect it, Barreiro rode along his line, yelling at his men to stand firm as the patriots drew ever closer.

At 50 yards, Peacock and Mackintosh called the halt. *MAKE READY! ... PRESENT! ... FIRE!* Gunpowder flashes rippled up and down the line. White-coated royalist infantry were thrown bloodily to the ground and the patriots soon began to gain the upper hand. Peacock and Mackintosh edged their troops forward as the 2nd Numancia Battalion facing them ceded ground. Then the Spanish cavalry reserve appeared. Wheeling round their infantry, 300 'splendidly mounted' riders of the 3rd and 5th companies of the Dragoons of Granada bore down on the patriot left with swords aloft.[6] As the thunder of pounding hooves drew closer, a wave of panic passed along the line.

There was nothing the Napoleonic infantrymen feared more than being caught in the open by enemy cavalry. The speed of the charge and sheer weight of the horses and riders hurtling towards them could cause panic. Many would fire too early, a mistake which only urged the cavalry on, whilst at the same time lessening the confidence of those around them. Unless formed in square, or exceptionally well-disciplined and led, foot soldiers were invariably routed in such a situation.[7] The patriot line at Boyacá was marshalled by Anzoátegui, however, and, whilst the Spanish Dragoons may have looked the part, their morale was low and their officers uncommitted.

As the enemy cavalry closed on his line, Anzoátegui ordered Rondón's Lancers to counter-attack. Trotting up the slope, with their horses snorting in the damp air, the patriot cavalry split into two. Half advanced against the Spanish infantry and the rest went to engage the cavalry threatening the patriot left. Seeing the legendary Llaneros emerge from the dead ground, the Dragoons hesitated; but the sight inspired the British volunteers to hold firm. When Rondón's men smashed into the Spanish riders, those not killed in the initial clash turned their horses and fled. The left flank broke first and the panic spread until all the Dragoons were flying back towards the moor. Rondón's

Lancers, meanwhile, continued their charge, their momentum carrying them into the troops guarding Loño's cannon. Some tried to hold off the riders with muskets and bayonets, but the rest ran or took cover under the guns. Many were lanced in the back as they fled and those that went to ground were soon killed or captured.[8]

The second squadron of Lancers charged against the infantry in the centre of Barreiro's position. Having seen their cavalry routed, several units of foot soldiers also turned and ran before the Lancers crashed home. The patriot riders then pursued the scattered bands, leaving the steadier formations to their infantry waiting a little way down the slope. With royalist morale broken, Anzoátegui ordered his entire line forward. To their sergeants' hollered commands the infantry fixed bayonets. A cheer rose from the ranks and they rushed up the slope. The royalists managed a few scattered shots as they closed. At the head of his company, Captain John Johnstone, who had thrown his boots into the Arauca 64 days earlier, suffered 'a desperate wound', the ball drilling right through his 'left arm and breast'.[9] Johnstone collapsed to the turf, but his men ran on.[10]

With the patriots closing, the rout became general, spreading from right to left along the royalist line. Barreiro dispatched an aide to the capital to warn Viceroy Sámano that Bolívar would soon be with him, then dismounted in a forlorn attempt to hold his panicked troops. His efforts proved in vain. Although a few scattered clusters of men fought on round their colours, entire regiments threw down their weapons, whilst most of the cavalry spurred their horses into flight without even drawing their sabres. Only Colonel López managed to maintain some order. Rallying 500 men, he made a stand on a hill to the rear, but Anzoátegui's entire division joined forces to defeat them.

Away to the south-west, Santander had also made a breakthrough. Having found an undefended ford, his cavalry had got behind the Spanish vanguard. After splashing across the river, they thundered into the royalists' flank. Simultaneously, Santander launched his infantry across the bridge. Assailed on two sides and seeing their comrades under Barreiro fleeing the field, Jiménez's men surrendered en masse.

Even before López's last stand, some of the patriots had begun to loot their prisoners. In the chaos several Spanish officers were killed with bayonets. Not wishing to suffer the humiliation of surrendering it to the 'insurgents', Barreiro threw his sword away and was later captured by Pedro Martinez, a private from the Black Rifles. Leaving Anzoátegui to marshal the prisoners, Bolívar then took off in pursuit of those that had fled. At the head of a Llanero cavalry squadron, The Liberator rode 20 miles before nightfall, a trumpeter by his side frequently sounding the advance. As the cavalry overtook bands of fugitives, he dispatched his men to escort them back to the battlefield. By the time the party galloped into the town of Ventaquemada, where they rested for the night, Bolívar's escort had shrunk to just seven riders. One of those run down on the chase was the Italian-born turncoat Vinoni, whose betrayal seven years earlier at Puerto Cabello had led to the downfall of the First Republic. Recognizing the traitor amongst his captives the next morning, Bolívar had him strung up to a nearby tree. With his body hanging by the roadside, The Liberator gathered his escort and returned to Boyacá.

Hundreds of prisoners were brought into the patriot camp in the days following the victory. Having picked up the muskets discarded by Barreiro's men, bands of local peasants scoured the countryside, rounding up any fugitives they found. The scale of the royalists' defeat was unparalleled. The entire 3rd Division had ceased to exist. Hundreds of royalists lay dead on the field. Their artillery, colours, arms, ammunition and baggage had all been captured. As well as Barreiro and the hated Jiménez, 1,600 men, five colonels and 34 other officers had been taken prisoner. Fewer than 100 patriots had died. Both Bolívar and Morillo were quick to realize the significance of the battle. The Spaniard later wrote that the defeat meant the loss of an entire province, never to be regained. Bolívar, on the other hand, would look back on the campaign as his 'most complete victory'. The day after the battle, the patriots set out for Santafé. The capital, which had been in royalist hands for the last four years, now lay virtually undefended a mere 70 miles to the south-west. Its capture would be the most significant victory in the history of the Third Republic.

Chapter 18

THE SIEGE OF AGUA SANTA

A
t the end of July, General English's British Legion abandoned Barcelona. The bridge was destroyed and the army marched back across the marsh to the bay of Pozuelas where the fleet was waiting. After the sick and wounded had been ferried back to Margarita, the rest sailed east to Cumaná. Aboard a brig of war named in his honour, General English spent the 50-mile voyage feeling 'very unwell, and in a weak state of health'.[1] On the second day the ships were becalmed. The next morning the wind picked up and soon the dark peak of the Brigantín Mountain to the south of Cumaná appeared on the horizon. By nightfall, the ships had dropped anchor in the Bay of Bordones, three miles to the west of the city. Although too ill to disembark, English still dreamed of leading his troops to victory. 'If not sufficiently strong to ride on horseback,' he wrote as he lay in his cabin, he should be carried at the head of the Legion in his hammock.[2] In the darkness, the men were rowed ashore, landing 'upon a beach of shingles', where they made camp.[3] Too nervous to sleep, Captain Chesterton spent the night listening to 'the ceaseless roar of the sea' and imagining the dangers that lay ahead.[4]

Founded in 1521 on the site of an old Franciscan mission, where the river Manzanares meets the sea, Cumaná was the first European settlement built in South America. Standing amongst 60ft coconut groves, the city was framed by the cloud-wreathed mountains of New Andalucia rising up to the south. Although destroyed on several occasions by earthquakes, by 1819 Cumaná was 'large, well-built, and populous', boasted 'many handsome edifices worthy of notice' and supported a population of 20,000.[5] Its wide, sheltered bay was home to the Spanish fleet and protected by hundreds of cannon. Dominating the city on a hill rising from the plain was the star-shaped Castillo de Santa Maria. Covered trenches connected the castle to strong outlying blockhouses and numerous batteries.

The morning after the landing, the volunteers awoke to 'a cloudless sun' and 200 reinforcements.[6] The mounted guerrillas of Colonel Montes, who operated from a base in the mountains to the south, failed to impress the British officers, however, one of whom compared them contemptuously to 'a horde of Italian banditti'.[7] After the officers' horses and baggage mules had arrived from their overland trek from Barcelona, the troops marched on Cumaná. The first leg would see them loop round the city behind the Colorado hill whilst the fleet sailed into the harbour. Orders had been given that the men should march 'six paces apart ... to cajole the Spaniards' into thinking that they faced a greater enemy.[8] Heading uphill away from the beach, they hiked eastwards, passing through groves of stunted trees and cacti.[9] It was a 'close and sultry' day. Little water and few rations were available.[10] Several men collapsed in exhaustion and one of Urdaneta's aides died of fatigue.

Watching their progress from the city walls was Lieutenant Sevilla, one of the dwindling band of Spaniards who had sailed from Cádiz with Morillo in 1815. Having interrogated a drunken English deserter, Sevilla was unsurprised by the Legion's sudden arrival, but was impressed by the soldiers' discipline on the march. As he watched the advance, he realized they were 'troops with a good level of training', in contrast to the American irregulars he had frequently faced over the last four years.[11] The lieutenant's commander, Brigadier Tomás de Cires, was also worried. His garrison was heavily outnumbered and scores of men were languishing in hospital suffering from tropical diseases. Like many of the royalist troops in the country, his men had lost faith in the cause and their morale was desperately low. Watching the 1,000-strong column snaking its way towards the city whilst Brion's fleet entered the bay, the brigadier feared the worst.

Aboard one of the patriot brigs of war, General English gathered his strength and hauled himself up onto the deck to observe the enemy position. 'At three o'clock' in the afternoon, they passed the Spanish fortifications and gunboats anchored beneath them.[12] Skirting the far shore, the ships opened fire, unleashing 'broadsides' at extreme range.[13] Startled by the sudden gunfire, flocks of 'brown pelicans, egrets and flamingoes' took to the air.[14] Dense smoke clung to the water, stabbed through with flame as the round shot hurtled towards the forts. The patriot column on the hills above the bay paused to watch the spectacle. Colonel Low thought it 'had an exquisite panoramic effect', but at such long range Brion's fire caused little damage.[15] Speaking to the colonel the following day, English joked that he would arrange a donation of 'three and six pence a man ... for contributing so highly to ... [the troops'] amusement'.[16]

As the sun sank beneath the horizon, the patriot column reached the river Cumaná. Swollen by rainfall in the mountains to the south, the river was deep and fast flowing, and the troops had to wade up 'to their necks' to get to the other side.[17] Setting up camp on the far bank, they passed the night tormented by hordes of mosquitoes.[18] Waking the next morning, they crossed 'an extended sandy plain, thinly skirted with wood' which offered little shade.[19] The volunteers' skin blistered and burnt and their thirst raged uncontrollably. Having looped round the city, the troops then passed close to the enemy batteries on the walls. The royalists hurled insults, but saved their powder for the main attack. Stopping on a 'marshy plain' to the east of the city known as Cantaro, the patriots then set up camp as it began to rain.[20] For the fourth consecutive night Captain Chesterton lay awake, listening to occasional shots as skirmishes broke out between the pickets under the walls.

Later that night, Colonel Low and Lieutenant Oben of the Legion reconnoitred the enemy positions with Colonel Montilla of Urdaneta's staff. Crossing a series of gentle hills that lay between them and the city, the officers crept up to the ridge line and surveyed the fortifications ahead. Low was pleased with what he saw. Cannon placed on the heights could be used to pound the royalists' positions into submission, whilst an infantry assault against Agua Santa, a strong house built on a commanding hill, stood a good chance of success. Returning to the camp, the officers presented Urdaneta with their report, fully expecting him to approve the attack.

The next morning, however, Urdaneta proposed that they abandon the assault and reiterated his plan to march south-east to Maturín, a town on the edge of Los Llanos halfway to Angostura. As soon as General English heard of Urdaneta's proposal, he disembarked and convened a meeting to convince Urdaneta to change his mind, believing that the men would mutiny if they left without a fight.[21] After a lengthy discussion, Urdaneta 'reluctantly' conceded, but insisted that responsibility for the action should be English's alone.[22] The general had never commanded men in action before and was loath to risk his reputation, but under pressure from his officers, 'at length, [and] with a doleful countenance he agreed'.[23]

Having made their decision, English and his staff then rode round the city, studying the fortifications until they were driven off by a company of enemy Grenadiers. Having seen what they were up against, the officers concurred with Low and Oben's conclusions and began planning a pre-dawn assault on Agua Santa. Men were then called for to form a Forlorn Hope. To his delight, English was swamped with volunteers and 150 were accepted. Captain Sadler, a young man from Tipperary, was given the honour of spearheading the attack, whilst Lewis Lyons, a popular lieutenant 'of the most sterling bravery, and ... engaging manners' was chosen as his second in command.[24] A body of 100 Hanoverian riflemen, under Major Friedhenthal, and the expedition's two light cannon were to provide covering fire. In the first of a series of moves seemingly designed to undermine the attack's chances of success, Urdaneta insisted that overall command should be given to Lieutenant-Colonel Harrison, the officer responsible for prematurely springing the ambush at El Morro. Colonel Low was stunned by the decision. Nor was he alone in believing him 'the worst ... [officer] that could ... [have been] chosen' to lead the attack.[25]

Agua Santa was just one of a string of fortifications ringing the city, but due to its prominent position atop a steep 'sugar-loaf hill' it was the key to unlocking the entire defence.[26] Nevertheless, it was far from impressive, being no more than a 'miserably built' single-storey blockhouse, loosely constructed of 'wood and mud'.[27] Two large cannon had been placed behind ramparts at the foot of the walls. The rest of the garrison held the rooftop, from where they could retreat through a trap door into the heart of the building as a last resort. Loopholes had been cut in the walls, and besides their muskets, the defenders were also armed with rudimentary grenades. A ditch surrounded the fort and a covered communication trench, connecting to the castle of San Juan, provided an escape route should the blockhouse be overrun.

Before dawn on 4 August, the storming party set out. Led by two local guides they marched through ravines to keep out of sight, whilst the officers passed up and down the line urging the men to keep quiet. Captain Chesterton was impressed. 'Not a word was spoken, and so light was the tread of this obedient band, that nothing ... denoted their measured footsteps.'[28] Unknown to the British officers, however, their guides had betrayed them. Instead of leading them to Agua Santa, they emerged near the main defences where they were in danger of being cut to pieces by the cannon lining the walls. Fortunately for the volunteers, Major Friedhenthal immediately realized their predicament. Drawing his sword, he killed one of the guides on the spot. The other escaped and raced towards the walls. The men then retraced their steps. At dawn they were still approaching their target, and the rising sun revealed their position to the sentries at Agua Santa. Meanwhile, General English had manhandled the two 6-pdrs into position on a nearby rise to support the assault. To his consternation, however, Urdaneta ordered the guns away, saying the British had no authority to use them. Colonel Low looked on in disbelief, knowing that 'in a short time' the guns 'would have knocked ... [Agua Santa] to pieces'.[29] Far from being 'of no use' as the Creoles claimed, they 'were the very article ... that [they] ... were alone in want of'.[30]

Unaware of the bitter argument raging just a few hundred yards away, the storming party charged up the slope into a maelstrom of musket and cannon fire. Grapeshot scythed through the ranks killing an officer and a handful of men. Before the Spanish gunners could reload, the survivors hurled themselves into the ditch. The enemy on the roof then threw grenades down amongst them. Meanwhile Friedhenthal's riflemen had taken up position and the accuracy of their Baker rifles soon made the rooftop a living hell. Defenders who 'appeared at the loopholes, the gangways, or on the ramparts ... were picked off in a moment'.[31] Emboldened by the covering fire, the Forlorn Hope charged the guns. As they closed, the defenders dared to squeeze off a volley. Hit in the head, Captain Sadler was killed instantly along with three others. The rest reached the barricades where hand-to-hand fighting broke out. Whilst wrenching a musket from the hands of his opponent, Lieutenant Lyons was also shot dead. Dozens more attackers took his place and the defenders were quickly overwhelmed.[32] Hunted down, they were killed with bayonet thrusts to the chest. After the initial bloodshed, a stalemate ensued. Although safe under Friedhenthal's covering fire, the storming party had no way of getting at the Spaniards inside. English had failed to provide ladders to scale the battlements, or even axes to breach the walls.

As the attackers pondered their next move, the wounded were taken down the hill to 'an old uninhabited convent' where Surgeon Richard Murphy and his assistant, Mr Gray, had set up a field hospital.[33] With raw spirits the only anaesthetic, the patients felt every cut of the scalpel and pull of the saw. Shattered limbs were amputated, wounds probed and balls extracted with tongs. Heavy bleeding was stemmed with tourniquets; serious wounds were cauterized in the fire; whilst smaller cuts were covered with improvised dressings, moistened with water, vinegar or wine.[34]

Two hours after the assault had begun, Urdaneta's bugler sounded the retreat. At first, the volunteers refused to believe their ears. A second and third call went unanswered, but after the fourth, they reluctantly retreated down the hill. Freed from the blockhouse, the defenders rushed out to load their cannon and soon grapeshot was tearing into the men, whilst the gunners on the city walls joined in the slaughter with round shot. Fearing royalist cavalry would sally out and butcher the survivors, Blosset formed the rest of the Legion into column to receive them. Nearby, believing themselves out of range of the guns, English and his staff were picking over 'the miserable details' of the day when an 18lb shot came 'booming through the air' and thumped into the convent at their backs.[35] The building 'was knocked to atoms'. The wounded were showered with debris and a cloud of white plaster rose up around the general and his staff.[36] Within seconds more round shot came skimming towards them. Several near misses whistled overhead, causing ripples of involuntary 'ducking' to flow through the ranks.[37] Other shot smashed directly into the column. Ripping through the formation, they tore off heads and limbs and showered the survivors with gore. To prevent further bloodshed, English then ordered a general retreat. Although the American troops scattered, the men of the Legion left the field in good order. With 'the shot striking close [to the] right and left of [the] column', they marched back to camp. It was 8.00am. Three hours had passed since Captain Sadler had led the attack.[38]

In total, 77 men had fallen, most killed or wounded by cannon fire during the retreat. Three officers were amongst the dead and many of the wounded would succumb to their injuries. Morale was at an all-time low. On the march back to camp, the men openly voiced their contempt for English and Urdaneta, blaming them equally for the disaster. For his part, English had allowed them to go into action fatally unprepared. If the storming party had been supplied with siege ladders, then Agua Santa would surely have fallen. Although he would later blame his illness and Urdaneta for the defeat, English was simply not up to command. The former clerk was a kind man with the best interests of his troops as heart, but was hopelessly out of his depth and too proud to admit it.[39] Urdaneta's culpability is equally undeniable. But as an officer with several campaigns behind him, his failure cannot simply be blamed on inexperience. Several British officers even suggested that the disaster may have been by deliberate design. Jealousy of the success of others and fear that his cowardice could be exposed may well have led Urdaneta to stop English deploying the cannon. The order to retreat is otherwise difficult to explain.[40]

As the men of the British Legion marched back to their encampment, they intercepted a band of 40 royalists sent from Cariaco as reinforcements for Cumaná. At first Colonel Valdés, Urdaneta's second in command, mistook the troops for patriots. In the confusion, 20 dashed past the Legion and made it to safety. The remainder tried 'to cut their way through', but were hopelessly outnumbered. Most were killed by men keen to avenge their dead comrades, but a few were captured and taken back to camp. Amongst them was 'a fine' young Grenadier captain, born in Spain of British parents.[41] The 19-year old's plight attracted the sympathy of the Legion's officers and his bravery endeared him to the men. Although the British begged Urdaneta to spare him, that night he 'and his men [were] taken [some way from camp] ... and privately butchered'. Captain Chitty saw their bodies the next morning. After being stripped and bound together, 'their hands [had been] nearly severed from their bodies by ... machetti, and several light wounds inflicted upon them ... by way of torture, before the finishing stroke was given'.[42] Later that morning, other officers also went to gaze upon the captain's 'mutilated remains'.[43] The sight 'was a death-blow to all ... past enthusiasm' and from that moment on, several conspired to desert.[44]

The morning after the attack, General English sought out Urdaneta to berate him for his actions the previous day. As a heavy rain fell that would persist for ten days, he insisted that the troops should attack again, reasoning that with the aid of the cannon the fort would surely fall. Despite 'a warm debate', Urdaneta remained unconvinced and again proposed they abandon the attack and march inland.[45] As the division's supplies were running low, and the men now reduced to a diet of sugar cane and the occasional plantain, English was forced to concede defeat. The next day the men broke camp and marched south, heading for Maturín. His pride stung, English felt he could no longer serve alongside Urdaneta so he returned to Margarita with some of his staff, the artillery and the Legion's sick and wounded. With the jeers of his men ringing in his ears, he boarded a waiting boat and was rowed out to the *Henrietta*. It was an ignominious end for the general. To make matters worse, his health deteriorated during the voyage and he arrived 'wearied both in spirits and body'.[46] At midnight on 11 August 1819, as he stumbled ashore at Margarita, his only consolation was that his wife was awaiting him at Pampatar.

After seeing their general depart, the remnants of the Legion set off for Maturín. Whilst each officer was allotted an Indian porter to carry his knapsack, the men were afforded no such luxuries. Heavily laden, they struggled across the waterlogged plain, sinking up to their knees with every step. A grisly sight awaited them as they passed the city walls. The head of Lieutenant Lyons had been 'stuck on a pole on the battlements' to bid them a macabre farewell.[47] Later, the rain lightened to a steady drizzle, affording them a daunting vision of the dark peaks of the cordillera of New Andalucia. Whilst most looked upon the sight with dread, Chesterton was inspired, thinking that the 'mighty mountains' promised untold adventure.[48] Further inland, the sandy plains of the coast gave way to ever denser vegetation and soon they were marching through thick forest alive with the 'yells of myriads of monkey'.[49] Exhausted, the volunteers stopped for the night at the camp of Colonel Montes's guerrillas at the base of the cordillera. Cattle were slaughtered and the beef distributed. Chesterton watched with disgust as his Indian porter, 'a fine stout fellow', devoured mounds of raw offal left for anyone who had the stomach to eat it.[50] After finishing their meal, the men settled down for the night. Wrapped in their cloaks, they shivered as the rain lashed down, listening to tigers prowling through the forest around them.

The next morning, the Legion climbed along a mountain ridge 'devoid of vegetation' which led the soldiers to the highest peak, known as 'The Impossible'.[51] Whilst the stragglers caught up, Chesterton took in the view enjoyed by Humboldt 20 years earlier. A sea of green swept downwards towards the bleached coastal plains and the shimmering waters of the Caribbean beyond. The bay of Bordones and the city of Cumaná were clearly visible in the distance. After descending from the heights, they made camp in a natural jungle clearing, cooking their meat on gigantic boulders which filled the bottom of a leafy ravine. On the next day's march, the men forded several streams now swollen by the downpour into dangerous torrents. Their shoes began to break apart and soon they were leaving a trail of bloody footprints behind them. At the end of the second day, they reached the 'populous hamlet' of Cumanacoa, a scattering of farms and tobacco plantations surrounded by open plains.[52] The excessive heat and hardships on the march had taken their toll and when the column broke camp the next morning, 140 men were too weak to continue. The remaining 600 pushed on. Some had exchanged a few belongings with the Indians in Cumanacoa for more provisions, whilst others picked guavas or shot and butchered monkeys to supplement their rations.[53]

After a week's trek through the stifling humidity of the jungle, passing Chaima Indian missions en route, the men emerged onto the plains around San Antonio.[54] As they marched through the tall grasses, parasitic insects known as 'jiggers' attacked them, burrowing their way under the men's toe nails, where they laid their eggs. Unless carefully dug out with the tip of a knife, they released thousands of larvae under the skin which feasted on flesh and left the men lame. Others fell foul of piranha or snakes whilst quenching their thirsts in the streams they had to ford. Disgusted with service conditions, several soldiers deserted. Feigning exhaustion, they dropped towards the rear of the column and sneaked out of line, making their way back to Cumaná to join the Spanish. When the men were missed at roll call, Urdaneta dispatched Montes's riders to round them up. A skirmish broke out when the two groups met on the peak of 'The Impossible'. The Lancers killed 16 amongst the rocks before the survivors threw down their muskets and surrendered. After being dragged back to camp, they were court-martialled and shot.

Near the hamlet of Aragua, the column crossed the Guarapiche, a fast-flowing river 'more than 25 fathoms deep' (over 200ft).[55] Selecting a narrow point, the men lowered themselves into the water. Aided by hide ropes tied to trees on the far bank, most made it safely across, but five were not so fortunate. After losing their footing, they were snatched away 'like a shot', the current 'dashing [them] … against stumps of trees, jutting rocks, and loose stones' until they slipped into unconsciousness and drowned.[56] Having seen his comrades carried to their doom, one 'timid wretch' sat down on the far bank and refused to cross.[57] Six good swimmers were sent back to fetch him. After trussing him up with rawhide, they dragged him through the torrent. Emerging spluttering and half drowned, he was hauled forward, tied to a tree and given 100 lashes. Mercifully the river proved to be the final trial of the march, and 11 days after they had set out from Cumaná, the 500 men remaining with the Legion arrived at Maturín.

Chapter 19

SANTAFÉ DE BOGOTÁ

When Barreiro's aide-de-camp reached Santafé on 8 August with news of the defeat at Boyacá, Viceroy Sámano panicked. In his arrogance he had made no preparations for a patriot victory. That evening, to conceal his inner turmoil, he hosted a party in his palace. The viceroy assured his guests that the rumours of defeat were unfounded and informed them that, in fact, Barreiro had 'cut' the insurgent army 'to pieces'.[1] Sámano was fully aware of just how precarious his situation had become, however, and was merely telling his supporters what they wanted to hear to ensure his own plans for escape would not be hindered. That night he left the party early and hurried back to his quarters. Throwing together a few possessions, he sneaked out of the city at dawn disguised as 'a Capuchin friar', accompanied by his personal guard.[2] After leaving the cobbled streets of Santafé behind them, the fugitives galloped north-west. Their destination was the town of Honda on the Magdalena River, from where gunboats would carry them to the safety of the royalist strongholds on the Caribbean coast. Others fortunate or senior enough to have been alerted rode south to Pasto or Popayán. The exodus was so sudden that over 'half a million pesos' in coin and gold bars were left in the royal mint and thousands of muskets, cartridges, uniforms and barrels of gunpowder were abandoned in the armouries.[3] Sámano even left a bag of gold coins on his desk. On 9 August, hundreds of lower-ranking royalist refugees began to stream out of the city on foot. Struggling under the weight of their hurriedly gathered possessions, they made slow progress, and the narrow roads leading out of the capital were soon congested with human traffic.

The next day, whilst crossing the bridge of Común, 20 miles to the north of Santafé, the patriot vanguard got word of Sámano's flight. Anzoátegui and O'Leary were dispatched in pursuit, whilst Bolívar, with 60 Llanero Lancers under Lieutenant-Colonel

Infante, advanced to secure the capital. En route to Honda, Anzoátegui's party stopped at the 'miserable' village of Hato Viejo, where O'Leary fought a duel.[4] In his memoirs, the Irishman is coy about the details of the encounter and, as a result, both the identity of his opponent and the result are unknown. Afterwards, they continued the pursuit, but although several fugitives and mules 'laden with doubloons' were captured, by the time they reached Honda, Sámano had already escaped down-river.[5]

Back in Santafé, an opportunistic mob had begun looting the shops and houses abandoned by the royalists, whilst the rest of the inhabitants congregated in the main squares to 'give loose to their joy'.[6] Several royalist officers who had been left behind were seen racing through town, desperately searching for horses so they could flee before the patriots arrived. By the afternoon, 'crowds of all ranks thronged the streets, congratulating each other on an event they had hardly dared to hope for'. Some 'busied themselves preparing triumphal arches in the Plaza', whilst others hurried out to greet Bolívar. All the while the mob continued its work, but at 5.00pm, when The Liberator and his escort arrived, order was soon re-established.[7] The looters melted away and the crowd pushed forward, 'wanting to see … the president to convince themselves it was true'.[8]

Bolívar lost no time in consolidating his hold on the city. Soldiers were dispatched to occupy the palace, the mint and the armoury. Huge quantities of arms and ammunition were found, providing a massive boost for the war effort. Some were distributed amongst the army in New Granada. The rest were shipped overland and by river to Venezuela for the units still fighting in the plains. A search of the mint soon turned up the riches abandoned by Sámano. As was typical of the age, a proportion of the plunder was taken by the army. The money trickled down through the ranks, with the generals getting the lion's share and their subordinates receiving increasingly smaller divisions. One proclamation suggests that Bolívar was granted 25,000 pesos, colonels 10,000 each, lieutenants 4,000 and so on, down to a share of 500 pesos for private soldiers.[9] In a letter to his family, Lieutenant Lee of Mackintosh's corps boasted that his prize money 'amounted to eight hundred' pesos, the equivalent of a year's pay.[10] On 12 August the infantry arrived.[11] The Black Rifles and Mackintosh's men led the column through cheering crowds. Overjoyed, locals rushed up to thank them and offer the officers lodging in their homes.[12] With 'not a pair of shoes or stockings' between them, the volunteers paraded barefoot just as they had crossed the mountains several weeks before.[13] Outnumbering the troops were the prisoners taken at Boyacá. As Barreiro and his officers shuffled past, the crowd hurled insults and jeered a royalist band that was forced to belt out martial tunes.

With a population of over 20,000, Santafé was the most impressive city the volunteers had seen in South America.[14] Built on a high fertile plain 8,200ft above sea level, the capital was overlooked by the 'steep ... almost inaccessible hill' of Monserrate. Looming 2,300ft above the centre, it was capped by two chapels offering spectacular views.[15] The central square below was dominated by a huge cathedral. Constructed from shining white stone, it could be seen from miles around.[16] On the far side of the square stood the palace formerly occupied by Sámano. Although an ugly brick building, its interior was 'fitted up in ... vice-regal splendour' and glorious paintings adorned its walls.[17] Radiating out from the main square were 'narrow, ill paved streets' with open sewers, flanked by rows of whitewashed houses, their central courtyards perfumed by orange trees.[18] Nearby was the Alameda, a broad street lined with poplars and public gardens which came alive in the evenings, when troubadours strummed guitars for strolling lovers and horse-drawn carriages carrying the city's elite rattled by. On the outskirts, beyond the hovels of the poor, lay green valleys dotted with farmhouses, where, to Lieutenant McGuire's astonishment, the peasants were capable of producing 'two crops in the year'.[19]

After the hardships of the campaign, the volunteers enjoyed their stay in the capital immensely. They were regularly paid and provisions were plentiful. Captain O'Leary pronounced 'the climate delightful' and claimed the men had 'every comfort' that money could buy.[20] 'More than all,' as Mackintosh attested, they were 'elated with victory'.[21] In September official celebrations began. 'Nicely done up' in new uniforms and sporting gold campaign medals hung on yellow ribbon, the British officers attended balls and banquets, eating, drinking and dancing with the young ladies of the capital, who they thought 'remarkably lively ... pleasing in their manners ... and delicately formed'.[22] Several affairs began and hearts were broken.[23] Those unable to attract a local girl would no doubt have patronized one of the capital's many brothels, where their prize money made them very welcome indeed. On Monday 24 August, a memorial service was held to remember those who had fallen in the campaign.[24] *Te Deum*s were given in the cathedral, and later, a procession headed by Bolívar, Santander and Anzoátegui marched through the streets. Twenty young girls dressed in white presented Bolívar with a crown of laurels. He passed it on to his generals, who in turn threw it to a group of British officers from the Black Rifles who were standing nearby.

Even before the celebrations had finished, Bolívar set about re-forming his army. Many of the prisoners captured at Boyacá were incorporated into the ranks. Some 400, nearly all natives of Venezuela, joined the Black Rifles, whilst Mackintosh's unit, now renamed the Albion Battalion, was reinforced with the recruits from Tunja that O'Leary had helped to train. Several volunteers were promoted. Lieutenant-Colonel Sandes, still recovering from the wounds he had suffered at Vargas, received official confirmation of his brevet rank (a temporary rank, normally one degree higher than one's pay), Mackintosh was made a lieutenant-colonel, Captain Johnstone, with his left arm still shattered but recovering well, received his majority and the 20-year old Lieutenant Wright, having 'distinguished himself in both' battles, became a captain.[25]

With no immediate threat from the enemy, the men were given extended leave. Lieutenant McGuire used the time to write home, informing his family that he was 'in good health, and would be quite happy if only' he could pay 'Mother, Brothers, and Sisters a visit now and again'.[26] Others explored the local countryside. Captain Richard Vowell, who had by now rejoined his comrades, visited the village of Zipaquira, where he found a Spanish edition of *Gulliver's Travels* in the house of a local priest.[27] Later, he made a trip to the waterfall of Tequendama, 20 miles to the south-west of the capital. After falling 330ft, the river Fúno crashed into a projection of solid rock, sending spouts of water in all directions and leaving a fine 'column of mist' suspended in mid-air. Enterprising local Indians had set up an unusual business in the area. After collecting a small sum from curious passers-by, they hurled tree trunks into the river. 'Like an arrow from a bow' they shot along the gorge and were launched into the abyss, momentarily defying gravity before plunging into the boiling waters below.[28]

In Santafé, Bolívar was busy directing the ever-expanding republic. From his offices in the palace on the main square, he dispatched units to hold towns to the north, south and west of the capital, whilst organizing a provisional government. Although eager to return to the campaign trail, he reluctantly accepted the office of president, choosing Santander as his deputy. Bolívar was also concerned with providing for the voiceless victims of war. On 19 September, an edict was issued to set up a charitable school in the capital to educate orphans whose fathers had died in battle.[29] When not working in the palace, he retired to a villa halfway up the slope to Monserrate, a quiet haven of rose gardens where he could escape the pressures of command.

In victory, Bolívar could afford to be magnanimous to his prisoners. Whilst the Spanish-born rank and file were forcibly pressed into the army, the Americans who wished to return to their homes were allowed to do so. Only those who refused to renounce the royalist cause and the higher-ranking officers remained in custody. On 9 September, Bolívar wrote to Sámano at Cartagena, proposing a prisoner exchange. Amongst others, The Liberator asked for the release of MacGregor's volunteers captured at Portobelo. Santander, who had previously been a vehement opponent of reconciliation, appeared to back the deal and even visited Barreiro in his quarters to keep him abreast of the negotiations. After The Liberator had left the capital for Angostura, however, it became apparent that Santander's goodwill was merely a pretence.

On the night of 10 October, he told the 38 Spanish officers to prepare for their imminent execution. The next day, shortly before noon, they were marched from their quarters in shackles to the opposite side of the square. As Santander and his staff watched from the palace gates, they were ordered to kneel in rows of four and shot in the back of the head. When Barreiro's turn came, he asked Colonel Ambrosio Plaza, who was leading the parade, to pass on a final message to his fiancée. 'Moments later ... the volley was fired at his back.'[30] Bolívar was furious when he learnt what had happened. Having hoped to leave the 'War to the Death' behind him, Barreiro's execution was a major setback to his plans. More worryingly, Santander's wilful disobedience was a sign of the turmoil that was to come. Like Páez and Piar before him, the New Granadan had his own political agenda and was already looking beyond the end of the war to the power scramble that peace would bring.

Chapter 20

THE THIRD WAVE

B ack in Britain, a further wave of volunteers, divided into two separate expeditions, was preparing to leave for South America. New troops for General MacGregor made up the first group. As news of his defeat at Portobelo had yet to reach Europe, the general's reputation had remained intact and recruits were still being attracted into Colonel Maceroni's offices at a tremendous rate. Aided by Colonel Eyre, another Irish veteran of the Napoleonic Wars, Maceroni recruited a further 1,000 men in the summer of 1819. Before they left British shores, the captains of the seven ships that would carry the new volunteers had been told to make for Aux Cayes in Santo Domingo, where it was promised patriot representatives would be waiting for them.

The second body of troops to leave Britain that summer was 'General' John Devereux's Irish Legion.[1] 'A handsome … fine looking man,' and 'eminently endowed with … eloquence', Devereux impressed all those he met.[2] Beneath the charm, however, lay a charlatan who was the least scrupulous and most profiteering of all those who enlisted men for the cause. As a young man, Devereux had been forced into exile in the United States after his father had become involved in the failed Irish Rebellion of 1798. In Baltimore, he worked as a merchant for the Oliver brothers for several years before turning up in Paris in 1812, where he began a hugely successful career as a con man. Posing as a representative of the United States government, he convinced the French authorities to sign over several confiscated cargoes held in the port of Naples, and returned to Baltimore a rich man. In 1815, learning of the wars raging in South America, he hired a schooner which he loaded with arms and ammunition and embarked for Cartagena, intending to sell the cargo to the patriots on arrival. Bolívar was delighted with the shipment and the two men went on to discuss the possibility of Devereux raising an Irish Legion for the republican cause. Despite his boasts to the contrary, Devereux had no military experience, however, and so on his return to Ireland in 1818, he enlisted the help of Colonel William Aylmer, a veteran of the Austrian Army, as his second in command. The recruiting flyer that they produced offered all 'effective and spirited Men … a most favourable opportunity to … acquire a handsome Provision for … Life'. As a further enticement, Devereux drew parallels between Ireland's struggle to throw off the yoke of English subjugation with Bolívar's fight against the Spaniards. These ideas were taken up by the Irish press thereby turning what was, in reality, extortion on a gigantic scale, into a focal point for national pride. Despite lacking the authority to ensure that his promises were kept, Devereux offered the following seven point package to any who volunteered:

1st   Four pence in the Shilling more than the British Army.

2nd   A passage to Head Quarters, with 60 pesos on arriving.

3rd   1lb of Beef or Pork, 1lb of Bread, 1 ½ lb of Potatoes, 1 Noggin of Whisky per day.

4th   Oatmeal and Butter, &c &c &c on the passage.

5th   A Proportionate share of Land, Captures and Prize Money.

6th   200 Acres of Land, with 80 Pesos to Purchase Implements of Agriculture.

7th   A Full Discharge and leave to sell the land, with a free passage home, if required, after 5 years service.[3]

Unlike previous commanders, Devereux sold the commissions for his Legion, thereby amassing the huge sum of £60,000.[4] As he only profited from recruiting officers rather than rank and file, this led to a ludicrous imbalance of power. One 'regiment' embarked with a single soldier commanded by over 20 officers. Initially, the higher ranks fetched as much as £1,000 each, but as the British Government became increasingly hostile towards enlistment, Devereux grew more anxious to conclude the business and the price fell to as little as £100.[5] Nevertheless, even after expending £7,000 on provisions and ships, he was left with a massive profit.[6] The vast majority of those recruited had little or no military experience. One volunteer wrote that 'a great number … were old men, and many others quite unfit for service'. Another described them as inexperienced 'feather-bed soldiers', whilst Captain Chitty, who saw them land at Margarita, thought them a 'confused, heterogeneous mass, varying from the peasant fresh from the ploughshare, to the artisan, whose close, sedentary occupation rendered him sickly and altogether unfit for the active duty of a soldier'.[7]

Although most of Devereux's senior officers would prove unfit for command, there were two notable exceptions. Brigadier General Middleton Power, a Napoleonic veteran of 22 years experience, raised the 1st Light Infantry, an excellent body of men led by a string of competent officers that would serve the republic well. The other officer of note was the second in command of the Irish Lancers, Lieutenant-Colonel Francis Burdett O'Connor. Although he had no experience of combat, O'Connor would prove to be an excellent leader and was utterly dedicated to his men. His career in Bolívar's army would span 20 years and take him from the Caribbean coast to the Altiplano of Bolivia.

Fuelled by the grinding poverty in Ireland, the efforts of the liberal press and the backing of prominent politicians such as Daniel O'Connell, Devereux's recruitment was exceedingly successful. Even the publication of Colonel Hippisley's narrative in late 1819, which was scathing in its criticism of Bolívar's republic, did little to curb the wave of enthusiasm that swept over Ireland and, in total, 1,728 men were enlisted.[8] By early 1819, the recruiting business had become so lucrative that the competition for signatures between the representatives of MacGregor and Devereux turned into a fierce rivalry. On 4 August, Devereux was attacked by MacGregor's brother whilst staying in a Dublin hotel. The general took legal action and his attacker narrowly escaped a prison sentence. Earlier in January 1819, an even more serious incident had occurred in Gravesend, when two rival parties encountered each other whilst waiting to embark for the New World. 'After getting drunk, they began to quarrel.' The argument escalated and 'ended in a regular battle, with swords and bayonets' being used. A number of the protaganists 'were apprehended and committed to Maidstone Gaol, for cutting and maiming some of the other party'. A report in the *British Monitor* concluded that 'should they die', the attackers 'will be tried for murder'.[9]

Eventually, such high-profile incidents forced the government to take action. In June 1819, the Prince Regent's proclamation was followed by the more resolute Foreign Enlistment Act, which forbade 'British subjects from taking part in disputes between the King of Spain and those who ... seek to govern ... parts of ... South America'. In response, a meeting was held at the George and Vulture Tavern near Saint Paul's, calling together 'some of the most respectable merchants ... engaged in the South American trade'.[10] Fearing business was coming to an end, they petitioned parliament, but despite their efforts, the bill was passed and recruitment in London ground to a halt. Beyond the capital, however, Westminster continued to turn a blind eye to the practice and the Irish Legion's activities were as blatant as ever. When the *Henry* sailed from Dublin, for example, 'crowds of people assembled' on both sides of the Liffey 'and followed the vessel as far as the point of the lighthouse, where three unanimous and loud cheers bespoke the parting farewell'.[11] In fact recruitment continued unchecked in Belfast, Dublin and Liverpool until the summer of 1820, when changing circumstances in South America, rather than government intervention, finally brought the practice to a close.

Chapter 21

DISASTER AT RIO DE LA HACHA

Following his escape from Portobelo, General Gregor MacGregor returned to his old base at San Andres. The *Hero* arrived on 5 May 1819. Of the 500 volunteers he had taken to Portobelo in April, only 11 remained. Desperate to retain their loyalty, MacGregor meted out meaningless promotions. The ship's master, Captain Hudson, was made rear admiral of the National Navy of New Granada, coronets Colclough and Semple were raised to lieutenants and even the division's carpenter and purser were given commissions. Captain Dunham, a roving privateer who had seen MacGregor's expedition leave several weeks earlier, was shocked by the change that had come over the general. Nursing two broken ribs from his leap from the balcony and dressed in the threadbare nightshirt he had escaped in, he thought the normally irrepressible Scot cut a 'forlorn and destitute figure'.[1]

Nevertheless, MacGregor was not prepared to give up on his dreams of wealth and glory. Even whilst at Portobelo he had been thinking about his next move, and on San Andres he began to set his plan in motion. Over the previous eight years he had built up contacts throughout the region and had recently received letters from acquaintances in Rio de la Hacha (Riohacha), a sizeable port on the coast of New Granada, inviting him to oust the Spanish garrison, promising he 'would be received with open arms'.[2] After leaving a few men on San Andres with assurances that he would be back within three weeks, he set sail for Rio de la Hacha with fresh optimism. Arriving in mid-May, Hudson dropped anchor well out of cannon range of the Spanish fort onshore. A boat was then lowered and sent towards the beach. As MacGregor looked on, a crowd streamed out of town to receive it. Unsure of their intentions, he ordered a warning shot from one of the *Hero*'s 18 cannon. The round shot went screaming overhead, the crowd fled in panic and the guns mounted in the fort returned fire. With the balls splashing about them,

MacGregor's sailors spun the boat round as fast as they could and were soon safely back on board. Unknown to the Scot, General Hore had discovered the letters from Rio de la Hacha's patriot sympathizers amongst the documents he had captured at Portobelo, and had informed José Solís, the Spanish governor at Rio de la Hacha, who had known about MacGregor's plan for some time.

With the governor alerted, MacGregor knew he would need more men to fulfil his ambitions and he set sail for Aux Cayes, Santo Domingo, where the second wave of volunteers recruited by Maceroni and Colonel Eyre had arrived. Rear Admiral Hudson was by now thoroughly sick of the whole affair and 'daily bickerings took place' as the *Hero* cut due north through the Caribbean.[3] To make matters worse, disease broke out shortly after Santo Domingo was sighted, prompting MacGregor to detour to Port-au-Prince to rid the ship of those infected. Fortunately for the Scot, his chief detractor was amongst them. After dumping Hudson and Colclough on the beach without even a single peso to support themselves, MacGregor renamed the ship the *MacGregor* in his own honour, and continued to Aux Cayes.[4] Despite his precautions, the fever stayed with them and Lieutenant Semple died as they approached their destination. Whilst the general looked on, 'smoking a cigar', Semple's body was thrown into Flamand Bay.[5] Doubtful of the reception he was to receive in Aux Cayes, MacGregor then anchored off the Isle de la Vache out of sight of the second wave of 350 volunteers who were awaiting him.

As the recruits had left London before news of Portobelo had broken, they had only heard of their comrades' fate after landing at Aux Cayes. To make matters worse, it soon became apparent that MacGregor had made no provision for their arrival. Amongst the new officers was Lieutenant-Colonel Michael Rafter, the brother of MacGregor's second in command at Portobelo who was now languishing in a Spanish dungeon in Panama. The colonel, who would later write a memoir about his experiences, was bitterly disappointed with the state of affairs at Aux Cayes. The men were desperately low on provisions, medicine, arms and ammunition, and disease had already broken out. One of the first victims was Major Lockyer. 'Well known to the public in consequence of a fatal duel … on the Isle of Wight', Lockyer had spent the last two years hiding from the authorities in England before embarking on his ill-fated adventure.[6] With the death toll mounting, several volunteers resigned and paid for their passage back to Europe. The majority, however, had not brought enough money for the voyage and were soon forced to seek employment on nearby plantations or beg in the streets of Aux Cayes to buy food. Others sold their uniforms and equipment. The 'richly laced' coats, 'polished helmets' and 'brilliant epaulettes' were snapped up by locals for a fraction of their original cost, leading to ridiculous scenes as the farmers of Santo Domingo 'proudly strutted about in their borrowed plumes'.[7]

Flamand Bay was an unlikely setting for such suffering. A perfect natural anchorage, it was surrounded by 'majestic hills' which rose around it 'in a varied amphitheatre … their lofty summits clothed in luxuriant hanging woods'.[8] The rainforest abounded with plantains, oranges, limes, tamarinds and coconuts, and the officers would go hunting for monkeys and wild pigs to supplement their meagre supplies. On 31 May, after a month spent skulking on the Isle de la Vache, MacGregor dared to join them. As he sailed into the bay, the *MacGregor* ran aground on a sandbank puncturing her hull. Although she took a full 36 hours to sink, not all of the sick on board were taken ashore and several drowned in their berths. Seemingly unconcerned, MacGregor set about selling the wreck as scrap. With the resulting 500 pesos, he set himself up in comfortable quarters in town with Colonel Eyre, whilst his men continued to suffer.

All the while new boatloads of volunteers were arriving and, by early August, 900 had gathered in town. On 14 June the *Amelia*, a schooner from London loaded with muskets, pistols, sabres and gunpowder had dropped anchor, briefly raising the men's hopes that the expedition could finally set sail. When word of her arrival reached the Haitian custom officials, however, the stores were seized. Then, on 18 September, the *Lovely Ann* arrived, with several French and Italian officers commanding British troops under Colonel de Lima. Their voyage across the Atlantic had been anything but easy. 'Mortified at the idea of being commanded by a foreigner', the men had been unruly from the moment they had left British shores.[9] At first their dissent 'was confined to abuse and invective', but by the morning of 3 August, it had turned into open mutiny.[10] Whilst the ship's master, Captain Gibson, stood to one side, the British and Continentals had lined up facing each other across the deck, 'armed with muskets, blunderbusses, pistols, sabres and boarding pikes'.[11] Just when bloodshed seemed inevitable, an officer of the Rifle corps had intervened, brokering an uneasy peace which lasted the remainder of the voyage.

Once at Aux Cayes, De Lima's officers realized that their problems had only just begun and with the sole exception of the colonel, they resigned en masse. Some found work as music, language or art teachers. Others returned to Europe. With no support amongst his troops, De Lima was transferred to MacGregor's staff. Captain Gibson tried to sail from the island, but was stopped by MacGregor's men who ransacked the *Lovely Ann*, stealing everything they could lay their hands on. In a letter published in the Irish press, Gibson complained that he was even 'compelled to give MacGregor what liquor [he] had left on board for [the Scot's] own use', even though he was already owed over £7,000 by Maceroni.[12] MacGregor, on the other hand, was delighted. The *Lovely Ann* had brought out sufficient provisions to last the volunteers 20 days and as the Scot now also had enough muskets to arm them, he decided to sail for Rio de la Hacha before his much reduced band disappeared entirely.[13]

On 27 September the fleet set sail. Of the seven ships that had arrived in Aux Cayes in the previous six months, only three left with MacGregor. The rest had sailed for England, the United States or Canada after their leases had expired. Just 258 of the 1,300 men, women and children who had come from Britain were on board, the majority only agreeing to sail 'from the absolute dread of perishing from want'.[14] The illnesses that had already claimed hundreds of lives at Aux Cayes continued to plague them as they sailed south. On board the *Lovely Ann*, ten men, three women and two children 'died in a very few days'.[15] Amongst the victims was one of Colonel Eyre's daughters, 'an amiable young creature, whose gentle manners' and good looks had caught the eye of many a volunteer.[16] A few days into the voyage, a 'pitiless storm' broke out. Whilst the women slept under cover, the men remained on deck. The high seas, wind and rain lasted for five days.[17] MacGregor responded by issuing more meaningless promotions. Amongst the beneficiaries were colonels de Lima and Eyre who both received general's commissions for their misplaced loyalty.

On the sixth day the volunteers awoke to a scene of unusual splendour. 'The wind had abated, the sea had fallen' and the horizon was clear. Lieutenant-Colonel Rafter trained his telescope southwards towards the coastline. 'Far away … appeared the Sierra Nevada, or snowy mountains of Santa Marta, their silvery pinnacles lighted up with the first beams of the rising sun.'[18] At 10.00am Rio de la Hacha was spotted, and by midnight the *Amelia* had dropped anchor in the bay. At first all was calm, but when MacGregor ran up the New Granadan flag, the Spanish gunners in the fort opened fire and the ships were forced to sail out of range.

Founded in 1545, Rio de la Hacha had once played a prominent role in the Spanish Empire. As well as being an important centre for trade, it had provided safe haven for the treasure galleons laden with Peruvian silver which passed by every year on their way to Cádiz. By 1819, however, its glory days were far behind. The galleons now sailed round Cape Horn and Rio de la Hacha's role as a trading port had been overshadowed by Santa Marta and Cartagena, its more prosperous neighbours to the south-west. The locals now scraped a precarious living dealing in wild horses, mules and long-horned cattle rounded up from the inland plains, or turtles taken from the mouth of the river which formed Rio de la Hacha's eastern boundary.[19] A small, square fort bristling with cannon pointing out to sea, and two shore batteries, one of which faced west along the beach, defended the town from raiders. To the south of the open harbour, several narrow, unpaved streets led to a central square. The low, timber houses were large and airy 'and thatched with the branches of the cocoa nut tree'.[20] The population of 2,500 were mainly Guajiro Indians, mixed with a handful of hardened Creole settlers and a garrison of 80 Spanish troops under the governor, José Solís. Traditionally loyal to the Spanish king, the Guajiros had a well-deserved reputation as fierce warriors and would often join the garrison as a local militia if the city came under attack. Dressed only in cotton loincloths or trousers, 'which did not reach below the knee', they wandered round town topless, with 'a profusion' of long 'lank' hair streaming down their 'dark copper' backs.[21] Some carried muskets and had cartridge boxes slung round their waists, but most favoured bows and arrows made of dried reeds, tipped with 'jagged fish-bones' and smeared with fast-acting nerve poison refined from the sap of local vines.[22]

Lying offshore out of range of the fort's cannon, MacGregor considered his plan of attack, whilst Lieutenant-Colonel Rafter trained his telescope on the town, witnessing the agitation their sudden arrival had caused. The white-coated Spanish soldiers, clearly distinguishable in the moonlight, were mobilizing the militia, whilst the women and children streamed out of town to hide in the surrounding forests. Having decided to attack, MacGregor sent the smallest ship of the flotilla, the *Alerta*, to find a suitable landing spot out of range of the shore batteries. Her mission completed, the *Alerta* then led the other ships three miles to leeward to a stretch of the coast called Mariangola.[23] Word was then passed round that the initial landing party should prepare to disembark. At 1.00am, 200 men under Lieutenant-Colonel Norcott boarded the boats and were rowed ashore. To everyone's surprise, the landing was unopposed. The men leapt from the boats, struggling to keep their feet in 'the violent surf', and splashed ashore. A company of riflemen was then sent to hold the wooded heights above the beach whilst the rest of the troops were landed. Two hours later they were ready to advance. Rafter's Rifles took the high ground on the right, Norcott led the guard of honour in the centre and Major Atkinson's Hibernia Battalion was on the left, its flank lapped by the waves breaking onshore. Whilst waiting for MacGregor to join them, Norcott drilled the men. The veterans were dismayed by their performance. Rafter complained that 'the greater number scarcely knew how even to shoulder their firelocks', let alone maintain discipline for a night attack.[24]

Just after 3.00am, a horde of Guajiro skirmishers came rushing through the woods. Rafter's troops met them with a steady fire. Several were killed and the rest fell back towards town. Down on the beach, Atkinson's men panicked when they heard the shooting and several opened fire towards the woods. A handful of riflemen were hit and the rest took cover until they ceased fire. After order had been re-established, Rafter pursued the fleeing Indians through the trees, whilst Norcott's and Atkinson's units advanced in column down the beach. 'An almost impenetrable forest of brushwood and branches … intersected by ravines and hollows' hindered Rafter's troops considerably. Advancing in pairs, one man forced his way forward, whilst his partner took cover, squinting along his rifle barrel into the gloom. At home in the undergrowth, the enemy easily kept ahead of them and maintained a harassing fire as they fell back. At sunrise, Rafter's men lost contact and the enemy melted back to its own lines. Still a mile from town, the men were ordered to halt whilst they waited for MacGregor and his staff to disembark.

Unknown to Rafter, Norcott and the others, the general and his staff had already been ashore. Shortly after landing they had approached a group of soldiers in the dark only realizing they were royalists when they opened fire. General de Lima, Lieutenant-Colonel Beridge and Captain Metsosa had all been wounded. The survivors had then struggled back to the boats and been rowed offshore. Meanwhile, Rafter's men were still waiting. Two hours passed. Whilst they gave voice to their frustration, the Guajiros crept through the undergrowth and surrounded them on three sides. Suddenly they opened fire. 'Five officers and fifteen men' were cut down by the first volley alone.[25] Norcott ordered the survivors to fix bayonets. As a 'smart, galling fire' rained down from the tree line, they dashed forward with a cheer.[26] Unused to such tactics, the Guajiros 'fled in confusion' before the attack hit home.[27] A series of 'huzzas' echoed up and down the lines and Norcott led the troops towards town, now visible for the first time in the distance.

As they neared the outskirts, the Spanish battery opened fire and 32lb iron shot scythed through the air. One skipped off the sand and hit Major Atkinson in the right thigh. The bone shattered and he died 'in extreme agony'. With the advance stuttering, the Indians closed in once more, 'their well aimed bullets and poisoned arrows' adding to the carnage caused by the guns. Amidst cries of 'we are betrayed' and 'where is MacGregor?' the British were pushed back three times. On each occasion their officers threw them back into the fray. Five hours into the action, the volunteers advanced into a clearing sheltered by tree stumps and rocks just 100 yards from the guns. In a moment of selfless lunacy, 2nd Lieutenant James Gibbons then leapt up from behind cover and charged, followed by 50 men. 'Thunderstruck' by their audacity, the Spaniards abandoned the guns and fell back. Norcott then beat off a hastily organized counter-attack, whilst Rafter led his riflemen into town. The house to house fighting that followed was perhaps the bloodiest of all. No quarter was given. Soldiers became trapped in houses, gardens or blocked roads with no escape, and bayonets were frequently used.[28] After five hours, the last of the defenders had either fled or been killed. The flag of New Granada was hoisted over the fort to 'heartfelt shouts of joy'.[29] A salute was then fired from the cannon. The volunteers' victory was complete.

Although they had won the battle, British losses had been considerably heavier than those of their enemy. Bodies littered the beach and woodland for three miles. One major, two lieutenants and 20 men had been killed, 41 had been wounded and six listed as missing. Only 50 Spaniards and Indians had fallen, most bayoneted in the street fighting at the end of the battle. The rest had fled into the woods surrounding town. Once the last shots had been fired, Lieutenant-Colonel Norcott set about organizing the defences. Considered to be too vulnerable to counter-attack, the outlying battery was abandoned after the cannon had been spiked. Houses were searched for supplies, and cattle were rounded up from the surrounding plains and corralled in the fort. Possession was taken of two schooners abandoned in the harbour and small parties of men were sent out into the woods to bring the wounded into town. Lieutenant-Colonel Norcott then rowed out to the *Hero* to report to MacGregor. Despite his reassurances, the Scot insisted on sailing closer into town to establish the security situation before disembarking. During Norcott's absence, discipline ashore broke down. 'The soldiers, and several of the officers' went rampaging through the abandoned houses searching for 'stores of wine and spirits'.[30] By the time Norcott returned, the troops were blind drunk.

The next morning Norcott and Rafter were summoned aboard the *Hero* and made full colonels for their bravery. Following the ceremony, MacGregor finally came ashore. Nursing hangovers from the previous night's excesses, the men greeted him with 'palpable … contempt'.[31] Some even spoke of shooting him for cowardice. Fearing for his life, MacGregor spent the day indoors, toasting the patriot cause and making speeches to his officers and the few locals that remained. That night he held a celebratory dinner. More drinking and speeches followed the feast. 'Elated by the sound of his own bombast', the Scot proclaimed himself 'Inca of New Granada', a title which bewildered all present.[32]

Meanwhile, the royalists were regrouping in the brushwood on the outskirts of town.[33] The volunteers were well aware of their presence as their camp was visible from the battlements and Guajiro warriors were frequently seen wandering through town. Lacking orders, the men allowed them to collect their wounded and secure any valuables that had been missed in the looting. MacGregor was unable or unwilling to take control and to make matters worse, the 80 locals he had armed and formed into a militia unit began to desert to the enemy. Soon only a handful were left. Realizing that it was only a matter of time before they were attacked, Colonel Rafter begged MacGregor to organize the town's defences, suggesting that he pull down the houses near the fort to clear the cannons' field of fire. MacGregor agreed to take care of matters, but did nothing other than arrange a meeting with Francisco, the leader of the Guajiros, who assured him his men meant them no harm. Their actions, however, betrayed their real intent. Whenever the volunteers ventured out of the centre they were fired upon. Several were killed and others chased back to town. Sensing that the situation was reaching breaking point, the last of the locals fled from their homes, leaving Rio de la Hacha eerily deserted.

On 7 October, a 'richly laden' Spanish schooner was sighted, her crew unaware that the town was no longer under royalist control.[34] Wearing a Spanish cocked hat as a disguise, Colonel Norcott took 15 men and rowed out towards her. The royalists were boarded before they had time to realize what was happening. Confronted with the heavily armed volunteers, they 'took shelter under the hatches' and surrendered without a fight.[35] The men, meanwhile, were growing increasingly unruly and as MacGregor did nothing to curb their behaviour, some of his officers decided to take matters into their own hands. One maimed a man who refused to stop looting and another shot a soldier dead for insubordination.[36] Colonels Rafter and Norcott, for their part, decided to abandon the mission altogether. On the night of 10 October, having gathered seven officers and 27 men to aid them, they crept out from their quarters, 'held a pistol at the watch' to stop them from raising the alarm, seized the captured Spanish schooner and sailed out of port.[37] Although the colonels intended to make directly for England, gales blew them off course and the ship was seized by the British authorities after limping into Jamaica. Penniless, the men were forced to join the garrison or find work on local plantations. The officers, on the other hand, had the money to pay for their passage home and reached Britain later that year.

On the morning of the 11th, MacGregor awoke to reports of Norcott and Rafter's betrayal along with credible rumours of an impending attack. Instead of alerting his men to the danger, the Scot chose to sacrifice them to ensure his own escape. After issuing orders allowing unrestricted plunder, he was rowed out to the ships, taking General Eyre's wife and children with him. Once on board, he ordered the captains to weigh anchor and sail offshore. In the meantime, any semblance of order that there had once been in town had disappeared entirely. Setting about an orgy of looting and destruction, the men didn't notice MacGregor had gone until it was too late.

With the *Amelia*'s cannon now well out of range and the volunteers in total disarray, the Guajiros realized the time to attack had come. Seeing what was about to happen, Lieutenant-Colonel Borel, one of the French officers recruited by Maceroni, tried to order the drunken looters into a makeshift defence. His poor English did little to aid his cause, however, and his pleas were ignored. The men continued plundering the houses and threatened to shoot the Frenchman if he got in their way. Meanwhile, the Indians were making their way towards the centre of town, firing on any volunteers who crossed their path. Those they encountered dropped their booty and ran. With their comrades encountering no organized resistance, hundreds more Indians poured into town with 'yells of savage horror'.[38] The volunteers panicked and fled in all directions. Many were killed in the streets. Others ran north to the beach and were butchered in the surf. Several who tried to swim out to the ships were shot amidst the breakers, whilst those who begged for quarter were bayoneted on their knees. Realizing there was no escape, 150 others headed for the fort. After barring the gates, they manned the cannon, answering single musket shots with 24lb round shot and grape. They held the enemy at bay for 30 minutes, but when one of the cannon was fired too near the powder store, a tremendous explosion ripped through the fort, killing or wounding 30 and leaving many others 'dreadfully scorched'.[39] Seeing all was lost, Lieutenant-Colonel Borel and two other officers slid down the ramparts into the waves and struck out for the fleet. They were hauled on board just as MacGregor gave the order to stand out to sea.

With General Eyre killed in the explosion, Lieutenant-Colonel Beridge took over command of the survivors in the fort. At first he was determined to fight on, but General de Lima persuaded him to negotiate. Stripping off his white shirt, he ran it up the flagpole to signal their surrender.[40] The gates were then opened and a swarm of Guajiros rushed in. Surrounded, the volunteers threw down their weapons and were locked in the dungeons beneath the fort. Fearing they would rise up and overthrow their guards, Governor José Solís decided to split his prisoners into two groups. Over the next few days 50 of the unwounded privates and NCOs and the women and children were marched inland to Valledupar. Solís then sent dispatches to Viceroy Sámano in Cartagena to ask for instructions as to what should be done with the remaining 61. The viceroy's reply was typically ruthless.

On 30 October, the three Catholics amongst the condemned were offered the last rites. General de Lima tried to bribe the Spanish when they entered his cell, but his offer of 2,000 pesos was refused. At 1.00am he was shot three times and died in his cell. The rest of the prisoners then had their hands bound and were taken down to the beach, where they were killed one by one. By 3.00am it was all over. The bodies were left to rot where they lay. The men who had been taken to Valledupar fared no better. At midday on 8 November, all but one were executed by firing squad. The survivor was a boy who convinced the Spaniards that he should be spared.[41] Along with the women and children he was then marched overland to Santa Marta.[42] Of the 250 volunteers who had disembarked at Rio de la Hacha, only 74 escaped with their lives.

Chapter 22

'I AM GOING THE WAY OF
ALL FLESH, SIR!'

In the summer of 1819, the first detachments of General John Devereux's Irish Legion sailed from Dublin, Liverpool and Belfast for the Venezuelan island of Margarita. To celebrate the occasion, several well-publicized farewell banquets were held at Morrison's, one of Dublin's most fashionable clubs. Local dignitaries such as Daniel O'Connell made patriotic speeches in the Great Room, accompanied by much 'cheering and waving of hats'.[1] Conditions on board the ships were far less harmonious. 'Insufficient' and 'inferior' rations caused protests on the *Hannah* and the teenaged commander of *La Forey*, Lieutenant-Colonel Robert Young, was faced with a potential mutiny just seven days after embarking.[2] With the Irish coastline still in sight, Young returned to shore where he dismissed the five officers and 42 men who had threatened to rebel before continuing for South America.

Once on the open sea, any excuse was used to alleviate the boredom of the daily routine. On 4 June the king's birthday was celebrated. The party went off 'in the usual manner ... and the men received an extra allowance of Grog'.[3] Lieutenant-Colonel Young then formed a gentlemen's club, which he named 'The Black Lion'. The organization had arcane rules. One stipulated that the president had 'to wear a cap, with the initial letters of the club ... marked with green ribbon'. Another decreed that each member had to memorize 'a song, or repeat a verse of Poetry' at every meeting. The real purpose, however, appears to have been to indulge in heavy drinking and most sessions ended with drunken dancing on deck.[4] On many of the ships, drinking and gambling were rife and on one no fewer than 'fifteen duels' were fought.[5] After landing at Margarita, matters continued to deteriorate. Due to the difficulty of maintaining communications between the island, Santafé and Angostura, the locals were unprepared for their arrival and no provision had been made to receive them. Many of the officers resigned within days. Hundreds more succumbed to fever and disease. Rations were poor and order broke down. Desertions and duels followed as the Legion tore itself apart.

One of the first to arrive was Captain Thomas O'Brien of the Irish Lancers. Unlike the majority of the Legion, the Lancers had enjoyed an uneventful voyage and when their ship anchored on 13 August 1819 after 40 days at sea, the men were 'in [the] greatest [of] health and spirits'. In Juan Griego, a village of 'sixty miserable huts, worse than the most wretched hovels in Ireland', it soon became apparent that all was not well, however.[6] For the first few nights O'Brien's men were forced to sleep in the streets. Wrapped in their cloaks, they shivered as the temperature plummeted and heavy morning dews soaked them to the skin.[7] Following their unsuccessful attack on Agua Santa, 150 sick and wounded from the British Legion, including their commander, General English, had reached the village two days before.[8] With no medicine, doctors, shelter, food or water they died in droves. The survivors further dispirited the Irish with tales of bad leadership and the terrible deprivations they had suffered on campaign. After two days, to O'Brien's relief, Admiral Brion requisitioned some mules to carry them to a makeshift hospital in El Norté. Several who fell from their mounts en route were left by the roadside and never got up again.[9]

Having believed Devereux's promises that they would be looked after on arrival, most of the Irish volunteers had brought little money with them and were soon reduced to selling their clothes and equipment to buy food. Captain William Adam 'gladly accepted 6 [pesos] … for the saddle and bridle which, in Dublin, had cost … [him] upwards of seven guineas'.[10] Another officer sold a sword worth over £21 for just 'one shilling worth of bread'.[11] Others deserted and made their way inland to look for work on local farms or signed up to serve on board the patriot privateers that regularly came into port. The rest took to fishing in the bay for sardines or, like Captain O'Brien, went hunting for deer and rabbit.[12] At the end of the month, lieutenant-colonels Harvey and Young arrived aboard the ships *Countess* and *La Forey*, enlarging the Irish presence on the island to some 600 men.

At the end of August 1819, a schooner named the *Simón Bolívar* appeared in the bay. Of the 120 British volunteers who had embarked from Angostura at the start of the month, 14 were veterans of the Apure campaign, the rest new arrivals recruited by Captain Elsom. According to Lieutenant Alexander Alexander, who had seen action with the Black Rifles at Caujaral the previous year, the journey had initially enjoyed a light-hearted air, with the newcomers teasing the old hands about their haggard appearance. Halfway down the Orinoco, however, yellow fever broke out. In the overcrowded conditions the disease spread with horrendous speed. Soon the majority of the 'unseasoned' troops were affected. The bleedings administered by their surgeons had little effect and by the time they reached the Gulf of Paria, between 'three and four' were dying daily.[13] Alexander tried to comfort the sick in their final moments. 'One of them said to me, with a look I shall never forget, "I am going the way of all flesh, sir." I was on the point of consoling him ... when he expired.'[14] The hurried funerals were tense affairs. 'Some of the officers ... called upon to read prayers' over the dead 'would grumble and put it off from one to another', fearful of contracting the disease themselves. Afterwards the bodies were slung overboard to be snapped up by waiting crocodiles and their personal effects were auctioned off in accordance with an old army tradition. The men 'bid ... with the greatest avidity'. The money raised was sent to their families at home.[15]

When the ship finally dropped anchor off Juan Griego, only 30 of the original 120 remained alive. Desperate to escape the 'death boat', they leapt into the water and swam for shore before the boats could come out to collect them. Captain O'Brien, who was watching from the beach, noted that 'their rum and clothes were all ... [they] took with them'.[16] Perhaps conveyed by mosquitoes infesting the water barrels on board, the *Simón Bolívar* had brought the fever with her, and soon it was making fresh inroads into the Irish onshore. In total a third of the Legion would die of the disease. Funeral processions occurred daily, with the victims interred in shallow graves on the beach, as the local priests refused them access to hallowed ground.[17] At night the locals dug up the dead and stole the clothes they had been buried in.

At midnight on 4 September, eight ships of the Spanish fleet appeared offshore.[18] After receiving word of the Legion's departure from their ambassador in London, the royalists had sailed from their base at Puerto Cabello to intercept the detachments yet to arrive. When the ships were sighted from the signal post above town, the drummers beat to arms and alarm guns were fired across the island. By 3.00am the defences 'were in perfect order'.[19] The defenders were a mixture of locals, Irish troops and American merchants resident in the village. Much to the disgust of some of the Irish officers, who believed gentlemen were above such things, all the soldiers from the rank of captain down were issued with muskets, powder and cartridges.[20] General English then set off round the island to gather all the foreign troops who had scattered in search of work. 'By six o'clock in the evening he returned, having rode fully sixty miles on one ... of the hottest days ever experienced on the island.'[21]

By the second day, 19 Spanish ships were visible offshore and the whole bay was in a state of panic. Locals were streaming out of the village, burying their valuables 'under every bush' and the road to the nearby village of Mota was packed with refugees.[22] Perhaps haunted by his failings at Agua Santa, General English was like a man possessed. After ordering a new central battery of 32-pdrs to be constructed, he took up a shovel and began digging the new earthworks himself.[23] 'The men [were] inspired … [and] carried on the work with Herculean strength.' Later, 'Mrs. English herself went to the battery, and gave … each man [working there] a glass of rum'.[24] That night huge bonfires were set alight to illuminate the bay whilst the troops worked on the battery in shifts.

During the blockade rations became scarcer than ever. Lieutenant O'Brien and his men had to survive on no more than 'a pint of oatmeal a day'.[25] By the third week, the volunteers were desperate. Some went inland to raid farmers' fields or steal provisions from locals' houses. The islanders took brutal revenge on anyone they caught. Several volunteers went missing, and the bodies of a few, including Lieutenant Byran of the Lancers, were later discovered in the hills to the east of town. The corpses were 'quite naked' and some had 'their heads cut off'.[26] Disease continued to decimate their ranks, and on 23 September, General English contracted yellow fever. At first he believed it was merely sunstroke brought on by his recent exertions, but whilst breakfasting with his wife he was struck down by excruciating pain.[27] Despite Mary's unstinting care and the close attentions of doctors Fitzgibbon and Main, the general's condition deteriorated rapidly. At 2.30pm he was given emetics and vomited 'full three pints of dark green bile'.[28] Then, after enduring a restless night, Fitzgibbon administered a dose of opium, mercifully rendering him 'insensible'.[29]

On 25 September, to the relief of those onshore, the royalist fleet weighed anchor and sailed away to the west, bringing the blockade to an end. In his official dispatch to Morillo, the Spanish Admiral, Fernando Lizarra, explained his actions. Supplies on board had been running low, his sailors were suffering from hunger, illness and low morale and, after three weeks at sea, his fleet had been reduced to just four serviceable vessels.[30] As soon as the ships had disappeared behind the headland, Colonel Harvey, Lieutenant-Colonel Young and several other 'holiday soldiers' abandoned the cause and set sail in three detachments.[31] The first made for Jamaica, where some found work on the plantations. Others enlisted in the local British Army battalion or paid for their passage home. The second sailed to Port of Spain in Trinidad. Whilst most of those on board returned to Europe, Captain William Adam and Lieutenant Jamieson sailed on to the Venezuelan mainland instead, intending to make their way overland to Angostura via Maturín to demand their back pay. The 30 unfortunates who sailed on the third ship, on the other hand, 'were destined never to see home again'.[32] Having been 'overtaken by a squall at St. Thomas's … the vessel was dashed to pieces' on the rocks. Only two of those on board survived.[33]

Back on Margarita, General English's disease was entering its final stages. On the third day, 'a few minutes before three o'clock', his weakened body was wracked by hour-long bouts of bloody vomiting. Unable to stand her husband's pain, Mary left the room.

The following day, 26 September, she was called back by the doctors when the general died. That afternoon his coffin was loaded onto a gun carriage draped with the Venezuelan and British flags. A total of 600 men, both locals and volunteers, marched behind to 'the mournful stroke of the muffled drum' as the procession wound its way inland.[34] At 5.00pm they arrived at the burial site – a beautiful spot 'in the centre of a large plain', surrounded by an amphitheatre of 'picturesque mountains'.[35] After the coffin had been lowered into the grave, the British troops fired three musket volleys. The report 'reverberated from the … mountains for many minutes'.[36] By this point, the whole of the island, 'men, women and children' had turned out to pay their respects – quite a tribute for a man who only two years earlier had been nothing more than a failed horse trader and military clerk.[37]

In the days after the funeral, the *Hannah*, with 200 officers and men of the 2nd Lancers, and the *Charlotte Gambier*, with Colonel Meade's Rifle Regiment on board, arrived at Juan Griego. With 1,000 volunteers now competing for the same limited resources, it was becoming increasingly difficult to maintain order in the village. The men 'lampooned their officers' and 'openly disobeyed them'. The commissioned ranks behaved little better.[38] Many passed the time drinking and playing 'Hazard and *Ving et Une*' at Black Sam's Inn or 'quarrelling and fighting duels' in the streets.[39] The officers' servants would spread the news of any upcoming challenges, so by the time the two parties met 'hundreds' of spectators had gathered.[40] Some were provoked by the most trivial of pretexts, one arising when a drunken officer claimed he had seen the Flying Dutchman, a legendary ghost ship said to haunt the Cape of Good Hope. His equally inebriated companion doubted his word and the storyteller immediately issued a challenge. They fired a pair of pistols apiece. All four shots went wide of the mark. The protagonists then resumed their conversation, 'as good friends as ever'.[41]

In late October the Legion marched to the town of Pampatar in an attempt to escape the epidemic at Juan Griego and the situation began to improve.[42] Merchant ships arrived daily, bringing fresh supplies to town.[43] Then a ship carrying cattle from Los Llanos appeared. Although 19 of the cows drowned during a difficult landing, the rest were coaxed ashore and that night the soldiers feasted on fresh beef.[44] Privateers towing captured ships were also frequent visitors to the bay. The captains sold the contents straight from the hull to the highest bidder. One of the prizes was a barque which had sailed from Portugal with gifts for the royal family in exile in Brazil. With luxuries intended for the crowned heads of Europe available at knock-down prices, the wealthier Irish officers began to enjoy themselves. Lieutenant Clair of the 1st Lancers, for example, wished he could remain on the island 'much longer', explaining in a letter home that he had an 'abundance of Beef, Mutton, Pork and fine bread, and all kinds of Wines of the finest description'.[45]

In early November Colonel Burke's light infantry arrived, and in December the *Borean* carrying Colonel Begg's regiment of 23 officers and 200 men was sighted offshore.[46] Although those who had been on the island for several months had built up a resistance to the local diseases, the newcomers had no such protection. Many died 'of flux' and others of fever.[47] Despite the hardships, there was 'a great deal of fandangoing during Christmas'. At improvised parties, the officers danced 'with the Native girls, some of whom … [they thought] very handsome'.[48] Indeed, relations with the Margaritans seem to have improved dramatically with the Legion's move to Pampatar. James Nangle, the commissary chief, wrote that he was often invited into the locals' houses, where he was greeted with hospitality and 'paid every attention'.[49]

In January 1820 Colonel Mariano Montilla, a 37-year old Creole, arrived at Pampatar to take command of the Legion in General Devereux's absence. Bolívar had instructed him to sail to the mainland and capture Rio de la Hacha, before marching south to link up with a body of troops under Colonel Lara. They were then to strike against either the New Granadan port of Santa Marta or the town of Maracaibo across the Venezuelan border. Montilla had been an active figure in the push for South American independence for 12 years. Following the collapse of the Second Republic in 1814, he had fled to Cartagena where he was promoted to colonel for his part in thwarting Morillo's siege. He had then joined Bolívar in Haiti, but had not taken part in The Liberator's landing on the Venezuelan coast the following year due to a disagreement between the two men. After spending two years on the fringes, Montilla had then been accepted back into the fold for the failed expedition against Cumaná, before being assigned his new role. He was an able commander and would win the respect of the majority of the Irish officers. Francis Burdett O'Connor, a 28-year old atheist from Cork and one of the few volunteers who would distinguish themselves in the forthcoming campaign, thought him a 'brave and gentlemanly officer'. The two would later become close friends.[50]

After his arrival in Pampatar, Montilla ordered the men to fall in on parade. As he knew no English and 'none of … the Legion spoke even a single word of Spanish', he gave his commands in French.[51] They were then translated by O'Connor. Montilla was shocked by 'the terrible quality of the men', their 'insubordination' and 'ineptitude' and 'the inexperience of the majority of the officers'.[52] To make matters worse, Devereux had failed to equip them and Montilla was forced to delay his mission until he could procure sufficient arms and ammunition. To this end he immediately set sail for Saint Thomas's, where he acquired 1,000 muskets and bayonets from the merchants at Bendetti and Company for 14 pesos a piece. By the time he returned to Pampatar in February, the situation had deteriorated even further. The Irish rank and file had been looting the locals' houses to supplement their rations and were almost entirely out of control. Since the first detachments had landed six months previously, roughly 600 had died of fever and 100 others had deserted.[53] After fleeing into the interior they had formed armed bands that were now preying on passing travellers.[54] Knowing that to delay further would result in the complete disintegration of his command, Montilla marched the 678 remaining men back across the island to Juan Griego to embark for the Main.[55] Before leaving, Captain Parsons visited General English's grave, 'thinking it might be the last time … [he] would ever see it'.[56]

On 6 March they arrived at Juan Griego and the men boarded three transports waiting in the bay. Conditions on board were horrendous, with eight men crammed into every four-bunk berth. Alongside was a flotilla of 11 warships and two gunboats which was to escort them to Rio de la Hacha. At 3.00pm, Brion gave the signal to set sail. During the first two days at sea, several volunteers died of fever and their bodies were hurled overboard. On the third day they encountered 'very rough weather'. A tornado developed and threatened to engulf the fleet.[57] As Captain Parsons looked on from the deck of the *Urdaneta*, water was sucked upwards 'in clouds in a circular manner, higher than our masts and as white as snow'.[58] 'Leaning over the ship's side' to get a better view, Parsons 'heard a dreadful splash … and … saw a poor sailor emerge out of the waves'.[59] The man had fallen from 'the top-gallant yard', one of the highest spars on the ship. A boat was lowered to attempt a rescue, but in vain. For the next few nights Parsons was haunted by the event. As soon as he closed his eyes he saw the poor sailor struggling in his dreams.[60]

After an uncomfortable night on the quarterdeck, 'with an eighteen pound shot under … [his] head, by means of a pillow', Parsons awoke to the sound of the band calling the men for their morning ration of grog.[61] Shortly afterwards, Rio de la Hacha hove into view. Sailing closer into shore, Brion gave the order for the fleet to drop anchor. The Spaniards responded by opening fire with the 32-pdrs mounted in the fort. Although the first few shots dropped short, the range increased as the barrels heated up and round shot were soon falling all about them causing a fine spray to pass across the decks. Whilst the fleet prudently withdrew, Brion sent a flag of truce ashore to demand the governor's surrender. This was promptly refused and the men of the Irish Legion prepared to disembark.

At 4.00am the next day, the volunteers were rowed ashore. Several wooden houses had been set ablaze by flaming wadding discharged from the shore battery's cannon and the flames lit up the entire town. Colonel O'Connor's boat was the first to reach the beach. 'To avoid a soaking in the brine', he paid a sailor a gold coin to carry him ashore.[62] After his Lancers had joined him, he drew his sword and led them in a charge against a tower flying the Spanish flag, yet there was no cannon fire to receive them, nor musket volleys to decimate their ranks. Learning from their encounters with MacGregor's men six months earlier (that their Indian irregulars were better suited to skirmishes and ambush than to pitched battles against European troops), the royalists had abandoned town and melted away into the surrounding forests.[63] Notwithstanding, O'Connor was not to be denied his moment of glory. Racing up the stairs to the top of the tower, he tore down the Spanish banner and 'ran up the Lancers' standard ... with the Irish harp in its centre' in its place.[64] Spying it waving from the battlements through his telescope, Brion ordered a volley from the fleet's cannon to salute the 'victory' and the celebrations began. It was a promising beginning for the Irish Legion, but the capture of Rio de la Hacha was just the first objective. Taking the town of Valledupar, a 100-mile march to the south through difficult terrain teeming with enemy guerrillas, would prove a much more demanding proposition.

Chapter 23

'A DREADFUL SERVICE' – THE BRITISH LEGION IN MATURÍN

Following its cross-country march from Cumaná, the British Legion arrived in Maturín in late August 1819. Once prosperous as the country playground of Venezuela's elite, the town's fortunes had faded since the outbreak of hostilities. Having acquired a reputation for its pro-patriot stance, Maturín had been burnt to the ground three times by royalist raiding parties from the coast. The locals had rebuilt it on each occasion, but as the richer inhabitants had fled, it had emerged from the ashes with little of its former glory. When the Legion staggered into town, the soldiers found an impoverished, forgotten backwater, where, to Captain Chesterton's annoyance, not even 'a sheet of paper, or a single pen [could] be purchased'.[1]

Built on an extensive plain stretching south from the coastal mountain range of New Andalucia, the grandly titled 'Head Quarters of the Department of the East' was a small town of 600–700 inhabitants situated beside an arm of the Guarapiche River.[2] In the centre was a vast square, covered with 'a fine sod', where Colonel Blosset drilled the men in the mornings to avoid the burning heat of midday.[3] Each side of the plaza was 'a furlong in length' and lined with houses 'built with tolerable regularity, one storey high'.[4] Although a few were stout, stone-walled constructions, roofed with bamboo, the majority were 'formed simply of … stakes, interwoven with rank dried leaves' and plastered with mud from the banks of the river. On the perimeter of the town were three forts, each mounting a single pivot gun. Whilst Blosset and his staff took possession of the finer buildings, the field officers were quartered in the 'mud built hovels' round the square.[5] In place of furniture, they used blocks of wood. Lengths of cowhide slung from the beams served as crude hammocks.[6] Next to the square stood a large unfinished building 'resembling an English barn', where the rank and file slept whilst mosquitoes buzzed about them and 'innumerable' rats scratched for food in the dark.[7]

Following its defeat at Cumaná, the Legion's morale was at rock bottom. The men had not been paid and although rations had improved in quantity, the monotonous supplies of raw unsalted beef and cassava cake did little to raise their spirits. To make matters worse their clothes were falling apart, and barely a man had shoes or stockings to protect his feet from the injurious thorn bushes of the plains when sent out on patrol.[8] Of the 500 who had arrived in August, 25 per cent were soon suffering from fever or infected with flesh-eating ticks.[9] Surgeon Richard Murphy and Assistant Surgeon Gray could do little for their charges and the line of graves outside town grew with each passing day. In despair, several officers applied to General Urdaneta for permission to resign. Not only were their requests refused, but they were also threatened with imprisonment in the fortress at Old Guyana where Colonel Wilson had been held for several months in 1818. Faced with this ultimatum, Chesterton and Murphy decided to desert, planning to sail up the Guarapiche with 'a young Canadian trader' they had met in town, before crossing the Gulf of Paria and making for Trinidad.[10] Before their plan could be put into effect, the trader caught fever and the conspirators were forced to bide their time.

Frustrated by the relentless heat and terrible conditions, tempers began to fray and a series of duels followed. One of the first arose from 'a trifling quarrel' between Major Davy and Assistant Surgeon Gray.[11] Just 30 minutes before the contest was due to begin, Gray asked Chesterton's advice about which jacket he should wear for the occasion. Dressed entirely in white, as per the captain's suggestion, he then went out to face his foe. Watched by their respective seconds in a grove outside town, the men paced out the distance, turned and fired. Gray missed, but Davy's aim was truer. His bullet passed directly 'through … [the assistant surgeon's] heart', killing him instantly.[12] As he stood over the body, something inside Davy snapped. From that moment on it was said that he never smiled again.[13] A second duel, which took place at the end of November 1819, was contested by Captain Rupert Hand and Lieutenant Lynch. 'The ball of the latter took effect, passing through the back part of [Hand's] right thigh, grazing the left, and taking with it, in its passage, the testes, which were completely cut away.'[14]

The Legion's new commander, Colonel John Blosset, made 'not a single effort to allay the torments' of his men and soon became the focus of their anger.[15] In Margarita, where he had enjoyed sole command of the 1st Division before English's arrival, Blosset had been feted for his firm control, but since the disaster at Agua Santa his personality had undergone a radical transformation. 'His mind became enerrated, and he envinced a most unpardonable apathy towards the interests and comforts of those under his command.'[16] Blosset had cut himself off from his men's problems and a three-tiered society had emerged within the Legion. While he and his staff enjoyed comparative luxury, the field officers struggled and the rank and file suffered endlessly. When 'a present of wines, rum, porter, flour and other provinces' arrived from some British merchants in Trinidad as a gift for the entire regiment, it was immediately appropriated by Blosset and his staff and exclusively reserved for their table. This 'selfishness bordering on inhumanity' infuriated the men and junior officers alike. Unconcerned, Blosset and his staff continued to flaunt their superior lifestyle, regularly picnicking in a nearby orange grove accompanied by local ladies done up in 'gay and fantastic' dresses.[17] After feasting on 'Meats ... Coffee, Chocolate ... [and] a superabundance of fruits of every description', they would waltz to the music of the Legion's diminishing band under the shade of the orange tree boughs. Dinner was then served 'in a similarly sumptuous style', before the party returned to Maturín.[18]

Towards the end of 1819, General Rafael Urdaneta was ordered back to Angostura. His departure was celebrated by the volunteers, who almost universally despised the haughty Creole. The recall was part of a major upheaval taking place in the capital which had begun when Bolívar had left for the front in April 1819. With The Liberator away on what most presumed to be an impossible mission in New Granada, the Caudillos, led by General Bermúdez, had staged a bloodless *coup d'état*.[19] Vice-President Zea had been replaced by General Arismendi, the former governor of Margarita. Once in power, Arismendi immediately took revenge on his old nemesis; he recalled Rafael Urdaneta to Angostura to face trial, whilst an ally of the new regime, Santiago Mariño, was sent to Maturín to replace him.

A 'stout, fair-haired man, of ... gentle manners' as well as 'great military skill and undoubted bravery', Mariño was well received by the Legion.[20] His distant Irish ancestry further endeared him to his new charges.[21] Whilst on a tour of inspection, he showed his compassion by weeping aloud at the suffering in the hospitals.[22] Afterwards he petitioned congress for medicine and supplies and the situation in Maturín began to improve. He also rescinded Urdaneta's policy of refusing to issue passports to those who wished to resign. Whilst Captain Chesterton took advantage of this reverse, Surgeon Murphy, a 34-year old from County Sligo, had a change of heart. Following Gray's death in his duel with Major Davy, Murphy (a graduate from Trinity College Dublin) was now the only remaining surgeon and he 'could not think of leaving so many ... without medical assistance'.[23] Mariño rewarded the Irishman with a money order granting him half a peso a day. Murphy was delighted. He no longer had to wash his own shirt and could now afford a little coffee with his breakfast.[24]

In January the Legion was ordered to join Páez's army of the west in Los Llanos and, having passed through Angostura, the men sailed on up the Orinoco and Apure.

One afternoon, after the boats had stopped to pick up supplies, an ugly incident occurred in which a British private angered a Creole staff officer. Enraged by his insolence, the officer drew his sword and wounded the volunteer 'severely in the arm'.[25] The men were furious and it was all Blosset could do to prevent them from exacting a brutal revenge. The Legion then proceeded up-river, disembarking at San Fernando, where the troops set off overland on the last leg of their journey. As they neared Achaguas, they forded the Apurito River. It was unusually high for the season and three officers, captains Fred and Lyte and Lieutenant Hill, were swept away by the current and drowned.[26] The rest marched on to Achaguas, arriving in early January 1820.[27] Having arrived at Maturín with 500 men, the Legion was now reduced to just 200.[28] Before the end of the year a full-scale mutiny would tear what remained of the regiment apart.

Chapter 24

THE BLACK RIFLES MOVE NORTH

A s news of the battle of Boyacá spread through New Granada in the second half of 1819, huge swathes of the country spontaneously rose up, armed themselves and overthrew royalist garrisons. By the end of the year the entire central section of the country had sided with the patriots, but the cities of Pasto and Popayán in the southern highlands and the areas to the north and west of Cúcuta, stretching to the distant Caribbean coast, still remained loyal to King Ferdinand. Soon after his triumphant entrance into Santafé, Bolívar set about bringing these areas under his control. In September an expedition had marched south under Colonel Antonio Obando, and General Soublette had been ordered north to occupy the border city of Cúcuta. Soublette's mission had dual aims: firstly to prevent the royalists in Venezuela launching a counter-attack, and secondly to provide a springboard for future operations towards the north and west.

The men of Soublette's division soon came up against resistance. After they had repulsed a few pushes across the border from General La Torre, Bolívar ordered a second column into the area to reinforce them. In mid-October it set out from Santafé.[1] Led by General Anzoátegui, with Captain Daniel O'Leary serving as his aide-de-camp, two veteran units made up the column. Colonel Rondon led the cavalry squadron that had distinguished itself at Boyacá and the Black Rifles marched under Arthur Sandes. Having recovered from the two wounds he had suffered at Vargas, the lieutenant-colonel was once again fit for active service so Major Peacock returned to the post of second in command. The Rifles' ranks had been filled with prisoners taken on the field at Boyacá and the unit now numbered 600 men. Of the 16 European officers who had arrived in Angostura in July 1818, only eight remained. Four had died of fever in Venezuela, Colonel Piggot had been given leave to recover from illness after the battle of Gamarra,

Captain Harris had been left behind during the winter march across the flooded Los Llanos, Lieutenant Westbrook had perished on the Paramo of Pisba and Captain Byrne had been killed at Boyacá.[2] Battle scarred and toughened by countless marches, the survivors bore little resemblance to the idealistic young men who had left Fowey two years earlier to the tune of 'The Girl I left Behind Me'.

With the cavalry scouting ahead, the column left the capital and wound its way northwest across the fertile plains and valleys of Boyacá. As the soldiers passed the villages, local peasants rushed out to give them bundles of food and drink and then cheered them on their way. In early November they reached the 300-year old town of Pamplona, spread out on 'a verdant carpet' in the shelter of two parallel mountain ranges.[3] Having prospered under the royalist regime, it boasted 'a handsome … church with other public edifices' built around a large central square. In 1810 the town had been amongst the first in South America to rebel against Spain. The people had been punished during Morillo's recapture, but this had only increased their support for the republican cause. When news of Bolívar's success at Boyacá had reached them, the garrison had been swiftly overthrown and Pamplona now served as an important staging post for patriot operations further north.

On 15 November, after celebrating his 30 birthday, General Anzoátegui died suddenly in his quarters near the main square. Captain Wright 'believed that he had been poisoned by some addict to the Spanish cause'.[4] This was never proved, however, and several other theories have since arisen, one of which suggested the general had died of a heart attack in the arms of his lover, Celia Gomez, following an all-night drinking session. When Bolívar found out, he was devastated. Almost uniquely amongst all the self-serving commanders The Liberator had been forced to rely on, Anzoátegui had been an example of devotion and loyalty.

His replacement, Colonel Bartolomé Salom, then spent a few frustrating weeks trying to secure provisions and round up cattle for the march to Cúcuta, eventually leaving Pamplona on 22 December.[5] Two days later, Rondon's cavalry encountered a picket of 50 royalists. Barely breaking stride, the Llaneros charged, killing four and wounding 14. The survivors were then chased northwards to the town of Las Cruces. On the 28th, Rondon's men saw 60 enemy scouts on the heights ahead of them. One straggler was killed. The rest eluded their pursuers in the labyrinthine streets of Capacho. The campaign continued in this vein for several days, with the enemy forces withdrawing northwards as Rondon's Lancers harassed their rear. Towards the end of the year, the royalists took a more determined stand at the bridge over the river Chámeza. The position was sufficiently fortified to dissuade the patriots from attacking and the skirmishing ground to a halt. The Rifles then spent the next six months at Tariba, a small town to the west of the Chámeza nestled in a high mountain valley. Troops were notoriously difficult to control when inactive for such long periods and the Rifles proved no exception. Throughout the winter 'disorder and horrendous excesses' were committed.[6] As no reports of the incidents survive, one can only speculate on the unit's behaviour. A combination of drunkenness, rape and theft seems likely, whilst court martials, floggings and firing squads would have been used to discipline those responsible.

In March, Bolívar arrived in Cúcuta having quashed the Caudillo uprising that had taken place in Angostura. When Bolívar had reached the Venezuelan capital after his success in New Granada, he was given a hero's welcome and popular support for the warlords soon evaporated. His subsequent election as the president of Gran Colombia was a formality and brought his dream of a united Venezuela, New Granada and Ecuador a step closer. With his plans back on track, The Liberator could afford to be magnanimous with the defeated rebels. Arismendi and Bermúdez were given military commands in the east of Venezuela, whilst the ever loyal Zea was reinstated as vice-president. His hegemony cemented, Bolívar then left for the front line.

After Anzoátegui's death, Captain O'Leary was assigned to Bolívar's staff. In his memoirs, the young Irishman detailed the general's daily routine in Cúcuta. After waking at six, Bolívar would inspect the horses in the stables, then return to his quarters where he read for two hours until breakfast, 'his favourite authors of the time' being 'Montesquieu and Rousseau'.[7] The Liberator ate at 9.00am, then dedicated the rest of the morning to 'official business', reading reports, consulting with staff and dictating dispatches to be sent to all four corners of his ever growing domain.[8] Once his work was concluded, he returned to his books, emerging at 5.00pm to eat supper. 'His table … was very frugal: soup, roast or stewed meat, poultry and simply prepared vegetables … finished with something sweet.' He invariably drank only water.[9] Afterwards 'he went riding accompanied by an aide, or … his secretary', then read until 11.00pm in his hammock, before retiring for the night.[10]

Uppermost amongst The Liberator's concerns at the time were the disastrous reports that had reached his headquarters from Colonel Obando's expedition in the south. On 24 January, Obando's troops had been defeated in Popayán. Attacking at dawn, the royalists had caught the patriot pickets unawares. Although his 600 men were vastly outnumbered, Obando had held out in the central square for two hours. But when the royalists moved round his flanks and surrounded him, his troops had panicked and fled. Only five officers and 100 men had escaped the massacre that followed. Determined to crush the troublesome Pastusos, Bolívar ordered Santander to dispatch a second expedition from Santafé. One of the units to march south was Mackintosh's Rifles, now renamed the Albion Battalion in honour of their heroics at Vargas.

Chapter 25

THE ALBION MARCH SOUTH

O n 2 March 1820, Urdaneta's old second in command, General Manuel Valdés, led 1,500 troops south-west from Santafé. At the head of the column, dressed in new red uniforms, marched the Albion Battalion under Colonel Mackintosh.[1] Behind the volunteers followed a second infantry unit, the battalion of Cundinamarca. Two cavalry squadrons of 100 riders each patrolled the flanks as they advanced. One of these, the Guias (Guides), was commanded by Colonel Lucas Carbajal, a veteran of Vargas and Boyacá.[2] Bringing up the rear were field guns pulled by mules and a lengthy baggage train complete with wives, children, dogs and cattle.

Fewer than 100 of the troops that Rooke had led over the Andes remained with the Albion Battalion; 50 had died on the Paramo of Pisba, seven had perished at Vargas and others had succumbed to their wounds. Several more had been killed at Boyacá or been left behind in the hospitals of Santafé.[3] To make up for these losses, 100 more volunteers had joined the unit, amongst them Captain Richard Vowell. Although the vast majority were British, two were German veterans of the Napoleonic Wars. The regiment had been further bolstered with 400 recruits from Tunja, bringing its total strength up to 600 men.[4] The New Granadans were proud to join the regiment that had so distinguished itself at Vargas and Boyacá. They 'thought themselves above the other [South American] soldiers' and 'called themselves English, and swore in English by way of keeping up the title'.[5]

Initially the column made swift progress. Marching along raised causeways through the marshland to the south-west of Santafé, the men passed the Indian village of Bogotá from which the capital took its name. At an area known as La Boca del Monte (the mouth of the mountain), they began the descent from the 8,200ft-high valleys of Cundinamarca to the tropical lowlands of the upper Magdalena basin. A series 'of broad stone steps, each a foot in height' known as *escaléra*, had been cut into the solid rock by Musica

Indians long ago to facilitate the journey.[6] This ancient staircase passed through a 'deep glen', flanked by 'magnificent' pine trees before reaching 'a rugged ridge', where the volunteers waited for the rear of the column to catch up.[7] The descent proved particularly treacherous for the artillery. The cannon had been dismantled and loaded onto the mules in sections. Several collapsed under the weight and fell to their deaths on the rocks below.

At the foot of the *escaléra*, the British found themselves in a completely different environment to the one they had left scarcely an hour before. Accustomed to the cool climate of the capital after their seven-month stay, they were shocked at the sudden increase in temperature and humidity. A traveller who passed through the region two years later noted that his thermometer rose to over 97 degrees.[8] The landscape had also undergone a dramatic transformation. In place of the open grasslands, hills and scattered trees of Cundinamarca, there stretched a blanket of near-impenetrable vegetation, only occasionally broken by pockets of farmland. After passing through the town of Tocaima, the troops came to the Magdalena River. Broad-bladed grasses, shrubs and squat trees lined its banks, their lower branches dipping into the muddy brown water. At 130ft wide, the river presented a serious obstacle. Careful not to disturb the alligators basking in the sun, the men boarded *zampanes* (Indian canoes) at the pebble beach of Flandez. They were swept several hundred yards downstream before reaching the far bank.[9] Once across they continued southwards. Following the west bank, the troops regularly passed 'villages and populous towns', whose inhabitants came out to greet them.[10]

Seven weeks after leaving Santafé, the division arrived at the stultifyingly hot town of Neiva. With a population of 2,000, it was the most important staging post between the capital and the column's destination of Popayán, a further 200 miles to the south-west over the Cordillera Central. Whilst the troops were resting, Major Johnstone, who had insisted on rejoining the unit despite not having fully recovered from the musket wound he had suffered at Boyacá, wrote to the *Gazeta de Santafé de Bogotá*, praising the locals for their hospitality. Well taken care of, the troops recuperated, whilst a locally recruited infantry battalion swelled their numbers to over 2,000 men. Vowell noticed that many of his new comrades were afflicted by a strange skin condition. Known as *caráte*, it 'produced white spots on different parts of their copper coloured skin; and, in some instances, turn[ed] even the hair white'.[11]

Soon after the column's arrival in Neiva, Valdés got word of a Spanish garrison of 280 men in La Plata, a town built in the foothills of the Cordillera Central 60 miles to the south-west, and he ordered his second in command, Colonel José Mires, to march out and attack it.[12] On 22 April Mires set off with the Albion Battalion and 100 of Colonel Carbajal's cavalry. After a four-day march they were within striking distance and on the 27th, they spent the whole day hiding in the shadows of a deep ravine. As soon as night had fallen, Mires's men moved out, reaching the edge of town at dawn. Believing the nearest patriot forces were still in Neiva, the royalist commander, Captain Domínguez, was caught unawares. He and his officers had been enjoying a party the night before and were still fast asleep when Mires made his move.

A fast-flowing, boulder-strewn river lay between the patriots and their objective. Spanning the torrent was a rickety bamboo bridge. The Spaniards had already cut several of its supports and were ready to send the rest of the structure plunging into the water at the first sign of trouble.[13] Realizing speed and surprise would be of the essence, Mires ordered a two-pronged attack. First Carbajal and 14 of his riders were sent to a ford down-river from where they would ride round to the back of town to cut off the royalists' retreat.[14] Once the cavalry were in place, the 200 Grenadiers of the Albion Battalion under Captain Rasch, one of the unit's two German officers, were to charge across the bridge. Awaiting the order to attack, the volunteers were hidden on a wooded slope overlooking town. Whilst the men fixed bayonets, the sergeants checked their gun flints and the officers loaded their pistols and drew their swords. When Mires gave the signal, they sprinted towards the bridge. Blinded by the rising sun, the sentry called a challenge. In reply a sergeant yelled 'les Ingleses!'[15] After hurriedly firing his musket, the sentry took to his heels, but was caught and bayoneted in the back.

Roused by the shot, Captain Domínguez turned out 'a strong … guard … at the foot of the bridge'. Forming up, the men fired a volley at their attackers, killing five Grenadiers and wounding three.[16] The rest piled in with fixed bayonets. The hand-to-hand fighting was brutal.[17] Captain Rasch killed 11 with his sabre, and nine more were killed by his men before the survivors fell back.[18] Rasch then held the far bank under fire, whilst the rest of the battalion, led by Mackintosh, crossed the bridge to join him. Once Rasch's men had been reinforced, the Spanish fell back to the main square. Mackintosh then gave the order to finish them. Outnumbered three to one, 100 of the Spaniards threw down their arms after a few volleys and ran into the hills, where Carbajal's Lancers cut them to pieces. Domínguez and 80 others refused to surrender. In the final struggle on the outskirts of town, Captain Kean bayoneted Domínguez in the groin.[19] Amidst the confusion, the Spaniard crawled away to an Indian hut in the mountains, where he bled to death.[20] With victory secured, the volunteers' thoughts turned to their empty stomachs. Having not eaten during the previous night's march, they burst into the royalists' quarters and fell upon the remains of their feast with relish.

The action at La Plata was a great success for the patriots. Some 100 Spaniards had been killed and 150 taken prisoner. Only 13 had escaped. Racing over the mountains to the west, they took word of the disaster to General Calzada in Popayán, who immediately began preparing a counter-attack. On 10 May he advanced to Guambia. After setting up camp, Calzada sent out scouts to keep track of the patriots' movements. Meanwhile, unknown to the royalists, Valdés had rendezvoused with the Albion in La Plata, then advanced westwards through the villages of Lame and Inza.[21] By the beginning of June they had reached the foot of the Cordillera Central. With just 25 miles separating them from the royalist camp, Valdés ordered his men into the mountains. The Grenadier Company of the Albion once again formed the van.

Winding upwards through rocky ravines, the troops climbed steeply, skirting mountain torrents which drenched them with a fine spray. Occasionally, when the wind snatched away the blanketing mist, impoverished hamlets appeared. Clinging to the slopes, they were surrounded by fields sowed with potatoes, barley and *aracacha* (a root vegetable) which the troops dug up and ate raw.[22] Later the path levelled out and crossed open moorland. The men struggled to catch their breath in the rarefied air. Several collapsed, some never to rise again. As the baggage mules died, local Indians acclimatized to the conditions were employed as bearers to replace them. Vowell fell in with their chief, a proud man by the name of Lorenzo, who boasted of the number of Spaniards he had killed with his own hands.[23] After passing several beautiful 'lagoons ... of an unfathomable depth', the path began to descend.[24] The mists evaporated and the Albion left the paramo behind them. On 5 June, as Mires's rearguard was still struggling over the moors with the baggage, the vanguard reached Pitayó, a cluster of Indian huts situated in a steep-sided hollow.[25] Once they had cleaned and reloaded their muskets, the troops scattered over the surrounding hills to dig for wild potatoes and *aracacha*.[26] Others were too exhausted to join in the search. 'One old soldier' of the 2nd Company 'by the name of Slattery' had only just made it over the moor. Collapsing in the corner of a local's hovel, he fell fast asleep.[27]

The next morning, whilst the main body of troops under Calzada was still several miles away, the 1,400 men of the royalist vanguard advanced on the outskirts of Pitayó, unaware that the patriots had arrived before them.[28] Marching with a company of skirmishers at the head of the column was Antonio López, a former patriot officer and veteran of the victories at Vargas and Boyacá. López had been captured at Popayán the year before, only escaping execution by agreeing to serve as a private in the royalists' ranks. At midday, as López's unit rounded a bend in the track just outside the village, it was challenged by the patriot picket. Both sides were stunned by the encounter, but it was the royalists who were the first to recover and open fire. Captain Pizarro, the patriot commander, was shot twice but stubbornly held his position, buying time for Valdés to organize the rest of the men.[29]

Back in Pitayó, Private Slattery was woken by the gunfire. Hearing that the enemy was 'driving in the out-post, and about to attack', he exclaimed 'then Slattery is well' and rushed out to join his comrades.[30] Meanwhile, still held up by Pizarro's pickets, the royalist commander ordered López's company and one other to outflank them. After discharging his musket into the air, López ran ahead and was soon clear of his company. Hiding in the shade of a copse of trees, he prepared to cross over to the patriot lines. Having seen the royalists try to move round his position, Valdés had sent 200 men of the Albion to counter them. The two sides now clashed across a ravine to the left of the track. Recognizing his former comrades, López turned his musket butt end up and ran across no man's land shouting in English for the troops to hold their fire. Some of the British were about to shoot until he was recognized by a Creole coronet. After embracing him, he sent López to report to Valdés.

Realizing he could hope for no support from Calzada, the royalist commander hoped to crush the patriots before they could fully deploy. Whilst his cavalry formed a rearguard, he ordered his infantry to spread out on both sides of the track and advance. The patriots, however, were ready for them. The two sides clashed in the woods and the battle became general. Volleys rippled up and down the lines. The patriots' priest, Padre Guzmán, distributed cartridges and gave the dying the last rites.[31] The firing continued for one hour before the British veterans began to get the upper hand. Valdés then decided to finish it. The men were ordered to fix bayonets and advance. With Mackintosh leading them, the volunteers crossed the ravine and advanced up the hill towards the royalist line, firing and reloading as they went. After ten minutes, as the Spaniards began to cede ground, Mackintosh gave the order to charge. With a cheer, the red-coated line surged forwards. Seeing the victors of Vargas rushing up the slope towards them, many fled before the steel-tipped ranks crashed home. Those who held were knocked to the ground and bayoneted or blasted with musketry at close-range. To the left of the British position, on the track leading to Guambia, the newly recruited battalion of Neiva was also fighting well. Having pushed the royalists back, the road was now clear for Carbajal's cavalry to deliver the *coup de grâce*. With their horns blowing, the 50 horsemen galloped up the track. The Spaniards scattered before them. 'Some died by the lance.' The remainder 'fled into the hills to save themselves'.[32] The cavalry forming the royalist rearguard had seen enough. Without even drawing their sabres, they galloped back to Guambia, soon outstripping their infantry who dropped their muskets as they ran.[33]

A total of 130 royalists were killed at Pitayó. Their corpses lay amongst the trees, face down on the track or strewn through the ravine. A further 80 were wounded and 150 captured. The tally would have been even higher, but as the patriots were still drained from their march over the moors, the scattered remnants of the royalist column were allowed to make their way back to Guambia unmolested. In retaliation for the executions Calzada had ordered after the patriot defeat in Popayán the year before, three captured

Engraving, A Llanero Rodeo. *The volunteers witnessed several of these rodeos whilst traversing the Venezuelan plains during the campaigns of 1818 and 1819. (© British Library Board)*

The Orinoco *by Louis Remy Mignot. South America's second largest river, the Orinoco carried the volunteers into the heartlands of Venezuela. (Bridgeman Art Library)*

The Descent from Santafé to Honda. This engraving depicts the torturous route from the capital of New Granada (Colombia) to the highest navigable point on the River Magdalena. (Marc Dechow, www.antique-prints.de)

The Bay of Rio de la Hache. *Rio de la Hacha was the sight of two British attacks, one by General MacGregor, the other by the Irish Legion. Both ended in disaster. (The Trustees of The National Library of Scotland)*

The tomb of General James Towers English, Juan Griego, Margarita. English's final resting place lies within a few hundred meters of the beach where so many of his men were buried in unmarked graves after succumbing to disease. (Author's Collection)

Close up of a memorial commemorating the British Legion's stand at the battle of Carabobo. One of the few signs of the British contribution to South American independence that remains on display today. (Author's Collection)

Fort at Juan Griego, Margarita, Venezuela. Juan Griego was home to both the British and Irish Legions. Both units were decimated by disease before the survivors moved on to military operations on the mainland. (Author's Collection)

Bust of Colonel Ferrier at Carabobo. The hero of Carabobo, Ferrier was a doctor's son from Manchester and veteran of the 43rd Foot who went on to lead the British Legion. (Author's Collection)

Memorial to the British Legion, Carabobo. This rarely visited memorial stands on the site of the Legion's valiant stand. One third were killed or wounded. (Author's Collection)

The Albion Battalion was one of the most celebrated of all the British units. This photo shows the river they crossed under royalist fire at the start of the battle of La Plata. (Author's Collection)

The British Cemetery, Bogotá. Hidden away behind a high wall at the corner of a busy intersection in downtown Bogotá, the British Cemetery houses the remains of Major Mackintosh amongst others. (Author's Collection)

Soldier's Lake, Paramo de Pisba. This forlorn site, 4,000 metres up in Cordillera Central of the Andes, once witnessed the passage of Bolívar's army en-route to the battles of Vargas and Boyacá. (Author's Collection)

The battlefield of Boyacá, where Bolívar won his greatest victory. The reconstructed bridge can be seen in the centre, whilst the obelisk in the background marks the site of the army's attack against Barreiro's rearguard. (Author's Collection)

officers were shot by firing squad. Their bodies were then decapitated for good measure.[34] Patriot casualties had been light. Just 30 men from the battalions of Albion and Neiva had been killed and 60 more had been wounded. Private Slattery was amongst the survivors. Returning to his hovel, he was seen with a 'prisoner in one hand, and his musket and two [captured] doubloons in the other'.[35]

After receiving word of the defeat at Pitayó, Calzada withdrew his army south towards Popayán. Rather than pursue him directly, Valdés first went north-west to rendezvous with reinforcements. From Pitayó, the patriots marched through 'gloomy woods' on their way down from the mountains. As there were not enough mules to carry the powder and wounded, many officers were obliged to give up their horses and continue on foot. Vowell found the conditions 'very fatiguing'. The passage of thousands of men and cattle had churned the muddy paths into a 'succession of deep furrows' and the Englishman slipped and fell several times 'up to the middle in mud'. Vowell's problems were nothing next to the hardships endured by the prisoners. Forced to carry the wounded who 'could not sit a horse', they 'suffered severely'.[36] On 11 June the troops reached a steep hill near the village of Caloto overlooking the 'fertile valley of Cauca'.[37] Having survived for several weeks in the highlands on nothing but 'scanty fare', the men's spirits were lifted by the sight. The temperature and humidity soared as they descended into the valley. Coffee bushes the size of cherry trees, fields of sugar cane, cacao, maize, cotton, tobacco and plantains grew beside the track. On reaching Caloto, they rested for three days. On the 13th, Valdés issued a proclamation to the slaves of the Cauca valley, offering emancipation to any who would join his army for three years.[38] The division then continued to Quilichao where the men paused for 'some weeks' to regain their energy.

Quilichao was surrounded by abandoned gold mines. As the male slaves that had worked them had long since been pressed into one army or another, only a few 'wretchedly poor women and children' remained, living in the caves where the metal had once been dug.[39] When the troops arrived, they emerged to trade small quantities of gold grain packed inside vultures' quills for the heads and offal of bullocks slaughtered for the army. In the second week at Quilichao, Valdés's men were joined by 2,000 reinforcements raised in the city of Cali, 80 miles to the north. The next few weeks were spent drilling the new arrivals and tracking those who deserted. The problem became so pronounced that a permanent court martial was established. Captain Vowell was amongst those who sat in judgement. There was little room for leniency in Spanish military law and executions were common. If Valdés was in a 'merciful humour', however, he allowed the condemned to throw dice on a drum head for their lives. The winners were pardoned. The losers were shot. 'On one occasion, twin brothers' named Florez 'threw against each other'. Shaking with fear, 'they were … incapable … of holding the dice-box', so the 'officers who conducted their defence, threw for them'. As the first rolls were equal, the officers threw again. For a second time the dice failed to find a winner.[40] Suspecting divine intervention, Colonel Mires sought a pardon from Valdés. To Vowell's relief, both men were spared.

After three weeks at Quilichao, the division established new headquarters in Cali. Then on 9 July 1820, the men headed south for Popayán. The three-day march took them along an undulating road through evergreen woods, before emerging at the banks of the river Cauca on the edge of the city. The five-arch stone bridge surrounded by crumbling pleasure houses once owned by Popayán's elite was held by a royalist picket who fled after a short skirmish. On hearing that the enemy was at the gates, Calzada withdrew southwards to the arid scrublands of Patia. To the volunteers' annoyance, Valdés and his staff then spent three days stripping the city of its remaining wealth before they were allowed to enter. Unlike Neiva, where the patriots had enjoyed local hospitality, Popayán had strong royalist sympathies. Their reception would be of an entirely different calibre.

* * *

Meanwhile, in General Morillo's headquarters over the border in Venezuela, rumours were arriving of dramatic events in Spain that would have major repercussions on the war in South America. On 1 January 1820, after refusing to sail for the New World, an expeditionary force in Cádiz under colonels Rafael del Riego and Antonio Quiroga had revolted. Whilst Quiroga barricaded himself inside the city and a fortress stronghold on the Isle of Leon, Riego marched through Andalucía gathering support.[41] On hearing the news, King Ferdinand VII ordered General Frever to counter the insurrection.[42] On 9 February, his attack on the Isle of Leon was repulsed, but Cádiz itself fell after a month-long siege.[43] Hundreds of mutineers and civilians were massacred in the reprisals that followed.[44] The martyrs inspired the rebels and the revolt spread. As well as Riego, who was still at large in Andalucía, other officers rebelled in Asturias, Pamplona, Barcelona and Zaragoza.[45] In the meantime, bands of guerrillas were mobilizing in the countryside and rumours of a plot to execute the king swept through Madrid.[46] Seeing the tide turning against him, on 7 March King Ferdinand VII appeared on the balcony of the Palacio Real to address the mob and agree to the rebels' key demands. The constitution of 1812 was reinstated and order returned to Spain.

To understand the reasons behind the Spanish liberal revolution, it is necessary to look back to the Napoleonic Wars. In 1812, when Ferdinand was forced to abdicate by the French, a new Spanish government, known as the Cortes, had been formed in Cádiz, the only city on the mainland which had been able to resist Napoleon's forces.

Influenced by the fashionable ideals championed by the new republics of France and the United States of America, and freed by Ferdinand's absence, the Cortes wrote a new constitution. It abolished the Inquisition, greatly reduced the influence of the church and the aristocracy, limited the power of the king and created a system of electoral representation. But when Wellington's triumphs over the French had allowed Ferdinand to return to Madrid, he immediately overturned the innovations of the Cortes and returned Spain to a system of absolute monarchy. Caught up in a rush of patriotic fervour following liberation, the people initially welcomed the return of the king, but the euphoria was not to last.

Ferdinand's second term was increasingly despotic. As more and more political opponents were thrown into prison, the people began to turn against him, realizing they had merely replaced one tyrant with another. The army in particular grew to resent his return. When Morillo had set off for Venezuela with his 'pacifying army' in 1815, crowds of jubilant supporters had thronged the quayside at Cádiz to show their support, but by 1818 the war had lost its popularity.[47] Official propaganda that had boasted of victory was undermined by the 'melancholy contents' of letters sent home by the troops and reports published in British newspapers.[48] The people had no wish to see their sons killed in battle or die of fever hundreds of miles across the Atlantic. Nevertheless, the king continued to send reinforcements, prompting a series of minor mutinies. As early as 1815, General Juan Diez Porlier had inspired the garrison at La Coruña to revolt. His rebellion fell apart at Santiago de Compostela, but was followed by further uprisings in 1817 by generals Lacy in Catalonia and Vidal in Valencia. These too were put down, but a spirit of indignation was growing. Ferdinand's arrogance and brutality had lost him the support of his people. Riego's rebellion was the result.

For Morillo the consequences were profound. He could no longer hope for reinforcements, his authority was undermined by the decentralization of power in Spain, and his long-held position of refusing to recognize the legitimacy of the republicans was overturned by the new players in Madrid. In April 1820, orders from the Cortes arrived in Caracas. Morillo was instructed to hold talks with the rebels and offer them limited self-representation if they would put down their arms. At first negotiations were tentative, and there would be six more months of fighting before an armistice was agreed.

Chapter 26

A 'SERIES OF SURREPTITIOUS ASSAULTS'

At the end of May 1820, Sandes's Black Rifles were ordered to Ocaña to meet up with Colonel Lara, who had been operating around the lower Magdalena. The ten-day march from Tariba took the troops 100 miles to the north-west. After passing through the arid valleys around Cúcuta, they moved towards a distant range of cloud-covered peaks. The road wound upwards into green foothills, following rapid, boulder-filled rivers. After cresting the heights, they descended towards Ocaña, entering a landscape of scrub and lightly forested hills, crisscrossed by countless rivers. A week into their stay at Ocaña, Colonel Lara arrived, leading the Flanqueadores and Pamplona infantry battalions as well as the cavalry of Colonel Infante. The combined column then marched towards the royalist-held lower Magdalena. Lara had orders to unite with Colonel Montilla and the Irish Legion at Valledupar, 200 miles to the north. The two expeditions were then to make a combined assault on Santa Marta, on the New Granadan coast, or the city of Maracaibo in Venezuela.

Marching north-west from Ocaña, Lara's column crossed the Cordillera Oriental. From the ridge line there was a magnificent view of the Magdalena River, a wide, brown band, snaking its way sluggishly across an immense, forested plain thousands of feet below them. As the men descended, the temperature and humidity rose. Sweating heavily in their dark green uniforms, the Rifle officers were plagued by clouds of mosquitoes as they hacked their way through tangled scrub and woodland. Nearing the river, they turned north. Then, on 24 June, the vanguard encountered an enemy picket near a farmhouse several miles south of the village of Chiriguaná. After firing a few shots at Lara's men, the royalists dispersed to the north. Wary of ambush, Lara then dispatched carbine-armed cavalry to reconnoitre the woods ahead. They returned with news that the enemy was gathering in strength at Chiriguaná.

At dawn the next day the advance continued. Spread out in skirmish formation, the 1st Company of the Rifles led the way through the woods. At 3.00pm the troops emerged onto a plain, where a local woman told them that the royalists had taken up positions to the west of Chiriguaná. Lara sent his infantry forward in column with the cavalry covering the flanks. As they neared the enemy, the Rifles of the 1st Company opened fire, their musketry pushing the royalists back into the woods. To cover their withdrawal, 50 cavalry appeared, forcing the riflemen to close ranks in case they were charged. The 2nd Company was then deployed and together their fire drove the horsemen back. With the enemy retreating all over the field, the patriots advanced, pursuing their opponents for ten miles through the woods until nightfall and heavy rain brought the encounter to a close. Sandes then re-formed his scattered companies, the band playing to call them together in the dark.[1] That night, whilst the patriots slept under cover in Chiriguaná, the royalists regrouped to the north.

Following their defeat, the royalists would restrict themselves to guerrilla tactics for the rest of the campaign. Using hit-and-run raids, they picked off small groups as the patriots pushed northwards. When writing his memoirs decades later, Captain Thomas Wright recalled 'a series of surreptitious assaults and clashes in skirmish order'.[2] Every 'inch of terrain was disputed' and the patriots were constantly on alert.[3] The enemy mainly comprised local Indians. Fiercely loyal, the majority of the Magdalena tribes, like those of the Caribbean, believed that King Ferdinand had a divine right to rule them. Capuchin friars, sent from Spain years before, coordinated the attacks from the safety of the deep woods. Wright remembered them as shadowy, mounted figures. A hangover from the day of the Inquisition, they 'carried a sword in one hand and a crucifix in the other'.[4]

For several days, the advance continued through thick 'virgin forest'. At nightfall, whilst clouds of mosquitoes buzzed about them, the troops set up their bivouacs under the boughs, and sentries were dispatched to the perimeters. Nearly every night the Indians would gather to attack them. When all was quiet, one would crawl 'along the ground like a serpent until he got within bowshot', then loose off an arrow with 'exceptional dexterity', which 'rarely, if ever, missed'. The assailant would then bound forward, snatch the sentry's musket and disappear before the alarm could be raised. On one occasion, after a guard had stubbornly refused to give up his weapon, his attacker leapt on him 'like a cat', drew 'a sharp dagger' and was 'about to decapitate' him when a sergeant came to his aid. As the attacker 'started to slice into the skin of the back of … [the sentry's] neck', the sergeant charged into the melee and bayoneted him. The Indian screamed 'when he felt the steel', leapt up and fled into the woods.[5] Following a trail of blood, the guards later found his corpse, whilst the sentry, who had served the royalists until his capture at Boyacá, was promoted to corporal for his bravery.

A few days later a more serious attack occurred. After the column had stopped for the night in a small village, Lieutenant Reynolds, one of the original Rifle officers who had sailed on the *Dowson*, was sent with four men to gather yucca and plantains from the fields. Minutes later just one returned, babbling incoherently about a 'horde of Indians' that had risen 'up like magic from the ground'. Sandes dispatched a company to investigate. Although the attackers had disappeared, the bodies of Reynolds and his men were soon found, covered with arrow wounds. 'Some [of the barbs] … had been pulled out [to be used again], but one or two were still firmly lodged in each body.'[6]

After this incident, patrols were routinely sent out to sweep the area around camp each night. Whilst leading one such mission, Captain Wright was attacked. Picking their way through the forest in the failing light, the 25 men of his patrol were ambushed. The Indians were all around them, firing arrows from behind trees and bushes. Wright was the first hit. An arrow struck his right shoulder, the barbs lodging under the bone and preventing any movement. Whilst he lay incapacitated amidst the foliage, his men returned fire, lighting up the gloom with musket flashes. Sergeant Carillo then came to his aid and managed to work the shaft free, but in the process was hit himself in the chest. The barb pierced his heart, killing him instantly. Three or four others were then hit before the attackers were driven off into the night.[7]

A few miles closer to Valledupar, the Indians launched an even more audacious attack. Having made several sweeps of the surrounding woods, Lara ordered the men to set up camp in an abandoned village. Believing they were safe for the night, the Rifles stacked their muskets in the main square, and settled down. Infante's cavalry, meanwhile, had ridden out to a nearby meadow to graze their horses. The cavalry had started to make fires to prepare their own food when one noticed a Capuchin friar on horseback in the distance. Realizing that an attack was imminent, he raised the alarm, but it was too late. The Indians had crawled through the long grass 'like ants' and rose up amongst them. The horses panicked, scattering through the trees, whilst their riders fled towards the village with the Indians in hot pursuit. Both groups reached the square simultaneously. Seeing the stacked muskets, the Indians rushed towards them. The Rifles ran to intercept them and hand-to-hand fighting broke out. Wrestling over the weapons, the patriots gouged and punched their opponents, who retaliated with their knives. Eventually the Indians were driven back by weight of numbers, leaving several dead or wounded in the square. The friar who had masterminded the attack was nowhere to be seen.

This incident was the last real challenge of the campaign. A few more attempts were made to snatch the cavalry horses, but musket volleys into the surrounding trees proved sufficient deterrent, and the column arrived at Valledupar in July largely unmolested. Expecting Montilla and the Irish Legion to be awaiting them, Lara and his officers were dumbstruck when they found the city deserted. What had become of Devereux's men?

Chapter 27

MUTINY!

Rio de la Hacha was all but deserted when the Irish Legion landed on 13 March 1820. Knowing that his Indian troops were better suited to skirmishing and laying ambushes in the forests, the royalist commander, Sanchez Lima, had withdrawn them eight miles into the interior. In town, 18 cannon were found spiked and abandoned along with a mass of Nicaraguan hardwood. Ready for export, the timber would command high prices in the markets of Jamaica. After posting a strong guard of sailors to protect it from the Irish, Admiral Brion issued an edict forbidding further looting. The order was ignored. The Irish and Creole troops went from house to house ransacking the interiors in their search for alcohol and plunder. 'A soldier and a black man' caught 'abusing some of the inhabitants' who had not fled into the woods, were later chosen to pay for the general indiscipline. Brion forced them 'to draw lots' to see which would 'be shot by firing squad'. As Colonel O'Connor looked on, 'the officer who had the straws in his hand tricked the Blackman'. The latter was executed without further ado. Cowed by the punishment, the rest of the men returned to their units, order was restored and the locals began to drift back to town.[1]

Meanwhile, Montilla set about preparing the defences.[2] The cannon were unspiked, guards were posted to hold the outlying batteries, the fort was garrisoned and outposts were set up on the edge of the forest. As a final precaution, the admiral ordered the fleet into the bay, close enough to provide covering fire should Sanchez Lima dare to launch an attack. Whilst patrolling the beach, the Irish came across the remains of MacGregor's men. Having been executed by the Spanish in November the previous year, the bodies had been left to rot where they lay.[3] A few days after the Legion's arrival, several British merchant ships sailed into the bay. Brion sold them the captured timber, whilst Colonel O'Connor bought 'a little tobacco, some foodstuffs and barrels of wine' to supplement his

Lancers' rations. The other Irish units had to rely on a seemingly inexhaustible supply of giant turtles, taken from the river to the east of town. They were 'so large that a single one … [was] sufficient to feed a hundred men'.[4] As Brion's aide-de-camp, Captain Parsons had access to the best supplies in town. His breakfast included 'wild ducks, cold venison [and] bullock's hearts … washed down with claret, port, or grog of either rum, brandy or gin'.[5] The Dubliner soon grew sick of this 'delicate food', however, and craved 'something in the shape of an Irish breakfast' of 'tea, bread, butter and eggs'.[6]

On 17 March Commander Padilla hosted a Saint Patrick's Day celebration. Whilst the band brought out from Dublin played 'Rule Britannia', 'God Save the King' and 'Saint Patrick's Day', the normally reserved Captain Parsons danced as if 'the Devil had got into [his] … heels'. The alcohol flowed and the party continued into the small hours of the morning.[7] Despite the festivities, the Legion's morale was going into decline. There was still no sign of the bonuses the men had been promised and several of the officers who had been assured promotion remained in junior positions. By way of protest, Colonel Aylmer, who was nominally in charge of O'Connor's Lancers, refused to leave his quarters, justifying his stand by claiming that Devereux 'had tricked him'. To calm the situation, Brion promised their bonuses would be paid once his brother-in-law had returned from Jamaica with the proceeds from the captured timber.[8] Meanwhile, O'Connor kept the men busy with drill and weapons training and on the afternoon of 23 March, before serious discontent could arise, the Legion was ordered to march for Valledupar.

The 430 Irish who remained well enough to march were divided into three units under the overall command of Colonel Aylmer. Colonel O'Lawler led a company of sharpshooters. Major Richard Rudd, a Waterloo veteran from County Wexford, headed the light battalion of Cundinamarca, and Colonel O'Connor commanded six under-strength companies of unmounted Lancers.[9] Completing the column was a unit of 100 marines from Brion's fleet, veterans of the attack on El Morro led by Colonel Jackson, and a small party of German engineers. Captain Parsons, who remained in Rio de la Hacha with 700 native troops under Commander Padilla, watched as his compatriots left town. They seemed 'in high spirits', were 'perfectly sober, and in tolerable good order'.[10]

Leaving the flat scrubland of the coast, the column marched due south for three days, entering a region of thickly forested valleys flanked by arid hills. The humidity built throughout the morning and by midday became unbearable. Little water was found and the men suffered terribly from thirst. As O'Connor was aware, they were marching through hostile Guajiro territory. The Indians abandoned their villages as the patriots approached, the women and children going deep into the forest, whilst the warriors shadowed the column, constantly keeping out of sight. At the end of each day the Irish commanders formed up their units for a headcount. Invariably several men were missing.

On the march, the weakest lagged behind and others went off to look for water. Each evening search parties were sent out, 'but never was a single [one] … brought back alive; those that went to look for them found them murdered on the path', having been mutilated 'in the most barbarous manner'.[11]

After three days the column reached the village of Moreno. Then on 29 March, scouts detected an enemy presence on the outskirts of Fonseca. The royalists held a strong position to the right of the road, defended by earthworks and barricades. At 8.00am the next day, Montilla ordered his skirmishers to advance. Keeping up a steady fire from the woods for an hour, they dropped several of the defenders before the marines and the light company of Cundinamarca fixed bayonets and charged. Seeing the line hurtling towards them, the royalists fled back to their main position in the village.[12] The defence of Fonseca was organized by a handful of Spanish officers, who positioned their Indian allies in the houses and behind barricades thrown up across the main streets. Following up their success on the outskirts, Jackson's marines and Rudd's light company arrived on the heels of the routed defenders and ran straight into the volley fire of the royalist reserve. They fell back in disorder, but when the rest of Montilla's division caught up, vicious street fighting ensued. The royalists defended tenaciously, keeping up a tremendous fire 'from the windows … and down all the streets from the outskirts to the central square'.[13] In the middle of the fight, Major Rudd's horse was startled by musketry. Whilst he struggled to regain control, the men of the Cundinamarca Regiment wavered to the point of breaking. Displaying 'coolness and promptitude' under fire, Lieutenant Ternan took control, formed the regiment into line and advanced.[14] Moving steadily from house to house using bayonets and musket butts, the troops drove off the last of the defenders after two hours of fighting. The survivors fled through the woods to the south-west, whilst the Irish counted their losses. Two officers and five men had been killed and ten wounded. Royalist casualties were 'much more considerable'.[15] Impressed with his bravery, Montilla promoted Lieutenant Ternan to captain and transferred him to his personal staff.

Only after the fighting had finished did they realize that the German engineers were missing. Scouts later came across their remains. Having entered Fonseca by a different track to the rest of the division, the Germans had been wiped out whilst their comrades were pinned down on the far side of the village.[16] Their bodies had been mutilated. Fingers, toes, noses, limbs, ears and genitalia had all been removed. In his memoirs, O'Connor coolly remarked 'it was war to the death and neither side took prisoners'.[17] After the victory the patriots rested for three days, then continued their march at daybreak on 2 April. Following the valley 15 miles south-west, they encountered the enemy again at the village of San Juan. The royalist commander, Colonel Diaz, had placed his men behind a ravine in the woods three miles outside town but 30 minutes of musketry dislodged them. Falling back to San Juan, the royalists barricaded themselves into the houses. As O'Connor later recalled, the street fighting that followed was intense. 'As we entered down the main street, they opened fire from the windows, my horse [was hit and] fell flat on his face: I picked him up with the reins, but ... hardly got him to the square [before he died].'[18] After two hours the last defenders were driven out by repeated bayonet charges. The survivors fled over a river and dispersed into the woods to the south.

The morning after the battle, O'Connor paid one of his soldiers to carry his saddle and another to struggle with his hammock and trunk, then left San Juan on foot at the head of his Lancers. Noticing his discomfort, Montilla lent him his remount, 'a heroic animal from the plains of the Orinoco'.[19] O'Connor was overjoyed. The horse had incredible stamina and would serve him well for the remainder of the campaign. As the column drew closer to Valledupar, the landscape changed yet again. The virgin forests of the north were replaced by monotonous fields of sugar cane, where the troops rested in the shade at the end of each day's march. On one occasion, seated on the floor of a peasant's shack, O'Connor and Montilla were sharing a meal of unseasoned beef with a plantain leaf as a tablecloth, when an aide burst in. A snake had bitten one of the Lancers on the foot and his comrades feared that he would die. The victim was 'in dreadful pain ... bleeding from his mouth, nose and ears and in convulsions'.[20] Amongst the onlookers was the owner of the house that O'Connor had occupied. Through an interpreter, Montilla demanded that he cure the soldier, threatening him with execution if he failed. Escorted by a soldier, the Indian returned a short while later with a *vejuco* root which he rubbed on the bite, before giving the victim an infusion made from the same plant. He made a swift recovery and the column continued its advance.[21]

In early April they arrived at Valledupar. On their approach the locals had fled, leaving the town deserted. With little to do whilst awaiting Lara's division advancing from the south, Montilla settled the troops into a routine of drill and weapons training. As the days passed, provisions became scarce. Now 100 miles from their base at Rio de la Hacha, the supply lines were stretched to breaking point. Although Montilla made every effort to acquire what he could, and even paid from his own pocket for luxuries such as rum and sugar when they were available, the mood in town began to turn sour.[22]

The situation at Rio de la Hacha was also growing tense. With Montilla's troops far to the south, Brion and Padilla had just 700 men to defend the town against the increasingly hostile locals. To make matters worse, 70 of the garrison were sick and of the rest, a large proportion were sailors from the fleet and ill prepared for such duties. Scattered shots were regularly heard outside the walls and gangs of armed Indians and Creoles of dubious allegiance were seen on the outskirts of town after dark. Fearing attack, Captains Parsons slept fully clothed with his sword, pistols and carbine by his side. Plans were put in place to torch the houses should the troops have to make a rapid departure, and new units were recruited from amongst the local Indians to bolster the defence. Parsons doubted their loyalty, however, believing that 'they would change from one side to another for a glass of grog'.[23] His lack of faith would prove well founded.

Meanwhile, back in Valledupar, Montilla's scouts reported enemy forces gathering in Molinos, a village 20 miles to the north. By positioning his troops between the column and Rio de la Hacha, the royalist commander, Sanchez de Lima, had cut the lines of supply. Montilla had no option but to break camp and march against them. As they approached, De Lima's troops dispersed to the north. Not wishing to take on the Irish in battle after their two recent defeats, the royalists confined their activities to harassing the rear and flanks of the enemy column as it fell back to Fonseca. On arrival at the village, Montilla received reports of a massacre at Moreno, three days march further north. A mixed unit of 50 Irishmen, who had been discharged from the hospital in Rio de la Hacha, and 100 locally recruited Creoles under Colonel Garcia had been ambushed at the village on 13 April. En route to reinforce Montilla's column, Garcia's troops had been caught completely off guard. Creeping into the village whilst the patriots were sleeping, Guajiros had set fire to their huts. Several men had been burnt alive. In the confused fighting that followed, the patriots' Creole contingent had gone over to the enemy, leaving the Irish to form up round their colours and fight their way out. Half made it back to Rio de la Hacha, the rest had been killed in the village or cut down during the retreat. Captain Sinnot and Assistant Surgeon McEldery were amongst the dead. Captain Murray of the Lancers was horrendously wounded, but despite a sword blow that had nearly decapitated him, he somehow struggled back to the coast.[24]

Expecting the royalists to attack his column next, Montilla decided to await them in Fonseca, whilst sending the sick and wounded back to Rio de la Hacha by a little-used route. Unknown to the colonel, 15 healthy Irish officers accompanied them.[25] When he heard, Montilla was furious and dispatched troops to bring them back. The next day a court martial dismissed them from the service, effective on reaching the coast. Four days had now passed since the ambush at Moreno and, as there was still no sign of the enemy, Montilla held a council of war. With Jackson acting as his interpreter, the colonel outlined their position. The ambush at Moreno had cut them off from the coast and the latest intelligence suggested that their opponents were gathering in strength somewhere to the north. Believing the men would mutiny if they were ordered back to Rio de la Hacha with nothing to show for their endeavours, O'Connor proposed they march back to Valledupar to wait for Lara's column to join them from the south, but the majority wanted to head for the coast without delay. The massacre at Moreno had rattled them.

Faced with the prospect of being cut off in enemy territory in command of an unruly mob threatening to mutiny, Montilla was only too happy to oblige them.

With the decision made, the column headed for Rio de la Hacha. As he had predicted, O'Connor 'heard several soldiers complaining about the retreat' even before they had left the outskirts of town.[26] On the march, rumours of Brion's profiteering caused further discontent. Some claimed that he had made a profit of 'sixty thousand' pesos on the sale of the timber, and the men were determined to claim their share.[27] To make matters worse, supplies of food and water were growing scarcer. When the troops reached the site of the massacre at Moreno, their morale took another blow. Amidst the ashes were the mutilated and charred corpses of old comrades who had fallen in the fight. After their remains had been buried, the column pushed on, arriving at Rio de la Hacha on 16 May. Any hopes of a share of Brion's profits were soon dashed. Insisting that the money was needed to pay the government's debts, Brion refused the Legion's requests for compensation. Furious, the Irish retired to their quarters around the main square to discuss their next move. Many were convinced that Brion was lying to them and some even wanted to rise up in revolt. Despite their anger, however, the men and officers alike proceeded with caution, each group sending petitions to Montilla expressing their views. The letter from the rank and file asked for their dismissal from the service and transportation to a British colony. As it was anonymous, Montilla ignored their request. The second petition was signed by 52 officers and was taken very seriously indeed. Complaining 'of their wants', they demanded their bonuses and back pay, threatening to take action if they received an unfavourable answer.[28] On 19 May a meeting of senior officers was held in Montilla's headquarters to discuss the situation. Whilst writing to Bolívar of their 'spirit of insubordination and insolence', Montilla was not unsympathetic to their cause and did all he could to take care of their daily needs.[29] With a credit note to be paid by his family in France, he 'contracted with … [one] merchant … for shoes and clothing', acquired 25 barrels of flour from another and even sold his gold watch to obtain tobacco for the men.[30] Nevertheless, with no sign of the Irishmen's bonuses, the rumblings of discontent rolled on.

Whilst Montilla attempted to hold the division together, Brion's actions only exacerbated the situation. Rumours of his contempt for the Irish were rife. He regularly referred to them as 'thieves and cowards' and when they applied for standards to carry on campaign he dismissed the idea, stating that 'broom sticks only were fit for them'.[31] A visiting merchant, whose vessel the *Betsy Ann* along with several others had been detained in the harbour for the use of the troops, kept a diary which gives an insight into the atmosphere in town. Mr Low recorded that the Irish 'all spoke very favourably of Colonel Montilla, but I didn't hear any man speak well of the admiral'. He went on to admit 'that his conduct, while I was in port, was well calculated to give a bad impression of his prudence, or aptitude for such an important role'.[32] A few days after the officers had written their letter, 32 of the signatories resigned. Combined with the losses caused by sickness or combat, the resignations were devastating for the Legion. Only six officers out of an original complement of 47 remained with the Cundinamarca Regiment. The Lancers and sharpshooters were comparably reduced. Those who stayed were far from satisfied with their lot and the rumblings amongst the men continued unabated. The next day, however, the sudden appearance of the enemy outside town put the issue temporarily on hold.

Emboldened by reports of the Legion's discontent, Sanchez de Lima ordered 800 cavalry to advance against the patriots' outposts early in the morning of 20 May.[33] By 8.00am the pickets had been overwhelmed and were rushing back to town with the cavalry in pursuit. Several locals spontaneously took up arms to drive them off. The Legion's band which was quartered in the vicinity also joined the counter-attack. Roused by the 'sharp fire' on the other side of town, colonels O'Connor and Aylmer gathered the Lancers and a single company of sharpshooters in the square.[34] Montilla then ordered them to engage the enemy. Supported by a single 6-pdr, the 200-strong column marched towards the fight. By the time it arrived, the majority of the locals and the band had fled. Under cover in the bushes previously occupied by the patriot pickets, the royalists were firing on the few troops who remained. Aylmer led his men out against them. After firing a few scattered shots the enemy retreated, regrouping just over half a mile away from town. With the remains of the band formed up on their flanks, the Lancers pursued them at the double, soon leaving the artillery far behind. Minutes later they came up to the royalists' position. De Lima had lined his men on level ground near a saltwater lagoon with dense woodland a few hundred yards to their rear. The Irish halted 400 yards out and Aylmer gave the order to fire. By the time the smoke had cleared, the royalists had retreated to the tree line. Meanwhile Montilla's artillery had hauled their 6-pdr into position. Two or three round shot were fired in quick succession. The Irish then fixed bayonets and charged through 'a smoke so thick' that O'Connor 'couldn't see a thing'.[35] Before the bayonets could bite home the royalist line broke and fled. The corpses of 'eight or nine men' were found. The Irish had lost just three.

With no cavalry to follow up the victory, the battle proved indecisive. Nevertheless, it momentarily overshadowed the Legion's complaints and for the next four days there were no further disturbances. On 24 May, however, the situation deteriorated. That morning Montilla ordered the drummers and buglers to play the men in on parade, planning to advance into the countryside to seek a decisive showdown with the enemy. Colonel Jackson's marines, a locally recruited infantry regiment, the artillery and a cavalry picket formed up. But of the Irish Legion, only O'Connor and his Lancers answered the call. Dreading a protracted march chasing shadows in the burning heat of the day, the Cundinamarca and sharpshooter regiments refused to leave their barracks until they received pay. Without their support, Montilla dared not risk an engagement. Furious with their disobedience, he dismissed the parade.

Early the next morning O'Connor rode out to check on the pickets. At daybreak, he noticed smoke rising from a copse of trees a little way beyond the town's perimeter. Riding closer, he clearly heard 'the strokes of the hatchet cutting wood'.[36] De Lima's men had returned. After informing Montilla, O'Connor tried to persuade the Legion to take the field.[37] To everyone's surprise the troops agreed.[38] The division formed up on the outskirts of town and marched on De Lima's encampment. The column was 870-strong. Colonel Jackson's marines and the artillery's two cannon led the line. Following them were Padilla's Rio de la Hacha Regiment. The Irish came next, with Aylmer's Lancers marching on foot ahead of Rudd's Cundinamarca unit and the sharpshooters under Colonel O'Lawler. In the rear were a few mounted cavalry pickets, both Irish and Creole, commanded by Lieutenant-Colonel Hobkirk. On the march the column became strung out and soon Jackson's marines and Montilla and his staff were well ahead of the rest. Unknown to the patriots, De Lima had hidden 300 troops in the bushes to the right of their line of advance. As the marines neared the encampment, the trap was sprung. Thirty were killed or wounded in the first volley alone. Whilst Jackson tried to rally his men, Montilla sent Colonel Stopford, his chief of staff, to bring up reinforcements. Unsure of where the fire was coming from, the marines blazed away blindly as the enemy volleys tore through their ranks. All was smoke, screams and confusion.

When Stopford galloped up to Aylmer and breathlessly asked for his help, the colonel acted decisively. Separating his men from the rest of the column, he advanced at the double on a looping march to outflank the ambuscade. Deafened by the noise of their own musketry and blinded by the smoke, the royalists failed to notice the approaching danger until it was too late. Just 20 yards away from their position, the Lancers opened fire. Three volleys crashed out in little over a minute, killing 37, including the royalist commander. Without giving them a chance to recover, Aylmer then charged. Several royalists were bayoneted, the rest fled back to their main line. After re-forming his men, Montilla continued the advance, with the cavalry, Cundinamarca Regiment and sharpshooters still some way to the rear. Following the fleeing enemy troops, they marched two miles down a narrow path through the woods before emerging onto a grassy plain, known as the Savana del Patron, where De Lima had taken up position. With 3,000 men, the royalists were drawn up in line with a screen of skirmishers in the woods on either flank. Montilla ordered his men to halt and each regiment deployed in column. The enemy opened fire, but at such long range did little damage. When the regiment of

Cundinamarca and the sharpshooters finally arrived, the patriots advanced. As the range closed, the royalists' fire began to tell. Aylmer was wounded by a skirmisher sniping from the woods and O'Connor was slowed by a glancing blow to the shoulder. The patriots closed to within a few dozen yards before firing. For 30 minutes the lines blasted volleys at each other across the plain. At first neither side gained the advantage. But when the artillerymen brought up their 6-pdr, the fight turned against De Lima's men. Seeing a shiver pass through the royalists with every load of grapeshot, Montilla switched from columns into line and gave the order to fix bayonets. 'With a terrible cheer' the patriots charged.[39] Not waiting to receive them, the enemy broke ranks and dispersed into the woods to the south. When the Irish emerged through the smoke, nothing but a few head of cattle and the dead and wounded remained. Determined to score a decisive victory, Montilla ordered the pursuit. Hobkirk's cavalry galloped into the woods in one direction, whilst Jackson led his marines in another. At home in the forest, the royalists easily evaded the pursuit. Despite suffering over 300 dead, captured and wounded, De Lima's army would live to fight another day.

Amongst the prisoners was a Spanish officer who had surrendered to Montilla's Irish aides, captains Byrne and Ternan. As they were accompanying him across the battlefield, a Creole captain blocked their path. 'Are you one of Ferdinand's officers?' he demanded. 'Yes,' replied the Spaniard, punctuating his defiance with a cry of 'Long live the King!'[40] Without a moment's hesitation, the captain drew a pistol and shot him dead. The Irish were appalled. As they stared in disbelief, the Creole turned on his heel and casually walked away. Despite such scenes, the men were in buoyant spirits after the victory and agreed to go out in search of the enemy the next morning. The march took them 15 miles inland to the village of El Passa. There was no sign of De Lima's forces so Montilla gave up and turned back to the coast. The men were exhausted and had not eaten all day. With the midday sun burning overhead, the return march was horrendous. Several died of fatigue. The rest limped back to Rio de la Hacha with spirits broken. Collapsing in their barracks that evening, they vowed never to leave town again.

On 27 May, with the Irish rank and file still skulking in their quarters, Montilla held a dinner to celebrate the victory at Savana del Patron. Each officer who had fought in the action was presented with a pair of shoes as a reward. A few days later an American schooner brought news from Santa Marta. According to the captain, when word of Montilla's victory had reached the city, the locals had considered switching allegiance. The captain was convinced that if the patriot flotilla appeared off the coast, they would rise up in rebellion, handing an easy victory to Montilla's men. Enticed by the prospect of plundering one of Spain's most important possessions, the Irish were keen at first, but when Brion delayed by objecting to certain details, their enthusiasm waned. Distrustful of the admiral, the men feared that he would once again rob them of their spoils. Montilla decided to bring matters to a head by organizing a vote. The decision split the Legion. Half were willing to continue. The rest insisted that they still wanted to resign.

On 2 June, a drunken Brion entered Montilla's headquarters and began insulting Major Bourne and captains Boardman and Ternan. He declared that all the Irish were 'rascally, cowardly and mutinous' and a 'disgrace to the patriot service'. His pride stung, Bourne countered 'that the Irish were never known to be cowards [and] … had achieved more for the cause … than he with his fleet had ever been able to perform'.[41] Furious, Brion rushed upon the major, snatched the cigar from between his lips and dashed it against him. Before he could cause further mischief, Ternan restrained him. Two of Brion's men then appeared and demanded his release, threatening to cut Ternan down if he refused. Just when bloodshed seemed inevitable, Montilla arrived and ordered the Irish to back down. Unable to bring the enemy to a decisive action and with his troops beginning to turn on one another, Montilla finally lost patience and decided to abandon the campaign.

On the night of 4 June the evacuation began. The sick and wounded were the first to be rowed out to the ships. Next to depart were a crowd of local civilians, fearful of royalist retribution should they remain behind. All the while the troops were confined to their quarters and growing increasingly impatient. Around midnight discipline finally collapsed. Breaking out of their quarters, the Irish and Creoles alike rampaged through town in search of loot and liquor. Even some of Brion's marines took part. Sergeant William Burke discovered a hidden cache of gold that he would later use to set himself up in business in Jamaica.[42] Others found 'large quantities of rum' in the abandoned houses. The barrels were broken apart and the booze carried off 'in all kinds of vessels'.[43] According to O'Connor, the Lancers were the only Irish unit not to take part. Convinced that the enemy would take advantage of the confusion to launch an attack, they remained on guard on the perimeter of town as the chaos played out around them.

In the small hours of the morning several buildings on the southern outskirts of town caught fire. Lieutenant White of the Cundinamarca Regiment claimed that the locals set them ablaze, preferring to leave nothing but ashes for the royalists. Others blamed Brion's marines and some said gangs of drunken Irish looters were responsible. O'Connor heard some of the Legion had laid gunpowder trails leading up to the houses and Montilla's report to Bolívar makes mention of Irish arsonists threatening to kill any officers who tried to stop them.[44] The fire spread with alarming speed. Leaping between the wooden houses, the flames pushed north towards the town centre and the sea. Several Irish troops were so intoxicated that they perished in the blaze.[45] Fearing they would be cut off, O'Connor and his Lancers withdrew to the main square. Only then was the Legion given permission to embark. After the last of the sharpshooters and Cundinamarca Regiment had been rowed offshore, the men of O'Connor's rearguard made their way to the beach. By now the town was an inferno. As they dashed through the streets, flames leapt into the night sky. Clouds of black smoke spiralled upwards and ashes rained down. Aside from a unit of marines under Major Graham that was holding the fort, the Lancers were the last to leave town. At 3.00am they were rowed offshore. Passing from ship to ship in the bay, they tried to find a captain who would take them. Most, however, were already packed with soldiers, sailors and civilian refugees. By the time Captain McCormick of the *Lord Rodney* finally allowed them aboard, the sun had appeared on the eastern horizon and a new day had dawned.

All was confusion on board the ships. In the chaos of the night before, the units had been divided and each vessel now contained a mixture of men. Most were unsure of their destination. Several believed the plan to capture Santa Marta would still go ahead. To make matters worse, the rations had been poorly distributed. Whilst the *Lord Rodney* was supplied with 'plenty of water, ten barrels of flour and four casks of beef' the *Dash* 'had not a [single] cask of water onboard'.[46] Incensed that their ships had been taken over by drunken, mutinous Irishmen, the merchant captains struck their colours to signal that they were no longer in command.[47] Throughout the morning, Brion's gunboats sailed between the ships, pausing at each vessel to insist that the Irish troops give up their arms. Only then did the men realize that they were bound for a British colony. Nevertheless, many were reluctant to part with their muskets and in several cases the warships had to threaten 'to blow them out of the water' before they complied.[48]

Fearing that his Lancers would be disbanded along with the rest of the Legion, O'Connor commandeered a boat and was rowed over to the *Urdaneta* to discuss the situation with Montilla. Insisting that his regiment had played no part in the mutiny, O'Connor persuaded the colonel to allow the Lancers to remain in service. He then shuttled back and forth between the ships all morning, reiterating the offer to his men. Although some were content to proceed to Jamaica, 72 accepted and were transferred to Brion's ships. At 5.00am Major Graham's marines abandoned the fort. After lighting fuses leading to the magazine, they hurried to the beach and were rowed out into the bay as the explosion rent the air. Flames flew upwards, a column of dust and debris rose into the sky and fragments of stone and wood splashed about them. With the fort in ruins and the town ablaze, Brion's fleet departed. The admiral and his warships sailed west along the coast, whilst the merchantmen carrying 544 mutinous Irishmen steered north for Jamaica.[49]

Chapter 28

THE EVE OF SAINT SIMÓN

I n early 1820, news of the conditions faced by the Irish Legion at Margarita began
to filter back to Dublin. At first the reports were disbelieved, but as more letters
arrived the weight of evidence became overwhelming. In time the public would turn
against Devereux and an inquiry headed by his former supporter, Daniel O'Connell,
would be launched to investigate the matter. Initially, however, the early returnees were
ridiculed as feather-bed soldiers. Detachments continued to set off for the New World
and 'the general' enjoyed widespread support. When the *Nicolai Pollewitch* left Belfast in
February 1820, for example, Brigadier General Middleton Power, the commander of the
150 troops of the Irish 1st Light Infantry, did not hesitate to set sail. A veteran of the 28th
Foot, Power had seen action 'in Holland, Germany, Egypt … Portugal and Spain'.[1]
It would take more than a few letters to dissuade him from his latest adventure. His sole
concession to the rumours was to alter the *Pollewitch*'s destination. Rather than head for
Margarita, he decided to proceed directly to Angostura, believing that his men would be
better received there.

Once under way, the *Pollewitch* proved 'a true and faithful servant' and Power's unit
arrived in the New World without losing a single man.[2] After reaching the Gulf of Paria,
the detachment proceeded up the Orinoco, dropping anchor off Angostura at 3.00pm on
14 April 1820.[3] As the first forces of the Irish Legion to arrive at the capital, they caused
considerable commotion. Cannon and small arms were fired in salute and grand
preparations were made to receive them.[4] After a final night on the river, the men
disembarked, parading on the beach in front of a crowd of locals. A party was held that
night in the palace on the main square.[5] In the weeks that followed, the Irish officers
swiftly settled into Angostura's expatriate community. Major Hodges was quartered with
Mr Thompson, a North American merchant, whilst Power and several others stayed

with the Scot, James Hamilton. Their daily routine was one of luxury and leisure. In the cool of the early morning they went riding in the countryside, returning to a breakfast of fruit, eggs and coffee. Dinners of 'fresh meat and fish' served with wine were eaten at 5.00pm.[6] 'Scarce a night … passed without a ball, and dinner parties … [were] frequent.'[7] Rations for the rank and file were also plentiful. Each man received '3lb of beef and 1lb of bread, equal to half-a-pint of rum, salt, vegetables and tobacco' and some pay was available 'to defray … [their] expenses'.[8]

In early May two horse races took place on the outskirts of town. 'All the native Officers and respectable inhabitants were there.'[9] The first pitted Power, mounted on a fine thoroughbred named Devereux, against Major Thomas Manby, who was back in the capital on leave after campaigning in New Granada. Major Egan 'acted as steward and judge'.[10] Galloping between two rows of cheering spectators, Power crossed the finishing line ahead of his rival.[11] Mr Thompson, the owner of the horse, was especially pleased, having backed the brigadier general to the value of 500 pesos. A second race, held immediately afterwards, was won by Egan's groom.

Two weeks later Power and his men left the capital for the front line. They reached San Juan de Payara, the headquarters of General Páez's army of the west, in early June 'without losing a man, except one by an Alligator' and were promptly incorporated into the British Legion under Colonel Blosset.[12] In late August the regiment moved yet again, this time heading for Achaguas, a Llanero town built between two rivers, which was to be its base for the next eight months.[13]

At first, the volunteers were content in their new home. The officers and men alike thought Páez 'a fine … fellow' and the appreciation proved mutual.[14] Rations of flour and beef were plentiful as was rum 'when it … [could] be procured', and half pay was issued 'as help for subsistence'.[15] With their immediate needs taken care of, the Legion's officers indulged their passions in their free time. Captain James Paterson organized an amateur dramatics club which regularly performed plays, particularly those by Shakespeare. His efforts were 'very well' received. Others enjoyed far baser entertainments. Gambling was extremely popular and cockfights and bull-baiting were well attended by all ranks.[16] Perhaps the most exciting events were the jaguar and panther hunts, designed to clear 'the woods of as many of the wild beasts as possible'. If not regularly culled, their confidence around humans would grow and they became *cebádos* (man-eaters) – a threat to anyone wandering in the wilds alone.[17] After arming themselves with tough hide lassos and bamboo lances, the mounted hunters would set out accompanied by beaters on foot leading 'tall stout limbed tiger dogs of Cumana', a powerful breed of bloodhound introduced by the Conquistadores.[18] The beaters then surrounded the woods, leaving a single escape route leading to a glade where the hunters would be waiting. When all were in position the beaters advanced, driving the quarry from the woods in ones and twos. The hunters worked in pairs to intercept them. Lassoing a single feline simultaneously from opposite directions, they tightened their ropes, thus rendering the animal incapable of charging either one, before closing in and finishing it off with repeated lance thrusts.[19]

A couple of months after the British Legion had arrived, conditions in Achaguas began to deteriorate. The supplies of rum and flour slowed to a trickle and then dried up entirely. By September bad beef and water were all that was available, and in November the men stopped receiving pay.[20] With no signs of the situation improving, the volunteers took out their frustrations on Colonel Blosset. Although at first his disciplined approach had held the Legion together, he had grown increasingly apathetic and withdrawn since the defeat at Cumaná. Isolated from the men and field officers, he became susceptible to flattery from his staff, a fault exploited by the man who would become the real power behind the Legion, Captain Traynor. A former corporal in the British Army, Traynor had 'wormed himself into the colonel's confidence' to such a degree that he became 'his sole advisor' and was rewarded with an influential role as brigade major.[21] His fellow officers despised him. One thought him 'an illiterate man of low, vulgar habits' with an 'overbearing arrogance and insolent assumption', whose 'only redeeming qualities were a bustling activity and tolerably soldier-like appearance'.[22] The rank and file were also against him as a deeply ingrained snobbery led them to resent those who rose from the ranks. Hated by all, Traynor grew increasingly embittered and commanded with 'a severity that astonished'.[23] The officers blamed Blosset for indulging his petty acts of cruelty and his behaviour eventually led them to threaten mass resignation.[24] When Blosset ignored all criticism, however, the feeling of discontent spread to the ranks and soon the stage was set for another mutiny.

The spark was struck on 27 October 1820, the eve of Saint Simón's day. That morning Achaguas was a hive of activity. South Americans and Europeans alike were busy preparing for a grand celebration to be held the following day. A bullfight and illuminations were planned and a play was to be put on by Captain Paterson. Traynor had ordered the Legion's light company to build the stage. The officers in charge of the work party, Captain Hodgkinson and Lieutenant Risdale, had been born into privilege and as such despised Traynor for his lowly background. The major reciprocated their animosity and habitually gave the light company the most gruelling tasks as a result.[25] That morning the sun rose 'bright and glorious'.[26] By mid-afternoon the heat and humidity were intense. Felling trees on the outskirts of town, the men of the light company were soon exhausted. Hodgkinson doled out 'ardent spirits … twice or thrice' to cheer them and by the time their work was done the men were drunk.[27] 'Noisy and riotous' they hauled the logs back to town.[28] When Traynor saw them he was furious and drove 'the inebriated and unarmed men' back to their quarters, beating any who resisted with the flat of his sword.[29] When he later came across Lieutenant Risdale, he blamed him for the commotion. Risdale's denial of the charges, issued with effortlessly 'amiable manners' and 'gentlemanlike … conduct' drove Traynor to distraction.[30] Thundering 'You, sir are as drunk as those whose cause you espouse!' he placed the lieutenant under arrest and confined him to quarters.[31]

Inside the Legion's barracks on the main square, a heated argument was in full flow. Sick of the deteriorating conditions and Traynor's tyranny, several of the men wanted to petition Páez for Blosset's replacement, whilst others called for open mutiny. When news of Risdale's arrest came in, there was uproar. The bugler sounded the call to arms and all 500 men rushed into the plaza with fixed bayonets, shouting 'Down with Blosset!' and 'Death to Traynor!' The commotion woke several British officers from their midday siestas. Leaping from their beds they ran towards the square, pulling on shirts and breeches. At first the officers were unsure how best to deal with the situation, but when Colonel Davy arrived he took control. Moving towards the mutineers, he 'endeavoured to pacify' them, but several rushed from the ranks and bayoneted him in three places before his fellow officers could drag him clear.[32] When Blosset appeared, 'well armed and determined to restore order', he was also set upon by the men. It fell to Páez to calm the situation.[33]

Proceeded by cries of 'Paez! Paez!' the Caudillo galloped into the square, his mere presence causing a hush to fall over the mutineers.[34] 'Calm and collected … his eye flashing indignation', he called his American troops to arms. With the mutineers frozen to the spot, the regiment of Apure formed up facing them and awaited the order to fire. Páez then called for Captain Wiltheu, his English aide, to announce his commands. Standing before the mob, Wiltheu declared that if any man had a complaint he should step forward and make himself known. A hushed conference took place amongst the mutineers and at length six sergeants advanced to represent them. As soon as they left the ranks, they were seized by Páez's troops and disarmed. With the situation under control, Traynor made a belated appearance. As the six sergeants stood by 'in mute despair', he ordered Captain Hodgkinson to select 12 men from the light company to form the firing squad. The captain refused. Proudly defiant, he told Páez: '*My* fate depends on *your* will; my disgrace or honour upon my *own*.' Páez had him arrested, stripped of his rank and sent under escort to the guard room. The firing squad was then formed and the sergeants lined up against a low stone wall. As the men levelled their muskets a shout went up, the six leapt the wall and made a break for freedom. Before they had even reached the woods, the Llanero cavalry was upon them. Five were lanced in the back as they ran. One survivor rushed up to Páez to beg for mercy, but was dispatched by Traynor with a sword thrust through the chest. The rest of the soldiers were ordered back to quarters and the dead were left where they fell.

Early the next morning the Legion was formed into a three-sided square in the plaza. Páez and Blosset stood alone by the wall that made up the fourth side. No trace of the previous day's executions remained. A heavy rain had fallen overnight washing the blood from the ground, and the bodies had been furtively buried by their comrades. As the men stood to attention wondering what fresh indignity the day would bring, a muffled drum was heard approaching. Expecting the execution of the privates who had wounded Colonel Davy, the officers were confused. Why would such ceremony be wasted on the rank and file? When the procession turned into the square, the question was answered. Twelve men, with their arms reversed, led the column, followed by six drummers and the Legion's band. Behind were the privates with their hands tightly bound. Risdale and Traynor brought up the rear.

First, the privates were ordered to kneel by the wall. Then Risdale was commanded to join them. Only then did he realize his fate. As the officer in charge of the drunken work party the day before, he was to be the scapegoat for the Legion's indiscipline. 'Am I really … to die?' he asked incredulously.[35] Colonel Blosset's only reply was to advise him to accept his fate like a man. Perhaps inspired by Paterson's amateur dramatics, Risdale replied, misquoting Macduff: 'I shall, but must likewise feel it as a man.' Stripping off his red jacket, he looked round and begged his friend, Captain Scott, to intervene. 'Scott … sprung towards him' but was held back and 'compelled to resume his post'. Risdale's last request was that his family be informed. He then walked to the wall and knelt before it. Traynor ordered the firing squad to load. The two ranks of six bit open the cartridges and rammed the balls home. As they brought the muskets up to their shoulders, Risdale crossed his arms over his breast 'in a token of resignation'.[36] The order to fire was then given.

The night after the execution all the officers in town were invited to Páez's quarters to celebrate Saint Simón's day. After dinner, toasts were made and the hall soon rang with 'vivas!' With the alcohol flowing, the men managed to put the image of Risdale's body out of their minds, but further tragedy was about to strike. In an effort to patch up relations with his officers following the mutiny, Blosset had invited Power to have a drink with him. The colonel 'courteously refused'. Blosset, who had been drinking heavily, took offence at the perceived rebuff and demanded satisfaction.[37] Although Páez intervened and the matter appeared to have been settled amicably, Blosset continued to goad Power in the weeks that followed. Unknown to many of those present, the two men had a long history of acrimony. In 1801 both had served in Sir Ralph Abercrombie's Egyptian expedition. It is not known what passed between them on the sands outside Alexandria, but it appears that Blosset had still not forgotten 19 years later. To make matters worse, Power had his own reasons for bearing a grudge. In Ireland, Devereux had promised him the rank of brigadier general but upon his arrival in South America, he was informed that such a high rank would never be granted to a foreigner. Not only was he forced to serve alongside his old rival, but he also had to suffer the indignity of holding an inferior rank.

In spite of Blosset's taunts, Power was initially a model of restraint. But with a gentleman's honour on the line, 'the [end] result was inevitable'.[38] Early one morning at the beginning of December, the two men strode out of Achaguas to a secluded spot. Minutes later two pistol shots rang out. Although Power escaped unhurt, Blosset was mortally wounded. On his deathbed several witnesses heard him exonerate Power of all blame. Nevertheless, Páez had the colonel arrested and sent to Bolívar's headquarters. After trial by a council of war, Power was found not guilty. Disillusioned with the service, he resigned and made his way back to Europe. Meanwhile, back in Achaguas, Blosset had lingered on for three days before finally breathing his last. His body was interred in the aisle of the church on the main square. Although the funeral was held 'with all the pomp of military and Masonic honours', his death passed 'unlamented'.[39]

Chapter 29

THE FALL OF SANTA MARTA

Back in Dublin, the pressure was mounting on General Devereux. The founder of the Irish Legion had been in hiding since January, when a series of angry letters had appeared in the press relating the fate of his men in Margarita. In March, when some embittered survivors returned, Judge Fletcher launched an investigation into his recruiting practices.[1] As Devereux had gone to ground, his military secretary, Colonel Sutton, was arrested in his stead and subjected to severe questioning. Meanwhile, the search for the real culprit went on and 'one or two spirited young men' even issued public challenges, demanding satisfaction for his lies.[2] Feeling himself 'in imminent danger of being arrested or shot', Devereux realized it was time to get out of town.[3] With an escort of 25 staff officers, he disappeared to Liverpool where he hired an old 'coal brig'. After renaming her the *Ariel*, he set sail for South America in May 1820.[4]

In mid-Atlantic they spoke with a passing ship whose captain gave them the latest reports from Margarita. The news did not bode well for Devereux. As the voyage continued his anxiety deepened, and by the time they reached the Windward Islands, he feared he would be put to death.[5] Nevertheless, the *Ariel* dropped anchor off Juan Griego on 12 June. At first Devereux refused to disembark and eventually the port captain had to row out to see who the unexpected visitors were. Father John O'Mullen, the Legion's spiritual advisor, was as shocked as anyone by the Creole captain's reaction. 'When he understood … we had Gen. D'Evereux on board, nothing could equal [his] … joy.'[6] News of the mutiny at Rio de la Hacha had yet to reach Margarita and despite the Legion's problems, the locals treated him like a hero. Two Creole officers were immediately sent out to act as his aides and the next day the general 'landed under a grand salute … amidst loud huzzas from the … spectators that lined the shore'.[7]

Lieutenant Alexander, now serving with Admiral Brion's marines, was at Juan Griego when Devereux's retinue arrived. The general cut 'a tall vain figure', affected 'all the pomp of a sovereign' and was 'so covered with ... [gold] that he looked like a lace merchant's pattern card'.[8] Whilst riding off the beach, his arrival degenerated further into farce. Having been confined in the *Ariel*'s hold for several weeks, his horse leapt into a pond by the side of the track to free its coat of fleas, in the process covering the general in mud. Moments later, still dripping with filth, he delivered a speech to a flock of local dignitaries. Waving his sword to punctuate each point, he vowed to kill every Spaniard who crossed his path and promised never to rest until South America was free. His audience, who spoke not a word of English, were left dumbfounded.[9]

Following this inauspicious opening, a series of inspections, balls and banquets were laid on in Devereux's honour. Morgan O'Connell, the 14-year old son of the Dublin lawyer and statesman, accompanied the general as one of his numerous aides. Used to the cream of Dublin's high society, O'Connell was delighted when the governor of the island, 'a man of no education whatever', served champagne in tumblers rather than the saucers fashionable at the time. Later that evening the revellers went dancing in Government House.[10] Amongst several others, Mrs English was there. According to O'Connell, she looked 'very handsome', but to the young rake's disappointment, 'did not dance [as] she was [still] in mourning'. After drinking heavily for several hours, Morgan's cousin, Maurice, yet another of Devereux's seemingly inexhaustable retinue, 'went to dance a fandango', but 'got through it very miserably; and tore a lady's gown with his spur'.[11]

After the celebrations had wound down, Devereux issued a proclamation pardoning any British deserters still at large on the island. Several turned themselves in. Others were rounded up from the interior by local militia or seized from the privateers they had joined since deserting.[12] Father O'Mullen, meanwhile, was taking care of the spiritual needs of the islanders. Scores of baptisms were carried out and a mass was held that Sunday in the church. O'Mullen later recounted, 'to my great satisfaction ... I had a most numerous and respectable congregation'.[13] The service signalled the end of Devereux's visit to the island. Afterwards the general, his staff and the 200 deserters were rowed out to the *Ariel*. Still unaware of the mutiny that had taken place a few weeks before, the captain set sail for Rio de la Hacha, where Devereux intended to assume command of his men. When they arrived offshore, the officers scanned the defences with their telescopes. There was no sign of life. The captain's signals also went unanswered. No doubt the royalists were hoping their silence would lure the ship within range of their guns. Devereux was nothing if not cautious, however, and decided to sail for Jamaica 'for information' instead.[14]

By the time the *Ariel* arrived at Kingston on 1 July 1820, the mutineers had already been there for several weeks. Some had found employment as slave drivers or pickers on the sugar plantations. Others who had once had a trade in London were offered work and William Burke, the sergeant who had found gold in Rio de la Hacha, opened a 'grog' shop in Kingston with his ill-gotten gains.[15] Others paid for a berth to Europe. The majority were not so fortunate, however, prompting Colonel O'Connor to hold a meeting with the British governor, William Montagu, to discuss what was to be done with them. As Canada needed colonists to prevent the expansion of the United States, the governor suggested that some should begin a new life in the frozen north. Subsequently, 130 took up the offer.[16] A few others were allowed to join the local British Army battalion, but, fully aware of their recent history, its colonel was loath to take on any more. A further 60 were admitted to hospital with a variety of ailments, leaving a few hundred unable to find employment or a way to get home. 'Pale and thin from hunger', they supported themselves by begging and thieving and became a 'perfect nuisance to the inhabitants'. At night they slept 'on board the old, rotten, abandoned vessels' in the 'wherry wharf'. The authorities soon lost interest in their plight.[17]

Predictably, life was easier for the officers, who were able to borrow money to pay for their passage home. Some left direct for Dublin. Others made their way 40 miles across the island to Salt River from where the *Janet* took them to Greenock in Scotland.[18] A handful, including O'Connor and Stopford, were keen to rejoin the patriots, but had to wait several weeks until Montilla sent a ship to collect them. In the meantime, the two colonels lodged with a Scottish resident named Mr Grimshaw, who had also taken in Colonel Aylmer, still seriously ill from the wounds he had suffered at Rio de la Hacha. His condition deteriorating, Aylmer eventually died on the morning of 20 June. O'Connor paid 500 pesos for his burial and sent a letter informing the family in Ireland of his death.[19] After the funeral, the colonels went hunting in the Blue Mountains and visited 'coffee and sugar cane plantations' around the island, finally sailing for New Granada at the end of the month.[20]

When Devereux arrived in Kingston he attempted to gather the remnants of his Legion, but was thwarted by Governor Montagu as his actions contravened the Foreign Enlistment Act. Still he refused to give up on his dream of command, and when he learnt that 100 of his Lancers still remained in patriot employ near the town of Baranquilla, he decided to join them. Accompanied by his staff and the 200 men he had gathered from Margarita, Devereux left Kingston on a chartered schooner on 18 July.[21] After a 'tedious' passage of several weeks, the *Frederick* arrived at Savanilla in early August.[22] The port lay at the mouth of the Magdalena River, a few miles downstream from Baranquilla, where patriot forces were massing for a strike against Santa Marta. Brion's fleet was in the bay as the schooner arrived. Whilst Devereux's 'reception by [the] admiral ... was most cordial', Colonel Montilla, in charge of the land forces, wisely refused to cede command.[23] In response, Devereux dispatched two aides to Cúcuta to take up the matter with Bolívar.

Whilst awaiting transport up-river, the Irish were billeted in local houses. Three pounds of beef, 'a good loaf' of bread, rice and candles were provided for each man.[24] After a week, a barge took them to Baranquilla. On 22 August Bolívar arrived to inspect the fleet gathering for the upcoming offensive. When he heard of The Liberator's approach, young Morgan O'Connell could not contain his excitement. Mounting up alongside Devereux and Colonel Stopford, he galloped out of town to intercept him. 'The President wore a splendid red uniform and was surrounded by a splendid staff.'[25] After doffing his cap to Bolívar, O'Connell was approached by Daniel O'Leary. The two had previously met in Dublin and were soon fast friends. After they reached the city, a tour of the navy yard and stores was conducted. The largest fleet of river-borne gunboats ever seen on the Magdalena had been gathered for the imminent assault.[26] As they inspected the boats, torrential downpours frequently sent the officers running for cover. Within minutes the streets were transformed into rivers, but just as suddenly the skies cleared and the sun burnt off the haze.

The next stop on Bolívar's tour was Turbaco, a small town 60 miles to the south-west near the city of Cartagena where Montilla's ground forces were based. The army consisted of 1,000 inexperienced American troops, 100 of O'Connor's Irish Lancers and Colonel Jackson's marines. As well as being a holding post for the troops, Turbaco was also the base for the ongoing siege of Cartagena. The infantry and cavalry had formed a loose cordon surrounding the city, whilst Commander Padilla headed a fleet blockading the bay. The siege had been under way for some months and the situation inside the city was becoming desperate. When the royalist commander Brigadier Torres heard of Bolívar's arrival, he sent word proposing a meeting. Knowing his troops clearly had the upper hand, The Liberator was unwilling to negotiate unless the royalists officially recognised Gran Colombia as an independent state. Insulted by the rebuff, Torres vowed to get his revenge.

At dawn on 1 September, the regiment of León slunk past the cordon of troops encircling Cartagena and marched on Turbaco, hoping to kill or capture Bolívar. Unknown to his adversaries, The Liberator had already left with Montilla and most of the troops, but the rest of the garrison was caught unawares. Its commander, Colonel Ayala, was an ageing veteran whose spine and spirit had been broken in the Caracas earthquake of 1812.[27] When the first shots rang out, most of the Irish Lancers were foraging outside town and the infantry in the main square barely had time to form up before the main body of the enemy appeared. Advancing down several side streets simultaneously, the royalists opened 'a heavy and destructive fire'.[28] The conscripts gathered in the plaza soon broke and fled. Ayala, who would later be dismissed for his cowardice, took off after them followed by his second, Commander Garcine. Nevertheless, 25 Irish infantry under Captain Du Verney, Jackson's marines and an artillery detachment led by Lieutenant Barnes decided to fight on.

For three hours they held out. Protected by a line of barricades, Lieutenant Barnes' gunners performed heroically, firing round after round of canister from their twin 4-pdrs. Gradually, however, the royalists' fire began to take its toll. A ball drilled through both of Lieutenant Sexton's legs, Colonel Jackson was wounded and Doctor O'Reilly was hit 'on the side of the neck', the ball passing 'through … his cheek [and] taking a couple of teeth with it'.[29] By the time he recovered his senses, most of the patriots had either been killed or had fled, and the small knot of men left holding the square were hopelessly outnumbered. Choosing discretion over valour, Captain Du Verney ordered the retreat.[30] O'Reilly and the others shot their way out, whilst Lieutenant Barnes and his gunners stayed behind to cover them. As the lieutenant was loading a final case of cannister, a Spanish officer came galloping through the smoke and cut him down with his sabre. Before he could charge the crew of the second gun, however, his horse was shot beneath him. Sent clattering across the cobble stones, he was finished off with bayonets.[31] Barnes was then dragged from the square and the last of the patriots retreated into the woods outside town. Finding The Liberator had eluded them, the royalists took out their frustrations on a host of civilians who had sought sanctuary in the church; 130 men, women and children were slaughtered. The royalists looted, raped and burned for two hours before the foraging patriot cavalry returned. Seeing the town ablaze and overrun by the enemy, the cavalry charged down the narrow streets, driving the disorganized royalists before them. With the town recaptured, the pursuit was called off. The royalists withdrew to Cartagena, the cordon was re-established and the siege wore on.

Back in Baranquilla, Devereux had become seriously ill with fever and the Black Rifles had arrived to bolster the forces massing for the attack on Santa Marta. Ever since setting out from Valledupar several weeks before, Sandes's men had been cutting their way through the jungle, harassed by royalist Indians at every turn. After reaching El Banco, they had sailed down the Magdalena for Baranquilla. By the time they arrived they were exhausted, and their clothes were hanging from them in threads.[32] Also in town was Captain Alexander, who had not seen his old comrades from the Black Rifles since the battle at Caujaral in February 1819. Delighted to see one another, the men spent the evenings swapping stories of their adventures. Sandes's men talked of the beauty of central New Granada and the parties, women and pay they had enjoyed in Santafé. Alexander, for his part, spoke of the 'death ship' that had taken him to Margarita and his subsequent adventures with the marines. Later Alexander was invited to rejoin the unit, but when it emerged that he had served in the rank and file with the British Artillery, the Rifle officers ostracized him. Their 'behaviour … became wholly changed to me', he noted with sadness. 'I was passed on the streets, or only got a slight and distant nod.'[33] Maurice O'Connell, majors Rudd and Powell and Doctor O'Reilly (who had made a full recovery from his wounds) evidently came from better stock. Tired of Devereux's inactivity, all were made welcome by Sandes and his fellow officers and absorbed into the Black Rifles for the forthcoming campaign.[34]

With the arrival of the Rifles, the campaign could finally begin. Bolívar hoped to crush the army of Sanchez de Lima and expel the royalists from the northern region entirely. As Colonel Lara had been taken ill, his second in command, Colonel Carreño, was to lead the land forces through the flooded jungles of the lower Magdalena, whilst Commander Padilla would sail with his gunboats across the Ciénega, a giant saltwater lagoon, to attack Santa Marta from the sea. Carreño's troops began their march at the village of Sabana Grande, a few miles up-river from Baranquilla. The Rifles (now kitted out with new green uniforms) along with a detachment of cavalry under Colonel Infante formed the backbone of the 1,500-strong force, which was also bulked up with a scattering of 'loose companies' from various American units.[35] Having recently arrived from Jamaica, Colonel Francis Burdett O'Connor was appointed chief of staff.

In mid-October the operation began. On the first day the troops marched south, cutting their way through the undergrowth beside the Magdalena, before being ferried to the eastern side by canoe. The river was a couple of miles wide and the current swift and dangerous.[36] The area was teeming with wildlife. Flocks of waterfowl glided overhead, whilst crocodiles followed the canoes looking for an easy meal. They were not to be disappointed. The boats were dreadfully overcrowded and, as the troops jostled for space, some fell into the water and were devoured.[37] That night, the men camped near a ranch on the riverbank, plagued by an 'abundance of mosquitoes', before heading east through swampland blanketed by dense shrubs.[38] Progress was slow. Whilst most of the officers were mounted, the rank and file waded 'with the water up to their chests for long stints again and again'.[39] Meanwhile, Infante's cavalry ranged ahead rounding up wild cattle. The horsemen then set up camp and butchered the beef whilst waiting for the infantry to arrive. The 'only ration … was a pound and a half of … meat without salt'. There was no bread and the men were not paid. After dinner, the officers slung hammocks and the men slept on the bare ground.[40] Besides the insects, the greatest difficulty the volunteers faced was the intense heat and humidity, which soared to levels that the Rifle officers had not experienced since the Amacuro Delta. On 30 October, following the path as it began to climb out of the swampland, the column arrived on the outskirts of San Carlos de Fundación, where the Spaniards were lying in wait.

Some 300 Spanish infantry were dug in behind barricades on the north bank of a 65ft-wide river running through town. When patriot scouts reached the far side they were fired upon. Battle commenced at 10.00am. Soon the rest of Carreño's troops came up and the fighting became widespread. Despite being heavily outnumbered, Sanchez de Lima's position was a formidable one. At first, neither side gained the upper hand. Then, after one hour of 'smart firing', with the casualties building on both sides, eight of Infante's horsemen plunged into the river downstream and swam to the far bank, outflanking the royalist line. Realizing the position was lost, De Lima fell back five miles to a low hill, known as El Codo, whilst Infante's riders waited for their infantry to wade across the river and join them. By the time the patriots had caught up, the royalists had taken up firing positions behind stone walls on the summit.[41] Sandes led the 1st and 2nd Companies of the Rifles against them. Supported by the cavalry, they fanned out in skirmish formation and took the hill after a 15-minute fight. When the final bayonet charge swept across the summit, the surviving royalists fled to the north. Only 15 mounted officers, including Sanchez de Lima, escaped the slaughter. Many royalists died in the firefight, but the majority were cut down in the rout or executed after capture. The patriot rank and file were intent on killing all the Spaniards they found. Only 15 were spared. Patriot casualties, on the other hand, were surprisingly light. Just two lost their lives and 16 were wounded.[42]

That night O'Connor and Sandes lodged with Carreño in the principal house in town, which belonged to a local family named Collins. The Irishmen found several English books in the library, which they perused by candlelight before retiring.[43] Early the next morning, the infantry searched the surrounding fields for any royalists who had escaped the bloodshed. An enemy standard and 80 muskets were gathered from the field and, now that the patriots' bloodlust had eased, a further 115 prisoners were taken. The column then moved north to Santa Marta. As the men cut their way through the jungle, an occasional break in the canopy revealed the jagged line of the Sierra Nevada de Santa Marta rearing above them five miles to the east. Increasing in height as it neared the sea, the cordillera culminated in twin snow-capped peaks soaring to over 18,700ft. A few days into the march, Carreño was informed that 200 of the enemy were preparing to make a stand at Rio Frio, a swift-flowing river fed by melt water cascading down from the heights. Although specifically ordered not to lose contact, the vanguard formed by the 1st Company of the Rifles was nearly a mile ahead when it encountered the enemy. Following with the main body, O'Connor heard shots in the distance and ordered the men to quicken their pace. When they emerged from the trees, they saw the 1st Company had managed to cross the river but was pinned down on the beach on the far bank. The royalists had built parapets on the ridge of a steep slope overlooking the crossing, affording them a commanding field of fire. Several riflemen had already paid the price for their impetuosity. Knowing the position would be too costly to assault head-on, Carreño sent Lieutenant Alcalá with a half company down-river to look for a second ford. Once the troops had crossed, the royalists fell back yet again, this time making for the coastal town of Ciénega, 15 miles to the north. In their haste to escape, the Spaniards left two wounded comrades by the barricades where they had fallen. One of Carreño's aides asked for permission to finish them off. Colonel O'Connor's objections proved in vain. The aide, named Hormachea, tied the prisoners up by their ankles and hoisted them over the river. They were left hanging upside down for some time before he decapitated them with his sword.[44]

The morning after the skirmish, the column pressed on, arriving within sight of the fortifications of Ciénega before nightfall on 9 November. The royalists had gathered to make a final stand. Overlooked by the mountains of the Sierra Nevada to the east, the sea to the north and a vast saltwater lagoon to the west, the only land approach was covered by three lines of defence. Carreño's men would first have to cover 'a flat, sandy beach' under fire from four cannon and two mortar sighted in a dry river bed.[45] Beyond lay more open ground, another battery, and a ditch and palisade of sharpened stakes held by the bulk of the royalist infantry. Several other gun positions, boasting cannon of up to 24lb in calibre, had been built further back, covering the sea approaches.[46] The task seemed daunting, but Carreño's men were not alone. Commander Padilla's flotilla of gunboats was anchored in the lagoon ready to provide covering fire.

After exchanging prearranged signals, Padilla's gunboats opened fire against the enemy batteries at 9.00am the next morning, whilst Carreño launched his men against the open ground to the south. The patriot troops were divided into three groups. Mixed units of 200 infantry and cavalry advanced against the centre and right wing in a diversionary feint, whilst Carreño and Sandes led 600 in the main attack against the left of the position.[47] Racing across the sands, the troops were met by a 'furious cannonade'.[48] Despite the covering fire of the gunboats, several were cut down. Musketry and grapeshot scythed through the air and mortar shells sent shrapnel screaming into the ranks. As the sergeants closed up the line, Sandes, mounted at the front before the colours, urged his men on.[49] The majority remained resolute but a few lost heart. Dragging wounded comrades behind them, they slunk away from the fight. Major Powell, one of the Irish officers who had joined the Rifles at Baranquilla, was amongst those who fled.[50]

Following Wellington's doctrine, Sandes ordered the Rifles to hold their fire as they closed with the enemy, then unleashed a devastating volley at pistol range.[51] When the smoke cleared, the bayonet-tipped line poured into the dry river bed and overran the surviving royalist gunners. A handful fled towards their second line. The rest were 'cut down with their spunges in their hands' or bayoneted as they cowered beneath the guns.[52] No prisoners were taken. The patriots then spun the captured cannon round and exchanged counter-battery fire with the field pieces in front of the pallisades. A few rounds of grapeshot forced the royalists to flee.[53] The attacking wave swept forward once more. Many of the Indian defenders awaiting them were roaring drunk. De Lima had supplied them with barrels of grog before the battle to boost their fighting spirit, but the tactic was about to backfire. In several places the royalists abandoned their defences and blindly counter-attacked, falling upon the patriots 'like tigers'.[54] Their bravery was no match for the Rifles' discipline. Volley fire cut them down in swathes. In other areas, the ditch and palisades had to be stormed. Pistols were discharged at point-blank range and sabres and bayonets used to force the enemy back. Once inside the defences, the Rifles slaughtered all they found. Several Indian women who had been handing out ammunition were also killed.[55] Within ten minutes the main defences were taken and the surviving royalists fell back. Meanwhile most of the lagoon-side batteries had been knocked out by Padilla's gunboats.[56] The rest were overwhelmed by Carreño's men. The flotilla then sailed into shore and the marines disembarked, joining the infantry for the final assault on the centre of town. Inching forward, the patriots cleared the streets with volley fire, whilst others fought their way through the houses. Very few of the enemy were spared and the final stages of the battle turned into a massacre.

Carreño's subsequent casualty report listed 253 enemy wounded to nearly 600 dead. A total of 29 royalist officers were killed and only eight allowed to surrender. The patriots had also suffered heavily, with 50 killed and over 100 wounded. Amongst the latter were two of the Black Rifles' original officers. Sandes's second in command, Major William Peacock, was lightly wounded and Captain Jamie Phelan, the British Artillery veteran whose Spanish wife was awaiting him in Angostura, had been hit in the leg.[57] For his part, Major Powell was branded a coward by his comrades for fleeing from the field. He was later given his passport and dismissed. By midday, as the temperature rocketed, a horrendous stench began to rise from the bodies littering the field. Lacking both the will and energy to bury them, the patriots burnt the corpses in piles, using stakes from the palisade as kindling. The wood was consumed before all had been disposed of. The rest were left where they lay. For weeks the reek of rotting flesh hung over the town. Sandes's veterans, however, had long since lost their finer sensibilities. One had become so inured that he was even able to laugh about seeing dogs and pigs munching the bones.[58]

In the immediate aftermath of the battle, Carreño consolidated his position. After securing the arms and ammunition abandoned on the field, he penned a dispatch to his superiors, then sent O'Connor with an escort of Lancers to Santa Marta to demand the city's surrender. The vast majority of the royalist troops had been deployed at Ciénega, leaving the governor with little choice but to comply. With the city's capitulation, the only areas remaining in royalist hands in New Granada were the coastal city of Cartagena and Pasto in the far south. Realizing their grip on the continent was unravelling, the Spaniards were finally ready to listen to Bolívar's demands. Even as the patriots had launched their attack at Ciénega, the final terms of an armistice were being ironed out and the two greatest generals of the war were about to meet face to face.

PART FOUR

VICTORY!
1821

Next to a battle lost the greatest misery is a battle gained.

The Duke of Wellington

Chapter 30

THE ARMISTICE OF SANTA ANA
AND THE BATTLE OF GENOY

Ever since the liberal revolution in Cádiz, the Spanish had been keen to negotiate. As they were still unwilling to countenance Bolívar's demands for absolute independence, however, the Cortes instructed Morillo to deal with the secondary patriot commanders instead, hoping to cause rifts in the unstable alliance. Anticipating this strategy, Bolívar strictly forbade independent negotiation with the enemy. Following his successes in New Granada and the overthrow of Arismendi's rebel government, not even Páez dared disobey. Nevertheless, various royalist delegations, some of which had travelled all the way from Spain, approached the Caudillo in Los Llanos, sailed up the Orinoco to meet congress at Angostura, and even made overtures to Montilla and several other chiefs around the coast.[1] All their attempts were rebuffed, however, and it soon became clear that the Spaniards would have to deal directly with Bolívar if they were to stand any chance of success.

With the triumphant progress of his armies in New Granada, The Liberator was in no rush to negotiate. As he confided to Soublette in June, 'they have everything to lose and nothing to gain. We have nothing to lose and want everything they possess:... So we must offer only peace in return for [full] Independence.'[2] Bolívar continued to stall through the second half of 1820, whilst Lara's men pushed the royalists before them in the north, and Valdés's southern division was victorious at La Plata and Pitayó. To make matters worse for the royalists, their American troops throughout the region were deserting en masse or siding with the patriots. The entire Creole garrison at Cumaná marched out of the city straight into Colonel Montes's camp and the Indian Caudillo, Juan de los Reyes Vargas, also switched allegiance.[3] With his position strengthening daily, Bolívar eventually agreed to a meeting in October, but by then it was Morillo's turn to prevaricate whilst he manoeuvred his remaining forces to back up his negotiating position. Finally, in November 1820, both sides were ready to talk.

After six years campaigning, Morillo was glad that the bloodshed finally appeared to be coming to an end. His position had become increasingly untenable since the defeat at Boyacá, and he had still not fully recovered from the lance wound he had suffered at Semen two years before. Furthermore, his troops' morale had gone into freefall and those remaining were beginning to separate into two camps. The ultra-conservatives were appalled that Morillo had even entered into negotiations and, at his headquarters in Valencia, an assassination plot was uncovered. According to one report in the *Dublin Evening Post*, his own mistress, Tabletta, was to have administered the poison. Along with the local mayor, she was executed by firing squad. Over 100 others were imprisoned.

In November 1820 Captain O'Leary and other members of The Liberator's staff held a series of preliminary meetings with a royalist delegation. These led to the signing of a six-month armistice and, on the 27th, Bolívar and Morillo met face to face in the village of Santa Ana to ratify the decision. When O'Leary pointed out Bolívar to Morillo, the general was a little disappointed, asking, 'What, that little man in the blue frock coat and forage cap riding a mule?'[4] Despite his initial misgivings, the two leaders got on famously and the meeting was an unqualified success. Morillo later called it 'one of the most joyful days of my life'.[5] After embracing 'with the heartiest good will', the Spaniard dismissed his military escort and the two parties sat down to business. Ironically, the treaty was ironed out in the very same house where Bolívar had declared 'War to the Death' seven years earlier.[6] Each side promised to keep to their current territories and freeze all troop movements whilst the truce endured. Conditions for prisoners were agreed and the 'War to the Death' was officially brought to an end. Then dinner was served and as bottles of wine were passed round the table, campaign stories were exchanged. Later, both commanders climbed onto the table to drink to peace. Volleys of 'vivas!' echoed round the hall and by the end of the night, it seemed as though the gathering was one of old friends rather than bitter enemies. In the early hours of the morning, as the celebrations rumbled on, the generals decided that a monument should be erected to mark the occasion. Stumbling into the street, they selected 'a large stone' and carried it 'between them' to the centre of the square, where it was placed with all the gravitas that they could muster.[7]

The next morning messengers were dispatched to Madrid, Santafé, Calabozo and Margarita to spread the news and, as a sign of goodwill, Morillo granted 40 passports to patriot officers, allowing them to travel through royalist territory to visit family and friends. The delegations then returned to their respective lines. In a letter written the next day, Morillo referred to the whole occasion as if it had been a dream. His words would prove prophetic. Even as celebrations were taking place in Santa Ana, Valdés's men were preparing for a new campaign far to the south. The messengers had hundreds of miles of difficult terrain to cross before reaching them and would not arrive in time to prevent further bloodshed.

* * *

Since arriving in Popayán on 12 July 1820, Valdés's army of the south had endured a virtual state of siege. Royalist guerrillas controlled the surrounding countryside, and by September the patriots' provisions were running dangerously low. Rations were reduced to meat, firewood and occasional supplies of salt. Eventually even the beef became scarce and luxuries such as tobacco and sugar were almost impossible to come by. To satisfy their cravings during the 'drought', the locals boiled dried figs to sweeten their *chocoláte* and even 'respectable inhabitants' were reduced to searching the streets for cigar butts.[8] With no money left to purchase medicine for the troops, the cold climate and poor diet took a heavy toll. Hundreds of soldiers fell ill. Soon there were not enough beds in the hospitals to accommodate them.[9] Emboldened by the pitiful state of their enemies, royalist guerrillas from the neighbouring region of Patia began to infiltrate the city. Several officers 'returning late and unaccompanied to their quarters' were snatched from the streets and never seen again.[10] To make matters worse, desertion was becoming evermore commonplace. On one night alone, Coronet Ramoncito of Carbajal's cavalry fled with 25 of his men. After cutting a bloody trail across the province, committing various atrocities en route, the deserters were captured, taken to Neiva and shot by firing squad. Their fate did little to deter the rest, however, and soon as many as 60 were absconding each night.[11]

Founded in 1537, Popayán had become an important political, cultural and religious centre and boasted 'several handsome public buildings'. Of special interest to Captain Richard Vowell was the *Compañia* (college of Jesuits).[12] A colonial gem, the building had spacious courts, corridors and apartments, and a 'large library, well supplied with books, telescopes, and mathematical instruments', where the young undergraduate spent the long, cold nights.[13] During his stay, Vowell also befriended the Mosqueras, a prominent local family with four sons, two of whom would go on to be Colombian presidents. On one occasion, the youngest invited the Englishman and his fellow officers to take part in a hunting trip.[14] The aristocrat's peons had seen a *danta* (mountain tapir) in the peaks surrounding the volcano of Puracé and the band set off in eager anticipation of a kill. After passing the first night at a plantation near the Indian village of Coconuco, they set out before daybreak. Climbing upwards towards the snowline, they reached the forested ravine where the animal had last been seen. Suddenly, the hunting party caught sight of the 500lb beast grazing amongst the trees. Sensing them, it charged. The officers took cover and opened fire. Although the *danta* was hit by 'two or three musket balls' as it thundered past, Vowell was astonished to see it race on 'with no apparent effect' and disappear into 'the woods'.[15]

For Valdés in Popayán, the situation continued to deteriorate. Desertion had reached new heights, there was little hope of improvement in the state of supply and the royalists were growing ever bolder in their nocturnal attacks. In response, Valdés decided to withdraw to the north, where the locals were better disposed to his cause, rather than risk the all-out assault which seemed imminent. After marching to Quilichao, the units were distributed around the towns in the region. The regiments of Cauca and Neiva, and Carbajal's cavalry, were sent to Llanogrande; the Cundinamarca Regiment was assigned quarters in Buga; whilst Valdés, his staff, the hospital and the Albion Battalion returned to the city of Cali. Soon after the troops had settled into their new homes, three issues arose between Valdés and the volunteers. The first concerned the receipt of a letter from General Santander ordering him to double the size of the Albion Battalion to 800 troops. This would require several new officers. As no British ones were available, Creoles would have to be appointed. Insisting that they would never be accepted, the British threatened to resign should Valdés force the issue. Knowing that the Albion was his best regiment and the mere mention of its name could strike fear into the hearts of his enemies, Valdés was forced to comply.[16] The second point of contention was the sad fate of Captain Weaver.[17] Following his death from fever, Valdés had forbidden the captain's burial from taking place on hallowed ground. His final resting place was a shallow grave scraped from the sand by the banks of the river Cali. This infuriated his fellow volunteers, who saw the move as a deliberate slight.

The third and most serious complaint concerned Valdés's corruption. To feed his gambling habit, the general had begun to embezzle funds intended to feed and clothe the men and had even plundered the pay chest. Matters reached a head when the commissary of the army openly accused him of theft. Colonel Mackintosh then threatened to resign, march the Albion back to the capital and petition Bolívar to have him replaced. With the British officers, the commissary of the army and Colonel Carbajal all united against him, Valdés 'became as abject as he had been before insolent and overbearing'. He 'wept like a child, and offered to give up command' to his second, Colonel Mires, who had won the respect of the British following his success at La Plata. Instead of taking command, however, Mires chose to defend his superior and 'at length [he] succeeded in appeasing Col. McIntosh's just resentment'.[18] On the surface, Valdés appeared to continue in command much as before, but his authority had been weakened. Despite these issues, the division's situation improved during its stay in the valley of Cauca. As had previously been the case, the people proved far more open to the patriot cause than those at Popayán. Rations improved, new troops were recruited and morale picked up. By the end of the year the division was 3,000 strong and ready for action. In December the troops reunited at Quilichao, and then marched to Popayán. After resting in the city for two days, Valdés led them out through the gates on 2 January 1821. Their destination was Pasto, the capital of the royalist heartland of the south.[19]

The road from Popayán descended through wooded valleys, flanked by twin Andean mountain ranges, just visible in the distance through the haze. After several days they emerged into the low-lying region of Patia, where the forests gave way to an arid landscape of sand, cacti and scrub. The cool climate was replaced by a burning heat and relentless sun. Even more unwelcome were the royalist guerrillas who shadowed the column, ready to pick off any who fell behind. On the march a certain parity emerged between the ranks. Nearly all the officers were on foot, few had shoes or a change of clothes and most carried no baggage. Like the men, they now washed their own uniforms. The entire division would then wait naked by the riverbank whilst the soldiers' clothes dried in the sun. All ranks from captain down carried a musket, and the only food distributed to officers and men alike was unsalted beef.[20]

On 21 January, three weeks after setting out from Popayán, the column reached the river Mayo.[21] 'An impetuous torrent … with precipitous banks, and scarcely in any part fordable', the river was easily defended.[22] A detachment of 100 royalists held the only bridge, its mission being to delay the patriot advance. The Grenadier Company of the Albion, which formed the patriot vanguard throughout the campaign, approached through a thick wood. To hinder the van's passage, several trees had been cut down to from an *abbatis*, a barricade constructed with interlocking tree trunks studded with sabre blades or bayonets. After breaching the barrier under light fire, the Grenadiers advanced to the river. On the far bank waited a body of the enemy, supported by a second line positioned on a hill behind them. Once on the 'narrow … stone bridge', the volunteers opened fire.[23] The royalists had little heart for the fight. After exchanging a few volleys, they abandoned the position and fell back to the south.

Beyond the river, the column climbed steadily into the forested mountains of San Lorenzo. Vowell thought the roads were as bad as any he had seen since leaving Santafé. Numerous freshwater springs rendered the route so marshy that the rearguard became bogged down with the ammunition and was soon separated from the main body by a full day's march. Further on, the column passed a landslide of more than two miles in length. The topsoil had concertinaed into a series of 'irregular ridges' which reminded Vowell of 'the waves of the sea'.[24] A week after crossing the Mayo, the patriots reached the Juanambu. Of great depth and prone to flash flooding, the river had long served as the de facto northern boundary of the Pastusos, an indigenous people whose land had once formed the northern limits of the Incan Empire. Having been converted by Catholic missionaries generations before, they strictly adhered to the church's pro-royalist policies. When news of Valdés's presence reached Pasto, they flocked to enlist in the army, determined to defend their homeland against the republican advance.

Whilst the Spaniards equipped the new recruits, an advance guard of 400, armed with muskets, slings and axes and led by a handful of Spanish officers, had gathered to contest the passage of the Juanambu.[25] They held a series of trenches and breastworks built on a bluff on the far bank, overlooking the only ford. As the current proved too strong for the patriot infantry to keep their footing, all but the strongest had to be carried over by Carbajal's cavalry. They crossed the river again and again under a most 'galling fire' from the royalists on the bluff.[26] Several were killed by musketry or had their skulls crushed by slingshot stones the size of grapefruit.[27] Eventually enough troops had crossed to launch a counter-attack. Climbing the slopes to one side of the ford, 200 of the Albion formed up on the heights and fell upon the flank of the enemy position. As they poured into the trench system, firing muskets and pistols and killing with bayonets, Valdés ordered 25 of Carbajal's Lancers to charge the position from the front. Assailed on two sides, the Pastusos ran. Several were cut down or shot as they fled. The rest dispersed into the woods to the south. Swollen with pride, Valdés now began to underestimate his enemy. Little did he realize that he was falling into a trap.[28]

The patriots spent the rest of the day ferrying the rearguard and baggage across the river. Pickets were posted to watch the woods and a camp was set up on the heights. The next morning, scouts were dispatched seeking word of the royalists' strength and latest movements. The locals were reluctant to aid them, however, and they returned none the wiser. Valdés pushed on regardless, confident that his men were more than a match for whatever the enemy could throw against them. There was good reason for his impetuosity. Advance notice of the armistice had been sent by Santander, along with orders to take and hold the far bank of the Juanambu before the official messengers arrived and hostilities were suspended.[29] Having already achieved this objective, Valdés now had even more ambitious plans. Following Mackintosh's threatened mutiny at Cali and the multitude of desertions over the winter, he knew that he could only be sure of maintaining command if he scored a decisive success. Capturing Pasto, the hub of royalist resistance in the south, was just the victory that he needed.

On 1 February the division reached Tambopintado, the town which Santander had named as the maximum point of advance for the campaign. Nevertheless, at just over 30 miles away, Pasto was tantalizingly close. Realizing he had no time to lose if he was to take the city before the peace delegation arrived, Valdés pushed on. The track climbed steeply from Tambopintado, taking the men to over 6,500ft above sea level into a landscape of jagged peaks and sheer precipices plunging thousands of feet to icy streams below. As low clouds rolled in around them, the altitude and cold began to take their toll. Exhausted, men fell out of the line and were left behind. Valdés urged the rest to press on. After spending a restless night exposed on the heights, the troops broke camp at dawn. At first light the sun cast 'gigantic shadows' of the marching men on the clouds rising 'out of the vallies beneath' them. Vowell noted that 'each individual saw his own shadow only, and not that of any other'. Whilst the Englishman was delighted with the spectacle, several of his superstitious South American comrades thought it a 'vision of the *Vulto*, or evil genius of the Cordilléra'. It was a bad omen on the eve of battle and whispers of an imminent defeat spread down the line.[30]

Just before noon, as the column was working its way up the northern flanks of Mount Chaguarbamba, the British vanguard came across a handful of enemy skirmishers who had taken up positions behind rocks and trees on either side of the track. After a brief exchange of fire, the royalists were driven back by a determined cavalry charge and the patriots pressed on. Regrouping a short way to the south, the royalists were reinforced. For the next few hours they executed an 'obstinate' fighting withdrawal.[31] Progress was slow and Valdés soon lost patience. In desperation, he ordered the cavalry to drive the enemy before them. The Pastusos ceded ground easily enough, but Carbajal's Lancers soon lost contact with their infantry who were forced to jog up the hillside behind them in an attempt to keep pace. For three leagues (approximately nine miles) the chase continued, and the troops were soon strung out along the path. Valdés had pushed them too far. The advantage now lay with his opponent.

Bacilio Garcia, the Spanish officer in charge of the defenders, had spent months constructing a series of trenches, bulwarks and barricades along the patriots' line of advance. The Pastusos held each one long enough to fire a few volleys before racing back to the next. Five positions were captured before Carbajal's cavalry were forced to a halt at 1.00pm.[32] After galloping round a bend in the track on the outskirts of the village of Genoy, the colonel suddenly found himself face to face with the entire royalist army. Garcia had chosen the position well. Two companies of veteran Spanish skirmishers screened the main line. Beyond them the field narrowed into a bottleneck ravine, leading to an open maize field. At the far side was a v-shaped ditch with a breastwork of tree trunks defended by 600 well-armed Pastusos.[33] The flanks were also well protected. To one side was a marsh. To the other stood a copse of trees climbing the slopes of the 13,000ft-high Galeras volcano which dominated the field. The patriots were left with no option but to attack the position head-on.

Carbajal's cavalry were soon driven back by the Spanish skirmishers, firing at them from 'pistol range' from behind rocks and scrub.[34] A short while later the first of the Albion Battalion appeared. Gasping for air after their scramble up the track, the volunteers were hastily organized and thrown into the attack. For two hours they tried to dislodge the skirmishers, but the men from Aragon tenaciously held their position. Tiring of the stalemate, Mackintosh ordered his men to fix bayonets and form line. On the colonel's command they charged through the woods, brushing the Spaniards aside. Several were shot or bayoneted. The rest scrambled through the ravine to the safety of the trenches and took up position in the centre of the line. Back down the track, scattered bands of infantry from the Albion, Neiva, Cundinamarca and Cali regiments were still arriving. As soon as they appeared, they were herded together by Valdés's staff and thrown into the battle.[35]

Despite the chaos, the patriots forced their way through the bottleneck by sheer weight of numbers. Climbing over their own dead into a maelstrom of musketry, they pushed into the maize field beyond, where the officers formed them into line of battle. The Albion Battalion and the cavalry were ordered to assault the centre, whilst the rest of the infantry, in mixed units, attacked the flanks. The valley soon filled with smoke, blotting out the sun. Small fires broke out amidst the ripening corn stalks, sparked by smouldering musket wadding. Caught in the open, the tightly packed patriot formations presented an easy target. Scores fell. The dead were left on the field, whilst the wounded were dragged into cover by their comrades. Despite the volume of fire, some managed to leap the ditch and reach the barricades. One captain of the Albion actually had his foot on top of the parapet before he was hurled backwards by a dozen musket balls. His sacrifice inspired his comrades and the patriots surged forward once more.

As the shadows lengthened over the field, Vowell felt the tide of battle was beginning to swing their way. But just when it seemed that the royalists would break, Valdés committed a gross tactical error, inexplicably launching Carbajal's cavalry against the breastworks. The Lancers' horses could neither leap the trench nor scale the parapet, and made easy targets as they milled in front of the massed muskets of the Pastusos. At the head of his men, Carbajal was amongst the first to be hit. A musket ball ripped through his chest, killing him instantly. As his body slipped from the saddle his troops panicked. Robbed of their leader, they turned and fled, riding over the British troops to their rear. Several were knocked to the ground and crushed under hoof. The rest were thrown into confusion. Despite the best efforts of the officers to make them stand firm, the panic spread down the line and the rout became general.

When the patriots fled, the Pastusos broke cover to pursue them. Sallying from their defences they tore across the field, hacking the wounded to death with their axes. If it hadn't been for a rearguard of 15 cavalry who covered the retreat with a series of desperate charges, the bottleneck ravine would have turned the defeat into a massacre reminiscent of Semen. As it was, the battle would prove costly enough. Whilst Valdés and his staff galloped clear with the surviving cavalry, the infantry fled in small groups through the trees.[36] Many were butchered by bands of Indians 'blowing conch-shells and cow-horns'. Others escaped in the gathering gloom, eventually making their way back to where Valdés was marshalling the survivors on the banks of the river Mayo.

Bacilio Garcia was delighted with the victory, especially as the enemy had been led by the Albion Battalion, the 'brave champions' of Vargas whom his men had thought indestructible.[37] Aside from suffering 100 casualties, his only disappointment was that he didn't have sufficient cavalry to follow up his success. The royalists had captured 500 muskets and 20 boxes of ammunition, and had killed 360 patriots. Over 100 wounded had been dragged from the field by their comrades, leaving a bloody trail marking the line of the patriot retreat. Forty of the Albion (10 per cent of the regiment's strength) had been lost.[38] Lieutenant Peter Paumier was amongst the dead and Mackintosh had been injured in the left hand.[39] Those taken prisoner faced a terrifying fate. After being marched to Pasto, they were paraded through the streets, tied to posts in the main square in front of a jeering crowd and executed with axe blows to the back of the head.[40]

Pasto had been a step too far for Valdés. His career would never recover. After returning to Santafé to face a court martial, he was dismissed in disgrace. General Sucre, the officer dispatched to replace him, arrived at the same time as the official messengers brought news of the armistice. Although 1821 was to be a momentous year for the patriots, the focus of the war would swing away from Vowell and his companions back to the Venezuelan plains where their adventures had begun two years before. Bolívar was to have a final showdown with the royalists near Caracas. This time it would be General English's British Legion who would win the day.

Chapter 31

CAPTIVE!

After the battle of Genoy, the armistice established an uneasy truce throughout northern South America. Morillo, who had long been looking for a way out of the war, took advantage of the lull to resign. Whilst a schooner was being fitted out to carry Morillo home, 'a great number of officers' came to bid him farewell.[1] Despite his lessening enthusiasm for the cause, especially since Semen, Morillo had served his country well and was highly respected by his peers. Tactically flawless, with boundless energy and drive, his departure weakened the royalists considerably. When he stopped in Havana, however, his reception was of an entirely different nature. Cuba would be the final bastion of Spain's American Empire and the city was dominated by ultra-conservatives, who were furious that Morillo had even dealt with the insurgents at all. Believing his life was in danger, Morillo fled in disguise, eventually escaping on board a British brig, the *Blücher*. After reaching London, he continued on to Spain where he was given a hero's reception.[2]

Meanwhile, in South America, the armistice had led to an economic boom, to the delight of James Hamilton and his fellow merchants based in Angostura. With no Spanish warships blockading the Gulf of Paria, the trade in mules, cattle and arms conducted with the British colonies became 'extremely lively'.[3] Enterprising locals based as far inland as Los Llanos were also taking advantage of the ceasefire. In Achaguas one officer with the British Legion was amazed when mule trains arrived from Caracas and began trading 'as though they had never been enemies'.[4]

Another consequence of the peace was the mass release of prisoners of war. One of the first to benefit was Colonel Uslar, the Hanoverian whose riflemen had served alongside the British Legion in the disastrous action at Cumaná. A few months after the defeat, he had been captured by a royalist gunboat whilst sailing across the Gulf of Paria.[5]

After being stripped and beaten, he was chained to the deck for the 24-hour voyage to Güiria.[6] Upon landing, his hands were bound and a piece of 'old rug' thrown over his head as his only covering. He was then marched to the capital 'like a slave'.[7] After four months in prison he was granted an interview with General Morillo, who offered him command of a cavalry regiment in the royalist army. Uslar refused, claiming he would 'sooner die than be guilty of treachery to the cause … [he] espoused'. At a subsequent court martial in which deserters gave evidence against him, he was 'condemned to be shot' as an insurgent sympathizer, but was later saved by the intervention of fellow freemasons amongst the royalist elite. After eight months of solitary confinement, he was released as part of the armistice agreement and reached patriot headquarters on 25 January 1821.[8]

Another volunteer who endured captivity was Captain Chesterton, the memoirist who had fought with the British Legion's light company. In contrast to Uslar, Chesterton was treated well. After resigning his commission in English's regiment at Maturín, he was taken prisoner whilst crossing the Gulf of Paria. Although Chesterton threw his papers overboard, the Creole captain of the intercepting gunboat discovered his identity and had him arrested. His possessions were stolen by the crew, but once in the hands of the Spanish governor at Cumaná, Brigadier Tomás de Cires, he was well treated and later surmised 'that the Spaniards were not the fiends … [his former employers had] represented them to be'.[9] Cires took his parole and permitted him 'to roam through … town' unmolested.[10] A few weeks later Chesterton and his escort embarked for Caracas. En route, at El Morro de Barcelona, he fell ill with a bout of fever, but was saved by a Spanish colonel who nursed him with 'zealous care'.[11] Afterwards the small group continued, arriving at the port of La Guaira where Chesterton was imprisoned once more, this time with a daily allowance of three *reals*, 'which amounted … to something exceeding one shilling'.[12] Twelve days later he was transferred to Caracas, where he was put up in a local inn, granted parole and given freedom of the city. His arrival was reported in the local newspaper. Soon 'multitudes of people, urged by curiosity, crowded the *posada* in order to get a glimpse' at the 'English Captain'.[13] Chesterton spent three days exploring the capital before Morillo ordered him to be taken to his headquarters at Pao, near Valencia. As soon as he arrived, Chesterton was ushered into the general's presence and the reasons behind his jailers' benevolence became clear. As a veteran of the Peninsular War, Chesterton had several friends in the Spanish Army, one of whom had written to Morillo asking that he 'be treated with consideration'. On the understanding that he would not take up arms against the Spanish again, Morillo waived all charges against him. He returned to La Guaira, where he drew the pay of a Spanish captain for six weeks, before embarking for Europe on a British ship of war on 23 April 1820.

In sharp contrast to Chesterton's tale is that of the 340 volunteers who were taken prisoner at Portobelo. After MacGregor had abandoned them, they were imprisoned in the town's magazine for the first few nights of what would prove to be a year-and-a-half-long ordeal. The royalists were initially undecided as to what to do with their new charges. Some favoured ridding themselves of the problem entirely with a mass execution, but eventually it was decided that they should be marched across the isthmus to the Pacific coast and imprisoned near Panama. The 40-mile trek began on 2 May 1819. On the first morning, the prisoners were woken early and paraded through the streets of Portobelo watched by lines of curious locals. After being searched for weapons on the outskirts of town, they entered the 'gloomy forests' of the interior and were soon climbing the foothills of the Cordillera Central, the mountain range which runs like a spine through the centre of Panama.[14] The march was extremely fatiguing. At times they 'were obliged to ascend ... [on their] hands and feet' and 'in other places ... sank up to the knees in mud'. All the while the guards forced them onwards with the butt ends of their muskets to contemptuous cries of 'Vamos MacGregor!'[15] The column spent the first night in the jungle. 'A small quantity of rice and biscuit' was doled out to each man. Colonel Rafter then led them in a spirit-rousing chorus of 'God Save the King'.[16] Four more days of marches followed, frequently through pouring rain. The men were searched once more at the town of San Juan where Colonel Rafter's 'fine old gold watch' was amongst the items confiscated.[17] On the ninth day they ascended the main mountain range and were rewarded with stunning views over both the Pacific and the Caribbean. It was the first time the majority had seen the far side of the world. The sight inspired them and the next day they set off with renewed optimism.

Early on the morning of 10 May, the church spires of Panama were seen rising above the tree tops in the distance. The forest began to thin out, and at 1.00pm, as the drummers and buglers at the head of the column struck up a tune, they were marched into town. 'All the inhabitants ... were on the streets, or crowding the balconies and windows of the houses.'[18] After two circuits of the streets, they were led to a barracks by the sea, which became the home of the rank and file for the next 17 months. On their first full day, the Catholics amongst them were offered their freedom on the condition that they would join the locally based Catalonia Regiment on five-year contracts; 50 accepted the offer. On the 13th, the rest of the officers were taken by canoe to the town of Canne deep in the Darien rainforest. There they were imprisoned under the guard of Sergeant Bos, infamous amongst the volunteers for the murder of Captain Acton and his performing poodle, Leo. On arrival, the doctors and surgeons were sent to work in a nearby hospital where they treated the royalist sick and wounded. The rest were assigned quarters in 'a few reed huts, situated on the banks of a large river'.[19]

Although the officers were treated well and several were allowed to live and work in town, Colonel Rafter decided to make a break for freedom. His plan was audacious. First the men would capture a shore battery, then turn the guns on the city to create a diversion. Only then would they seize a Spanish brig, the *Venturosa*, which was lying at anchor in the bay, and sail south to join Lord Cochrane's Chilean squadron. Unfortunately for Rafter, his plan was uncovered. The conspirators were then imprisoned whilst Hore awaited orders from Sámano. The viceroy's instructions were all too predictable.[20] Early one morning, Rafter and 11 others were executed by firing squad and buried in the sands by the shore, an ignoble end for a man of such talent and experience.[21] As a consequence of the escape attempt, a stricter regime was imposed. The prisoners were beaten with sticks 'on very trifling pretences' and rations were reduced.[22] One newspaper reported that a single bullock's head boiled in water served as a day's rations for 15 men. Every morning the prisoners were chained together and forced to perform public works. 'In a state bordering on nakedness', they toiled from dawn to dusk, building causeways and fortifications, draining marshes, cutting down brushwood and repairing roads and bridges, whilst the guards encouraged them with their bayonets.[23] Unsurprisingly, sickness spread rapidly and the row of graves scraped out of the sand grew with every passing day.[24]

On 16 September 1819, a 350-ton frigate flying Spanish colours dropped anchor in the bay. The next morning she sailed up to a fort on the island of Taboga, seven miles offshore. Then, to the horror of the defenders, the sailors ran up the flag of the fledgling Chilean republic and opened fire. The frigate was the 36-gun *La Rosa de los Andes*, part of Lord Cochrane's Pacific squadron. After half an hour of thunderous broadsides the Spanish gunners fled and 200 Chilean sailors and marines were then rowed ashore. A bayonet charge killed or captured a few stubborn defenders and the rest were soon rounded up and taken prisoner.[25] The Spaniards were furious, but were impotent against the might of *La Rosa*'s cannon. As they fumed behind their fortifications, the frigate blockaded the bay for several days, capturing any unsuspecting merchantman that attempted to land. Her captain, an Englishman named John Illingworth, soon learnt of the British captives onshore and proposed a prisoner exchange. Hore refused and when he later heard rumours of a rescue attempt, he moved the prisoners further inland and warned that he would have them shot as soon as Illingworth's men landed. Despite Hore's threats, the sight of the friendly frigate so close at hand was too much for the captives to resist and a second escape plan, this time the brainchild of Doctor Phythian, was put into action.

At 8.00pm, the doctor and nine companions slunk into a shed behind the prison. Then, cutting across the yard, they reached the wall unseen. A rope was fixed to a nearby embrasure and they lowered themselves one by one into the ditch below. Creeping along the beach they boarded a canoe and began paddling out to the frigate. At that moment, disaster struck. An offshore gale was blowing and several huge waves swamped the boat, driving the men spluttering back to the beach. After months of poor rations and forced labour, all but one were too weak to climb back into the prison. At 11.00pm the guards raised the alarm. Private John Lewis and sergeants Leard and Hughes ran off, whilst Phythian and three others hid themselves beneath some bushes next to the wall. The guards scoured the area all night and, with daylight, their hiding place was revealed. Lewis was also recaptured, but when Hughes saw the soldiers approaching, he swam four miles to a tiny island exposed by the retreating tide, where the razor-sharp coral cut his hands and feet to ribbons. As the guards rowed towards him, Hughes picked up a stick to defend himself. The guards shot him, then dragged him back to prison.

Later that day, after refusing the services of a Catholic priest, the eight would-be escapees were led into a yard behind the prison where a firing squad and crowd of onlookers awaited them. Doctor Phythian 'looked at the Catalonian officers, in a manner prophetic of a day of retribution', but his fate had already been decided. The prisoners were forced to kneel with their backs to the assembly and the order to fire was given. When the smoke cleared, it became apparent that the muskets had failed to do their job. Phythian was still alive. On a signal from the officers, the soldiers finished him off with their bayonets.[26]

The last of the escapees, Sergeant Leard, was considerably more fortunate. As a Peninsular veteran, he could speak Spanish and had made several friends in town. In his hour of need one took him in, and hid him from the authorities until a passing American frigate, the *Macedonian*, agreed to take him on board. The captain, a sympathetic man by the name of Mr Downs, managed to convince Hore to release four more prisoners into his custody to serve as replacement crew. Later, two more managed to dupe the guards and slip on board; Mr Hawkins wore a sailor's uniform and Assistant Surgeon Kirnan disguised himself as a woman. Shortly afterwards the *Macedonian* upped anchor and sailed away.

On 20 September 1820, after a full 17 months in captivity, the rest of the prisoners held at Panama were released by order of the new liberal government in Madrid. They were shipped to Jamaica by the British authorities before finally returning home. Out of the 340 men that MacGregor had abandoned at the end of April 1819, only 121 survived. A total of 23 had been executed by the Spaniards and the rest had died of exhaustion, malnutrition or disease.[27]

Chapter 32

THE BATTLE OF CARABOBO

In early 1821 both sides violated the terms of the armistice. For the royalists, belligerent cargoes arrived from Cádiz. Guns and ammunition were unloaded at Puerto Cabello and 1,200 Spanish troops disembarked in Coro and Cumaná.[1] The patriots were equally culpable. Firstly, 1,000 infantry from General Sucre's army of the south, including 100 of the Albion, were sent to the Ecuadorian city of Guayaquil to support a local uprising. Then, in a similar incident, Bolívar covertly sent troops to support patriots in the Venezuelan city of Maracaibo. After they had overthrown the royalist garrison, General Urdaneta was ordered to move his entire division into the city to consolidate patriot control. Faced with such flagrant aggression, the royalists made an official complaint. Bolívar made no reply and hostilities recommenced on 28 April 1821.

Bolívar was unconcerned, having never had any intention of maintaining a long-lasting peace. Ever since his meeting with Morillo in December 1820, he had been planning to force the royalists into a decisive showdown by concentrating all his forces and marching on Caracas. With five separate divisions involved, it was to be a masterpiece of coordination. Two were used in diversionary strikes, whilst the others gathered for the main attack. In the east, General Bermúdez advanced against Caracas from Cumaná with 1,200 troops on 28 April. Although only intended as a feint, the attack enjoyed spectacular success. Catching the royalists unprepared, Bermúdez's troops took and held the capital for 12 days before being driven back by a counter-attack. General Urdaneta, in command of the second diversionary division, also began operations on the 28th. Leaving Maracaibo, he marched against the coastal city of Coro. Meanwhile, the three divisions involved in the main strike were converging on San Carlos, a town on the edge of Los Llanos 100 miles to the south-west of Caracas. Bolívar advanced from Cúcuta with General Cedeño's 2nd Division, whilst the 3rd, under Colonel Ambrosio Plaza, marched from Barinas. The last to set out was Páez's 1st Division. Based at Achaguas, it was 2,500 strong and included the British Legion.

The Legion's morale had picked up considerably since Blosset's death, principally through the introduction of new personnel. Colonel Thomas Ferrier, the new commander, was a veteran of the 43rd Foot, who had originally sailed to South America with Colonel Gillmore's artillery in January 1818.[2] Having seen action at the skirmish in Caujaral and numerous encounters in Los Llanos under Páez, the doctor's son from Manchester also had considerable experience of the war in South America. He was liked and respected by his men and his energy and commitment were in stark contrast to Blosset's apathy. Another new addition to the regiment was Captain Charles Minchin, originally one of Captain Elsom's recruits. As one of four Irish brothers who had volunteered in 1819, Charles was the only one left in the service two years later. Two of his brothers had died of fever and the third had resigned his commission in the Irish Legion and returned home. Minchin's dedication and endurance were beyond doubt.[3] As well as an influx of new arrivals, the Legion's morale had also been boosted by a vast improvement in conditions. In November 1820, 500 new uniforms had been issued and rations had begun to improve.[4] For the first time in months, the men were able to take pride in their appearance. According to one report, the morning and evening parades held every Sunday were a sight to behold.[5] Since March that year, the Legion had been receiving pay and on the 21st of the month, Bolívar himself arrived in town.[6] After inspecting the troops he made a stirring speech, announcing that they would be in Caracas within 50 days. The prospect of action and plunder lifted the men after months spent idling in the plains, and the camp became a hive of activity.[7] Whilst the British oiled their muskets, made up cartridges and checked their flints, the Llaneros sharpened swords and lance heads.[8] More than 2,000 horses and 4,000 calves were rounded up from the surrounding plains.[9] On the morning of 10 May, Páez prayed for the Virgin's blessing at the church in Achaguas. The order to march was then given and the column filed out onto the plain.

Although the troops were unmolested by the enemy who had been lured back to Caracas by Bermúdez's feint, the march coincided with the start of the rainy season and soon became an ordeal. The downpour was incessant. For hours on end the men had to march 'up to the knees' in water.[10] To make matters worse, Páez was obliged to drive them at the double to keep to Bolívar's schedule. Near the start of their march, the patriots had to cross the river Apurito. Later they contended with numerous streams 'swarming with alligators' and voracious 'Caribe fish' whose teeth could 'penetrate a coat of steel'.[11] Some fell prey to snake bites or died of fatigue. At night the troops slept on the open plain 'with no ... covering ... but the canopy of Heaven'.[12] They were grateful if the rain ceased long enough for the cattle to be butchered and cooking fires to be lit. Inevitably, after the men had settled for the night, the wild horses would escape 'in a mad rush' and each morning hours were spent herding them back to camp.[13] On 31 May, the division reached Tucupido, where it split into two. Páez rode ahead with the cavalry and arrived at San Carlos on 7 June. The infantry struggled in four days later. Bolívar and the 2nd Division had already arrived. At an inspection, The Liberator paid Colonel Ferrier 'many handsome compliments' on the 'appearance' and 'discipline' of his men.[14] The volunteers were then allowed to rest for a few days whilst awaiting the arrival of Plaza's 3rd Division from Barinas.

San Carlos had been abandoned by the royalists a few days before. Most of the locals had been evacuated and General La Torre, now in charge following Morillo's departure, had taken everything of value before falling back towards Caracas.[15] The day after the British Legion arrived, a Spanish colonel rode in under a flag of truce. The days of the 'War to the Death' were over and the visitor was received with cordiality. In a scene reminiscent of the battlefields of Europe, a table was laid and formal introductions made before the company sat down to eat. After the meal, the Spaniard proposed a new armistice with the river Portuguesa as the demarcation line. Certain he was on the verge of a decisive victory, Bolívar refused. For his part, Páez believed that the Spaniards had already known that the truce would be turned down and the colonel was little more than a glorified spy.[16]

On 19 June Colonel Plaza's 3rd Division arrived. The army was now complete. It was the largest concentration of patriot troops South America had ever seen. A total of 6,500 men, 4,500 horses and 4,000 cattle were spread around town and across the neighbouring plains. Amongst the new arrivals were the Black Rifles. After their victory at the battle of Ciénega, the regiment had taken up quarters in Santa Marta, where several British officers had died. Major Peacock had succumbed to his wounds and Captain Phelan had died whilst having his leg amputated. Yellow fever had further decimated the ranks. Captain Bunbury died in mid-December, despite the attentions of Doctor O'Reilly, who later fell victim to the disease himself along with the Swiss-born Captain Schwitzgibel and lieutenants Macnamara and French.[17] By the time they left Santa Marta, only three of the 35 officers who had sailed on the *Dowson* were still alive. Besides those in the ranks of the British Legion and the Black Rifles, there were 30 other British privates, NCOs and officers at San Carlos. Captain O'Leary, Surgeon Murphy and Colonel Woodberry were all attached to Bolívar's staff. Lieutenant Charles Church, who had originally been recruited by Elsom and had served with the Legion for some time in Los Llanos around San Juan, now commanded a Creole cavalry unit and Major Joseph Farrar, who had previously served as commandant for Angostura, was with the 1st Division as General Páez's aide-de-camp.

On 20 June the army advanced down the main road to Caracas. An officer with the British Legion thought the plains they passed through 'a fine country'. The grassland was spotted with trees and scrub, and alive with birdsong.[18] The following day, Páez's vanguard clashed with enemy scouts near the village of Tinaco. The Spanish commander and four of his men were killed. The rest surrendered and were brought back to camp.[19] The patriots then crossed the river Chirigua. Fearing that they would suffer the same fate as the scouts at Tinaco, La Torre withdrew a second picket that he had placed on the heights of Buenavista and, at midday, patriot vedettes occupied the position. The heights afforded Bolívar and his staff a fine view of La Torre's army formed up on a high plateau a mile to the north-east.

Numbering 4,500 men, La Torre's army held the high ground of Carabobo, blocking the road to the capital. The Spaniard had chosen his position well. The only obvious line of attack ran straight into the fire of the two 4-pdr cannon he had placed on a hill overlooking the main road. Positioned behind the ridge line to the gunners' rear were 2,500 infantry and the whole force was backed up by a cavalry reserve of 1,500 men. Of these, 200 were Spanish Hussars and the rest were royalist Llaneros under General Francisco Tomás Morales. Despite his commanding position, La Torre was not confident of victory. Following the liberal revolution and Morillo's departure, his troops had little will to fight. Furthermore, there was a lack of support from his senior commander. General Morales had felt slighted when he had not been given overall command of the army and La Torre knew that he could no longer rely on him. Denied his cavalry reserve, the Spaniard knew he would have to hold the patriots at arm's length if he were to win the battle. If Bolívar's troops managed to get up to the plateau in strength, a general collapse seemed likely.

On the plains below, the patriots formed into line of battle. Páez's men were on the right, Cedeño held the left and Plaza's division was in the centre. Offering words of encouragement, The Liberator rode down the line accompanied by Captain O'Leary and a huddle of mounted staff officers. When he reached the British Legion, his words were met with 'three hurrahs' that carried to the Spanish lines.[20] The troops were ready, but although it was only 1.00pm, Bolívar decided to postpone the attack until the next morning. Captain Charles Minchin, the commander of the Legion's Grenadier company, thought the delay 'was either to give us a rest or because he thought it would be lucky to fight on San Juan's day'.[21] As the news passed down the line, the troops fell out and prepared to spend another night on the plain. That evening, 'the rain fell in torrents'.[22] Although the ground was soon churned into a morass and the men soaked to the skin, the British took the weather as a good omen. During Wellington's campaigns, it had often rained the night before a battle and a particularly memorable downpour had preceded

Waterloo. As they huddled under cover, Sandes, Rudd, Uslar and the other veterans reassured their comrades that it was 'a prelude to victory'.[23]

Early in the morning of 24 June, the volunteers awoke to a cloudless sky. Whilst the officers of the British Legion gathered to talk over 'the chances of the day', Bolívar and his staff reconnoitred the field.[24] It was clear that La Torre's position was too strong to attack head-on: his cannon would rake their line of march as they climbed up to the heights and their left would be exposed to a flanking attack from the royalist infantry on the plateau. Nevertheless, the terrain appeared to offer little alternative.[25] At a council of war later that morning, the senior patriot officers were at a loss until a local guide mentioned a little-used path that led round to the royalists' right. The Liberator seized upon the idea and soon a plan to send Páez's division to outflank the enemy had been formulated. The Bravos de Apure, closely supported by the British Legion, were to spearhead the attack, whilst the Caudillo's cavalry and Cedeño's 2nd Division followed on behind. If the infantry could push back La Torre's right and establish themselves on the high ground, the cavalry could pour onto the plateau and roll up the royalist line. Meanwhile, the 3rd Division was to be held in reserve on the main road

THE BATTLE OF CARABOBO

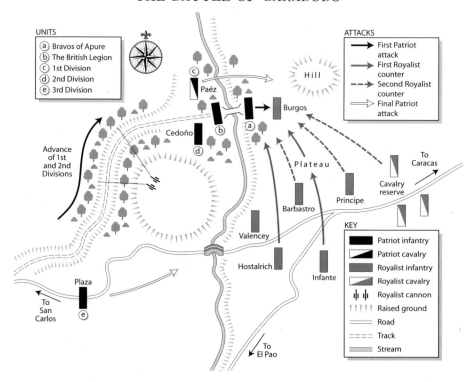

302

to Valencia, ready to mop up after the 1st and 2nd divisions had broken the royalists' will to fight.

The path wound round to the north for two miles, following the bottom of a wooded gulley.[26] It was so deep that the British Legion and Bravos de Apure soon lost sight of the enemy regiments above them, and so narrow that they were frequently forced into single file. The track was covered in sharp stones that cut their shoes to pieces and 'deeply' wounded their feet.[27] As they cleared a path through the tangled undergrowth with machetes, the cool of dawn was replaced by a fierce mid-morning heat.[28] Minchin remembered that 'all was calm and still', the only sounds the chattering of monkeys and the buzz of insects. Meanwhile, the royalists had become aware of their presence and La Torre was busy realigning his troops to meet the threat. The 2nd Battalion of Burgos, an 800-strong infantry unit with a core of Spanish veterans, was ordered to move from the centre to the right to hold the ridge line where the enemy forces were expected to emerge.

At one point the ravine the patriots were following crossed an area of open ground, briefly exposing them to Spanish cannon fire from the heights above. Bolívar sent O'Leary ahead to make sure the men got through. As each company appeared, he ordered them to form into small groups under cover, then dash across at the double.[29] Each time the Spanish gunners opened fire with a shower of round shot and grape. At least ten men in each regiment were killed, studding the trail with broken bodies. The survivors re-formed on the far side and pressed on. At 11.00am the Bravos de Apure emerged from the ravine. Ahead of them was the narrow stream of Carabobo, beyond which lay a steep scrub-covered slope leading to the plateau where the battalion of Burgos awaited them. Whilst the rest of the troops remained on the far bank, the Bravos de Apure crossed the stream and advanced up the hillside in column into scattered fire. They got to within pistol range of the royalists before forming line. As they completed the manoeuvre, the Spaniards poured a volley into them. The slope enabled the rear ranks to shoot over the heads of their comrades, producing a terrifying volume of fire. The close-range volley was devastating. Scores fell dead and wounded. The survivors retreated back to the stream where their officers managed to re-form them. Again they pushed up the wooded slope, but once more were thrown back in confusion. This time there was little their commanders could do. With the Spaniards' fire still playing upon their rear, they sprinted down the hill 'in headlong disorder' and crashed into the British Legion who had been sent to support them.[30]

Wide-eyed with terror, the Bravos elbowed their way through the British ranks. For a moment it seemed as if the panic would spread and the whole division would flee in disorder, but Colonel Ferrier coolly took command. Towering over his men on horseback, the Mancunian urged them to hold, whilst his officers and NCOs manhandled the weak-hearted back into line. Eventually order was re-established and the Legion advanced, pushing up the hill by companies with Minchin's Grenadiers leading the way. The incline was so pronounced that the captain 'was glad to catch hold of the tail' of a passing officer's horse to haul himself to the summit.[31] From the ridge line ahead, the Burgos Battalion opened fire. With the musketry whistling through the air, several volunteers were killed or wounded. The rest struggled on up the slope. At the head of the regiment, Colonel Ferrier was hit a glancing blow in the leg. Then Minchin received a 'severe' blow to his right thigh.[32] Gritting his teeth against the pain, he formed his men into line on the lip of the plateau and gave the order to fire. The enemy formation seemed to shiver as the volley bit home. Each of the Legion's eight companies then formed alongside them and unloaded into the royalist ranks. Faced with the fearsome red-coated 'veterans of Waterloo', the Spaniards began to inch backwards. Ferrier sensed victory would soon be his.

From his position in the royalist centre, La Torre could see his right wing engulfed in fire and smoke. The 2nd Burgos Battalion was ceding ground and a few men were already fleeing to the rear. Realizing urgent reinforcements were needed, the Spaniard ordered the battalions of Hostalrich and Infante, initially positioned on his left flank, to support them. By the time they had formed up and opened fire on the Legion, it was past midday. The British troops were now outnumbered four to one and enveloped in fire from the front and both flanks.[33] To make matters worse, their ammunition was beginning to run low. Nevertheless, amidst the storm of lead, smoke and flame, the volunteers maintained their cool. Biting open their cartridges, they rammed the balls home and fired off volleys twice a minute to Ferrier's barked command. In the ebb and flow of the battle, several bayonet charges were made by both sides, but beaten back on each occasion after fierce hand-to-hand fighting. The volunteers paid a horrendous price for their bravery. Colonel Ferrier was hit for a second time, whilst yelling at his men to hold firm. The ball 'splintered the bone below his knee most dreadfully' while 'at the same moment, his horse was bayoneted and dropped under him'.[34] The colonel's second, Lieutenant-Colonel Davy, 'was [also] wounded in several places'.[35] Major Edward Brand then briefly took over, but fled the field after his horse had been killed.[36] With Ferrier, Davy and Brand all out of the fight, Captain James Scott, the reverend's son from Perthshire, took up command.[37]

Although outwardly calm as he called out orders to his ever shrinking company, Captain Minchin was seething with anger inside. Whilst his 'comrades were falling in all directions', the bulk of the patriot army was as yet uncommitted.[38] Looking behind him he could see Páez's cavalry and the entire 2nd Division watching the bloodshed from the safety of the far side of the stream. Although the cavalry could be excused as the wooded slope was not suitable for mounted troops, the patriot foot had no reason for holding back.[39] With 'curses … loud and deep', the men shared Minchin's frustration, but it only strengthened their resolve 'to carry the enemy position or perish'.[40] Twenty minutes after the Spanish reinforcements had arrived, the Legion's situation was becoming critical. Running low on ammunition, the men were reduced to fishing through their dead comrades' pouches for spare cartridges, and keeping the royalists back with their bayonets. An aide had been sent back to Páez to beg for more ammunition, and the men fired their ramrods high into the air in a recognized signal of distress. The officers were being killed and wounded at an alarming rate. After a few minutes at the head of the Legion, Captain Scott was shot through the head, leaving Minchin as the senior surviving captain to take command. On sighting Spanish cavalry approaching from the north-east, his first order was to form square. In the centre, the men holding the colours were singled out by Spanish sharpshooters firing from the high ground. The banners were 'cut to ribands [by their musketry] and [soon] dyed with the blood' of the six men who would die bearing them.[41] Next to the colours was Private John Hill, a former labourer from Kent now serving as a bandsman with the Grenadiers.[42] Despite being wounded in both an arm and a leg, he refused to be taken to the rear.[43] With his bugle clamped between bloodstained lips, he continued playing the order to hold. One third of the 300 were now casualties. Nevertheless, the Legion held firm.

As the volume of musketry fired against them lessened, the royalist infantry grew bolder. A company of 100 advanced to within a few dozen yards of the Legion's left flank to pour in a close-range volley. One British lieutenant reacted quickly to disperse the threat. Gathering 30 men around him, he led them in an uphill charge. The royalist troops buckled under the impact. Several were stabbed or bludgeoned to the ground and the rest fled back to their lines.[44] As the 30 rejoined the square, more ammunition arrived. In their desperation, the men tore open the boxes with their bare hands. The cartridges were handed out by companies and soon the hills echoed once more to the sound of British volleys. Eventually belated reinforcements began to appear. The Bravos de Apure and two companies of the Tiradores Battalion from the 2nd Division took station to the left of the British formation. Minchin then ordered his men to form line. They deployed 'as steadily as on a parade day', leaving the ground behind them carpeted with dead.[45] With three cheers the patriots charged. The Spaniards met them 'gallantly' and for a few moments, the outcome lay in the balance.[46] Opposing officers fought with sabres and pistols, whilst the men killed with their bayonets. Gradually the patriots gained the upper hand and the royalist regiments 'began to give ground'. Those in the front ranks tried to burrow into the heart of the formation, whilst others peeled away from the flanks and rear. The panic was infectious. Moments later the entire royalist right 'broke and fled'.[47]

Running back to a second line of hills to the rear, they re-formed, leaving the patriots battered, bloodied, but victorious.

With his right flank crumbling, La Torre dispatched two more infantry battalions, Principe and Barbastro, and two squadrons of the Queen's Hussars to shore up the defence. The momentum of the battle had already swung firmly in favour of the patriots, however, and with the way up to the plain now open, Páez's cavalry were able to join the fight. Passing the British Legion on their left, they looped round behind the hills now occupied by the remnants of the Spanish infantry and charged into their rear. Just when it seemed as if the battle had left the British Legion behind, the Spanish Hussars appeared. Again Minchin formed his men into square. Their mouths gritty from powder residue, the men closed ranks and loaded their muskets. With a start the cavalry appeared through the smoke. Galloping in line, they fired their carbines as they closed. The Legion met them with ordered volleys and a line of bayonets. The cavalry sheered off at the last moment. Flowing round the square, they fired more carbine shots from the saddle and slashed ineffectually at the line of bayonets. Standing in the heart of the formation, Minchin was hit. The ball drilled through his right shoulder and passed out through his back. Despite losing 'torrents' of blood, he fought on with his sword in his left hand until the royalists were repulsed.[48] As the Hussars retreated to the second line of hills, Minchin's vision clouded over and he collapsed to the ground.

Meanwhile the Spanish infantry were holding firm against Páez's cavalry. Leading the Caudillo's guard of honour, Captain Juan Ángel Bravo had his jacket pierced in 14 places by musketry and bayonets, but miraculously fought on unhurt.[49] When the royalists saw their Hussars fleeing from their brush with the Legion's square, it proved the final straw. The panic spread down the line and the entire mass routed. Whole regiments threw down their weapons and surrendered, while others scattered across the plains, fleeing in small clusters into the woodland to the north and east. The artillery on the heights which had harassed the patriots' morning advance were ordered to pull back before it was too late. With the tide of the battle now firmly against him, La Torre rode across to his rearguard cavalry and ordered them to cover the retreat. General Morales, the Spaniard's American rival for overall command, listened to his pleas 'with the utmost indifference', then wheeled his riders away from the fight. They rode for Valencia, 18 miles north-east on the road to Caracas, leaving La Torre fuming with rage.[50]

Despite the cavalry's shameful flight and the general collapse of the infantry, one royalist unit fought its way from the field. 'Made up entirely of veteran soldiers of the Motherland', the infantrymen of Valencey were determined to restore some pride to Spanish arms.[51] The regiment's colonel, a 'little dark looking fellow' from Scotland named Thomas Arbuthnot, formed a mobile square and retired from his position on the left wing towards Valencia in good order.[52] The unit acted as a beacon to the remnants of the other royalist regiments. Survivors flocked towards Arbuthnot's banners, strengthening the formation as it fell back.[53] Amongst the fugitives who made it safely inside the square were the artillery with one of their guns and several high-ranking officers including La Torre.

As the patriot infantry who had taken part in the preliminary assault were now exhausted, it fell to Páez's cavalry and the as yet uncommitted 2nd and 3rd divisions to break Arbuthnot's men. Bizarrely, it was at this stage in the fighting with the battle already won that several high-ranking patriot commanders lost their lives. One reason was overconfidence. Although other enemy infantry formations had surrendered with little resistance, the men of Valencey were determined to make it back to Valencia. Their resolve surprised their attackers, who charged them believing they would break long before they got within musket range. As the riders closed, the Spaniards stopped, levelled their muskets and fired. Several patriot officers paid the ultimate price. Colonel Ambrosio Plaza, the commander of the 3rd Division, was amongst those who fell. On hearing La Torre was escaping the field, he 'swore to drag him from the midst of his troops or perish in the attempt', then 'madly rode against the square and was shot in twenty places'.[54] General Cedeño was another high-profile casualty. 'Stung by a rebuke from Bolivar', he quitted the command post on the far side of the stream and set off after the Spaniards with a small body of riders.[55] Upon sighting the square, he cut back with his spurs and charged. Again the Spaniards coolly levelled and fired. Cedeño was shot through the head and died before his body hit the ground.[56]

The Black Rifles were also called into the pursuit. With each soldier mounted behind a cavalryman, they set off after the Spaniards to halt their retreat. On the ride they passed countless corpses littering the road, and encountered small, desperate skirmishes, where bands of royalist fugitives still held out. It was now late afternoon and the clear skies had given way to grey clouds and heavy rain. The road had been churned up by the retreating royalists and the horses struggled to keep their footing. By the time the Rifles caught up, dismounted and formed line, their opponents had already reached the outskirts of Valencia. After exchanging a few volleys near a string of windmills, Sandes led them in a bayonet charge.[57] The enemy broke before them and the Rifles swept through town. Some royalists were cut down or taken prisoner. Many more escaped down the road to Puerto Cabello. With them were several mounted officers, including La Torre, who made it safely back to the fortified coastal town. Up to 200 of Arbuthnot's infantry blasted their way through the ring of circling patriots to join them. Although a handful of patriot cavalry harassed them all the way, the majority of Bolívar's army stopped for the night in Valencia.

Even though the royalists would hold onto a few isolated towns on the coast for several years, the battle of Carabobo signalled the end of Spanish rule in the Venezuelan interior. A total of 122 officers and 2,786 men had been killed or captured.[58] The royalists' material losses were equally crippling. One of their two cannon was captured along with thousands of muskets, cartridges, barrels of powder, swords and bayonets. Patriot casualties, by comparison, had been remarkably light. Although the figure of 200 given in Bolívar's official dispatch was undoubtedly an underestimate, it seems likely that no more than 300–500 fell. Despite only fielding 5 per cent of the army, the British Legion had suffered 30 per cent of all patriot casualties. Of the 300-strong Legion that had marched out that morning, 33 per cent had been lost in just over an hour. Two officers and 28 men were killed on the field; 61 others were wounded, 12 of whom would later die in hospital.[59] The Legion's remarkable stand had undoubtedly been the decisive moment of the day. It had allowed the patriots to marshal their forces and later opened up the route onto the plains, where Páez's cavalry had proved unstoppable. Even before the Caudillo had entered the combat, however, the majority of the royalists had lost the will to resist. The stubbornness of the volunteers and their refusal to accept defeat, despite facing overwhelming odds, had sapped their energy and most surrendered to the Llaneros without a fight.

After the battle, the survivors of the British Legion were congratulated by Bolívar. Their faces were blackened by powder burns, their uniforms slashed and torn and their bayonets bent and stained with blood. As The Liberator watched them file past 'with trailed arms' as a sign of respect to their fallen comrades, he saluted them as 'Salvadores de mi Patria'.[60] His words were met by a single cheer. Later, whilst they were in barracks in Valencia, medals were awarded to all the survivors, and the regiment was renamed Battalón Carabobo. Three weeks after the battle, Colonel Ferrier died of his wounds. 'The whole of the brigade and most of the inhabitants' of the city attended the funeral.[61] Bolívar himself marched alongside the cortege. The survivors stood in silence as his corpse was consigned to the earth and ceremonial volleys thundered over his grave.

EPILOGUE

Subsequent to the battle of Carabobo, Spanish control of Venezuela and New Granada collapsed. Caracas was taken without a fight in the week following the victory, and pockets of resistance in Maracaibo and Coro were eliminated. Cartagena and Cumaná surrendered in October and on 28 November the province of Panama followed suit. The entire Caribbean coastline (with the exception of Puerto Cabello) was in patriot hands before the end of the year. On 24 May 1822, Ecuador's independence was sealed at the battle of Pichincha. This led to the surrender of the Pastusos in southern New Granada and rendered the liberation of Gran Colombia all but complete. Nevertheless, Bolívar's armies continued fighting in Peru and modern-day Bolivia for several more years, and it was not until 8 December 1824 at the battle of Ayacucho that the Spaniards were finally ousted from the continent.

Even before the final victory, The Liberator had realized that maintaining control of the newly independent states would be even more problematic than defeating the Spaniards. His pessimism proved well founded. Whilst he was campaigning in Peru, Santander and Páez turned against him and by the time he returned to Santafé in 1826, Gran Colombia was close to collapse. Further betrayals and civil war followed and in 1828 he was forced to leave the capital following an assassination attempt. His health went into decline with what would posthumously be diagnosed as tuberculosis, and two years later he resigned the presidency, planning to live out his remaining days in European exile. Without The Liberator at the helm, Gran Colombia split into its three constituent parts: Páez became president of Venezuela, Santander of New Granada and General Flores, a Venezuelan who had fought in the Wars of Independence, became head of an independent Ecuador. The Liberator, meanwhile, was growing weaker as he made his way to the coast. Subsequently, his doctors advised against travelling to Europe and when a wealthy Spaniard, Joaquín Mier, suggested that he and his shrinking entourage stay in his villa on the outskirts of Santa Marta, the offer was readily accepted. Bolívar was so weak that he had to be carried in on a sedan chair. His final days were restless as the disease ate away at his lungs. He died on 17 December 1830.[1]

In the same year, José Antonio Páez became the first president of Venezuela. Backed by popular support, the Caudillo proved a wise and fair leader and his 17-year rule is generally considered to have been a golden era in Venezuelan history. In 1847 he was succeeded by José Tadeo Monagas, another veteran of the war. Monagas's policies proved too liberal for Páez's liking, however, and in 1850 he led a rebellion against his former ally. The uprising was unsuccessful. Páez was arrested, briefly imprisoned then sent into exile. For the next eight years he toured Europe, lived in New York and became something of a celebrity, meeting such figures as the president of the United States. After returning to Venezuela he was re-elected, and served from 1861 to 1863. Exiled yet again following his second fall from power, he returned to New York where he died aged 82.

Following Carabobo, Arthur Sandes continued to lead the Black Rifles for five more years. In 1822 the regiment distinguished itself at the battle of Bomboná in northern Ecuador. After outflanking the enemy, Sandes led a bayonet charge that drove the royalists from the field and later received his full colonelcy as a reward.[2] Nine months later the unit fought an epic rearguard action in Peru after Sucre's army had been outmanoeuvred by the royalists in the build up to the battle of Ayacucho. Sandes and his men were given the unenviable task of holding the enemy back whilst the bulk of the army escaped over a river crossing. Although this bought enough time for their comrades to withdraw, 200 of his men were killed and 500 more were wounded or taken prisoner. After the encounter Sandes sat down on the riverbank and wept. Victory followed a few days later at Ayacucho and the colonel was promoted to general of brigade. Although it was the last major battle of the war, Sandes saw further action in the conflicts that the independent states fought amongst themselves in the late 1820s, distinguishing himself in his final action at Portete de Tarqui in 1829. After retiring from military life, he became one of 500 British veterans to settle in Gran Colombia.[3] He was appointed governor of a department of Ecuador and lived out the rest of his days in the town of Cuenca. Also resident were six other British veterans, including his old comrade, Thomas Wright.[4] His body worn out from years of campaigning, Sandes died at the age of 38 on 6 September 1832, 'after a tedious illness, which terminated in oropsy'.[5]

Francis O'Connor's military career also continued long after Carabobo. Following the battle of Ciénega in November 1820, he remained on the New Granadan coast throughout the armistice and took part in the siege of Cartagena in 1821. Three years later he was appointed chief of staff to Bolívar's 'United Army of Liberation in Peru', and fought in the battles of Junín and Ayacucho. After the final victory, he was appointed military governor of Tarija in Bolivia, where as well as regularly contributing to a local newspaper, he began to compose his memoirs. In 1827, at the age of 35, he married the 17-year old Francisca Ruyloba, who was to bear him several children. He had one final military hurrah 11 years later, when he co-commanded the Bolivian army at the battle of Montenegro. Victory consolidated the country's south-western frontier against Argentine encroachment, and enabled O'Connor to hang up his sword. Like many former officers he then moved into politics, becoming minister of war for Bolivia before retiring from public life to dedicate his remaining years to his farm in Tarija. He died at the age of 81.

John Mackintosh, John Johnstone, Thomas Manby and Laurence McGuire all fought with the Albion Battalion at the battle of Yaguchi under General Sucre in 1821. Victory sealed the independence of Guayaquil, Ecuador's second city. The battalion then took part in a disastrous encounter at Guachi. Sucre's army was routed. Mackintosh and Johnstone were wounded and captured along with dozens of other British volunteers. The former escaped and later rejoined the army.[6] Johnstone, on the other hand, would have to wait for a prisoner exchange. Nevertheless, he returned to the unit in time to take part in the battle of Pichincha on 24 May 1822. Fought on the flanks of a volcano on the outskirts of Quito, the encounter saw the royalist field marshal, Melchor de Aymerich, comprehensively defeated. The Albion, with the rearguard, once again played a crucial role. Standing firm after many of their comrades had fled, the battalion tore the heart out of the Spanish army with ordered volleys, turning what had looked like defeat into a memorable victory. It was their last significant contribution to the war. In 1823 the soldiers' five-year contracts expired and although a few such as Laurence McGuire continued with the army, the majority returned to Santafé to petition Santander for their back pay and the plots of land they had been promised by López Mendéz several years before. The senior officers' claims were supported by Creole comrades who held positions in high office. Those from the lower ranks, on the other hand, often had to wait months or even years before their cases were heard.

In 1823 Mackintosh, Johnstone and Manby were all awarded citizenship of New Granada in recognition of their services to the state.[7] Mackintosh then married Isabel Archer, his brother's sister-in-law, whom he had met five years previously when all four had shared a cabin on the *Prince*. After setting up house in Santafé, which now had a community of 100 British veterans complete with their own English language newspaper, Mackintosh and his wife sailed to England to seek medical attention for his old war wounds.[8] In 1829 they returned to the Gran Colombian capital to petition the government for the repayment of the loans his brother James had made in Angostura back in 1818. James's generosity had helped to keep the war effort afloat in the cash-strapped days of the early Third Republic and with interest, the debt now amounted to

£380,023 3s 11d. Negotiations advanced promisingly until 1830, when, with Bolívar's resignation, the country descended into chaos.[9]

Nearly all of the British veterans who remained in New Granada were affected by the upheavals. Whilst Páez in Venezuela and Flores in Ecuador generally honoured their commitments to the volunteers, Santander turned against them and attempted to erase from public memory the key role that many had played during the war. In 1837 Mackintosh wrote an open letter to *La Bandera Negra*, highlighting some of the president's most outrageous lies. In a widely publicized reconstruction of the battle of Vargas, Santander had claimed that it was his New Granadan troops rather than Rooke's Legion that had saved the patriots from defeat. In an attempt to set the record straight, Mackintosh pointed out that Santander's regiment had actually fled only 30 minutes into the fighting.[10] Not content with playing down the volunteers' contribution, the president also removed the names of those he saw as potential political enemies from the veterans' list, thereby denying them access to their pensions and associated benefits. The archives in Bogotá are filled with letters from Mackintosh, Johnstone, Manby and over 100 others from the period, pleading with the government to pay them their due.[11] Whilst claims by South Americans were processed rapidly and rarely, if ever, questioned, those by foreigners took several months or even years to resolve.[12] Eventually senior Creole officers came to their support and Santander was forced to back down. By 1836 the British had been re-inscribed on the list and were once again receiving their pensions. Sadly, Johnstone did not live long enough to benefit from this turnaround. In 1832 he left for England, exasperated by the president's lies and endless rounds of correspondence. He died a few weeks later in Panama, presumably of disease. Mackintosh, on the other hand, lived long enough to claim his pension for a further decade.[13] He died a year shy of his 50th birthday on 30 May 1846. Thomas Manby outlived both of his former comrades. In Santafé in 1836 he married Maria Fortoul, the daughter of a wealthy Creole general and cousin of President Santander. The couple went on to have several children. Having cemented his finances and social standing, Manby enjoyed a long retirement. In his old age he indulged his 'penchant' for composing 'long letters' to friends around the world.[14] When he passed away in 1881 at the age of 80, he was the last surviving volunteer.

After Carabobo, Daniel O'Leary travelled south with Bolívar as the focus of the war moved to Ecuador and Peru. He was used by The Liberator as both a military and political spokesman and became an increasingly close confidant. In 1827 he was promoted to colonel and a year later his position amongst the Creole elite was strengthened when he married Soledad Soublette, the sister of the patriots' pre-eminent staff officer. In 1830, as Bolívar entered his final decline, he rewarded his ever faithful servant with a promotion to general of brigade. O'Leary disobeyed Bolívar's final request that his extensive collection of documents be destroyed, however, and the Irishman would spend much of his later life compiling a 32-volume memoir.

Following The Liberator's death, Santander purged New Granada of all those considered pro-Bolívarian. Rather than face the witch-hunt, O'Leary chose voluntary exile in Jamaica instead. In Kingston he set himself up as a merchant and his wife gave birth to the first of nine children. After three years the situation in South America improved, and Soublette invited his son-in-law to move to Caracas. In 1835, O'Leary was appointed Venezuela's European ambassador and returned to his homeland after a 17-year absence. In the grip of the Industrial Revolution, Britain had changed considerably since he had left. Horse-drawn carriages and sailing ships had been superseded by trains and steamboats, the streets were lit by gas and numerous factories belched out smoke and noise. Later, on a visit to his native Cork, O'Leary was given a hero's welcome and was reacquainted with Catherine, his only surviving sibling. In total he was to spend six frustrating years as a diplomat in London, Paris, the Vatican and Madrid, attempting to gain recognition for the fledgling South American republics. Whilst in Spain he visited his old adversary General Morillo, who remembered him from their meeting at Santa Ana in 1820. After greeting each other like old friends, O'Leary told the general of his ambition to produce a history of the war. The Spaniard was delighted and handed over reams of documentation that his troops had captured following the rout at Semen in 1818. All the while O'Leary had been lobbying the British government for a political post in South America and in 1841 his persistence finally paid off. He spent the next ten years in Caracas, Puerto Cabello and Santafé, serving the government in a variety of diplomatic roles, before declining health prompted a return to Europe in 1851 at the age of 50. Sailing with two of his eldest daughters, he arrived in Southampton in September. After visiting doctors in Paris and Rome and making a final appearance in Cork to present Queen's College (now UCU) with a collection of South American minerals, birds and plants, he returned to Santafé via the United States, arriving in December 1853. The following February he died suddenly of 'apoplexy' and was given a grand state funeral in the cathedral in the city's central square.

Captain Charles Minchin, hero of Carabobo, defied all the surgeons' prognoses and survived his wounds. Two months after the battle he travelled to Caracas to rejoin the remnants of the British Legion. A carnival atmosphere had prevailed in the capital ever since Bolívar had ridden through the gates in triumph on 25 June.[15] The British troops, now on full pay for the first time since they had joined the service, were 'universally respected' and took full advantage of their new-found fame.[16] When Lieutenant Alexander reached the city a few weeks later, the party was in full swing. Devereux and his staff had also arrived and by late December, Caracas was full of British officers. In 1822, Minchin's Carabobo Battalion was sent to Coro to assist Soublette in his campaign against the remnants of the Spanish army holding out in Puerto Cabello. The following year the city was finally captured. Páez and his cavalry broke through the defences and after a brief skirmish in the square, the royalists surrendered. In 1827 Minchin married 'an American lady' in Coro, with whom he had several children.[17] He was later promoted to colonel, then general of brigade and assigned to a series of governmental posts including Minister of the Supreme Court Martial and Minister of the Army and Navy of Venezuela.[18] In his old age, he divided his days between a family home in Caracas and an inn he had set up near Carabobo, where he gave battlefield tours to interested travellers, an account of one of which was published in Charles Dickens' collection of short stories *All the Year Round* in 1859.[19] After a long retirement which was occasionally punctuated by public appearances at parades to celebrate the anniversaries of the battle, he died in Caracas on 3 June 1879 at the age of 82.

Lieutenant-Colonel Peter Grant, the giant Scot of captured clarinet fame, was also in Caracas following Carabobo. According to Lieutenant Alexander, he began an affair with a wealthy 'widow's daughter' whilst in the city, but his drunken 'misconduct' soon led to banishment and the poor girl was 'ruined' by the subsequent scandal. Grant later resurfaced in the town of Valencia 'dressed as gay as a prince' in the finery he had taken from her.[20] In 1822 he spent some time in Tocaima recovering from a serious illness and then travelled to Santafé, where he wrote several letters to the authorities requesting a pension. In mid-1826, whilst still in the capital, he was accused of assault. Nothing came of the charges, but a month later he was put on trial for the murder of Harris E. Fudger, a United States consul. Although many believed he had killed the consul with his own sword after a gin-soaked night at a local inn, Grant was eventually released owing to insufficient evidence.[21] In 1828 he returned to Caracas, where his activities attracted the attention of the Consul General of Great Britain, Sir Robert Ker Porter, who thought him 'a sad, worthless fellow … and a known thief'. Following a relapse of fever, Grant died on 9 May 1833.[22]

The merchant, James Hamilton, remained in Angostura long after the Spanish had been defeated. The 1820s saw continued foreign investment in the region and, in 1823, Hamilton was granted the sole concession to establish steamboat navigation on the Orinoco as a reward for his long commitment to the patriot cause. As ever, the flamboyant Scot was at the heart of the city's mercantile and social circles and regularly threw extravagant parties at his riverside address. In the 1830s, however, the bubble burst. Growing political upheaval foiled plans for modernization and repayments on several large European loans were defaulted. Investors grew timid and the economy went into decline. Nevertheless Hamilton stayed loyal to the city and was made British consul in 1836.[23] He remained in the post until his death in June 1840 of 'an apoplectic fit'.[24] His beloved Angostura would never reclaim the pre-eminence it had enjoyed during the war.

In late 1820, after the disaster at Rio de la Hacha, Gregor MacGregor returned to England with his reputation in tatters. Such was the belief in the investment potential of Latin America, however, that the unscrupulous Scot was able to put his most outrageous scheme to date into operation. Claiming that a local Indian chieftain had made him *Cazique* (Chieftan) of Poyais, an area of 12,500 square miles on the Caribbean coast of Honduras, he advertised for colonists to work the land and sought investment from merchants. Surprisingly his recent failings were ignored and MacGregor once again became the toast of fashionable society. The Lord Mayor of London, Christopher Magnay, even organized an official reception in the Guildhall, at which MacGregor spun outrageous tales of the beauty and fertility of Poyais. His stories were lapped up by eager investors and soon plots of land were being sold at 3s 3d an acre. By October 1822 he had raised £200,000, and in September and January of the following year two ships set sail from London and Leith carrying 240 colonists across the Atlantic. Only upon arrival did they begin to realize the magnitude of the Scot's lies. Saint Joseph, the so-called capital of Poyais, consisted of a couple of ruined huts inhabited by American hermits and was surrounded by untouched jungle. The colony had never existed, except in MacGregor's imagination. Fewer than 50 of the settlers would ever see home again. The rest died of disease or despair, or settled in nearby British Honduras.

When the survivors landed in London, their story was published in all its depressing detail. Amazingly, many of them still refused to believe that MacGregor was at fault, choosing instead to blame his advisors for their suffering. Major Richardson, MacGregor's partner, sued the papers for libel and for a while the Scot's reputation remained in the balance. Taking advantage of this vacillation, he fled the country for Paris. From here he contacted his old acquaintance, Gustavus Butler Hippisley, whom he persuaded to join him in selling the scheme to the French. Several shares were soon offloaded and a ship fitted out in Le Havre. The French authorities proved less gullible than their British counterparts, however, as the ship was impounded and Hippisley and several others arrested. MacGregor went into hiding, but was found and imprisoned in December. The trial took place the following year. Thanks to a skilled lawyer the two principal defendants were acquitted and returned to England. MacGregor continued to sell shares and land in his imaginary republic, but people were less and less inclined to invest. In 1839 he returned to Venezuela, where he applied for and was granted a military pension, and settled into a six-year retirement. He died in Caracas on 4 December 1845 at the age of 58.[25]

After recovering from his illness in Baranquilla, General John Devereux travelled to Santafé to take up a position on Bolívar's staff. Despite remaining in South American service until 1824, he managed to avoid combat entirely and seems to have spent all his time collecting money owed to him by the government. By the time he returned to Europe as an envoy for Gran Colombia, he had amassed a fortune of £150,000. His enemies in Ireland were unable to bring him to account for his crimes, and as he remained involved in mercantile activity between the two continents over the next decade, his wealth continued to grow. In 1840 he returned to New Granada and successfully petitioned for a state pension. Later he retired to the United States where he lived until his death in 1854.

In 1819, after his release from Fort San Francisco in Old Guyana, Colonel Henry Wilson returned to London. As the British press had already published accounts of his alleged sedition in Los Llanos, he felt compelled to reply to the charges and a public debate ensued. Wilson was made to look increasingly ridiculous and eventually felt obliged to move abroad. After four years of self-imposed exile in France, he briefly returned to London before disappearing from the historical record for some years.[26] In 1831 he re-emerged in Dublin, writing a letter to the *Literary Gazette* to defend himself against fresh allegations that had appeared in Alexander Alexander's memoirs. It was evident that Wilson would never be allowed to forget his disgrace as long as he stayed in Britain, and in 1832 he braved an eight-month voyage to Sydney, Australia, where it is said nepotism secured him the post of First Police Magistrate. Although Wilson initially enjoyed some success in this new role, his volatile temper soon led to him making several high-ranking enemies. In 1839, charges of corruption were brought against him and in 1840 he was formally removed from office. His decline continued the following year when an article he had written appeared in the *Free Press*. The piece enraged Major William Christie, a prominent member of Sydney society, who publicly horsewhipped Wilson and then challenged him to a duel. Although it is recorded that he ducked out of the engagement, what became of him afterwards is unknown.

Richard Vowell's adventures continued long after the Albion's defeat at Genoy. In 1821 he resigned from the battalion in Guayaquil, Ecuador, on account of 'a severe attack of rheumatism' and joined Lord Cochrane's Chilean fleet, which happened to be at anchor in the bay at the time.[27] The next nine years saw him sail the length of the Spanish Pacific, from Acapulco to the Chiloé Archipelago. After the royalist navy was defeated, Chile descended into civil war. Sick of conflict Vowell decided to return home, and in the spring of 1830, he landed in Portsmouth after an absence of 13 years.[28] A year later he published his memoirs and two semi-factual novellas set in Venezuela during the war. British interest in South America had faded, however, and his literary efforts, although more honest and finely observed than many of those that had come before, were met with a muted response. At the age of 36, Vowell made one final epic voyage to Australia, where he found work as a constable and clerk at the Number 2 Stockade near Cox's River. Two years after his appointment, he was accused of accepting a bribe to alter the sentence of two inmates from 12 to nine months. It seems his guilt was never in question. Vowell absconded from his post and was charged with forgery in his absence. A £20 reward for his capture was offered but the Englishman later gave himself up. Surprisingly he was allowed to return to his old position, but when the governor learnt of his transgression, he ordered that Vowell should be dismissed immediately. On 25 May, presumably upon hearing of the decision, Vowell once again fled the stockade, taking four convicts and four privates of the 4th King's Own Regiment with him. Travelling down the Murrumbidgee River, the fugitives spent several weeks surviving from the proceeds of a series of robberies before their eventual capture in August 1832. An 'emaciated', broken-toothed Vowell was hauled before the magistrates, convicted of theft and sentenced to death.[29] This was commuted to life at Norfolk Island and later reduced to seven years imprisonment.[30] Vowell was released in his late forties and remained in Australia for the rest of his days. He never married and although his nephew, the Reverend Michael Henry Becher, lived in Melbourne for the last nine years of his life, there is no evidence of any contact between the two men. It seems that Vowell grew old alone with his memories. He died in 1870 at the age of 76 in Bruk Bul, Victoria.[31]

Whilst the later careers of several officers can be pieced together, details regarding the rank and file are few and far between. Professor Matthew Brown's research has allowed some generalizations to be made, however. Of the 6,800 volunteers who sailed for South America between 1817 and 1820, a little less than half saw their homelands again. Of these, perhaps 1,000 returned to the Old World shortly after they had arrived in the New, whilst the rest left after the war had finished. Roughly 3,300 died during the conflict, of which half perished on campaign and half succumbed to disease. Only 500 survived to settle in South America.[32] Although they were spread across the entire northern and central part of the continent, Santafé de Bogotá and Caracas were by far the most popular locations. Roughly 350 made these cities their homes. Whilst 40 per cent retired, others took up a variety of professions, ranging from novelist to fisherman to jockey.[33] At least nine worked as doctors. Thomas Foley, who had amputated Rooke's arm after Vargas, became Bolívar's chief surgeon and Surgeon Richard Murphy of the British Legion set up a hospital for the poor in the town of Puerto Cabello, where he treated those unable to afford medical care until his death in 1834. Twenty others became farmers, enduring a 'precarious ... existence' reliant on small-scale local trade.[34] Others were involved in the post-war mining boom or set themselves up as merchants trading with the British colonies. Although both groups prospered in the early 1820s, by 1826 the economy had gone into decline and several went bankrupt. The men who retired spent the rest of their days surviving on meagre state pensions. For many, especially those crippled by the war or men who had wives and children to support, the payments were simply not enough. Some were reduced to begging. Others resorted to petty crime. Sir Ker Porter, the newly appointed British consul in Caracas, had little sympathy. Describing them as 'useless, invalid' and 'drunken', he complained that they stole money and jewellery from the city's elite and gave the rest of the British residents a bad name.[35]

A host of memoirs published in Britain in the early 1820s kept the memory of the volunteers alive for several years after the fighting had finished. Lieutenants Hackett and Brown and Colonel Hippisley were amongst the first to write of their experiences. These books were almost entirely negative in tone and merely reinforced the British public's comfortable stereotype of a continent populated by uncivilized barbarians. Nevertheless, they were eagerly digested by those who believed that South America offered great opportunities for investment. Even Hippisley's much maligned soporific was highly publicized and widely reviewed and read. Later publications, including those written by Vowell, Chesterton and Alexander, reached a considerably smaller audience.[36] By the time they were released, the public had lost interest in the continent as a result of its economic decline and continuing instability, a trend that has continued ever since.

In South America, the reasons why the volunteers are little known today are more insidious. As early as the 1840s Venezuelan and Colombian historians began to gloss over the part played by the British in favour of a less complex and more jingoistic version of events, with home-grown heroes alone taking centre stage. José Manuel Restrepo's history, for example, which was first published in the mid-19th century, briefly mentions Rooke, O'Leary and Ferrier, but ignores the vast majority of the volunteers and belittles the role that they played. This pattern was followed by later historians and in modern-day Colombia and Venezuela only a small fraction of the population have any idea that British troops took part in the war at all. Modern South American literature has also played a role in cleansing the national memory. In *El General en su Laberinto*, Colombia's most celebrated novelist, Gabriel García Márquez, imagines Bolívar's final days in Santa Marta. The Liberator's British confidants, including Daniel O'Leary, were amongst the closest figures to the general in this period. Nevertheless, they are ignored in the novel. Instead, Márquez uses the character of a fictional Colombian servant, José Palacios, as The Liberator's final sounding board, thereby neatly sidestepping the more complex reality.

In present-day Venezuela and Colombia a few signs of the volunteers' involvement in the war can still be seen. A monument near the bridge of Boyacá celebrates Rooke's

Legion and at Pantano de Vargas there is a plaque bearing the names of the officers who were killed or wounded during the battle. Dominating the area is a huge monument depicting the charge of Rondon's 14 Lancers. Although no special mention of Colonel Rooke is made on the battlefield, a bronze bust stands in the nearby town of Paipa and a second casting is hidden away in the courtyard of the monastery in Belencito where he died. The building, which now stands in the grounds of a Brazilian ironworks, is permanently closed to the public. In Venezuela, at the battlefield of Carabobo, a bust of Ferrier flanks the main avenue alongside those of Cedeño and Ambrosio Plaza. Just over a mile beyond the car park, at the end of a rarely used path, is an unmarked obelisk on the site of the Legion's superlative stand. Away from the battlefields, if one knows where to look, there are further reminders of the volunteers' involvement. Caracas and Bogotá both have plazas named after O'Leary, a bust of the Irishman stands in the town of Apure and his remains along with those of Charles Minchin lie alongside the tomb of The Liberator in the National Pantheon in Caracas. A school in Tovar, Venezuela, a hospital in Puerto Cabello and a street in Cuenca, Ecuador, are named after Gregor MacGregor, Surgeon Richard Murphy and Arthur Sandes respectively. The bench where Colonel Rooke lay as Foley amputated his arm is on display at the National Museum in Bogotá and in 1971 a commemorative stamp was issued by the Bolivian post office bearing the image of Francis Burdett O'Connor.[37] A regiment in the Colombian army is named in Rooke's honour and the Batallon de Ingenieros Thomas Ilderton Ferriar is stationed in Caracas.

One of the most poignant sites that I visited whilst researching this book was the British Cemetery in Bogotá. Its story is one of neglect that epitomizes the way in which the volunteers' memory has been allowed to fade. The original site was inaugurated by Vice-President Santander in 1825. It lay beside the road to Zipaquira on the outskirts of the capital. Later, it was moved to San Victorino, before eventually reaching its current home a few dozen blocks from the city centre. Sandwiched between two busy freeways, the cemetery is hidden behind a line of pine trees and a high wall. Its unmarked gate is never opened to the public. Inside is an oasis of calm. An inner iron fence, tipped with Spanish bayonets captured at Boyacá, guards the oldest graves. Although a plaque states that several volunteers, including John Mackintosh, were buried there, many of the gravestones have been so badly neglected as to render them illegible. Thousands of commuting Bogotános pass the site every day. Few, if any, are aware that some of their country's greatest unsung heroes lie a few hundred yards away.

NOTES

DRAMATIS PERSONAE

1   James Hackett, *Narrative of the Expedition which Sailed from England in 1817, to Join the South American Patriots: Comprising Every Particular Connected with its Formation, History, and Fate; with Observations and Authentic Information Elucidating the Real Character of the Contest, Mode of Warfare, State of the Armies etc...* (London, John Murray, 1818), p.119

2   James H. Robinson, *Journal of an Expedition 1400 Miles up the Orinoco and 300 up the Arauca: with an Account of the Country, the Manners of the People, Military Operations, &c* (London, Black, Young and Young, 1822), p.237

3   Richard Longeville Vowell, *Campaigns and Cruises, in Venezuela and New Grenada, and in the Pacific Ocean; From 1817 to 1830: with the Narrative of a March from the River Orinoco to San Buenaventura on the Coast of Chocó; and Sketches of the West Coast of South America from the Gulf of California to the Archipelago of Chilöe* (London, Longman and Co., 1831), p.49

4   The *Dublin Evening Post*, Dublin, 27 April 1820

5   Matthew Brown, *Adventuring Through Spanish Colonies: Simón Bolívar, Foreign Mercenaries and the Birth of New Nations* (Liverpool, Liverpool University Press, 2007), p.17

6   The English Papers, Suffolk County Record Office, HA 157,153,206

7   William Jackson Adam, *Journal of Voyages to Marguaritta, Trinidad, & Maturin: With the Author's Travels Across the Plains of the Llaneros, to Angustura, and Subsequent Descent of the Orinoco, in the Years 1819 & 1820* (London, J. Jones, 1824), pp.132, 133

8   Gustavus Mathias Hippisley, *A Narrative of the Expedition to the Rivers Orinoco and Apuré in South America: which Sailed from England in November 1817, and Joined the Patriotic Forces in Venezuela and Caraccas* (London, John Murray, 1819), p.470

9   Thomas Rourke, *Man of Glory: Simon Bolivar* (London, Joseph, 1940), p.197

10   Anon, *Recollections of a Service of Three Years During the War-of-Extermination in the Republics of Venezuela and Columbia* (London, Hunt and Clarke, 1828), p.66

11   Vowell, *Campaigns and Cruises*, p.214

12   George Laval Chesterton, *Peace, War and Adventure: An Autobiographical Memoir of George Laval Chesterton*, Volume 2 (London, Longman, Brown, Green and Longmans, 1853), p.140

PREFACE

1   Anon, *The Present State of Colombia: Containing an Account of the Principal Events of its Revolutionary War; the Expeditions Fitted Out in England to Assist in its Emancipation; its Constitution; Financial and Commercial Laws; Revenue, Expenditure and Public Debt; Agriculture; Mines; Mining and Other Concerns* (London, J. Murray, 1827), pp.85–86

PART 1

Poem: Roger Lonsdale (ed.), *New Oxford Book of 18th Century Verse* (Oxford, Oxford University Press, 1984), p.111

CHAPTER 1

Heading: George Laval Chesterton, *Peace, War and Adventure: An Autobiographical Memoir of George Laval Chesterton*, Volume 2 (London, Longman, Brown, Green and Longmans, 1853) p.23

1   William Pitt Lennox, *Three Years with the Duke or Wellington in Private Life. By an Ex-Aid-de-Camp* (London, Saunders and Otely, 1853), p.2

2   The *Quarterly Review*, Issue 28 (October 1822), pp.197–198

3   Ibid.

4   Ben Wilson, *Decency & Disorder: The Age of Cant 1789–1837* (London, Faber and Faber, 2008), pp.217–219

5   Sir John Fortescue, *The County Lieutenancies and the Army – 1803–1814* (London, Macmillan, 1909), p.293; Wilson, *Decency and Disorder*, p.255

6   Anon, *Recollections of a Service of Three Years During the War-of-Extermination in the Republics of Venezuela and Columbia* (London, Hunt and Clarke, 1828), p.8

7   Wilson, *Decency & Disorder*, p.220

8   There was no official police force in Britain until the Metropolitan service was founded in 1829. Prior to this the army was used to break up civil disturbances.

9   See John Charles Chasteen, *Americanos: Latin America's Struggle for Independence* (Oxford, Oxford University Press, 2008) for an overview of the rebellions across the continent. The Spanish interim government, known as the Cortes, spent the duration of the Peninsular War in Cadíz, the only part of mainland Spain to resist French occupation. Theoretically it governed the South American colonies in Ferdinand's absence, but in reality it lacked credibility in the eyes of many Creoles, who used the situation as an excuse to seek full independence.

10   George Dawson Flinter, *The History of the Revolution of Caracas Together with a Description of the Llaneros* (London, W. Glindon, 1819), p.29. Casualty estimates in primary sources vary from 10,000–30,000.

11   Chesterton, *Peace, War and Adventure*, p.148

12   Adam Zamoyski, *Holy Madness: Romantics, Patriots, and Revolutionaries, 1776–1871* (London, Phoenix Press, 2001) p.154

13   South and North America, Asia and Europe. An unabashed ladies' man, Miranda had a string of affairs on his travels. Amongst his conquests was said to be the Russian Empress, Catherine the Great.

14   Although the light cavalry of the Venezuelan interior made fine troops, Bolívar's infantry lacked discipline, training, equipment and arms, and were no match for Morillo's regulars.

15   Henri La Fayette Villaume Ducoudray Holstein, *Memoirs of Simon Bolivar: President Liberator of the Republic of Colombia, and of His Principal Generals: Secret History of the Revolution and the Events which Preceded It, from 1807 to the Present Time: with an Introduction Containing an Account of the Statistics and the Present Situation of the Country* (London, S. G. Goodrich, 1830), p.193

16   Ibid., p.226

17   Kew National Archives, FO 72/216, pp.139–144

18   Chesterton, *Peace, War and Adventure*, p.25

19   Gustavus Mathias Hippisley, *A Narrative of the Expedition to the Rivers Orinoco and Apuré in South America: which Sailed from England in November 1817, and Joined the Patriotic Forces in Venezuela and Caraccas* (London, John Murray, 1819), p.3

20   The evidence regarding Wellington's views on South American independence is contradictory. Although a lifelong Tory and therefore ideologically opposed to republicans and their revolutions, the duke made no objections when feted as a potential commander for a military expedition to liberate Venezuela in

1808. The plan was the brainchild of Miranda and backed by several influential politicians. However, Napoleon's invasion of Spain later that year radically refocused British interests, and the expedition once destined for South America was sent to Lisbon instead.

21 John Lynch, 'British Policy and Spanish America 1783–1808', in *Journal of Latin American Studies*, Volume 1 (1969), p.1

22 Chesterton, *Peace, War and Adventure*, pp.30, 31

23 Charles Brown, *Narrative of the Expedition to South America: Which Sailed from England at the Close of 1817, for the Service of the Spanish Patriots: Including the Military and Naval Transactions, and Ultimate Fate of that Expedition: Also the Arrival of Colonels Blosset and English* (London, John Booth, 1819) p.171

24 Kew National Archives, FO 72/216, pp.139–144. It has been suggested that Regency values can be multiplied by a factor of 50 to reach a modern equivalent. See Chapter 1, endnote 62, for more details.

25 Christopher Hibbert (ed.), *The Recollections of Rifleman Harris* (London, Orion Publishing Co., 2007), p.124

26 Wilson, *Decency & Disorder*, p.268

27 Ducoudray Holstein, *Memoirs of Simon Bolivar*, p.226

28 Richard Longeville Vowell, *Campaigns and Cruises, in Venezuela and New Grenada, and in the Pacific Ocean; From 1817 to 1830: with the Narrative of a March from the River Orinoco to San Buenaventura on the Coast of Chocó; and Sketches of the West Coast of South America from the Gulf of California to the Archipelago of Chilöe* (London, Longman and Co., 1831) p.111. The word 'regiment' denotes a body of armed men and does not equate in terms of size or structure to British military standards of the time. In fact, all the regiments initially raised in London were considerably smaller than the 800-man standard, as they contained only officers and NCOs. In his memoir, Hippisley recorded that 44 officers and 124 NCOs sailed in his detachment. The numbers of the other units varied from the 20 officers and 57 NCOs of Wilson's Red Hussars to the 37 officers and 200 NCOs of the rifle regiment led by Colonel Campbell.

29 Hippisley, *A Narrative of the Expedition*, p.52; Matthew Brown, *Adventuring Through Spanish Colonies: Simón Bolívar, Foreign Mercenaries and the Birth of New Nations* (Liverpool, Liverpool University Press, 2007), p.23

30 British Library Manuscripts, Add. 38268ff 106

31 Vowell, *Campaigns and Cruises*, p.49

32 According to Lieutenant Charles Brown, MacDonald served with the Portuguese Army as General Ballesteros's aide-de-camp in the Peninsular Campaign.

33 Hippisley, *A Narrative of the Expedition*, p.9

34 Archivo General de la Nación, Bogotá, Colombia (AGNC), Archivo Anexo, Fondo Historia, Tomo 23, Folio 179

35 The 3rd Infantry regiment of the line

36 Hippisley, *A Narrative of the Expedition*, p.15

37 Ibid., p.8

38 Ibid., p.7

39 These were the lowest commissioned ranks in the army. Coronets served in cavalry regiments. Ensigns were their infantry equivalent.

40 Hippisley, *A Narrative of the Expedition*, p.67

41 Brown, *Adventuring Through Spanish Colonies*, p.26

42 By way of comparison, the rank and file of the British Army in Bengal during the early 19th century were 48 per cent Irish, 34 per cent English and 11 per cent Scottish.

43 Brown, *Adventuring Through Spanish Colonies*, p.27

44 Ibid., pp.13–30

45 Wilson, *Decency & Disorder*, p.63; also Nick Foulkes, *Dancing into Battle: A Social History of the Battle of Waterloo* (London, Phoenix, 2007), p.56

46 Foulkes, *Dancing into Battle*, p.59

47 Wilson, *Decency & Disorder*

NOTES

NOTES

48 Richard Hopton, *Pistols at Dawn: A History of Duelling* (London, Portrait, 2007), p.213

49 William Pitt and the Duke of Wellington. The duels took place in 1798 and 1829 respectively. None of the participants were wounded.

50 Brown, *Narrative of the Expedition*, p.1

51 Anon, *Recollections of a Service*, p.9; *Carrick's Morning Post*, Dublin, 5 November 1817

52 Chesterton, *Peace, War and Adventure*, p.26

53 Ibid., p.140

54 http://freepages.genealogy.rootsweb.ancestry.com/~becher/vowell_family.htm

55 *The Sydney Gazette and New South Wales Advertiser*, Sydney, Australia, Saturday 6 June 1835; Chesterton, *Peace, War and Adventure*, p.141

56 Chesterton, *Peace, War and Adventure*, p.140

57 John Hamilton, *Travels Through the Interior Provinces of Colombia*, (London, John Murray, 1827), p.219

58 After Waterloo the daily half pay for infantry lieutenants was 2s 4d. Captains made 5s and lieutenant-colonels 8s 6d (Edward M. Brett, *The British Auxiliary Legion in the First Carlist War 1835–1838* (Dublin, Four Courts Press, 2005), p.28). Labourers of the period earned about 12s a week (Wilson, *Decency and Disorder*, p.392).

59 Anon, *Narrative of a Voyage to the Spanish Main, in the Ship 'Two Friends': The Occupation of Amelia Island by M'Gregor, &c. — Sketches of the Province of East Florida; and Anecdotes Illustrative of the Habits and Manners of the Seminole Indians: with an Appendix, Containing a Detail of the Seminole* (London, J. Miller, 1819), p.16; Hamilton, *Travels Through the Interior Provinces of Colombia*, p.219

60 Chesterton, *Peace, War and Adventure*, p.29

61 Officers led from the front and were frequently killed on the battlefield. All those junior in rank would have the opportunity of filling the dead man's shoes. During war officers could rise quickly through the ranks, but in peacetime the only sure way to attain promotion was by purchasing a commission, an option only available to the rich.

62 The volunteers referred to the currency used in South America as either dollars or pesos. All references in the text have been standardized and pesos are used throughout. Lieutenant Brown of Gillmore's artillery regiment estimated that 1 peso was equivalent to 2s 6d in British currency. Therefore the bounty of 200 pesos amounted to £25. Converting historical sums into their modern equivalents is notoriously difficult, but, as a rough estimate, if one multiplies the sum by 50 (Foulkes, *Dancing into Battle*, p.67) then a figure can be arrived at. This would mean that the bounty was worth roughly £1,250 in today's money. A better understanding of its real worth can be reached through a comparison of contemporary rates of pay. An infantry lieutenant in the British Army in 1815 earned an annual salary of roughly £80, captains made £175 and lieutenant-colonels £250. Therefore, the bonus money equates to a little over a month's wages for a lieutenant-colonel, a month and a half's pay for a captain and a quarter of a year's salary for a lieutenant. (Hippisley, *A Narrative of the Expedition*, p.59)

63 *The Courier*, London, 6 December 1817

64 Most of these supplies were provided by a small number of London based agents, such as Thompson and Mackintosh, who amassed a small fortune in the process.

65 James Hackett, *Narrative of the Expedition which Sailed from England in 1817, to Join the South American Patriots: Comprising Every Particular Connected with its Formation, History, and Fate; with Observations and Authentic Information Elucidating the Real Character of the Contest, Mode of Warfare, State of the Armies etc...* (London, John Murray, 1818), Preliminary Observation. A gold coin minted throughout the Georgian period, roughly equivalent in value to £1. Hippisley, *A Narrative of the Expedition*, pp.12–13

66 One such investor was William Walton, the editor of the *Morning Chronicle*, who put £100 of his personal savings towards obtaining firearms for MacDonald's Lancers.

67 English Papers, Suffolk County Record Office, HA 157/6/36

68 Eric Lambert (ed.), *Voluntarios Británicos e Irlandeses en la Gesta Bolivariana*, Volume 1 (Caracas, Ministerio de la Defensa, Dirección de Artes Graficas, 1993)

69   Hippisley, *A Narrative of the Expedition*, pp.48, 49

70   Ibid., p.15; Archivo General de la Nación, Bogotá, Colombia (AGNC), Archivo Anexo, Fondo Historia, Tomo 23, Folio 179

71   Archivo del Libertador, Caracas, Venezuela, Sección Juan de Francisco Martin, Volume 14, Doc. 15

72   AGNC, Sección Archivo Anexo, Fondo Historia, Tomo 24, Doc. 102

73   Brown, *Adventuring Through Spanish Colonies*, p.17

74   Archivo del Libertador, Sección Juan de Francisco Martin, Volume 14, Doc. 12

75   Hippisley, *A Narrative of the Expedition*, p.123. Officers and men taking their spouses on campaign was common practice amongst the armies of the age. Often a specific quota was assigned to each regiment, but such rules were frequently broken.

76   Ibid., p.45

77   Ibid., pp.399, 272

78   Vowell, *Campaigns and Cruises*, p.127

79   John Howell (ed.), *The Life of Alexander Alexander, Written by Himself and Edited by John Howell*, Volume 2 (Edinburgh, William Blackwood, 1830) p.86

CHAPTER 2

Heading: James H. Robinson, *Journal of an Expedition 1400 Miles up the Orinoco and 300 up the Arauca: with an Account of the Country, the Manners of the People, Military Operations, &c* (London, Black, Young and Young, 1822), p.4

1   Gustavus Mathias Hippisley, *A Narrative of the Expedition to the Rivers Orinoco and Apuré in South America: which Sailed from England in November 1817, and Joined the Patriotic Forces in Venezuela and Caraccas* (London, John Murray, 1819), pp.67–68

2   Ibid., pp.67–69

3   Ibid., p.25

4   Archivo General de la Nación, Caracas, Venezuela (AGNV), Gobernación de Guayana (GDG), Tomo 9, Folio 121

5   Hippisley, *A Narrative of the Expedition*, p.65

6   Ibid., p.53

7   Ibid., p.64

8   Anon, *Narrative of a Voyage to the Spanish Main, in the Ship 'Two Friends': The Occupation of Amelia Island by M'Gregor, &c.—Sketches of the Province of East Florida; and Anecdotes Illustrative of the Habits and Manners of the Seminole Indians: with an Appendix, Containing a Detail of the Seminole* (London, J. Miller, 1819), p.10

9   Archivo General de la Nación, Bogotá, Colombia (AGNC), Sección La Republica, Fondo Secretaria de Guerra y Marina, Tomo 323, Folio 87; Robinson, *Journal of an Expedition*, p.1

10   Robinson, *Journal of an Expedition*, p.5

11   Anon, *Narrative of a Voyage*, p.33

12   Robinson, *Journal of an Expedition*, p.6

13   *Carrick's Morning Post*, Dublin, 22 December 1817

14   Ibid.

15   Ibid.

16   National Archives, Kew, Foreign Office Papers, FO/72/216, p.40

17   The *Morning Chronicle*, London, 17 December 1817; Robinson, *Journal of an Expedition*, p.7

18   James Hackett, *Narrative of the Expedition which Sailed from England in 1817, to Join the South American Patriots: Comprising Every Particular Connected with its Formation, History, and Fate; with Observations and Authentic Information Elucidating the Real Character of the Contest, Mode of Warfare, State of the Armies etc...* (London, John Murray, 1818), pp.14–15

19   Robinson, *Journal of an Expedition*, p.4

20   *The Courier*, London, 3 January 1818

21   Tim Clayton, *Tars: The Men who Made Britain Rule the Waves* (London, Hodder and Stoughton Ltd., 2007), p.110. 'Ushant' is the English name for the island; in French it is 'Ouessant'.

22   *The Times*, London, 22 January 1818

23   The *Morning Chronicle*, London, 19 December 1817

24   *The Times*, London, 22 January 1818

25   Ibid., 17 February 1818

26   AGNC, Republica, Guerra y Marina, Volume 35, Folio 884–887

27   Robinson, *Journal of an Expedition*, pp.9–10

28   The *Dublin Evening Post*, Dublin, 27 April 1820

29   Alberot Eduardo Wright, *Destellos de gloria: biografía sintética de un prócer de la independencia, incorporando las 'Reminiscencias' del general de división don Tomás Carlos Wright* (Buenos Aires, Castorman, Oritz y Cia, 1949), p.20

30   There are several versions of this song. See http://www.musicanet.org/robokopp/usa/thegirli.html

31   AGNC, Sección Venezolana, BXXX 316

32   Ibid., W VI 19–24

33   Ibid.

34   Hippisley, *A Narrative of the Expedition*, pp.538–539

35   Ibid., p.539

36   Ibid., pp.538–539

37   Hackett, N*arrative of the Expedition*, p.21

38   Ibid., p.17

39   Robert James Young's diary, Public Record Office of Northern Ireland, D3045/6/3/2

40   Anon, *Narrative of a Voyage*, p.25

41   Ibid., p.24

42   Ibid.

43   Ibid., p.27

44   Ibid., p.37

45   William Douglas, *Duelling Days in the Army* (London, Ward and Downey, 1884), p.4 (quoted in Richard Hopton, *Pistols at Dawn: A History of Duelling* (London, Portrait, 2007), p.224)

46   Porter was an English ale. Hippisley, *A Narrative of the Expedition*, p.41

47   Francis Hall, *Colombia: its Present State, in Respect of Climate, Soil, Productions, Population, Government, Commerce, Revenue, Manufactures, Arts, Literature, Manners, Education, and Inducements to Emigration* (London, Baldwin, Craddock and Joy, 1824), p.99

48   Robert James Young's diary, Public Record Office of Northern Ireland, D3045/6/3/2

49   Hippisley, *A Narrative of the Expedition*, p.81

50   Ibid., p.79

51   Ibid., Appendix C, p.541

52   Ibid., p.67

53   Harry Hopkins, *The Strange Death of Private White: A Victorian Scandal that Made History* (London, Weidenfeld & Nicolson, 1977), pp.168–181

54   Symphisis is a cartilaginous fusion between the bones. W. Davidson Weatherhead, *An Account of the Late Expedition Against the Isthmus of Darien Under the Command of Sir Gregor McGregor; Together with the Events Subsequent to the Recapture of Porto Bello, till the Release of the Prisoners from Panama; Remarks on the Present State of the Patriot Cause and on the Climate and Diseases of South America* (London, Longman, Hurst, Rees, Orme and Brown, 1821), p.6

55   Hopton, *Pistols at Dawn*, p.251

56   Hackett, *Narrative of the Expedition*, p.19

57   Ibid. In Greek mythology, the Nereids were sea nymphs: daughters of Nereus and Doris, who often accompanied Neptune.

58   Ibid.

59   The *Dublin Evening Post*, Dublin, 7 August 1819

60   Hackett, *Narrative of the Expedition*, p.19

61   Robinson, *Journal of an Expedition*, p.35

CHAPTER 3

Heading: Anon, *Narrative of a Voyage to the Spanish Main, in the Ship 'Two Friends': The Occupation of Amelia Island by M'Gregor, &c.—Sketches of the Province of East Florida; and Anecdotes Illustrative of the Habits and Manners of the Seminole Indians: with an Appendix, Containing a Detail of the Seminole* (London, J. Miller, 1819), p.43

1   James Hackett, *Narrative of the Expedition which Sailed from England in 1817, to Join the South American Patriots: Comprising Every Particular Connected with its Formation, History, and Fate; with Observations and Authentic Information Elucidating the Real Character of the Contest, Mode of Warfare, State of the Armies etc...* (London, John Murray, 1818), p.119

2   Anon, *Narrative of a Voyage*, p.43

3   Ibid.

4   James H. Robinson, *Journal of an Expedition 1400 Miles up the Orinoco and 300 up the Arauca: with an Account of the Country, the Manners of the People, Military Operations, &c* (London, Black, Young and Young, 1822), p.38

5   Hackett, *Narrative of the Expedition*, p.55

6   Gustavus Mathias Hippisley, *A Narrative of the Expedition to the Rivers Orinoco and Apuré in South America: which Sailed from England in November 1817, and Joined the Patriotic Forces in Venezuela and Caraccas* (London, John Murray, 1819), p.127

7   Hackett, *Narrative of the Expedition*, p.24

8   Charles, or Karl, XII ascended the Swedish throne in 1697 aged 15. Three years later he led his country to victory over the combined forces of Denmark, Russia, Saxony and Poland. After capturing Copenhagen, Charles received the surrender of the Danish and Polish commanders and returned to his country to defeat the forces of Peter the Great, which had been besieging the Swedish town of Narva. Although heavily outnumbered the Swedes gained yet another victory, forcing the Russians from their shores. Hackett, *Narrative of the Expedition*, p.24

9   Ibid., p.36.

10   Robinson, *Journal of an Expedition*, p.48

11   Vowell, *Campaigns and Cruises, in Venezuela and New Grenada, and in the Pacific Ocean; From 1817 to 1830: with the Narrative of a March from the River Orinoco to San Buenaventura on the Coast of Chocó; and Sketches of the West Coast of South America from the Gulf of California to the Archipelago of Chilöe* (London, Longman and Co., 1831), p.3; Anon, *Narrative of a Voyage*, p.52

12   Vowell, *Campaigns and Cruises*, p.3

13   Hackett, *Narrative of the Expedition*, pp.30–31

14   Vowell, *Campaigns and Cruises*, p.5

15   *The Times*, London, 5 February 1819

16   Ibid., 18 January 1819

17   Ibid.

18   Ibid.

19   Kew National Archives, FO 72/216, Folio 183

20 Michael Rafter, *Memoirs of Gregor M'Gregor: Comprising a Sketch of the Revolution in New Granada and Venezuela, with Biographical Notices of Generals Miranda, Bolívar, Morillo and Horé, and a Narrative of the Expeditions to Amelia Island, Porto Bello, and Rio de la Hache, Interspersed with Revolutionary Anecdotes* (London, J. J. Stockdale, 1820), p.110

21 The details of this raid are described in Chapter 13.

22 Vowell, *Campaigns and Cruises*, pp.12–13

23 *The Times*, London, 13 January 1819

24 Hackett, *Narrative of the Expedition*, p.31

25 Ibid.

26 Archivo General de la Nación, Bogotá, Colombia (AGNC), Sección Archivo Anexo, Fondo Historia, Tomo 24, Doc. 102

27 Robinson, *Journal of an Expedition*, p.38

28 The officers of the 1st Hussars who resigned at Grenada were Captain H. Hebden, lieutenants MacDonald and Simons, Coronet Gunnel and Paymaster Batchelor.

29 The *Morning Chronicle*, London, 28 March 1818

30 Ibid.

31 Kew National Archives, CO 101/58

32 Although flogging was not banned by the British Army until 1881, Hippisley was considered a civilian by the government and, therefore, his actions were illegal.

33 Hippisley, *A Narrative of the Expedition*, p.200

34 *The Times*, London, 31 March 1818

35 Woodford made two proclamations, without orders from Westminster, threatening anyone caught taking arms to the republicans with confiscation of property and imprisonment.

36 Hippisley, *A Narrative of the Expedition*, pp.140, 217

37 Although Harris and Watson had originally intended to serve the patriots in Venezuela, they were actually in the employ of a Trinidad-based merchant, Mr Littlepage, at the time of their deaths. Having decided to quit the patriot service whilst in Port of Spain, the two men had been contracted by Littlepage to run shipments of arms and ammunition up-river, returning with mules to sell in the British colonies.

38 The *Morning Chronicle*, London, 12 September 1818

39 *Carrick's Morning Post*, Dublin, 23 June 1818

40 Archivo del Libertador, Caracas, Venezuela, Sección de Juan Francisco de Martin, Volume 14, Doc. 15

41 *The Times*, London, 3 September 1818

42 Hackett, *Narrative of the Expedition*, pp.118–119

43 Charles Brown, *Narrative of the Expedition to South America: Which Sailed from England at the Close of 1817, for the Service of the Spanish Patriots: Including the Military and Naval Transactions, and Ultimate Fate of that Expedition: Also the Arrival of Colonels Blosset and English* (London, John Booth, 1819), p.47

44 Eric Lambert, *Voluntarios Británicos e Irlandeses en la Gesta Bolivariana*, Volume 1 (Caracas, Ministerio de la Defensa, Dirección de Artes Graficas, 1993), p.227

45 Matthew Brown, *Adventuring Through Spanish Colonies: Simón Bolívar, Foreign Mercenaries and the Birth of New Nations* (Liverpool, Liverpool University Press, 2007), p.40

PART 2

CHAPTER 4

Heading: Edward Backhouse Eastwick, *Venezuela: or, Sketches of Life in a South-American Republic: with the History of the Loan of 1864. By Edward B. Eastwick, with a Map* (London, Chapman and Hall, 1868), p.81

1   Gustavus Mathias Hippisley, *A Narrative of the Expedition to the Rivers Orinoco and Apuré in South America: which Sailed from England in November 1817, and Joined the Patriotic Forces in Venezuela and Caraccas* (London, John Murray, 1819), p.218

2   Ibid., pp.218–219.

3   John Howell, (ed.), *The Life of Alexander Alexander, Written by Himself and Edited by John Howell* (Edinburgh, William Blackwood, 1830) p.24

4   Richard Longeville Vowell, *Campaigns and Cruises, in Venezuela and New Grenada, and in the Pacific Ocean; From 1817 to 1830: with the Narrative of a March from the River Orinoco to San Buenaventura on the Coast of Chocó; and Sketches of the West Coast of South America from the Gulf of California to the Archipelago of Chilóe* (London, Longman and Co., 1831), p.19

5   This fee, which was for a return journey to Angostura, or roughly 20 days work, was enough to buy a tenth of an ox in the republican capital, or one forty-fifth of a mule.

6   Hippisley, *A Narrative of the Expedition*, p.225

7   Yellow fever is a viral disease spread by mosquitoes in tropical regions. Following an incubatory period of three to six days, the disease is characterized by fever, headaches and vomiting. The virus then spreads to the internal organs, especially attacking the liver, which causes the jaundice to which the disease owes its name. Between 50 and 70 per cent of those affected recover after three or four days of exhibiting symptoms, but others deteriorate and death can follow shortly afterwards.

8   Maria Graham made her way back to London and later received £100 by way of compensation from Antonio Zea, Bolívar's vice-president. Hippisley, *A Narrative of the Expedition*, p.123

9   Charles Brown, *Narrative of the Expedition to South America: Which Sailed from England at the Close of 1817, for the Service of the Spanish Patriots: Including the Military and Naval Transactions, and Ultimate Fate of that Expedition: Also the Arrival of Colonels Blosset and English* (London, John Booth, 1819), p.53

10 Hippisley, *A Narrative of the Expedition*, p.226; Eastwick, *Venezuela*, p.81

11 James H. Robinson, *Journal of an Expedition 1400 Miles up the Orinoco and 300 up the Arauca: with an Account of the Country, the Manners of the People, Military Operations, &c* (London, Black, Young and Young, 1822), p.63

12 Ibid., p.66

13 Brown, *Narrative of the Expedition*, p.61

14 Hippisley, *A Narrative of the Expedition*, p.355

15 Eastwick, *Venezuela*, p.81

16 Vowell, *Campaigns and Cruises*, p.20

17 Robinson, *Journal of an Expedition*, p.68

18 Vowell, *Campaigns and Cruises*, p.22

19 Robinson, *Journal of an Expedition*, p.56

20 Vowell, *Campaigns and Cruises*, p.23; Brown, *Narrative of the Expedition*, p.67

21 Brown, *Narrative of the Expedition*, p.67

22 The *Dublin Evening Post*, Dublin, 29 June 1820

23 Brown, *Narrative of the Expedition*, p.67

24 George Laval Chesterton, *Peace, War and Adventure: An Autobiographical Memoir of George Laval Chesterton*, Volume 2 (London, Longman, Brown, Green and Longmans, 1853), p.122

25 Vowell, *Campaigns and Cruises*, p.24

26 Hippisley, *A Narrative of the Expedition*, p.237

27 Brown, *Narrative of the Expedition*, pp.72–73

28 Ibid., p.72

29 Ibid., p.71

30 Bolívar would later claim to have had no part in the killings, which he denounced as the work of 'madmen of the army'. Nevertheless, the officers who had given the order, Colonel Jacinto Lara and Captain Juan de Dios Monzón, were later promoted by The Liberator.

31 Vowell, *Campaigns and Cruises*, p.24

32   Ibid., pp.25–26

33   Ibid., p.25

34   Hippisley, *A Narrative of the Expedition*, p.233

35   Ibid., p.240

36   Ibid., p.561

37   Robinson, *Journal of an Expedition*, p.269

38   Hippisley, *A Narrative of the Expedition*, p.327

39   Ibid, p.353; Vowell, *Campaigns and Cruises*, p.20

40   Hippisley, *A Narrative of the Expedition*, p.353

41   Ibid., p.353; Vowell, *Campaigns and Cruises*, p.45

42   Vowell, *Campaigns and Cruises*, p.45

43   The *Dublin Evening Post*, Dublin, 29 July 1820

44   Chesterton, *Peace, War and Adventure*, p.132

45   Ibid.

46   William Jackson Adam, *Journal of Voyages to Marguaritta, Trinidad, & Maturin: With the Author's Travels Across the Plains of the Llaneros, to Angustura, and Subsequent Descent of the Orinoco, in the Years 1819 & 1820* (London, J. Jones, 1824), pp.111, 142

47   Chesterton, *Peace, War and Adventure*, p.129

48   Adam, *Journal of Voyages*, p.114

49   Hippisley, *A Narrative of the Expedition*, p.340

50   Brown, *Narrative of the Expedition*, pp.96–97

51   Robinson, *Journal of an Expedition*, pp.92–93

52   Ibid., p.93

53   Although Bolívar's junior officers were ethnically diverse, the highest ranking generals in 1817 were all white with the sole exception of Piar.

54   Brown, *Narrative of the Expedition*, p.83

55   Archivo del Libertador, Caracas, Venezuela, Sección Juan Francisco de Martin, Volume 14, Doc. 161

56   Adam, *Journal of Voyages*, p.109

57   Robinson, *Journal of an Expedition*, pp.123–124

58   Hippisley, *A Narrative of the Expedition*, p.279

59   Archivo General de la Nación, Caracas, Venezuela (AGNV), Gobernación de Guayana (GDG), Tomo III, Doc. 42

60   As well as his trading activities, Hamilton also envisaged founding an Irish colony on the banks of the Orinoco, named New Erin, where immigrants would pay for plots of farmland in and around the proposed capital, New Dublin. Although a nine-year land rental contract was eventually agreed with the republican authorities in 1820, Hamilton's dream of a Gaelic colony in the middle of the South American jungle would never get off the ground. (Archivo Historico de Guayana (AHG) Ciudad Bolívar, Fondo 1820, Doc. 1.3.4.89.1; Matthew Brown, *Adventuring Through Spanish Colonies: Simón Bolívar, Foreign Mercenaries and the Birth of New Nations* (Liverpool, Liverpool University Press, 2007), p.20)

61   Vowell, *Campaigns and Cruises*, p.152

62   Adam, *Journal of Voyages*, p.116

63   Ibid., p.117

64   Hippisley, *A Narrative of the Expedition*, p.272

65   Ibid.

66   Ibid., p.376

67   Ibid.

68   Archivo General de la Nación, Bogotá, Colombia (AGNC), Sección Archivo Anexo, Fondo Historia, Tomo 24, Doc. 102

69   AGNV, GDG, Tomo V, Folio 848

70   Hippisley, *A Narrative of the Expedition*, pp.352–353

71   Robinson and many of his fellow memoirists were rather inaccurate when naming the animals they saw. The term tiger was frequently used without distinction to describe either of South America's great felines, the jaguar and the panther. Howell (ed.), *The Life of Alexander*, pp.75–76

72   AGNV, GDG, Tomo VI, Doc. 246; 247; 256, Folio 266–276

73   Robinson, *Journal of an Expedition*, p.147

74   Ibid., pp.147–148

75   Vowell, *Campaigns and Cruises*, p.49

76   Hippisley, *A Narrative of the Expedition*, p.369

77   Ibid.

78   Alexander Humboldt, *Personal Narrative of a Journey to the Equatorial Regions of the New Continent* (London, Penguin, 1995), pp.175, 178

CHAPTER 5

Heading: Richard Longeville Vowell, *Campaigns and Cruises, in Venezuela and New Grenada, and in the Pacific Ocean; From 1817 to 1830: with the Narrative of a March from the River Orinoco to San Buenaventura on the Coast of Chocó; and Sketches of the West Coast of South America from the Gulf of California to the Archipelago of Chilöe* (London, Longman and Co., 1831), p.84

1   Alexander Humboldt, *Personal Narrative of a Journey to the Equatorial Regions of the New Continent* (London, Penguin, 1995), p.162

2   At the turn of the 19th century, Humboldt met a resident of Caracas, a Monsieur Depons, who estimated that there were '1,200,000 oxen, 180,000 horses and 90,000 mules' spread across the plains.

3   Humboldt, *Personal Narrative*, p.179; Vowell, *Campaigns and Cruises*, p.150

4   Vowell, *Campaigns and Cruises*, p.150

5   John Howell (ed.), *The Life of Alexander Alexander, Written by Himself and Edited by John Howell* (Edinburgh, William Blackwood, 1830), p.85

6   Vowell, *Campaigns and Cruises*, p.59

7   Ibid., p.60

8   Ibid.

9   Humboldt, *Personal Narrative*, p.163

10   George Dawson Flinter, *The History of the Revolution of Caracas Together with a Description of the Llaneros* (London, W. Glindon, 1819), p.96

11   Richard Longeville Vowell, *The Savannas of Varinas* (London, Longman and Co., 1831), p.108

12   *Carrick's Morning Post*, Dublin, 29 June 1818

13   Vowell, *Campaigns and Cruises*, p.65

14   Anon, *Narrative of a Voyage to the Spanish Main, in the Ship 'Two Friends': The Occupation of Amelia Island by M'Gregor, &c. — Sketches of the Province of East Florida; and Anecdotes Illustrative of the Habits and Manners of the Seminole Indians: with an Appendix, Containing a Detail of the Seminole* (London, J. Miller, 1819), p.15

15   Vowell, *Campaigns and Cruises*, pp.82–85

16   Ibid., p.84

17   Ibid., p.65

18   Ibid., p.68

19   Ibid., p.67

20   Thomas Rourke, *Man of Glory: Simon Bolívar* (London, Joseph, 1940), p.197

21   Gustavus Mathias Hippisley, *A Narrative of the Expedition to the Rivers Orinoco and Apuré in South America: which Sailed from England in November 1817, and Joined the Patriotic Forces in Venezuela and Caraccas* (London, John Murray, 1819), p.470

22   Archivo del Libertador, Caracas, Venezuela, Sección Juan de Francisco Martin, Volume 14, Doc. 40

23   Vowell, *Campaigns and Cruises*, p.69

24   Ibid., p.68

25   Vowell, *The Savannas of Varinas*, pp.39–40

26   Howell (ed.), *The Life of Alexander*, p.28; O'Leary, *Memorias de General Daniel Florencio O'Leary*, Volume 2 (Caracas, Imprenta de la Gaceta Oficial, 1879–1887), p.38; Gustavus Butler Hippisley, 'The Eve of Saint Simón', in *Godey's Magazine*, 1830, Volume XI, p.246

27   This title was earlier ascribed to Toussaint L'Ouverture, the ex-slave who led the Haitian revolution. Whether Páez or his followers were aware of this is impossible to gauge. C. L. R. James, *The Black Jacobins* (London, Alison Busby Limited, 1984)

28   Daniel O'Leary, R. A. Humphreys (ed.), *The Detached Recollections of General D. F. O'Leary* (London, The Athlone Press, 1969), p.11

29   Vowell, *Campaigns and Cruises*, p.74

30   George Laval Chesterton, *Peace, War and Adventure: An Autobiographical Memoir of George Laval Chesterton*, Volume 2 (London, Longman, Brown, Green and Longmans, 1853), p.207

31   Gustavus Butler Hippisley, 'The Ruse de Guerre', in *Colborn's United Service Magazine*, Arthur William Alsager Pollock (ed.), Third Edition (London 1847)

32   Chesterton, *Peace, War and Adventure*, p.213

33   O'Leary, *The Detached Recollections*, Volume 15, p.569; Vergara y Velasco, Francisco Javier, *1818: (Guerra de Independencia)* (Bogotá, Librería Americana, 1897), p.116, footnote 1, Chapter VII

34   José Páez, *Autobiografía* (Madrid, Editorial America, 1916), p.183

35   Vowell, *Campaigns and Cruises*, p.72

36   José Páez, *Autobiografía* (Madrid, Editorial America, 1916), p.183

37   James H. Robinson, *Journal of an Expedition 1400 Miles up the Orinoco and 300 up the Arauca: with an Account of the Country, the Manners of the People, Military Operations, &c* (London, Black, Young and Young, 1822), p.237

38   Howell (ed.), *The Life of Alexander*, Volume 2, pp.36, 388

39   W. Dupouy (ed.), *Sir Robert Ker Porter's Caracas Diary, 1825–1842: a British Diplomat in a Newborn Nation* (Caracas, Editorial Arte, 1966), p.730; Vowell, *Campaigns and Cruises*, p.72

40   Vowell, *Campaigns and Cruises*, p.71

41   Chesterton, *Peace, War and Adventure*, p.202

CHAPTER 6

1   Pablo Morillo (traducidas del frances por Arturo Gomez Jaramillo), *Memorias* (Bogota, Editorial Incunables, 1991), p.66

2   Richard Longeville Vowell, *Campaigns and Cruises, in Venezuela and New Grenada, and in the Pacific Ocean; From 1817 to 1830: with the Narrative of a March from the River Orinoco to San Buenaventura on the Coast of Chocó; and Sketches of the West Coast of South America from the Gulf of California to the Archipelago of Chilöe* (London, Longman and Co., 1831), p.76

3   Morillo, *Memorias*, p.67

4   B. P. Hughes, *Firepower, Weapons' Effectiveness on the Battlefield, 1630–1850* (London, Arms & Armour, 1974), p.59. Hughes estimates that 15 per cent of musket shots misfired in dry weather, rising to 25 per cent in wet conditions.

5   For a discussion of the musket's accuracy see Richard Holmes, *Redcoat: The British Soldier in the Age of the Horse and Musket* (London, Harper Collins, 2002), pp.198–199

6   Antonio Rodriguez Villa, *El teniente general don Pablo Morillo primer conde de Cartagena, marqués de la Puerta (1778–1837)* (Editorial America, 1920), p.508

7   Vowell, *Campaigns and Cruises*, p.77

8   Ibid., p.75

9   The *Morning Chronicle*, London, 1 July 1818

10   Vowell, *Campaigns and Cruises*, p.78.

11   Ibid.

12   Ibid.

13   Ibid.

14   Ibid., p.79

15   Ibid.

16   Ibid.

17   Ibid., pp.81–82

CHAPTER 7

Heading: The *Morning Chronicle*, London, 22 October 1818

1   Although Spanish born, Boves had been raised in Calabozo, Venezuela. As a young man, he became a powerful Caudillo made rich by the region's cattle trade. When the war broke out in 1811, he sided with the patriots, but, following several disagreements with the republican command, swapped allegiance and rallied the people of the plains to the royalist banner. Boves's brief military career was phenomenally successful, but cut short when he died of a lance wound received at the battle of Urica on 5 December 1814. Following Boves's demise, Páez filled the power vacuum in the plains.

2   An aide-de-camp was typically a junior staff officer, assigned to a superior to act as his personal messenger on the battlefield.

3   George Laval Chesterton, *Peace, War and Adventure: An Autobiographical Memoir of George Laval Chesterton*, Volume 2 (London, Longman, Brown, Green and Longmans, 1853), p.157

4   George Robert Gleig, *The Subaltern* (London, W. Blackwood and Sons, 1868), p.51

5   Rory Muir, *Tactics and the Experience of Battle in the Age of Napoleon* (London, Yale University Press, 2002), p.52

6   Gustavus Mathias Hippisley, *A Narrative of the Expedition to the Rivers Orinoco and Apuré in South America: which Sailed from England in November 1817, and Joined the Patriotic Forces in Venezuela and Caraccas* (London, John Murray, 1819), p.286

7   Ibid., p.288

8   Ibid.

9   Richard Longeville Vowell, *Campaigns and Cruises, in Venezuela and New Grenada, and in the Pacific Ocean; From 1817 to 1830: with the Narrative of a March from the River Orinoco to San Buenaventura on the Coast of Chocó; and Sketches of the West Coast of South America from the Gulf of California to the Archipelago of Chilöe* (London, Longman and Co., 1831), p.86

10   Pablo Morillo (traducidas del frances por Arturo Gomez Jaramillo), *Memorias* (Bogotà, Editorial Incunables, 1991), p.72

11   *Gazeta de Caracas*, Caracas, 15 April 1818

12   Vowell, *Campaigns and Cruises*, p.87

13   *Gazeta de Caracas*, Caracas, 15 April 1818

14   *The Times*, London, 12 June 1818

15   *The Courier*, London, 18 May 1818

16   Andrés Montaña (ed.), *Santander y los Ejercitos Patriotas: 1819* (Bogotá, Fundación de Paula Santander, 1989), Doc. 424

17   Vowell, *Campaigns and Cruises*, p.88

18   Ibid., p.89

19   Ibid.

20   Ibid., p.91

21   Ibid.; Alexander Humboldt, *Personal Narrative of a Journey to the Equatorial Regions of the New Continent* (London, Penguin, 1995), p.112

22   Chesterton, *Peace, War and Adventure*, p.141

23   A valise is a small bag used for carrying ammunition, tobacco and other personal possessions. Vowell, *Campaigns and Cruises*, p.100

24   Ibid., p.108

25   Chesterton, *Peace, War and Adventure*, p.143

26   Vowell, *Campaigns and Cruises*, p.109

27   Daniel O'Leary, *Memorias de General Daniel Florencio O'Leary*, Volume 12 (Caracas, Imprenta de la Gaceta Oficial, 1879–1887), pp.217–218

28   Henri La Fayette Villaume Ducoudray Holstein, *Memoirs of Simon Bolivar: President Liberator of the Republic of Colombia, and of His Principal Generals: Secret History of the Revolution and the Events which Preceded It, from 1807 to the Present Time: with an Introduction Containing an Account of the Statistics and the Present Situation of the Country* (London, S. G. Goodrich, 1830), p.130

29   Hippisley, *A Narrative of the Expedition*, p.419

30   Ibid., p.420

31   Ibid., p.572

32   The *Morning Chronicle*, London, 22 October 1818

CHAPTER 8

Heading: Gustavus Mathias Hippisley, *A Narrative of the Expedition to the Rivers Orinoco and Apuré in South America: which Sailed from England in November 1817, and Joined the Patriotic Forces in Venezuela and Caraccas* (London, John Murray, 1819), p.399

1   Ibid., p.379

2   Ibid., p.382

3   *Gazeta de Caracas*, Caracas, 15 July 1818

4   Richard Longeville Vowell, *Campaigns and Cruises, in Venezuela and New Grenada, and in the Pacific Ocean; From 1817 to 1830: with the Narrative of a March from the River Orinoco to San Buenaventura on the Coast of Chocó; and Sketches of the West Coast of South America from the Gulf of California to the Archipelago of Chilöe* (London, Longman and Co., 1831), pp.106–107, footnote 20

5   Hippisley, *A Narrative of the Expedition*, p.383

6   Ibid., p.384

7   Vowell, *Campaigns and Cruises*, p.110

8   Daniel O'Leary, R. A. Humphreys (eds.), *The Detached Recollections of General D. F. O'Leary* (London, The Athlone Press, 1969), pp.19–20

9   Vowell, *Campaigns and Cruises*, pp.110–111

10   Ibid., p.112

11   Hippisley, *A Narrative of the Expedition*, p.399

12   Ibid., p.398

13   Archivo General de la Nación, Caracas, Venezuela (AGNV) Gobernación de Guayana (GDG), Tomo VIII, Folio 55, Doc.10

14   Hippisley, *A Narrative of the Expedition*, p.403

15   James H. Robinson, *Journal of an Expedition 1400 Miles up the Orinoco and 300 up the Arauca: with an Account of the Country, the Manners of the People, Military Operations, &c* (London, Black, Young and Young, 1822), p.121

16   Archivo General de la Nación, Bogotá, Colombia (AGNC), Sección Archivo Anexo, Fondo Historia, Tomo 28, Folio 626

17   Ibid.

18   O'Leary, *The Detached Recollections*, pp.19–20

19 AGNC, Sección Archivo Anexo, Fondo Historia, Tomo 28, Folio 626

20 Ibid.

21 The *Morning Chronicle*, London, 13 January 1819

22 Hippisley, *A Narrative of the Expedition*, p.516

23 The *Dublin Evening Post*, Dublin, 15 March 1819

24 O'Leary, *The Detached Recollections*, pp.19–20

25 AGNC, Sección La Republica, Fondo Secretaria de Guerra y Marina, Tomo 323, Folio 212–213

26 The *Dublin Evening Post*, Dublin, 2 February 1819

27 O'Leary, *The Detached Recollections*, p.21

28 Vowell, *Campaigns and Cruises*, p.116

29 Ibid.

30 William Jackson Adam, *Journal of Voyages to Marguaritta, Trinidad, & Maturin: With the Author's Travels Across the Plains of the Llaneros, to Angustura, and Subsequent Descent of the Orinoco, in the Years 1819 & 1820* (London, J. Jones, 1824), p.21; Anon, *Recollections of a Service of Three Years During the War-of-Extermination in the Republics of Venezuela and Columbia* (London, Hunt and Clarke, 1828), p.90

31 Anon, *Recollections of a Service*, p.90

32 Ibid.

33 The *Morning Chronicle*, London, 26 January 1819; Vowell, *Campaigns and Cruises*, p.116

34 Vowell, *Campaigns and Cruises*, p.116

35 Ibid., p.114

36 Ibid.

37 AGNV, GDG, Volume VI, Doc. 2343–236, Folio 254–256

38 The *Dublin Evening Post*, Dublin, 2 November 1819

39 Vowell, *Campaigns and Cruises*, p.116

40 Ibid., p.127

41 Ibid., p.117

42 Ibid., pp.117–118, *Guarápo* is a potent sugar cane-based hooch.

43 Ibid., p.119

44 Ibid, p.136

45 Ibid.

CHAPTER 9

1 Archivo General de la Nación, Caracas, Venezuela (AGNV) Gobernación de Guayana (GDG), Tomo VIII, Folio 55, Doc. 10

2 Gustavus Mathias Hippisley, *A Narrative of the Expedition to the Rivers Orinoco and Apuré in South America: which Sailed from England in November 1817, and Joined the Patriotic Forces in Venezuela and Caraccas* (London, John Murray, 1819), p.408

3 Ibid., p.423

4 Ibid., p.424

5 Ibid., p.437

6 AGNV, GDG, Tomo VI, Docs. 4, 6, 7, 9–11

7 Charles Brown, *Narrative of the Expedition to South America: Which Sailed from England at the Close of 1817, for the Service of the Spanish Patriots: Including the Military and Naval Transactions, and Ultimate Fate of that Expedition: Also the Arrival of Colonels Blosset and English* (London, John Booth, 1819), p.111

8 The *Morning Chronicle*, London, 23 October 1818

9 Rory Muir, *Tactics and the Experience of Battle in the Age of Napoleon* (London, Yale University Press, 2002), p.34

10   Hippisley, *A Narrative of the Expedition*, p.640

11   Ibid., p.641

12   Ibid.

13   The *Morning Chronicle*, London, 5 November 1818

14   Ibid., 23 October 1818

15   Hippisley, *A Narrative of the Expedition*, p.642

16   The *Morning Chronicle*, London, 5 November 1818

17   Hippisley, *A Narrative of the Expedition*, p.642

18   Brown, *Narrative of the Expedition*, p.113

19   The *Morning Chronicle*, London, 5 November 1818

20   Ibid.

21   Ibid., 5 December 1818

22   Brown, *Narrative of the Expedition*, p.114

23   The *Morning Chronicle*, London, 23 October 1818

24   Hippisley, *A Narrative of the Expedition*, p.643

25   William Jackson Adam, *Journal of Voyages to Marguaritta, Trinidad, & Maturin: With the Author's Travels Across the Plains of the Llaneros, to Angustura, and Subsequent Descent of the Orinoco, in the Years 1819 & 1820* (London, J. Jones, 1824), pp.132, 3

26   Brown, *Narrative of the Expedition*, p.90

27   Ibid.

28   Adam, *Journal of Voyages*, p.120

29   Richard Longeville Vowell, *Campaigns and Cruises, in Venezuela and New Grenada, and in the Pacific Ocean; From 1817 to 1830: with the Narrative of a March from the River Orinoco to San Buenaventura on the Coast of Chocó; and Sketches of the West Coast of South America from the Gulf of California to the Archipelago of Chilöe* (London, Longman and Co., 1831), p.20

30   Ibid., p.21

31   John Lynch, *Simon Bolívar: A Life* (London, Yale University Press, 2007), pp.9–12

32   AGNV, GDG, Volume VI, Doc. 224, Folio 244; John Princep, *Diario de un Viaje de Santo Tome de Angostura en la Guayana Espanola a las Misiones Capuchinas del Caroni*, trans. Jaime Tello (Caracas, Ediciones de la Presidencia de la República, 1975), p.11

33   Muir, *Tactics and the Experience of Battle*, pp.73–76

34   AGNV, GDG, Tomo 9, Folio 121

35   Ibid.

36   Brown, *Narrative of the Expedition*, p.100; AGNV, GDG, Tomo V, Folios 663, 703

37   Brown, *Narrative of the Expedition*, pp.100, 101

38   Ibid., p.101

39   James H. Robinson, *Journal of an Expedition 1400 Miles up the Orinoco and 300 up the Arauca: with an Account of the Country, the Manners of the People, Military Operations, &c* (London, Black, Young and Young, 1822), p.164

40   The *Dublin Evening Post*, Dublin, 2 February 1819

CHAPTER 10

1   English Papers, Suffolk County Record Office, HA 156/6/30

2   Eric Lambert, *Voluntarios Británicos e Irlandeses en la Gesta Bolivariana*, Volume 3 (Caracas, Ministerio de la Defensa, Dirección de Artes Graficas, 1993), p.5

3   The *Morning Chronicle*, London, 22 October 1818

4   Kew National Archives, HO 79/3, p.324

5   Ibid., pp.324–325

6   George Laval Chesterton, *Peace, War and Adventure: An Autobiographical Memoir of George Laval Chesterton*, Volume 2 (London, Longman, Brown, Green and Longmans, 1853), p.26

7   Ibid.

8   Ibid., p.27

9   Ibid.

10   Ibid., p.28

11   Ibid.

12   The English Papers, Suffolk County Record Office, HA157/6/36

13   Chesterton, *Peace, War and Adventure*, p.38

14   Matthew Brown, *Adventuring Through Spanish Colonies: Simón Bolívar, Foreign Mercenaries and the Birth of New Nations* (Liverpool, Liverpool University Press, 2007), p.29

15   Chesterton, *Peace, War and Adventure*, p.38

16   Ibid.

17   Ibid., p.39

18   Lambert, *Voluntarios*, Volume 1, pp.272–276

19   Lieutenant Brown of Gillmore's artillery regiment estimated that 1 Venezuelan peso was equivalent to 2s 6d in British currency. Therefore the bounty of 300 pesos amounted to £37.50. See Chapter 1, note 62 for more details.

20   Archivo General de la Nación, Bogotá, Colombia (AGNC), Hojas de Servicio, Tomo 31, Folio 533

21   *The Times*, London, 30 August 1817

22   Michael Rafter, *Memoirs of Gregor M'Gregor: Comprising a Sketch of the Revolution in New Granada and Venezuela, with Biographical Notices of Generals Miranda, Bolivar, Morillo and Horé, and a Narrative of the Expeditions to Amelia Island, Porto Bello, and Rio de la Hache, Interspersed with Revolutionary Anecdotes* (London, J. J. Stockdale, 1820), p.389

CHAPTER 11

Heading: John Howell (ed.), *The Life of Alexander Alexander, Written by Himself and Edited by John Howell*, Volume 2 (Edinburgh, William Blackwood, 1830), p.96

1   *Blackwood's Edinburgh Magazine*, Volume XI, January–June 1822, p.122; Alfred Hasbrouck, *Foreign Legionaries in the Liberation of Spanish South America* (Columbia University Press, 1928), p.79

2   As ever, contradictory sources exist as regards the number of men under Rooke's command. Some put the figure as high as 140.

3   Richard Longeville Vowell, *Campaigns and Cruises, in Venezuela and New Grenada, and in the Pacific Ocean; From 1817 to 1830: with the Narrative of a March from the River Orinoco to San Buenaventura on the Coast of Chocó; and Sketches of the West Coast of South America from the Gulf of California to the Archipelago of Chilöe* (London, Longman and Co., 1831), p.139

4   Ibid.

5   Ibid., p.143

6   Ibid.

7   George Laval Chesterton, *Peace, War and Adventure: An Autobiographical Memoir of George Laval Chesterton*, Volume 2 (London, Longman, Brown, Green and Longmans, 1853), p.141

8   James H. Robinson, *Journal of an Expedition 1400 Miles up the Orinoco and 300 up the Arauca: with an Account of the Country, the Manners of the People, Military Operations, &c* (London, Black, Young and Young, 1822), p.150

9   Simón Bolívar, Vicente Lecuna (ed.), *Cartas del Libertador* (Caracas, Banco de Venezuela, Fundacion Vincente Lecuna, 1964), Second Edition, Tomo 2, Doc. 459, pp.164–167

10   Antonio Rodriguez Villa, *El teniente general don Pablo Morillo primer conde de Cartagena, marqués de la Puerta (1778–1837)*, Volume 4 (Editorial America, 1920), Doc. 765, p.5

11   Richard Longeville Vowell, *The Savannas of Varinas* (London, Longman and Co., 1831), p.104

12   Vowell, *Campaigns and Cruises*, p.146

13   *The Patriot*, Dublin, 24 July 1819

14   Charles Stuart Cochrane, *Journal of a Residence and Travels in Colombia*, Volume 1 (London, Henry Colburn, 1825), pp.498–499

15   Vowell, *Campaigns and Cruises*, p.136

16   *Correo del Orinoco*, Angostura, 3 April 1819

17   *The Patriot*, Dublin, 24 July 1819

18   Howell (ed.), *The Life of Alexander*, Volume 1, pp.85–86

19   Ibid., p.86

20   Ibid.

21   Vowell, *The Savannas of Varinas*, p.164

22   Ibid., p.163

23   Ibid., p.146

24   Robinson, *Journal of an Expedition*, p.184

25   Ibid., pp.178–179

26   Howell (ed.), *The Life of Alexander*, Volume 1, p.88

27   Ibid., p.89

28   Robinson, *Journal of an Expedition*, p.175

29   Howell (ed.), *The Life of Alexander*, Volume 1, p.90

30   Vowell, *Campaigns and Cruises*, p.147

31   Robinson, *Journal of an Expedition*, p.194

32   Ibid.

33   Howell (ed.), *The Life of Alexander*, Volume 1, p.90

34   Robinson, *Journal of an Expedition*, p.196; Alexander Humboldt, *Personal Narrative of a Journey to the Equatorial Regions of the New Continent* (London, Penguin, 1995), p.178

35   Vowell, *The Savannas of Varinas*, p.39

36   Howell (ed.), *The Life of Alexander*, Volume 1, p.92

37   Ibid.

38   Ibid.

39   The *Dublin Evening Post*, Dublin, 23 November 1820

40   Howell (ed.), *The Life of Alexander*, Volume 1, p.92

41   Robinson, *Journal of an Expedition*, p.208

42   Vowell, *The Savannas of Varinas*, pp.183–185

43   Howell (ed.), *The Life of Alexander*, Volume 1, pp.93–94

44   Ibid., p.95

45   Ibid.

46   Ibid., p.96

47   Cochrane, *Journal of a Residence*, p.470

48   Robinson, *Journal of an Expedition*, p.201

49   Robinson does not name the 'son of Hibernia' he spoke to, but as he later mentions that the officer was part of Páez's guard of honour, it is fair to make the assumption that he was indeed Captain Peter Grant.

50   Robinson, *Journal of an Expedition*, pp.234–235

51   Ibid. p.226

52 O'Leary, *Memorias de General Daniel Florencio O'Leary*, Volume 1 (Caracas, Imprenta de la Gaceta Oficial, 1879–1887), p.659

53 Ibid.

54 Robinson, *Journal of an Expedition*, p.216

55 Ibid.

56 Ibid., pp.216–217

57 Ibid., p.217

58 Cochrane, *Journal of a Residence*, p.472

59 Howell (ed.), *The Life of Alexander*, Volume 1, pp.34–35

60 Ibid.

61 Ibid., p.63

62 Ibid., p.102; Robinson, *Journal of an Expedition*, p.225

63 Howell (ed.), *The Life of Alexander*, Volume 1, p.63

64 Chesterton, *Peace, War and Adventure*, p.158

65 Anon, *Recollections of a Service of Three Years During the War-of-Extermination in the Republics of Venezuela and Columbia* (London, Hunt and Clarke, 1828), p.184

66 Howell (ed.), *The Life of Alexander*, Volume 1, pp.96–97

67 Ibid., p.96

68 Ibid., p.97

69 Vowell, *Campaigns and Cruises*, pp.57–58

70 Robinson, *Journal of an Expedition*, p.235

71 Howell (ed.), *The Life of Alexander*, Volume 1, p.104

72 Vowell, *The Savannas of Varinas*, p.265

73 O'Leary, *Memorias*, Volume 16, Doc. 592, pp.270–271

74 Vowell, *The Savannas of Varinas*, p.267

CHAPTER 12

1 Eric Lambert, *Voluntarios Británicos e Irlandeses en la Gesta Bolivariana*, Volume 1 (Caracas, Ministerio de la Defensa, Dirección de Artes Graficas, 1993), p.291

2 Archivo General de la Nación, Bogotá, Colombia (AGNC), Sección Republica, Hojas de Servicio, Tomo 30, Folio 973

3 The *Dublin Evening Post*, Dublin, 27 April 1820

4 Ibid., 10 June 1819

5 Ibid.

6 The English Papers, Suffolk County Record Office, HA 157,153,206

7 AGNC, Sección Republica, Hojas de Servicio, Tomo 31, Folio 131

8 Matthew Brown, *Adventuring Through Spanish Colonies: Simón Bolívar, Foreign Mercenaries and the Birth of New Nations* (Liverpool, Liverpool University Press, 2007), p.26; Matthew Brown, Martín Alonso Roa, *Militares extranjeros en la independencia de Colombia: nuevas perspectivas* (Bogotá, Museo Nacional de Colombia, 2005), Doc. 5

9 Archivo del Libertador, Caracas, Venezuela, Sección Juan Francisco de Martin, Volume 14, Doc. 21

10 John Howell (ed.), *The Life of Alexander Alexander, Written by Himself and Edited by John Howell*, Volume 1 (Edinburgh, William Blackwood, 1830), p.87

11 Archivo General de la Nación, Caracas, Venezuela (AGNV) Gobernación de Guayana (GDG) Tomo 7, Folio 1

12 Howell (ed.), *The Life of Alexander*, Volume 1, p.87

13 AGNV, GDG, Tomo VIII, Doc. 101

NOTES

14   Brown, *Adventuring Through Spanish Colonies*, p.42

15   *Correo del Orinoco*, Angostura, 6 March 1819

16   Howell (ed.), *The Life of Alexander*, Volume 1, p.106

17   Ibid., p.113

18   Ibid., p.27

19   Archivo del Libertador, Sección Juan de Francisco Martin, Volume 14, Doc. 40; Lambert, *Voluntarios*, Volume 1, p.175

20   Archivo del Libertador, Sección Juan de Francisco Martin, Volume 14, Doc. 10

21   AGNV, GDG, Tomo 1, Doc. 58–59, Folio 65–66

22   Archivo del Libertador, Sección Juan de Francisco Martin, Volume 14, Doc. 40

23   Ibid.

24   Ibid.

25   AGNV, GDG, Tomo V, Doc. 868

26   Ibid., Doc. 482, Folio 98

27   *The Times*, London, 23 October 1819

28   AGNV, GDG, Legajo 12, Folio 88

29   Ibid., Volume 3, Folio 126

30   Ibid.

31   John Lynch, *Simón Bolívar: A Life* (London, Yale University Press, 2007), p.121

32   Ibid.

33   AGNV, GDG, Tomo VIII, Doc. 104

34   *The Times*, London, 23 October 1819

35   *Carrick's Morning Post*, Dublin, 23 November 1820

36   Richard Longeville Vowell, *The Savannas of Varinas* (London, Longman and Co., 1831) p.180

37   Howell (ed.), *The Life of Alexander*, Volume 1, pp.82–83

38   Lieutenant Chesterton would later compare the Valancay Regiment to the 43rd British Light Infantry – 'the most perfect regiment … [he] ever saw under arms'. (George Laval Chesterton, *Peace, War and Adventure: An Autobiographical Memoir of George Laval Chesterton*, Volume 2 (London, Longman, Brown, Green and Longmans, 1853), p.213)

39   Daniel O'Leary, *Memorias de General Daniel Florencio O'Leary*, Volume 16 (Caracas, Imprenta de la Gaceta Oficial, 1879–1887), p.290

40   AGNC, Archivo Anexo, Fondo Historia, Tomo 23, Folio 179

41   Anon, *The Present State of Colombia: Containing an Account of the Principal Events of its Revolutionary War; the Expeditions Fitted Out in England to Assist in its Emancipation; its Constitution; Financial and Commercial Laws; Revenue, Expenditure and Public Debt; Agriculture; Mines; Mining and Other Concerns* (London, J. Murray, 1827), p.93

42   http://irishargentine.org/mcginnperu3.htm

43   Antonio Rodriguez Villa, *El teniente general don Pablo Morillo primer conde de Cartagena, marqués de la Puerta (1778–1837)*, Volume 4 (Editorial America, 1920), Doc. 770, p.23

44   *The Patriot*, Dublin, 24 July 1819

45   The *Dublin Evening Post*, Dublin, 15 July 1819

46   Ibid.

47   Ibid.

48   Ibid.

49   Richard Longeville Vowell, *Campaigns and Cruises, in Venezuela and New Grenada, and in the Pacific Ocean; From 1817 to 1830: with the Narrative of a March from the River Orinoco to San Buenaventura on the Coast of Chocó; and Sketches of the West Coast of South America from the Gulf of California to the Archipelago of Chilöe* (London, Longman and Co., 1831), pp.128–129

CHAPTER 13

1   Michael Rafter, *Memoirs of Gregor M'Gregor: Comprising a Sketch of the Revolution in New Granada and Venezuela, with Biographical Notices of Generals Miranda, Bolivar, Morillo and Horé, and a Narrative of the Expeditions to Amelia Island, Porto Bello, and Rio de la Hache, Interspersed with Revolutionary Anecdotes* (London, J. J. Stockdale, 1820), p.143

2   The *Dublin Evening Post,* Dublin, 17 June 1819

3   Ibid.

4   Rafter, *Memoirs of Gregor M'Gregor,* p.143

5   Jacob Dunham, *Journal of Voyages: Containing an Account of the Author's Being Twice Captured by the English and Once by Gibbs the Pirate* (New York, 1850), p.142

6   Rafter, *Memoirs of Gregor M'Gregor,* p.143

7   W. Davidson Weatherhead, *An Account of the Late Expedition Against the Isthmus of Darien Under the Command of Sir Gregor McGregor; Together with the Events Subsequent to the Recapture of Porto Bello, till the Release of the Prisoners from Panama; Remarks on the Present State of the Patriot Cause and on the Climate and Diseases of South America* (London, Longman, Hurst, Rees, Orme and Brown, 1821), p.10

8   Ibid., p.11

9   Ibid.

10 Ibid.

11 The *Morning Chronicle,* London, 24 April 1819

12 Rafter, *Memoirs of Gregor M'Gregor,* p.157

13 John Bezant, *Narrative of the Expedition under General MacGregor against Porto Bello: Including an Account of the Voyage; And of the Causes which Led to its Final Overthrow, (By an Officer who Miracoulously Escaped)* (London and Edinburgh, C. and J. Ollier, and T. and J. Allman, 1820), p.25; Rafter, *Memoirs of Gregor M'Gregor,* p.157

14 Weatherhead, *An Account of the Late Expedition,* p.12

15 Eric Lambert, *Voluntarios Británicos e Irlandeses en la Gesta Bolivariana,* Volume 3 (Caracas, Ministerio de la Defensa, Dirección de Artes Graficas, 1993), p.164

16 Weatherhead, *An Account of the Late Expedition,* p.11

17 Ibid., p.13

18 Lambert, *Voluntarios,* Volume 3, p.153

19 Weatherhead, *An Account of the Late Expedition,* p.14

20 Ibid., pp.14–15

21 Ibid., p.16

22 Ibid., p.21

23 Rafter, *Memoirs of Gregor M'Gregor,* pp.173–174

24 Dunham, *Journal of Voyages,* p.142

25 Weatherhead, *An Account of the Late Expedition,* p.19

26 Ibid., p.18

27 Lambert, *Voluntarios,* Volume 3, p.154

28 Weatherhead, *An Account of the Late Expedition,* p.19

29 Dunham, *Journal of Voyages,* p.143; Weatherhead, *An Account of the Late Expedition,* p.20

30 Weatherhead, *An Account of the Late Expedition,* p.33

31 Rafter, *Memoirs of Gregor M'Gregor,* p.195

32 Weatherhead, *An Account of the Late Expedition,* p.23

33 Rafter, *Memoirs of Gregor M'Gregor,* p.195

34 Alexander Humboldt (ed.), *Personal Narrative of a Journey to the Equatorial Regions of the New Continent* (London, Penguin, 1995), p.180

35 The *Dublin Evening Post,* Dublin, 19 June 1819

36   Ibid.

37   Ibid., 14 May 1819

38   Weatherhead, *An Account of the Late Expedition*, p.25

39   Lambert, *Voluntarios*, Volume 3, p.160

40   Rafter, *Memoirs of Gregor M'Gregor*, p.197

41   Weatherhead, *An Account of the Late Expedition*, p.25

42   Ibid., pp.25–26

43   Ibid., p.26

44   Ibid.

45   Ibid., p.27

46   Ibid.

47   Ibid.

48   Rafter, *Memoirs of Gregor M'Gregor*, p.198

49   Weatherhead, *An Account of the Late Expedition*, p.28

50   Francis Maceroni, *Memoirs of the Life and Adventures of Colonel Maceroni, Late Aide-de-Camp to Joachim Murat, King of Naples; Knight of the Legion of Honour, and of St. George of the Two Sicilies; Ex-General of Brigade, in the Service of the Republic of Colombia ect. ect, with a Portrait* (London, J. Macrone, 1838), p.438

51   Rafter, *Memoirs of Gregor M'Gregor*, p.200

52   Bezant, *Narrative of the Expedition*, p.45

53   Weatherhead, *An Account of the Late Expedition*, p.30

54   Bezant, *Narrative of the Expedition*, p.42

55   Weatherhead, *An Account of the Late Expedition*, p.31

56   Maceroni, *Memoirs of the Life and Adventures of Colonel Maceroni*, p.440

57   Rafter, *Memoirs of Gregor M'Gregor*, p.210

58   Weatherhead, *An Account of the Late Expedition*, p.40

59   Ibid., p.43

60   Ibid., p.39

61   Rafter, *Memoirs of Gregor M'Gregor*, p.216

62   Weatherhead, *An Account of the Late Expedition*, p.40

63   Ibid.

64   Rafter, *Memoirs of Gregor M'Gregor*, p.218

65   Weatherhead, *An Account of the Late Expedition*, p.45

66   Ibid.

67   Ibid., p.49

68   Lambert, *Voluntarios*, Volume 3, p.164

69   Weatherhead, *An Account of the Late Expedition*, p.49

70   Ibid., p.47

71   Ibid.

72   Ibid., p.48

73   The *Dublin Evening Post*, Dublin, 20 July 1819

74   Weatherhead, *An Account of the Late Expedition*, p.51

75   Ibid., p.52

76   Ibid.

77   Ibid.

78   Maceroni, *Memoirs of the Life and Adventures of Colonel Maceroni*, p.441; Weatherhead, *An Account of the Late Expedition*, p.49

79   Bezant, *Narrative of the Expedition*, p.52

80   Weatherhead, *An Account of the Late Expedition*, p.50

81   Ibid., p.52; Rafter, *Memoirs of Gregor M'Gregor*, p.225

82   Lambert, *Voluntarios*, Volume 3, p.164

83   Weatherhead, *An Account of the Late Expedition*, p.53

84   Ibid., p.54

85   Ibid.

86   Ibid.

87   Ibid.

88   Ibid, pp.56–57

89   Ibid., p.55

90   Ibid., p.57

91   Ibid., p.58

92   Ibid.

93   Ibid.

94   Ibid, pp.60–61

PART 3

John Kincaid, *Random Shots from a Rifleman* (London, T. and W. Boone, 1847), pp.90–91

CHAPTER 14

1   Rebecca Earle, *Spain and the Independence of Colombia 1810–1825* (Exeter, University of Exeter Press, 2000), p.133

2   Daniel O'Leary, R. A. Humphreys (eds.), *The Detached Recollections of General D. F. O'Leary* (London, The Athlone Press, 1969), p.54

3   Ibid., p.22

4   Ibid.

5   Richard Longeville Vowell, *Campaigns and Cruises, in Venezuela and New Grenada, and in the Pacific Ocean; From 1817 to 1830: with the Narrative of a March from the River Orinoco to San Buenaventura on the Coast of Chocó; and Sketches of the West Coast of South America from the Gulf of California to the Archipelago of Chilöe* (London, Longman and Co., 1831), p.154

6   Including Major Ferrier of the artillery and Captain Peter Grant.

7   Vowell, *Campaigns and* Cruises, p.158

8   Alberot Eduardo Wright, *Destellos de gloria: biografía sintética de un prócer de la independencia, incorporando las 'Reminiscencias' del general de división don Tomás Carlos Wright* (Buenos Aires, Castorman, Oritz y Cia, 1949), p.32

9   Ibid.

10   Charles Stuart Cochrane, *Journal of a Residence and Travels in Colombia*, (London, Henry Colburn, 1825), p.478

11   Archivo General de la Nación, Bogotá, Colombia (AGNC), Sección Colecciones, Fondo Enrique Ortega Ricuarte, Caja 79, Carpeta 1, Doc. 11

12   George Laval Chesterton, *Peace, War and Adventure: An Autobiographical Memoir of George Laval Chesterton*, Volume 2 (London, Longman, Brown, Green and Longmans, 1853), p.157

13   Vowell, *Campaigns and Cruises*, p.158

14   Ibid., p.159

15   Daniel O'Leary, *Memorias de General Daniel Florencio O'Leary*, Volume 1 (Caracas, Imprenta de la Gaceta Oficial, 1879–1887), p.666; AGNC, Fondo Sección Guerra y Marina, Sección La Republica, Tomo 778, Folio 83; The *Dublin Evening Post*, Dublin, 27 April 1820

16   O'Leary, *Memorias*, Volume 1, p.666

17   Vowell, *Campaigns and Cruises*, p.161

18   O'Leary, *Memorias*, Volume 1, p.667

19   Vowell, *Campaigns and Cruises*, p.159

20   O'Leary, *Memorias*, Volume 1, p.667

21   Ibid, Volume 16, p.411, Doc. 716

22   Vowell, *Campaigns and Cruises*, p.163

23   Ibid.

24   Ibid., p.164

25   John Hamilton, *Travels Through the Interior Provinces of Colombia*, Volume 2 (London, John Murray, 1827), p.16

26   Ibid.

27   Vowell, *Campaigns and Cruises*, p.164

28   Anon, *The Present State of Colombia: Containing an Account of the Principal Events of its Revolutionary War; the Expedition Fitted Out in England to Assist in its Emancipation; its Constitution; Financial and Commercial Laws; Revenue, Expenditure and Public Debt; Agriculture; Mines; Mining and Other Concerns* (London, J. Murray, 1827), p.96

29   Vowell, *Campaigns and Cruises*, p.166

30   Cochrane, *Journal of a Residence*, p.483

31   O'Leary, *Memorias*, Volume 1, p.671

32   Ibid.

33   Ibid.

34   Ibid.

35   Ibid. p.675

36   Cochrane, *Journal of a Residence*, p.487

37   O'Leary, *Memorias*, Volume 1, p.676

CHAPTER 15

1   Archivo del Libertador, Caracas, Venezuela, Sección Juan de Francisco Martin, Volume 14, Doc. 1

2   George Laval Chesterton, *Peace, War and Adventure: An Autobiographical Memoir of George Laval Chesterton*, Volume 2 (London, Longman, Brown, Green and Longmans, 1853), p.41

3   Edward M. Brett, *The British Auxiliary Legion in the First Carlist War 1835–1838* (Dublin, Four Courts Press, 2005), pp.70–72

4   Eric Lambert, *Voluntarios Británicos e Irlandeses en la Gesta Bolivariana*, Volume 3 (Caracas, Ministerio de la Defensa, Dirección de Artes Graficas, 1993), p.36

5   Chesterton, *Peace, War and Adventure*, p.42

6   Ibid., p.43

7   Ibid., p.44

8   *The Times*, London, 3 September 1818

9   Chesterton, *Peace, War and Adventure*, p.47

10   Charles Brown, *Narrative of the Expedition to South America: Which Sailed from England at the Close of 1817, for the Service of the Spanish Patriots: Including the Military and Naval Transactions, and Ultimate Fate of that Expedition: Also the Arrival of Colonels Blosset and English* (London, John Booth, 1819), p.162

11   Ibid. p.135; *The Times*, London, 3 September 1818

12   Chesterton, *Peace, War and Adventure*, p.54

13   Brown, *Narrative of the Expedition*, p.121

14   William Jackson Adam, *Journal of Voyages to Marguaritta, Trinidad, & Maturin: With the Author's Travels Across the Plains of the Llaneros, to Angustura, and Subsequent Descent of the Orinoco, in the Years 1819 & 1820* (London, J. Jones, 1824), p.23

15   Ibid.

16   Brown, *Narrative of the Expedition*, p.120

17   Ibid., pp.120–121

18   Adam, *Journal of Voyages*, p.24

19   Brown, *Narrative of the Expedition*, p.120

20   The couple were married on 28 January 1819. (Drusilla Scott, *Mary English: A Friend of Bolivar* (Sussex, The Book Guild, 1991), p.26)

21   Lambert, *Voluntarios*, Volume 3, p.55

22   Chesterton, *Peace, War and Adventure*, p.48

23   Lambert, *Voluntarios*, Volume 3, p.57

24   Chesterton, *Peace, War and Adventure*, p.49

25   Lambert, *Voluntarios*, Volume 3, p.57

26   Chesterton, *Peace, War and Adventure*, p.50

27   Ibid., p.51

28   Ibid., p.52

29   Ibid., p.53

30   The *Dublin Evening Post*, Dublin, 8 February 1820

31   Lambert, *Voluntarios*, Volume 3, p.61

32   Ibid. p.40

33   Brown, *Narrative of the Expedition*, p.175

34   Chesterton, *Peace, War and Adventure*, p.60

35   Ibid.; *Faulkner's Dublin Journal*, Dublin, 12 May 1820

36   Chesterton, *Peace, War and Adventure*, p.58

37   Anon, *Recollections of a Service of Three Years During the War-of-Extermination in the Republics of Venezuela and Columbia* (London, Hunt and Clarke, 1828), p.63

38   Ibid.

39   Ibid., p.66

40   Ibid.

41   Chesterton, *Peace, War and Adventure*, p.66

42   Ibid., p.61

43   Ibid.

44   Ibid.

45   Ibid.

46   Anon, *Recollections of a Service*, p.55; The *Dublin Evening Post*, Dublin, 8 February 1820

47   Anon, *Recollections of a Service*, p.69

48   The English Papers, Suffolk County Record Office, HA 157/6/1

49   Ibid., HA 156/6/29

50   Chesterton, *Peace, War and Adventure*, p.66

51   Anon, *Recollections of a Service*, p.72

52   Chesterton, *Peace, War and Adventure*, p.77

53   The English Papers, Suffolk County Record Office, HA 156/6/29; Chesterton, *Peace, War and Adventure*, p.77

54   Gustvus Butler Hippisley, *The Siege of Barcelona, a Poem in Three Cantos* (London, W. J. Cleaver, 1842), p.2

55   Anon, *Recollections of a Service*, p.76

56   Ibid., pp.80–81

57   The English Papers, Suffolk County Record Office, HA 156/6/29

58   Anon, *Recollections of a Service*, p.69
59   Ibid.
60   Chesterton, *Peace, War and Adventure*, p.63
61   Ibid.
62   *Faulkner's Dublin Journal*, Dublin, 12 May 1820
63   Chesterton, *Peace, War and Adventure*, p.64
64   Ibid.; Anon, *Recollections of a Service*, p.102
65   Chesterton, *Peace, War and Adventure*, p.65
66   Ibid.
67   Ibid.
68   *Faulkner's Dublin Journal*, Dublin, 17 May 1820
69   The English Papers, Suffolk County Record Office, HA 156/6/29
70   Chesterton, *Peace, War and Adventure*, p.70
71   Ibid., p.66
72   The English Papers, Suffolk County Record Office, HA 156/6/29
73   Anon, *Recollections of a Service*, p.94
74   *Faulkner's Dublin Journal*, Dublin, 12 May 1820
75   Ibid.
76   The English Papers, Suffolk County Record Office, HA 156/6/29
77   *Faulkner's Dublin Journal*, Dublin, 12 May 1820
78   Chesterton, *Peace, War and Adventure*, p.67
79   Anon, *Recollections of a Service*, p.105
80   *Faulkner's Dublin Journal*, Dublin, 17 May 1820
81   The English Papers, Suffolk County Record Office, HA 156/6/29
82   *Faulkner's Dublin Journal*, Dublin, 17 May 1820
83   Ibid.
84   Ibid.
85   Anon, *Recollections of a Service*, p.78
86   Ibid., p.84; Chesterton, *Peace, War and Adventure*, p.77
87   *Faulkner's Dublin Journal*, Dublin, 17 May 1820
88   Anon, *Recollections of a Service*, p.84
89   Ibid.
90   Chesterton, *Peace, War and Adventure*, p.77

CHAPTER 16

1   Alberot Eduardo Wright, *Destellos de gloria: biografía sintética de un prócer de la independencia, incorporando las 'Reminiscencias' del general de división don Tomás Carlos Wright* (Buenos Aires, Castorman, Oritz y Cia, 1949), p.31
2   *La Bandera Negra*, Bogotá, 25 December 1837
3   The *Dublin Evening Post*, Dublin, 27 April 1820
4   Archivo General de la Nación, Bogotá, Colombia (AGNC), Sección Republica, Hojas De Servicio, Tomo 30, Folio 979
5   Ibid.
6   The *Dublin Evening Post*, Dublin, 27 April 1820
7   Ibid.

8   Andres Montaña (ed.), *Santander y los Ejercitos Patriotas: 1819* (Bogotá, Fundación de Paula Santander, 1989), Doc. 424

9   Daniel O'Leary, *Memorias de General Daniel Florencio O'Leary*, Volume 1 (Caracas, Imprenta de la Gaceta Oficial, 1879–1887), p.673

10 Montaña (ed.), *Santander y los Ejercitos Patriotas*, Doc. 424

11 The *Dublin Evening Post*, Dublin, 27 April 1820

12 *The Limerick Chronicle*, Limerick, 15 June 1833

13 *La Bandera Negra*, Bogotá, 25 December 1837

14 Ibid.

15 Gabriel Carmargo Pérez, 'Cuna, Muerte y Sepultura de Coronel Jaime Rooke', in David R. Iriarte (ed.), *Reportario Boyacanense* (Madrid, 1981), pp.181–182

16 O'Leary, *Memorias*, Volume 1, p.660

17 Foulkes, *Dancing into Battle: A Social History of the Battle of Waterloo* (London, Phoenix, 2007), p.203

18 La Flise, 'Pokhad Velikoi Armii v Rossiiu v 1812g, Zapiski de la Fliza', in *Russkaia Starina*, Volume LXXI, LXXII, LXXIII, July 1891–March 1892

19 According to one source, 70 per cent of those who had their legs removed at the thigh following the battle of Waterloo succumbed to their wounds (Holmes, *Redcoat: The British Soldier in the Age of the Horse and Musket* (London, Harper Collins, 2002), p.250). Whereas Kaufman (Matthew H. Kaufman, *Musket-ball and Sabre Injuries from the First Half of the Nineteenth Century*, Edinburgh, Royal College of Surgeons, 2003) cites far more favourable rates of survival for the same battle, with only one in nine patients dying following primary amputation of the upper limb.

20 John Howell (ed.), *The Life of Alexander Alexander, Written by Himself and Edited by John Howell* (Edinburgh, William Blackwood, 1830), p.51

21 O'Leary, *Memorias*, Volume 1, p.660

22 Sotomayor Tribin, and Hugo Armando, *Guerras, enfermedades y médicos en Colombia* (Bogotá, Escuela de Medicina Juan N. Corpas, 1997), p.190

23 Richard Longeville Vowell, *Campaigns and Cruises, in Venezuela and New Grenada, and in the Pacific Ocean; From 1817 to 1830: with the Narrative of a March from the River Orinoco to San Buenaventura on the Coast of Chocó; and Sketches of the West Coast of South America from the Gulf of California to the Archipelago of Chilöe* (London, Longman and Co., 1831), p.194

24 Ibid.

25 Rory Muir, *Tactics and the Experience of Battle in the Age of Napoleon* (London, Yale University Press, 2002), p.109

26 Richard Holmes calculates that casualty rates of 15 per cent to the victor, and 20 per cent to the loser were average for warfare in the Napoleonic period. (Holmes, *Redcoat*, p.250)

27 Matthew Brown, *Adventuring Through Spanish Colonies: Simón Bolívar, Foreign Mercenaries and the Birth of New Nations* (Liverpool, Liverpool University Press, 2007), p.26; Matthew Brown, Martín Alonso Roa, *Militares extranjeros en la independencia de Colombia: nuevas perspectivas* (Bogotá, Museo Nacional de Colombia, 2005), Doc. 5

28 The *Dublin Evening Post*, Dublin, 27 April 1820; Muir, *Tactics and the Experience of Battle*, p.8

29 Charles Stuart Cochrane, *Journal of a Residence and Travels in Colombia*, Volume 1 (London, Henry Colburn, 1825), p.488

CHAPTER 17

Heading: The *Dublin Evening Post*, Dublin, 27 April 1820

1   Richard Longeville Vowell, *Campaigns and Cruises, in Venezuela and New Grenada, and in the Pacific Ocean; From 1817 to 1830: with the Narrative of a March from the River Orinoco to San Buenaventura on the Coast of Chocó; and Sketches of the West Coast of South America from the Gulf of California to the Archipelago of Chilöe* (London, Longman and Co., 1831), p.175

2   Daniel O'Leary, *Memorias de General Daniel Florencio O'Leary*, Volume 1 (Caracas, Imprenta de la Gaceta Oficial, 1879–1887), p.680

3   Ibid.

4   Alberot Eduardo Wright, *Destellos de gloria: biografía sintética de un prócer de la independencia, incorporando las 'Reminiscencias' del general de división don Tomás Carlos Wright* (Buenos Aires, Castorman, Oritz y Cia, 1949), p.32

5   Vowell, *Campaigns and Cruises*, p.170

6   Wright, *Destellos de gloria*, p.33

7   Rory Muir, *Tactics and the Experience of Battle in the Age of Napoleon* (London, Yale University Press, 2002), Chapter 6

8   Ibid., pp.128–130

9   The *Dublin Evening Post*, Dublin, 27 April 1820

10   Ibid.

CHAPTER 18

1   *Faulkner's Dublin Journal*, Dublin, 17 May 1820

2   Ibid.

3   George Laval Chesterton, *Peace, War and Adventure: An Autobiographical Memoir of George Laval Chesterton*, Volume 2 (London, Longman, Brown, Green and Longmans, 1853), p.81

4   Ibid.

5   Eric Lambert, *Voluntarios Británicos e Irlandeses en la Gesta Bolivariana*, Volume 3 (Caracas, Ministerio de la Defensa, Dirección de Artes Graficas, 1993), p.82

6   Chesterton, *Peace, War and Adventure*, p.81

7   Anon, *Recollections of a Service of Three Years During the War-of-Extermination in the Republics of Venezuela and Columbia* (London, Hunt and Clarke, 1828), p.105

8   Chesterton, *Peace, War and Adventure*, p.81

9   Ibid., p.82

10   Ibid.

11   Rafael Sevilla, *Memorias de un oficial del ejercito espanol. Campanas contra Bolivar y los Separatistas de America. Apreciacion de la obra por R. Blanco-Fombona* (Madrid, Biblioteca Ayacucho, 1916), p.241

12   *Faulkner's Dublin Journal*, Dublin, 17 May 1820

13   Ibid.

14   Richard Henry Bonnycastle, *Spanish America; or, a Descriptive, Historical and Geographical Account of the Dominions of Spain in the Western Hemisphere, etc. [With maps.]* (London, Longman and Co., 1818), p.27

15   The English Papers, Suffolk County Record Office, HA 156/6/29

16   Ibid.

17   Ibid.; *Faulkner's Dublin Journal*, Dublin, 17 May 1820

18   Chesterton, *Peace, War and Adventure*, p.82

19   Ibid.

20   *Carrick's Morning Post*, Dublin, 11 February 1820

21   Anon, *Recollections of a Service*, p.114

22   Chesterton, *Peace, War and Adventure*, p.83

23   Anon, *Recollections of a Service*, p.115

24   *Carrick's Morning Post*, Dublin, 11 February 1820

25   The English Papers, Suffolk County Record Office, HA 156/6/29

26   Anon, *Recollections of a Service*, p.115

27   The English Papers, Suffolk County Record Office, HA 156/6/29

28   Chesterton, *Peace, War and Adventure*, p.83

29   The English Papers, Suffolk County Record Office, HA 156/6/29

30   Ibid.

31   Anon, *Recollections of a Service*, p.118

32   Ibid., p.121

33   Ibid., p.124

34   Dr Martin Howard, *Wellington's Doctors: The British Army Medical Services in the Napoleonic Wars* (Padstow, Spellmount, 2002), Chapters 1 and 5

35   Chesterton, *Peace, War and Adventure*, p.86.

36   The English Papers, Suffolk County Record Office, HA 156/6/29

37   Rory Muir, *Tactics and the Experience of Battle in the Age of Napoleon* (London, Yale University Press, 2002), pp.48–49

38   *Faulkner's Dublin Journal*, Dublin, 17 May 1820

39   Anon, *Recollections of a Service*, pp.68–69

40   Ibid., p.116

41   The English Papers, Suffolk County Record Office, HA 156/6/29

42   Anon, *Recollections of a Service*, p.126

43   Chesterton, *Peace, War and Adventure*, p.88

44   Ibid., p.89

45   *Faulkner's Dublin Journal*, Dublin, 17 May 1820

46   Ibid.

47   The *Dublin Evening Post*, Dublin, 13 April 1820

48   Chesterton, *Peace, War and Adventure*, p.91

49   Anon, *Recollections of a Service*, p.128

50   Chesterton, *Peace, War and Adventure*, p.92

51   Alexander Humboldt, *Personal Narrative of a Journey to the Equatorial Regions of the New Continent* (London, Penguin, 1995), p.81

52   Chesterton, *Peace, War and Adventure*, p.96

53   Ibid., p.98

54   Humboldt recorded the presence of this tribal branch of the Carib Indians in the area on his travels at the turn of the 19th century.

55   Humboldt, *Personal Narrative*, p.97; Chesterton, *Peace, War and Adventure*, p.110

56   Anon, *Recollections of a Service*, p.134

57   Chesterton, *Peace, War and Adventure*, p.100

CHAPTER 19

1   Richard Longeville Vowell, *Campaigns and Cruises, in Venezuela and New Grenada, and in the Pacific Ocean; From 1817 to 1830: with the Narrative of a March from the River Orinoco to San Buenaventura on the Coast of Chocó; and Sketches of the West Coast of South America from the Gulf of California to the Archipelago of Chilöe* (London, Longman and Co., 1831), p.176

2   Ibid.

3   Daniel O'Leary, *Memorias de General Daniel Florencio O'Leary*, Volume 16 (Caracas, Imprenta de la Gaceta Oficial, 1879–1887), p.431

4   Ibid, Volume 3, p.47

5   Vowell, *Campaigns and Cruises*, p.176

6   Ibid.; O'Leary, *Memorias*, Volume 2, p.36

7   O'Leary, *Memorias*, Volume 16, Doc. 730, p.431

8   Ibid.

9   *Gazeta de Santafé de Bogotá*, Bogotá, 2 July 1820

10   The *Dublin Evening Post*, Dublin, 6 November 1819

11   *Gazeta de Santafé de Bogotá*, Bogotá, 15 August 1819

12   Vowell, *Campaigns and Cruises*, p.178

13   John Hamilton, *Travels Through the Interior Provinces of Colombia* (London, John Murray, 1827), p.217

14   Gaspard Mollien estimated the capital's population to be 30,000 in 1823. (Gaspard Mollien, *Travels in the Republic of Colombia in the Years 1822 and 1823* (London, C. Knight, 1824)

15   Vowell, *Campaigns and Cruises*, p.180

16   Ibid., p.183

17   Ibid., p.184

18   Ibid., p.181

19   The *Dublin Evening Post*, Dublin, 27 April 1820

20   Ibid., 7 December 1819

21   *Freeman's Journal*, Dublin, 3 February 1820

22   Vowell, *Campaigns and Cruises*, p.178; Alberot Eduardo Wright, *Destellos de gloria: biografía sintética de un prócer de la independencia, incorporando las 'Reminiscencias' del general de división don Tomás Carlos Wright* (Buenos Aires, Castorman, Oritz y Cia, 1949), p.34

23   Manuel Pérez Vila, *Vida de Daniel Florencio O'Leary* (Caracas, 1957), p.237

24   *Gazeta de Santafé de Bogotá*, Bogotá, 29 August 1819

25   Archivo del Libertador, Caracas, Venezuela, Sección Juan Francisco de Martin, Volume 14, Doc. 45; The *Dublin Evening Post*, Dublin, 27 April 1820

26   The *Dublin Evening Post*, Dublin, 27 April 1820

27   Vowell, *Campaigns and Cruises*, footnote 22, p.466

28   Ibid., pp.188–189

29   *Gazeta de Santafé de Bogotá*, Bogotá, 10 October 1819

30   O'Leary, *Memorias*, Volume 1 pp.691–692

CHAPTER 20

1   The biography that follows is largely based on the opening pages of Eric Lambert's *Voluntarios Británicos e Irlandeses en la Gesta Bolivariana*, Volume 2 (Caracas, Ministerio de la Defensa, Dirección de Artes Graficas, 1993).

2   Henri La Fayette Villaume Ducoudray Holstein, *Memoirs of Simon Bolivar: President Liberator of the Republic of Colombia, and of His Principal Generals: Secret History of the Revolution and the Events which Preceded It, from 1807 to the Present Time: with an Introduction Containing an Account of the Statistics and the Present Situation of the Country* (London, S. G. Goodrich, 1830), p.229; Anon, *Recollections of a Service of Three Years During the War-of-Extermination in the Republics of Venezuela and Columbia* (London, Hunt and Clarke, 1828), p.172

3   Matthew Brown, Martín Alonso Roa, *Militares extranjeros en la independencia de Colombia: nuevas perspectivas* (Bogotá, Museo Nacional de Colombia, 2005), Doc. 2, p.263

4   The practice of selling commissions was common in the British Army and many other European forces of the age. In fact, this was how the vast majority of officers progressed up the ranks during peacetime. In the Venezuelan Army, however, men were commissioned on the basis of merit or influence, and the idea of buying promotion was considered bad practice.

5   Michael Rafter, *Memoirs of Gregor M'Gregor: Comprising a Sketch of the Revolution in New Granada and Venezuela, with Biographical Notices of Generals Miranda, Bolivar, Morillo and Horé, and a Narrative of the Expeditions to Amelia Island, Porto Bello, and Rio de la Hache, Interspersed with Revolutionary Anecdotes* (London, J. J. Stockdale, 1820), Chapter 11

6   Ibid., p.131; Francis Hall, *Colombia: its Present State, in Respect of Climate, Soil, Productions, Population, Government, Commerce, Revenue, Manufactures, Arts, Literature, Manners, Education, and Inducements to Emigration* (London, Baldwin, Craddock and Joy, 1824), p.108

7   William Jackson Adam, *Journal of Voyages to Marguaritta, Trinidad, & Maturin: With the Author's Travels Across the Plains of the Llaneros, to Angustura, and Subsequent Descent of the Orinoco, in the Years 1819 & 1820* (London, J. Jones, 1824), p.7, Preface; Anon, *Recollections of a Service*, p.174

8   Matthew Brown, *Adventuring Through Spanish Colonies: Simón Bolívar, Foreign Mercenaries and the Birth of New Nations* (Liverpool, Liverpool University Press, 2007), p.41

9   The *British Monitor*, London, 10 January 1819

10   The *Dublin Evening Post*, Dublin, 27 May 1819

11   Ibid., 13 May 1819

CHAPTER 21

1   Jacob Dunham, *Journal of Voyages: Containing an Account of the Author's Being Twice Captured by the English and Once by Gibbs the Pirate* (New York, 1850), pp.148–149

2   The *Dublin Evening Post*, Dublin, 16 November 1819

3   Michael Rafter, *Memoirs of Gregor M'Gregor: Comprising a Sketch of the Revolution in New Granada and Venezuela, with Biographical Notices of Generals Miranda, Bolivar, Morillo and Horé, and a Narrative of the Expeditions to Amelia Island, Porto Bello, and Rio de la Hache, Interspersed with Revolutionary Anecdotes* (London, J. J. Stockdale, 1820), p.253

4   Fortunately for those abandoned, a local Irish reverend, Father O'Flynn, took pity on their plight and nursed the men through their illness. Although Colclough succumbed to the disease shortly after MacGregor's departure, Hudson survived to write a series of damning letters berating his general's behaviour which appeared in the British press throughout 1819.

5   The *Dublin Evening Post*, Dublin, 16 September 1819

6   Rafter, *Memoirs of Gregor M'Gregor*, p.266

7   Ibid., p.263

8   Ibid., p.300

9   Ibid., p.291

10   Ibid.

11   Ibid., p.292

12   The *British Monitor*, Dublin, 26 December 1819

13   Rafter, *Memoirs of Gregor M'Gregor*, p.299

14   The *Dublin Evening Post*, Dublin, 28 December 1819

15   Rafter, *Memoirs of Gregor M'Gregor*, p.316

16   Ibid.

17   Ibid., p.317

18   Ibid., p.318

19   Eric Lambert, *Voluntarios Británicos e Irlandeses en la Gesta Bolivariana*, Volume 3 (Caracas, Ministerio de la Defensa, Dirección de Artes Graficas, 1993), p.217

20   The *Dublin Evening Post*, Dublin, 6 July 1820

21   Rafter, *Memoirs of Gregor M'Gregor*, p.367

22   Ibid., p.368; Alexander Humboldt, *Personal Narrative of a Journey to the Equatorial Regions of the New Continent* (London, Penguin, 1995), p.225

23   Lambert, *Voluntarios*, Volume 3, p.217

24   Rafter, *Memoirs of Gregor M'Gregor*, pp.323–324

25   Ibid., p.325

26 Ibid., pp.325–356

27 Ibid., p.326

28 Rory Muir, *Tactics and the Experience of Battle in the Age of Napoleon* (London, Yale University Press, 2002), p.17

29 Rafter, *Memoirs of Gregor M'Gregor*, p.330

30 The *Dublin Evening Post*, Dublin, 30 December 1819

31 Ibid.

32 Ibid.; Rafter, *Memoirs of Gregor M'Gregor*, p.338

33 The *Dublin Evening Post*, Dublin, 30 December 1819

34 Francis Maceroni, *Memoirs of the Life and Adventures of Colonel Maceroni, Late Aide-de-Camp to Joachim Murat, King of Naples; Knight of the Legion of Honour, and of St. George of the Two Sicilies; Ex-General of Brigade, in the Service of the Republic of Colombia ect. ect, with a Portrait* (London, J. Macrone, 1838), p.447

35 Rafter, *Memoirs of Gregor M'Gregor*, p.343

36 Ibid., p.345

37 The *British Monitor*, London, 26 December 1819

38 Rafter, *Memoirs of Gregor M'Gregor*, p.371

39 Maceroni, *Memoirs of the Life and Adventures of Colonel Maceroni*, p.451

40 Lambert, *Voluntarios*, Volume 3, p.227

41 Ibid., pp.228–236

42 John Howell, (ed.) *The Life of Alexander Alexander, Written by Himself and Edited by John Howell*, Volume 2 (Edinburgh, William Blackwood, 1830), p.203

CHAPTER 22

Heading: John Howell (ed.), *The Life of Alexander Alexander, Written by Himself and Edited by John Howell*, Volume 2 (Edinburgh, William Blackwood, 1830), p.118

1 *Carrick's Morning Post*, Dublin, 19 July 1819

2 William Jackson Adam, *Journal of Voyages to Marguaritta, Trinidad, & Maturin: With the Author's Travels Across the Plains of the Llaneros, to Angustura, and Subsequent Descent of the Orinoco, in the Years 1819 & 1820* (London, J. Jones, 1824), p.9

3 The *Dublin Evening Post*, Dublin, 7 August 1819

4 Robert James Young's diary, Public Record Office of Northern Ireland, D3045/6/3/2

5 Matthew Brown, Martin Alonso Roa, *Militares extranjeros en la independencia de Colombia: nuevas perspectivas* (Bogotá, Museo Nacional de Colombia, 2005), Doc. 55

6 The *Dublin Evening Post*, Dublin, 13 April 1820

7 Ibid., 4 March 1820

8 Adam, *Journal of Voyages*, p.16

9 Archivo General de la Nación, Bogotá, Colombia (AGNC), Sección Colecciones, Fondo Enrique Ortega Ricuarte, Caja 79, Carpeta 1, Doc. 500–502

10 Adam, *Journal of voyages*, p.20

11 *Carrick's Morning Post*, Dublin, 3 February 1820

12 The *Dublin Evening Post*, Dublin, 13 April 1820

13 Howell (ed.), *The Life of Alexander*, Volume 2, p.117

14 Ibid., p.118

15 Ibid.

16 Ibid., p.121

17 Ibid., pp.122–123; Francis Burdett O'Connor, *Un Irlandés con Bolívar: recuerdos de la independencia de América del Sur* (Caracas, El Cid, 1977), p.11

18   *Faulkner's Dublin Journal*, Dublin, 19 May 1820

19   Ibid.; *Carrick's Morning Post*, Dublin, 28 January 1820

20   *Carrick's Morning Post*, Dublin, 28 January 1820

21   *Faulkner's Dublin Journal*, Dublin, 19 May 1820

22   Ibid.

23   The *Dublin Evening Post*, Dublin, 2 December 1819

24   *Faulkner's Dublin Journal*, Dublin, 19 May 1820

25   The *Dublin Evening Post*, Dublin, 13 April 1820

26   Archivo del Libertador, Caracas, Venezuela, Sección Juan Francisco de Martin, Volume 14, Doc. 46; Robert James Young's diary, Public Record Office of Northern Ireland, D3045/6/3/2

27   *Faulkner's Dublin Journal*, Dublin, 29 May 1820

28   Ibid.

29   Ibid.

30   Antonio Rodriguez Villa, *El teniente general don Pablo Morillo primer conde de Cartagena, marqués de la Puerta (1778–1837)*, Volume 4 (Editorial America, 1920), Doc. 794

31   The *Dublin Evening Post*, Dublin, 2 December 1819

32   Ibid., 13 April 1820

33   Ibid.

34   Adam, *Journal of Voyages*, p.16

35   *Faulkner's Dublin Journal*, Dublin, 29 May 1820

36   Ibid.

37   Ibid.

38   Howell (ed.), *The Life of Alexander*, Volume 2, p.128

39   Ibid.; Adam, *Journal of Voyages*, p.21

40   Howell (ed.), *The Life of Alexander*, Volume 2, p.128

41   Ibid., p.132

42   The *Dublin Evening Post*, Dublin, 4 March 1820

43   Ibid., 27 April 1820

44   Daniel O'Leary, *Memorias de General Daniel Florencio O'Leary*, Volume 17 (Caracas, Imprenta de la Gaceta Oficial, 1879–1887), Doc. 14, p.22

45   The *Dublin Evening Post*, Dublin, 27 April 1820

46   Ibid., 17 February 1820, 4 March 1820

47   Ibid., 4 March 1820

48   Ibid., 6 April 1820

49   Ibid.

50   Francis Burdett O'Connor, *Un Irlandes con Bolívar: recuerdos de la independencia de América del Sur* (Caracas, El Cid, 1977), p.14

51   Ibid.

52   O'Leary, *Memorias*, Volume 17, Doc. 14, p.22

53   Matthew Brown, *Adventuring Through Spanish Colonies: Simón Bolívar, Foreign Mercenaries and the Birth of New Nations* (Liverpool, Liverpool University Press, 2007), p.41

54   O'Leary, *Memorias*, Volume 17, Doc. 61

55   Brown, *Adventuring Through Spanish Colonies*, p.41

56   The *Dublin Evening Post*, Dublin, 6 July 1820

57   Ibid., 24 June 1820

58   Ibid.

59   Ibid.

60   Ibid.

61   Ibid.

62   O'Connor, *Un Irlandés con Bolívar*, pp.15–16

63   The *Dublin Evening Post*, Dublin, 6 July 1820

64   O'Connor, *Un Irlandés con Bolívar*, pp.15–16

CHAPTER 23

Heading: *Carrick's Morning Post*, Dublin, 11 February 1820

1   George Laval Chesterton, *Peace, War and Adventure: An Autobiographical Memoir of George Laval Chesterton*, Volume 2 (London, Longman, Brown, Green and Longmans, 1853), p.106

2   William Jackson Adam, *Journal of Voyages to Marguaritta, Trinidad, & Maturin: With the Author's Travels Across the Plains of the Llaneros, to Angustura, and Subsequent Descent of the Orinoco, in the Years 1819 & 1820* (London, J. Jones, 1824), p.81

3   Ibid.

4   Ibid.

5   Anon, *Recollections of a Service of Three Years During the War-of-Extermination in the Republics of Venezuela and Columbia* (London, Hunt and Clarke, 1828), p.153

6   Chesterton, *Peace, War and Adventure*, p.106

7   Ibid., p.108; Adam, *Journal of Voyages*, p.82

8   Adam, *Journal of Voyages*, p.83

9   The *Dublin Evening Post*, Dublin, 4 January 1820

10   Chesterton, *Peace, War and Adventure*, p.112

11   Ibid., p.107

12   Ibid., p.108

13   Eric Lambert, *Voluntarios Británicos e Irlandeses en la Gesta Bolivariana*, Volume 3 (Caracas, Ministerio de la Defensa, Dirección de Artes Graficas, 1993), p.95

14   Adam, *Journal of Voyages*, p.85

15   Chesterton, *Peace, War and Adventure*, p.109

16   Gustavus Butler Hippisley, 'The Eve of Saint Simón', in *Godey's Magazine*, 1830, Volume X1, p.247; The *Dublin Evening Post*, Dublin, 12 February 1820

17   Adam, *Journal of Voyages*, p.71

18   Ibid., p.74

19   John Hambleton, 'The Voyage of the U.S. Schooner "Non-Such"', in *The Hispanic American Historical Review*, Volume 30, November 1950, p.487

20   Chesterton, *Peace, War and Adventure*, p.115; Anon, *Recollections of a Service*, p.168

21   Anon, *Recollections of a Service*, p.168; The *Dublin Evening Post*, Dublin, 8 February 1820

22   Chesterton, *Peace, War and Adventure*, p.115

23   William Duane, *A Visit to Colombia in the Years 1822 and 1823, by Laguayara and Caracas, over the Cordillera to Bogota, and thence by the Magdalena to Cartagena* (Philadelphia, Thomas H. Palmer, 1826), p.185; *Carrick's Morning Post*, Dublin, 11 February 1820

24   *Carrick's Morning Post*, Dublin, 11 February 1820

25   Archivo del Libertador, Caracas, Venezuela, Sección Juan de Francisco Martin, Volume 14, Doc. 62

26   The *Dublin Evening Post*, Dublin, 23 November 1820

27   Daniel O'Leary, *Memorias de General Daniel Florencio O'Leary*, Volume 17 (Caracas, Imprenta de la Gaceta Oficial, 1879–1887), Doc. 16

28   The *Dublin Evening Post*, Dublin, 12 May 1821

CHAPTER 24

1   Eric Lambert, *Voluntarios Británicos e Irlandeses en la Gesta Bolivariana*, Volume 3 (Caracas, Ministerio de la Defensa, Dirección de Artes Graficas, 1993), p.255

2   Alberot Eduardo Wright, *Destellos de gloria: biografía sintética de un prócer de la independencia, incorporando las 'Reminiscencias' del general de división don Tomás Carlos Wright* (Buenos Aires, Castorman, Oritz y Cia, 1949), p.54

3   William Duane, *A Visit to Colombia in the Years 1822 and 1823, by Laguayara and Caracas, over the Cordillera to Bogota, and thence by the Magdalena to Cartagena* (Philadelphia, Thomas H. Palmer, 1826), p.370

4   Wright, *Destellos de Gloria*, p.63

5   Daniel O'Leary, *Memorias de General Daniel Florencio O'Leary*, Volume 17 (Caracas, Imprenta de la Gaceta Oficial, 1879–1887), Doc. 11

6   Ibid., Doc. 202

7   Ibid., Volume 2, p.38

8   Ibid., p.39

9   Ibid., p.37

10 Ibid.; John Lynch, *Simon Bolívar: A Life* (London, Yale University Press, 2007), p.136

CHAPTER 25

1   Manuel Antonio López, *Recuerdos Históricos de la Guerra de la Independencia* (Madrid, Biblioteca Ayacucho, 1878), p.58; Charles Stuart Cochrane, *Journal of a Residence and Travels in Colombia* (London, Henry Colburn, 1825), p.495

2   Ibid., pp.54–55; Richard Longeville Vowell, *Campaigns and Cruises, in Venezuela and New Grenada, and in the Pacific Ocean; From 1817 to 1830: with the Narrative of a March from the River Orinoco to San Buenaventura on the Coast of Chocó; and Sketches of the West Coast of South America from the Gulf of California to the Archipelago of Chilöe* (London, Longman and Co., 1831), p.196

3   Archivo General de la Nación, Bogotá, Colombia (AGNC), Sección Republica, Secretaria de Guerra y Marina, Volume 35, Folio 884–887

4   Cochrane, *Journal of a Residence* (London, Henry Colburn, 1825) p.490; Eric Lambert, *Voluntarios Británicos e Irlandeses en la Gesta Bolivariana*, Volume 3 (Caracas, Ministerio de la Defensa, Dirección de Artes Graficas, 1993), p.360

5   Cochrane, *Journal of a Residence*, p.496

6   Vowell, *Campaigns and Cruises*, p.196

7   Ibid.

8   Ibid., p.197

9   Ibid.

10 Ibid.

11 Ibid. This skin condition, also known as *Pinta,* is caused by bacterial infection and is still found throughout South America.

12 AGNC, Archivo Restrepo, Caja 10, Folio 178

13 Vowell, *Campaigns and Cruises*, p.202

14 López, *Recuerdos Históricos*, p.55; Daniel O'Leary, *Memorias de General Daniel Florencio O'Leary*, Volume 17 (Caracas, Imprenta de la Gaceta Oficial, 1879–1887), Doc. 200

15 John Hamilton, *Travels Through the Interior Provinces of Colombia*, Volume 2 (London, John Murray, 1827), p.5

16 *Gazeta de Santafé de Bogotá*, Bogotá, 7 May 1820

17 Hamilton, *Travels through the Interior*, Volume 2, p.6

18 *Gazeta de Santafé de Bogotá*, Bogotá, 7 May 1820

19 AGNC, Archivo Restrepo, Caja 11, Folio 140

20 Hamilton, *Travels Through the Interior*, Volume 2, p.5

21 Archivo Historico de la Univesidad de Cali, Popayán, Sección Independencia, M1 4C, Signatura 6379, Folio 12

22 Vowell, *Campaigns and Cruises*, p.203

23 Ibid., p.204

24 Ibid.

25 *Gazeta de Santafé de Bogotá*, Bogotá, 25 June 1820; López, *Recuerdos Históricos*, p.56

26 López, *Recuerdos Históricos*, p.56

27 AGNC, Fondo, Sección Guerra y Marina, Sección La Republica, Tomo 778, Folio 82

28 López, *Recuerdos Históricos*, p.56

29 Ibid., p.57

30 Cochrane, *Journal of a Residence*, p.496

31 *Correo del Orinoco*, Angostura, 19 August 1820

32 López, *Recuerdos Históricos*, p.60

33 Vowell, *Campaigns and Cruises*, p.205

34 Ibid.; López, *Recuerdos Históricos*, p.60

35 Cochrane, *Journal of a Residence*, p.496

36 Vowell, *Campaigns and Cruises*, pp.205–206

37 Ibid., p.205; Archivo Central de Cauca (ACC), Sección Independencia, M1 4C, Signatura 6379, Folio 17

38 ACC, Sección Independencia, M1 4C, Signatura 6379, Folio 18

39 Vowell, *Campaigns and Cruises*, p.210

40 Ibid., p.211

41 The *Dublin Evening Post*, Dublin, 17 February 1820; Adam Zamoyski, *Holy Madness: Romantics, Patriots, and Revolutionaries, 1776–1871* (London, Phoenix Press, 2001), p.214

42 The *Dublin Evening Post*, Dublin, 19 February 1820

43 Ibid., 30 March 1820

44 Ibid., 11 April 1820

45 Zamoyski, *Holy Madness*, p.214

46 The *Dublin Evening Post*, Dublin, 26 February, 9 March, 16 March 1820

47 The *Morning Chronicle*, London, 21 November 1818

48 Ibid.

CHAPTER 26

Heading: Alberot Eduardo Wright, *Destellos de gloria: biografía sintética de un prócer de la independencia, incorporando las 'Reminiscencias' del general de división don Tomás Carlos Wright* (Buenos Aires, Castorman, Oritz y Cia, 1949), p.35; Daniel O'Leary, *Memorias de General Daniel Florencio O'Leary*, Volume 17 (Caracas, Imprenta de la Gaceta Oficial, 1879–1887), Docs. 202–203, 236

1 *Correo del Orinoco*, Angostura, 12 August 1820

2 Wright, *Destellos de Gloria*, p.35

3 Ibid.

4 Ibid.

5 Ibid.

6 Ibid., pp.36–37

7 Ibid., p.37

CHAPTER 27

1 The *Dublin Evening Post*, Dublin, 6 July 1820; O'Connor, *Un Irlandes con Bolívar: recuerdos de la independencia de América del Sur* (Caracas, El Cid, 1977), p.16

2 The *Dublin Evening Post*, Dublin, 6 July 1820

3 Francis Hall, *Colombia: its Present State, in Respect of Climate, Soil, Productions, Population, Government, Commerce, Revenue, Manufactures, Arts, Literature, Manners, Education, and Inducements to Emigration* (London, Baldwin, Craddock and Joy, 1824), p.102

4 O'Connor, *Un Irlandes con Bolívar*, p.17

5 The *Dublin Evening Post*, Dublin, 6 July 1820

6 Ibid.

7 Ibid.

8 Daniel O'Leary, *Memorias de General Daniel Florencio O'Leary*, Volume 17 (Caracas, Imprenta de la Gaceta Oficial, 1879–1887), Doc. 423

9 Eric Lambert, *Voluntarios Británicos e Irlandeses en la Gesta Bolivariana*, Volume 2 (Caracas, Ministerio de la Defensa, Dirección de Artes Graficas, 1993), p.281

10 The *Dublin Evening Post*, Dublin, 6 July 1820

11 O'Connor, *Un Irlandes con Bolívar*, p.17; Benjamin MacMahon, *amaica Plantership (a Description of Jamaica Planters, viz. Attorneys, Overseers, and Book-keepers, Compiled During a Residence of Eighteen Years in the Island)* (London, 1839), pp.11–19

12 The *Dublin Evening Post*, Dublin, 29 June 1820

13 Ibid.; O'Connor, *Un Irlandes con Bolívar*, p.17

14 The *Dublin Evening Post*, Dublin, 4 December 1820

15 Ibid., 29 June 1820

16 O'Connor, *Un Irlandes con Bolívar*, p.18

17 Ibid.

18 Ibid.

19 Ibid.

20 Ibid.

21 Ibid., p.19

22 The *Dublin Evening Post*, Dublin, 19 August 1820

23 Ibid., 6 July 1820

24 Ibid., 30 November 1820

25 Ibid., 4 December 1820

26 O'Connor, *Un Irlandes con Bolívar*, p.21

27 The *Dublin Evening Post*, Dublin, 19 August 1820

28 Ibid.

29 *Correo del Orinoco*, Angostura, 30 September 1820

30 The *Dublin Evening Post*, Dublin, 19 August 1820; O'Leary, *Memorias*, Volume 17, Doc. 423

31 O'Leary, *Memorias*, Volume 17, Doc. 423; *The Dublin Evening Post*, Dublin, 4 December 1820

32 O'Leary, *Memorias*, Volume 17, Doc. 423

33 The *Dublin Evening Post*, Dublin, 4 December 1820

34 Ibid., 19 August 1820

35 O'Connor, *Un Irlandes con Bolívar*, p.22

36 The *Dublin Evening Post*, Dublin, 19 August 1820

37 O'Leary, *Memorias*, Volume 17, Doc. 423

38 The *Dublin Evening Post*, Dublin, 4 December 1820

39 O'Connor, *Un Irlandes con Bolívar*, p.24

40   The *Dublin Evening Post*, Dublin, 4 December 1820

41   Ibid.

42   John Howell (ed.), *The Life of Alexander Alexander, Written by Himself and Edited by John Howell*, Volume 2 (Edinburgh, William Blackwood, 1830), p.241

43   The *Dublin Evening Post*, Dublin, 19 August 1820

44   *Correo del Orinoco*, Angostura, 30 September 1820

45   The *Dublin Evening Post*, Dublin, 5 August 1820

46   Ibid., 19 August 1820

47   Ibid., 27 July 1820

48   Ibid.

49   Ibid., 31 August 1820

CHAPTER 28

1   *Carrick's Morning Post*, Dublin, 13 July 1819

2   The *Dublin Evening Post*, Dublin, 29 June 1820

3   Ibid.

4   Ibid., 24 June 1820

5   Ibid., 29 June 1820

6   Ibid.

7   Ibid., 22 July 1820

8   Ibid., 29 July 1820

9   Ibid.

10   Ibid.

11   Ibid., 22 July 1820

12   Ibid., 23 November 1820

13   Eric Lambert, *Voluntarios Británicos e Irlandeses en la Gesta Bolivariana*, Volume 3 (Caracas, Ministerio de la Defensa, Dirección de Artes Graficas, 1993), p.96; Gustavus Butler Hippisley, 'The Eve of Saint Simón', in *Godey's Magazine*, 1830, Vol. X1, p.246

14   The *Dublin Evening Post*, Dublin, 22 February 1821

15   Ibid., 4 January 1821

16   Hippisley, 'The Eve of Saint Simón', p.246

17   Richard Longeville Vowell, *The Savannas of Varinas* (London, Longman and Co., 1831) pp.197–198

18   Ibid., p.201

19   Ibid., p.204

20   Archivo General de la Nación, Caracas, Venezuela (AGNV), Ilustres Próceres, Caja 29, Carpeta 9

21   Hippisley, 'The Eve of Saint Simón', p.247

22   Ibid.

23   Ibid.

24   The *Dublin Evening Post*, Dublin, 3 February 1821

25   Hippisley, 'The Eve of Saint Simón', p.248

26   Ibid.

27   Ibid.

28   Ibid.

29   Ibid.

30   Ibid. p.247

31   Ibid., p.249

32   Henri La Fayette Villaume Ducoudray Holstein, *Memoirs of Simon Bolívar: President Liberator of the Republic of Colombia, and of His Principal Generals: Secret History of the Revolution and the Events which Preceded It, from 1807 to the Present Time: with an Introduction Containing an Account of the Statistics and the Present Situation of the Country* (London, S. G. Goodrich, 1830), p.314

33   Ibid.

34   Hippisley, 'The Eve of Saint Simón', p.249

35   Ibid., p.251

36   Ibid.

37   www.simonbolivar.org/bolivar/rebelion-britanica.htm

38   Archivo General de la Nación, Bogotá, Colombia (AGNC), Sección Republica, Secretaria de Guerra y Marina, Volume 334, Folio 151–152

39   Hippisley, 'The Eve of Saint Simón', p.251

CHAPTER 29

1   *Carrick's Morning Post*, Dublin, 28 January 1820

2   Anon, *Recollections of a Service of Three Years During the War-of-Extermination in the Republics of Venezuela and Columbia* (London, Hunt and Clarke, 1828), p.176

3   Ibid.

4   Ibid.

5   Ibid.

6   The *Dublin Evening Post*, Dublin, 31 August 1820

7   Ibid.

8   John Howell (ed.), *The Life of Alexander Alexander, Written by Himself and Edited by John Howell*, Volume 2 (Edinburgh, William Blackwood, 1830), p.141

9   Ibid.

10   *Carrick's Morning Post*, Dublin, 29 August 1820

11   Ibid.

12   Howell (ed.), *The Life of Alexander*, Volume 2, p.141

13   The *Dublin Evening Post*, Dublin, 31 August 1820

14   Ibid., 22 August 1820

15   Howell (ed.), *The Life of Alexander*, Volume 2, p.242

16   The *Dublin Evening Post*, Dublin, 5 October 1820

17   Howell (ed.), *The Life of Alexander*, Volume 2, p.242

18   The *Dublin Evening Post*, Dublin, 19 August 1820

19   Ibid.; Francis Burdett O'Connor, *Un Irlandés con Bolívar: recuerdos de la independencia de América del Sur* (Caracas, El Cid, 1977), p.26

20   O'Connor, *Un Irlandés con Bolívar*, p.27

21   The *Dublin Evening Post*, Dublin, 5 October 1820

22   Ibid., 11 November 1820

23   Ibid., 5 October 1820

24   Ibid., 11 November 1820

25   Ibid., 23 November 1820

26   Ibid.

27   O'Connor, *Un Irlandés con Bolívar*, p.28

28   The *Dublin Evening Post*, Dublin, 23 November 1820

29   Eric Lambert, *Voluntarios Británicos e Irlandeses en la Gesta Bolivariana*, Volume 2 (Caracas, Ministerio de la Defensa, Dirección de Artes Graficas, 1993), p.369; The *Dublin Evening Post*, Dublin, 23 November 1820

30   The *Dublin Evening Post*, Dublin, 23 November 1820

31   Ibid.

32   Howell (ed.), *The Life of Alexander*, Volume 2, p.178

33   Ibid., p.180

34   It is not clear from the sources whether Major Powell was originally part of the Irish Legion, but there seems to be little other explanation for his presence in Baranquilla at this time.

35   O'Connor, *Un Irlandes con Bolívar*, p.29

36   Howell (ed.), *The Life of Alexander*, Volume 2, p.197

37   Lambert, *Voluntarios*, Volume 3, p.265

38   O'Connor, *Un Irlandes con Bolívar*, p.29

39   Ibid.

40   Lambert, *Voluntarios*, Volume 3, p.265

41   O'Connor, *Un Irlandes con Bolívar*, p.30

42   *Correo del Orinoco*, Angostura, 3 March 1821

43   O'Connor, *Un Irlandes con Bolívar*, p.31

44   Ibid.

45   *Correo del Orinoco*, Angostura, 3 March 1821

46   O'Connor, *Un Irlandes con Bolívar*, p.31

47   *Correo del Orinoco*, Angostura, 3 March 1821

48   Ibid.

49   Rory Muir, *Tactics and the Experience of Battle in the Age of Napoleon* (London, Yale University Press, 2002), p.182

50   *Correo del Orinoco*, Angostura, 3 March 1821

51   Ibid.

52   Howell (ed.), *The Life of Alexander*, Volume 2, p.201

53   The *Dublin Evening Post*, Dublin, 8 February 1821

54   O'Connor, *Un Irlandes con Bolívar*, p.32

55   Ibid.

56   Alberot Eduardo Wright, *Destellos de gloria: biografía sintética de un prócer de la independencia, incorporando las 'Reminiscencias' del general de división don Tomás Carlos Wright* (Buenos Aires, Castorman, Oritz y Cia, 1949), p.41

57   http://irishargentine.org/mcginnperu3.htm

58   Howell (ed.), *The Life of Alexander*, Volume 2, p.201

PART 4

Heading: Richard Holmes, *Wellington: The Iron Duke* (London, Harper Collins, 2003), p.254

CHAPTER 30

1   The *Dublin Evening Post*, Dublin, 16 September, 21 September, 9 November 1820

2   Daniel O'Leary, *Memorias de General Daniel Florencio O'Leary*, Volume 29 (Caracas, Imprenta de la Gaceta Oficial, 1879–1887), Doc. 162

3   The *Dublin Evening Post*, Dublin, 8 February 1821

4   O'Leary, *Memorias*, Volume 29, Doc. 177

5   The *Dublin Evening Post*, Dublin, 8 February 1821

6   John Charles Chasteen, *Americanos: Latin America's Struggle for Independence* (Oxford, Oxford University Press, 2008), p.143

7   The *Dublin Evening Post*, Dublin, 3 February 1821

8   Richard Longeville Vowell, *Campaigns and Cruises, in Venezuela and New Grenada, and in the Pacific Ocean; From 1817 to 1830: with the Narrative of a March from the River Orinoco to San Buenaventura on the Coast of Chocó; and Sketches of the West Coast of South America from the Gulf of California to the Archipelago of Chilöe* (London, Longman and Co., 1831), pp.218–219

9   Manuel Antonio López, *Recuerdos Históricos de la Guerra de la Independencia* (Madrid, Biblioteca Ayacucho, 1878), p.61

10   Vowell, *Campaigns and Cruises*, p.224

11   López, *Recuerdos Históricos*, p.61

12   Vowell, *Campaigns and Cruises*, p.215

13   Ibid., p.216

14   Ibid., p.222

15   Ibid.

16   Eric Lambert, *Voluntarios Británicos e Irlandeses en la Gesta Bolivariana*, Volume 3 (Caracas, Ministerio de la Defensa, Dirección de Artes Graficas, 1993), p.371

17   Archivo General de la Nación, Bogotá, Colombia (AGNC), Sección Republica, Secretaria de Guerra y Marina, Tomo 778, Folio 81; Vowell, *Campaigns and Cruises*, p.214

18   Vowell, *Campaigns and Cruises*, p.214

19   *Gazeta de Santafé de Bogotá*, Bogotá, 4 March 1821; López, *Recuerdos Históricos*, pp.62–63

20   López, *Recuerdos Históricos*, p.64

21   *Gazeta de Santafé de Bogotá*, Bogotá, 4 March 1821

22   Vowell, *Campaigns and Cruises*, p.224

23   Ibid.

24   Ibid., p.225

25   *Gazeta de Santafé de Bogotá*, Bogotá, 4 March 1821

26   Vowell, *Campaigns and Cruises*, p.227

27   Chasteen, *Americanos*, p.107

28   López, *Recuerdos Históricos*, p.64

29   Ibid.

30   Vowell, *Campaigns and Cruises*, p.227

31   Ibid.

32   *Gazeta de Santafé de Bogotá*, Bogotá, 4 March 1821

33   Vowell, *Campaigns and Cruises*, p.228

34   AGNC, Archivo Restrepo, Rollo 11, Fondo 1, Volume 24, Folios 233–235

35   López, *Recuerdos Históricos*, p.64

36   Vowell, *Campaigns and Cruises*, p.228

37   AGNC, Archivo Restrepo, Rollo 11, Fondo 1, Volume 24, Folios 229–230 and 233–235

38   Lambert, *Voluntarios*, Volume 3, p.400

39   Charles Stuart Cochrane, *Journal of a Residence and Travels in Colombia*, Volume 1 (London, Henry Colburn, 1825), p.491

40   Ibid.

CHAPTER 31

1   The *Dublin Evening Post*, Dublin, 8 February 1821

2   Ibid., 20 March 1821

3   Ibid., 28 April 1821

4   Ibid., 12 May 1821

5   George Laval Chesterton, *Peace, War and Adventure: An Autobiographical Memoir of George Laval Chesterton*, Volume 2 (London, Longman, Brown, Green and Longmans, 1853), p.217

6   Ibid., p.218

7   The *Dublin Evening Post*, Dublin, 26 June 1821

8   Ibid.

9   Chesterton, *Peace, War and Adventure*, p.178

10   Ibid., p.179

11   Ibid., p.180

12   Ibid., p.184

13   Ibid., p.190

14   W. Davidson Weatherhead, *An Account of the Late Expedition Against the Isthmus of Darien Under the Command of Sir Gregor McGregor; Together with the Events Subsequent to the Recapture of Porto Bello, till the Release of the Prisoners from Panama; Remarks on the Present State of the Patriot Cause and on the Climate and Diseases of South America* (London, Longman, Hurst, Rees, Orme and Brown, 1821), p.71

15   Ibid., p.72

16   Ibid.

17   Ibid., p.84

18   Ibid., pp.88–89

19   Ibid., p.96

20   *Gazeta de Santafé de Bogotá*, Bogotá, 17 September 1820

21   Michael Rafter, *Memoirs of Gregor M'Gregor: Comprising a Sketch of the Revolution in New Granada and Venezuela, with Biographical Notices of Generals Miranda, Bolivar, Morillo and Horé, and a Narrative of the Expeditions to Amelia Island, Porto Bello, and Rio de la Hache, Interspersed with Revolutionary Anecdotes* (London, J. J. Stockdale, 1820), p.242

22   Weatherhead, *An Account of the Late Expedition*, p.99

23   Rafter, *Memoirs of Gregor M'Gregor*, p.244

24   Weatherhead, *An Account of the Late Expedition*, p.99

25   Diego Barros Arana, *Historia General de Chile*, Volume 9 (Santiago, Editorial Universitaria, 2000), pp.436–437

26   Weatherhead, *An Account of the Late Expedition*, pp.105–106

27   Ibid., p.118

CHAPTER 32

1   The *Dublin Evening Post*, Dublin, 14 June 1821

2   Alfred Hasbrouck, *Foreign Legionaries in the Liberation of Spanish South America* (Columbia University Press, 1928), p.79

3   Archivo General de la Nación, Bogotá, Colombia (AGNC), Hojas de Servicio, Tomo 31, Folio 533

4   Eric Lambert, *Voluntarios Británicos e Irlandeses en la Gesta Bolivariana*, Volume 3 (Caracas, Ministerio de la Defensa, Dirección de Artes Graficas, 1993), p.302

5   Ibid., p.309

6   Archivo General de la Nación, Caracas, Venezuela (AGNV), Ilustres Próceres, Caja 29, Carpeta 9

7   The *Dublin Evening Post*, Dublin, 14 June 1821

8   Ibid., 28 July 1821

9   Páez, José, *Autobiografía* (Madrid, Editorial America, 1916), p.237

10   The *Dublin Evening Post*, Dublin, 29 December 1821

11   Eric Lambert (ed.), *Carabobo 24th June 1821: Some Accounts Written in English* (Caracas, Fundacion John Boulton, 1974), p.49

12   The *Dublin Evening Post*, Dublin, 29 December 1821

13   Ibid.; Páez, *Autobiografía*, p.237

14   The *Dublin Evening Post*, Dublin, 29 December 1821

15   Ibid.

16   Páez, *Autobiografía*, p.240

17   The *Dublin Evening Post*, Dublin, 8 February 1821

18   Ibid., 29 December 1821

19   *Correo del Orinoco*, Angostura, 28 July 1821

20   Lambert, *Carabobo*, p.49

21   Ibid.

22   Ibid.

23   Richard Holmes, *Wellington: The Iron Duke* (London, Harper Collins, 2003), pp.236–237

24   Lambert, *Carabobo*, p.50

25   Ibid.

26   The *Dublin Evening Post*, Dublin, 29 December 1821

27   Henri La Fayette Villaume Ducoudray Holstein, *Memoirs of Simon Bolivar: President Liberator of the Republic of Colombia, and of His Principal Generals: Secret History of the Revolution and the Events which Preceded It, from 1807 to the Present Time: with an Introduction Containing an Account of the Statistics and the Present Situation of the Country* (London, S. G. Goodrich, 1830), p.282

28   Lambert, *Carabobo*, p.50

29   *La Ilustracion*, Caracas, No.100, 24 June 1870

30   Lambert, *Carabobo*, p.51

31   Ibid.

32   AGNC, Sección Republica, Hojas de Servicio, Tomo 31, Folio 533

33   Lambert, *Carabobo*, p.51

34   The *Dublin Evening Post*, Dublin, 11 December 1821

35   Ibid., 29 December 1821

36   Ibid.

37   *Blackwood's Edinburgh Magazine*, Edinburgh, 1822, Obituaries, p.133

38   The *Dublin Evening Post*, Dublin, 29 December 1821

39   Lambert, *Carabobo* p.52

40   Ibid.; *The Dublin Evening Post*, Dublin, 29 December 1821

41   Lambert, *Carabobo*, p.51

42   AGNV, Ilustres Próceres, Volume 42, AHG G, Acta 2

43   *La Ilustracion*, Caracas, No.100, 24 June 1870

44   The *Dublin Evening Post*, Dublin, 29 December 1821

45   Lambert, *Carabobo*, p.52

46   Ibid.

47   Ibid.

48   Matthew Brown, Martín Alonso Roa, *Militares extranjeros en la independencia de Colombia: nuevas perspectivas* (Bogotá, Museo Nacional de Colombia, 2005), Doc. 56

49   Páez, *Autobiografía*, p.240

50   Lambert, *Carabobo*, p.52

51   Alberot Eduardo Wright, *Destellos de gloria: biografía sintética de un prócer de la independencia, incorporando las 'Reminiscencias' del general de división don Tomás Carlos Wright* (Buenos Aires, Castorman, Oritz y Cia, 1949), p.42

52 The *Dublin Evening Post*, Dublin, 13 September 1821

53 *Correo del Orinoco*, Angostura, 28 July 1821

54 The *Dublin Evening Post*, Dublin, 25 September 1821

55 Lambert, *Carabobo*, p.52

56 The *Dublin Evening Post*, Dublin, 25 September 1821

57 Páez, *Autobiografía*, p.240

58 Archivo General de Indias, Seville, Spain, Archivo del General Miguel de La Torre, Legajo 21, Paquete 73, Numero 129

59 Lambert, *Carabobo*, pp.31–43

60 Ibid., p.52

61 The *Dublin Evening Post*, Dublin, 11 December 1821

EPILOGUE

1 John Lynch, *Simon Bolívar: A Life* (London, Yale University Press, 2007), pp.276–278

2 Francis Burdett O'Connor, *Un Irlandes con Bolívar: recuerdos de la independencia de América del Sur* (Caracas, El Cid, 1977), p.105

3 Matthew Brown, *Adventuring Through Spanish Colonies: Simón Bolívar, Foreign Mercenaries and the Birth of New Nations* (Liverpool, Liverpool University Press, 2007), p.177

4 Ibid.

5 The *Limerick Chronicle*, Limerick, 15 June 1833

6 Archivo General de la Nación, Bogotá, Colombia (AGNC), Hojas de Servicio, Tomo 30, Folio 992

7 *Gaceta de Colombia*, Bogotá, 15 June 1823

8 Brown, *Adventuring Through Spanish Colonies*, p.177

9 AGNC, Hojas de Servicio, Tomo 30, Folio 992

10 *La Bandera Negra*, Bogotá, 25 December 1837

11 Brown, *Adventuring Through Spanish Colonies*, p.159

12 Ibid.

13 AGNC, Hojas de Servicio, Tomo 30, Folio 973

14 Archivo de Cartas del Coronel Thomas Manby, Doc. 5, Biblioteca Luis Angel Arango, Bogotá

15 The *Dublin Evening Post*, Dublin, 9 April 1822

16 Ibid., 29 December 1821

17 AGNC, Republica, Hojas de Servicio, Tomo 31, Folio 504; Brown, *Adventuring Through Spanish Colonies*, p.181

18 Eric Lambert, *Voluntarios Británicos e Irlandeses en la Gesta Bolivariana*, Volume 3 (Caracas, Ministerio de la Defensa, Dirección de Artes Graficas, 1993), Epilogue

19 Eric Lambert (ed.), *Carabobo 24th June 1821: Some Accounts Written in English* (Caracas, Fundacion John Boulton, 1974), p.46

20 John Howell (ed.), *The Life of Alexander Alexander, Written by Himself and Edited by John Howell* (Edinburgh, William Blackwood, 1830), p.291

21 AGNC, Sección República, Fondo Criminales, Legajo 86, 2879, 1826-1828, Folios 120–240

22 W. Dupouy (ed.), *Sir Robert Ker Porter's Caracas Diary, 1825–1842: a British Diplomat in a Newborn Nation* (Caracas, Editorial Arte, 1966), p.730

23 Ibid., p.922

24 Ibid., p.1073

25 For further details on MacGregor's post-war career see David Sinclair, *The Land That Never Was: Sir Gregor Macgregor and the Most Audacious Fraud in History* (Paw Prints, 2008)

26 Lambert, *Voluntarios*, Volume 1, p.213

27 Richard Longeville Vowell, *Campaigns and Cruises, in Venezuela and New Grenada, and in the Pacific Ocean; From 1817 to 1830: with the Narrative of a March from the River Orinoco to San Buenaventura on the Coast of Chocó; and Sketches of the West Coast of South America from the Gulf of California to the Archipelago of Chilöe* (London, Longman and Co., 1831), p.254

28 Ibid., p.458

29 The *Sydney Gazette and New South Wales Advertiser*, Sydney, Saturday 6 June 1835

30 See Sue Rosen's Thesis entitled 'The Cox's River Road Gang' available online at: http://www.phansw.org.au/ROPHO/stockade.pdf. The details on Vowell are to be found in Chapter 8.

31 http://freepages.genealogy.rootsweb.ancestry.com/~becher/vowell_family.htm

32 Brown, *Adventuring Through Spanish Colonies*, p.42

33 Ibid., p.174

34 Ibid., p.175; Anon, *The Present State of Colombia: Containing an Account of the Principal Events of its Revolutionary War; the Expeditions Fitted Out in England to Assist in its Emancipation; its Constitution; Financial and Commercial Laws; Revenue, Expenditure and Public Debt; Agriculture; Mines; Mining and Other Concerns* (London, J. Murray, 1827), p.177

35 Dupouy (ed.), *Sir Robert Ker Porter's Caracas Diary*, p.307

36 Brown, *Adventuring Through Spanish Colonies*, p.205

37 Lambert, *Voluntarios*, Volume 3, p.450

BIBLIOGRAPHY

ARCHIVES

Archivo Central de Cauca, Popayán, Colombia
Archivo del Libertador, Caracas, Venezuela
Archivo General de Indias, Seville, Spain
Archivo General de la Nación, Bogotá, Colombia
Archivo General de la Nación, Caracas, Venezuela
Archivo Histórico de Guayana, Ciudad Bolívar, Venezuela
Archivo Histórico de la Universidad de Cali, Popayán
Biblioteca Luis Angel Arango, Bogotá, Colombia
Biblioteca Nacional de Colombia, Bogotá, Colombia
British Library Manuscripts, London
National Archives, Kew, Home Office, War Office and Foreign Office sections
Public Record Office of Northern Ireland, Belfast, Robert James Young's diary
Suffolk County Record Office, Ipswich, James Towers English Papers

CONTEMPORARY NEWSPAPERS AND MAGAZINES

Blackwood's Edinburgh Magazine (1822)
Carrick's Morning Post (1820)
El Colombiano (1820)
El Correo del Orinoco (1818–1821)
Faulkner's Dublin Journal (1819–1821)
Freeman's Journal (1820)
Gazeta de Caracas (1818)
Gazeta de Santafé de Bogotá (1820)
La Bandera Negra (1837)
La Ilustración (1870)
The *British Monitor* (1819–1820)

The *Courier* (1817–1822)

The *Dublin Evening Post* (1817–1821)

The *Edinburgh Gazetteer* (1822)

The *Limerick Chronicle* (1833)

The *Literary Gazette* (1830)

The *Morning Chronicle* (1817–1822)

The Patriot (1819)

The *Quarterly Review* (1822)

The *Sydney Gazette and New South Wales Advertiser* (1835)

The Times (1817–1822)

The *United Service Magazine* (1847–1849)

PRIMARY SOURCES

Adam, William Jackson, *Journal of Voyages to Marguaritta, Trinidad, & Maturin: With the Author's Travels Across the Plains of the Llaneros, to Angustura, and Subsequent Descent of the Orinoco, in the Years 1819 & 1820* (London, J. Jones, 1824)

Anon (Francisco Antonio Zea and Alexander Walker), *Colombia – Being a Geographical, Statistical, Agricultural, Commercial and Political Account of that Country, Adapted for the General Reader, the Merchant and the Colonis* (London, Baldwin, Craddock and Joy, 1822)

Anon, *Letters Written from Colombia During a Journey from Caracas to Bogota and Thence to Santa Martha in 1823* (London, G. Cowie and Co., 1824)

Anon, *Narrative of a Voyage to the Spanish Main, in the Ship 'Two Friends': The Occupation of Amelia Island by M'Gregor, &c. – Sketches of the Province of East Florida; and Anecdotes Illustrative of the Habits and Manners of the Seminole Indians: with an Appendix, Containing a Detail of the Seminole* (London, J. Miller, 1819)

Anon, *The Present State of Colombia: Containing an Account of the Principal Events of its Revolutionary War; the Expeditions Fitted Out in England to Assist in its Emancipation; its Constitution; Financial and Commercial Laws; Revenue, Expenditure and Public Debt; Agriculture; Mines; Mining and Other Concerns* (London, J. Murray, 1827)

Anon, *Recollections of a Service of Three Years During the War-of-Extermination in the Republics of Venezuela and Columbia* (London, Hunt and Clarke, 1828)

Bache, Richard, *Notes on Colombia Taken in the Years 1822 –23; with an Itinerary of the Route from Carcas to Bogota, and an Appendix; by an Officer of the US Army* (Philadelphia, H. C. Carey and I. Lea, 1827)

Bezant, John, *Narrative of the Expedition under General MacGregor against Porto Bello: Including an Account of the Voyage; And of the Causes which Led to its Final Overthrow (By an Officer who Miracoulously Escaped)* (London and Edinburgh, C. and J. Ollier, and T. and J. Allman, 1820)

Bonnycastle, Richard Henry, *Spanish America; or, a Descriptive, Historical and Geographical Account of the Dominions of Spain in the Western Hemisphere, etc. [With maps.]* (London, Longman and Co., 1818)

Brown, Charles, *Narrative of the Expedition to South America: Which Sailed from England at the Close of 1817, for the Service of the Spanish Patriots: Including the Military and Naval Transactions, and Ultimate Fate of that Expedition: Also the Arrival of Colonels Blosset and English* (London, John Booth, 1819)

Chesterton, George Laval, *Peace, War and Adventure: An Autobiographical Memoir of George Laval Chesterton*, Volume 2 (London: Longman, Brown, Green and Longmans, 1853)

Cochrane, Charles Stuart, *Journal of a Residence and Travels in Colombia*, 2 Volumes (London, Henry Colburn, 1825)

Douglas, William, *Duelling Days in the Army* (London, Ward and Downey, 1884)

Duane, William, *A Visit to Colombia in the Years 1822 and 1823, by Laguayara and Caracas, over the Cordillera to Bogota, and thence by the Magdalena to Cartagena* (Philadelphia, Thomas H. Palmer, 1826)

Ducoudray Holstein, Henri La Fayette Villaume, *Memoirs of Simon Bolivar: President Liberator of the Republic of Colombia, and of His Principal Generals: Secret History of the Revolution and the Events which Preceded It, from 1807 to the Present Time: with an Introduction Containing an Account of the Statistics and the Present Situation of the Country* (London, S. G. Goodrich, 1830)

Dunham, Jacob, *Journal of Voyages: Containing an Account of the Author's Being Twice Captured by the English and Once by Gibbs the Pirate* (New York, 1850)

Dupouy, W. (ed.), *Sir Robert Ker Porter's Caracas Diary, 1825–1842: a British Diplomat in a Newborn Nation* (Caracas, Editorial Arte, 1966)

Eastwick, Edward Backhouse, *Venezuela: or, Sketches of Life in a South-American Republic: with the History of the Loan of 1864. By Edward B. Eastwick, with a Map* (London, Chapman and Hall, 1868)

Flinter, George Dawson, *The History of the Revolution of Caracas Together with a Description of the Llaneros* (London, W. Glindon, 1819)

Gleig, George Robert, *The Subaltern* (London, W. Blackwood and Sons, 1868)

Hackett, James, *Narrative of the Expedition which Sailed from England in 1817, to Join the South American Patriots: Comprising Every Particular Connected with its Formation, History, and Fate; with Observations and Authentic Information Elucidating the Real Character of the Contest, Mode of Warfare, State of the Armies etc…* (London, John Murray, 1818)

Hall, Francis, *Colombia: its Present State, in Respect of Climate, Soil, Productions, Population, Government, Commerce, Revenue, Manufactures, Arts, Literature, Manners, Education, and Inducements to Emigration* (London, Baldwin, Craddock and Joy, 1824)

Hambleton, John, *Diario del Viaje por el Orinoco hacia Angostura (julio 11–agosto 24 1819) Con las Instrucciones para el viaje dadas por el Secretario del Estado, John Quincy Adams* (Bogotá, Banco de la República, 1969)

Hamilton, John, *Travels Through the Interior Provinces of Colombia*, 2 Volumes (London, John Murray, 1827)

Hibbert, Christopher (ed.), *The Recollections of Rifleman Harris* (London, Orion Publishing Co., 2007)

Hippisley, Gustavus Butler, 'The Eve of Saint Simón', in *Godey's Magazine*, 1830, Volume X1

Hippisley, Gustavus Butler, 'The Ruse de Guerre', in *Colborn's United Service Magazine*, Arthur William Alsager Pollock (ed.), Third Edition (London 1847)

Hippisley, Gustavus Butler, *The Siege of Barcelona, a Poem in Three Cantos* (London, W. J. Cleaver, 1842)

Hippisley, Gustavus Mathias, *A Narrative of the Expedition to the Rivers Orinoco and Apuré in South America: which Sailed from England in November 1817, and Joined the Patriotic Forces in Venezuela and Caraccas* (London, John Murray, 1819)

Howell, John (ed.), *The Life of Alexander Alexander, Written by Himself and Edited by John Howell*, 2 Volumes (Edinburgh, William Blackwood, 1830)

Humboldt, Alexander, *Personal Narrative of a Journey to the Equatorial Regions of the New Continent* (London, Penguin, 1995)

Kincaid, Sir John, *Random Shots from a Rifleman* (London, T. and W. Boone, 1847)

Lambert, Eric (ed.), *Carabobo 24th June 1821: Some Accounts Written in English* (Caracas, Fundacion John Boulton, 1974)

Lonsdale, Roger (ed.), *New Oxford Book of 18th Century Verse* (Oxford, Oxford University Press, 1984)

López, Manuel Antonio, *Recuerdos Históricos de la Guerra de la Independencia* (Madrid, Biblioteca Ayacucho, 1878)

Maceroni, Francis, *Memoirs of the Life and Adventures of Colonel Maceroni, Late Aide-de-Camp to Joachim Murat, King of Naples; Knight of the Legion of Honour, and of St. George of the Two Sicilies; Ex-General of Brigade, in the Service of the Republic of Colombia ect. ect, with a Portrait* (London, J. Macrone, 1838)

MacMahon, Benjamin, *Jamaica Plantership (a Description of Jamaica Planters, viz. Attorneys, Overseers, and Book-keepers, Compiled During a Residence of Eighteen Years in the Island)* (London, 1839)

Mollien, Gaspard, *Travels in the Republic of Colombia in the Years 1822 and 1823* (London, C. Knight, 1824)

Montaña, Andres (ed.), *Santander y los Ejercitos Patriotas: 1819* (Bogotá, Fundación de Paula Santander, 1989)

Morillo, Pablo (traducidas del frances por Arturo Gomez Jaramillo), *Memorias* (Bogota, Editorial Incunables, 1991)

O'Connor, Francis Burdett, *Un Irlandes con Bolívar: recuerdos de la independencia de América del Sur* (Caracas, El Cid, 1977)

O'Leary, Daniel, *Memorias de General Daniel Florencio O'Leary* (Caracas, Imprenta de la Gaceta Oficial, 1879–1887)

O'Leary, Daniel, and Humphreys, R. A. (ed.), *The Detached Recollections of General D. F. O'Leary* (London, The Athlone Press, 1969)

Páez, José, *Autobiografía* (Madrid, Editorial America, 1916)

Princep, John, *Diario de un Viaje de Santo Tomé de Angosturaen la Guayana Españolaa los misiones Capuchinas de Caroní*, trans. Jaime Tello (Caracas, Ediciones de la Presedencia de la República, 1975)

Rafter, Michael, *Memoirs of Gregor M'Gregor: Comprising a Sketch of the Revolution in New Granada and Venezuela, with Biographical Notices of Generals Miranda, Bolívar, Morillo and Horé, and a Narrative of the Expeditions to Amelia Island, Porto Bello, and Rio de la Hache, Interspersed with Revolutionary Anecdotes* (London, J. J. Stockdale, 1820)

Restrepo, José Manuel, *Diario político y milita: Memorias sobre los sucesos importantes de la época para servir a la Historia de la Revolución de Colombia y de la Nueva Granada, desde 1819 para adelante*, 4 Volumes (Bogotá, Imprenta Nacional, 1954)

Robinson, James H., *Journal of an Expedition 1400 Miles up the Orinoco and 300 up the Arauca: with an Account of the Country, the Manners of the People, Military Operations, &c* (London, Black, Young and Young, 1822)

Sevilla, Rafael, *Memorias de un oficial del ejercito español. Campanas contra Bolívar y los Separatistas de America. Apreciacion de la obra por R. Blanco-Fombona* (Madrid, Biblioteca Ayacucho, 1916)

Urdaneta, Rafael, *Memorias del General Rafael Urdaneta (general en jefe y encargado del gobierno de la Gran Colombia)* (Madrid, Editorial América, 1916)

Vowell, Richard Longeville, *Campaigns and Cruises, in Venezuela and New Grenada, and in the Pacific Ocean; From 1817 to 1830: with the Narrative of a March from the River Orinoco to San Buenaventura on the Coast of Chocó; and Sketches of the West Coast of South America from the Gulf of California to the Archipelago of Chilöe* (London, Longman and Co., 1831)

Vowell, Richard Longeville, *The Savannas of Varinas* (London, Longman and Co., 1831)

Weatherhead, W. Davidson, *An Account of the Late Expedition Against the Isthmus of Darien Under the Command of Sir Gregor McGregor; Together with the Events Subsequent to the Recapture of Porto Bello, till the Release of the Prisoners from Panama; Remarks on the Present State of the Patriot Cause and on the Climate and Diseases of South America* (London, Longman, Hurst, Rees, Orme and Brown, 1821)

Wright, Alberot Eduardo, *Destellos de gloria: biografía sintética de un prócer de la independencia, incorporando las "Reminiscencias" del general de división don Tomás Carlos Wright* (Buenos Aires, Castorman, Oritz y Cia, 1949)

SELECTED SECONDARY SOURCES

Barros Arana, Diego, *Historia General de Chile*, Volume 9 (Santiago, Editorial Universitaria, 2000)

Bolívar, Simón, and Vicente Lecuna (ed.), *Cartas del Libertador*, Second Edition (Caracas, Banco de Venezuela, Fundacion Vincente Lecuna, 1964)

Brett, Edward M., *The British Auxiliary Legion in the First Carlist War 1835–1838* (Dublin, Four Courts Press, 2005)

Brown, Matthew, *Adventuring Through Spanish Colonies: Simón Bolívar, Foreign Mercenaries and the Birth of New Nations* (Liverpool, Liverpool University Press, 2007)

Brown, Matthew, Alonso Roa, Martín, *Militares extranjeros en la independencia de Colombia: nuevas perspectivas* (Bogotá, Museo Nacional de Colombia, 2005)

Chasteen, John Charles, *Americanos: Latin America's Struggle for Independence* (Oxford, Oxford University Press, 2008)

BIBLIOGRAPHY

Clayton, Tim, *Tars: The Men who Made Britain Rule the Waves* (London, Hodder and Stoughton Ltd., 2007)

Earle, Rebecca, *Spain and the Independence of Colombia 1810–1825* (Exeter, University of Exeter Press, 2000)

Fortescue, Sir John, *The County Lieutenancies and the Army – 1803–1814* (London, Macmillan, 1909)

Foulkes, Nick, *Dancing into Battle: A Social History of the Battle of Waterloo* (London, Phoenix, 2007)

Hambleton, John, 'The Voyage of the U.S. Schooner "Non-Such"', in *The Hispanic American Historical Review*, Volume 30, November 1950

Harvey, Robert, *Liberators: South America's Savage Wars of Freedom* (London, Constable and Robinson, 2000)

Hasbrouck, Alfred, *Foreign Legionaries in the Liberation of Spanish South America* (Columbia University Press, 1928)

Holmes, Richard, *Redcoat: The British Soldier in the Age of the Horse and Musket* (London, Harper Collins, 2002)

Holmes, Richard, *Wellington: The Iron Duke* (London, Harper Collins, 2003)

Hooker, Terry, and Poulter, Ron, Men-at-Arms 232, *The Armies of Bolivar and San Martín* (London, Osprey Publishing, 1991)

Hopkins, Harry, *The Strange Death of Private White: A Victorian Scandal that Made History* (London, Weidenfeld & Nicolson, 1977)

Hopton, Richard, *Pistols at Dawn: A History of Duelling* (London, Portrait, 2007)

Howard, Dr Martin, *Wellington's Doctors: The British Army Medical Services in the Napoleonic Wars* (Padstow, Spellmount, 2002)

Hughes, B. P., *Firepower, Weapons' Effectiveness on the Battlefield, 1630–1850* (London, Arms & Armour, 1974)

James, C. L. R., *The Black Jacobins* (London, Alison Busby Limited, 1984)

Kaufman, Matthew H., *Musket-ball and Sabre Injuries from the First Half of the Nineteenth Century* (Edinburgh, Royal College of Surgeons, 2003)

Lambert, Eric, *Voluntarios Británicos e Irlandeses en la Gesta Bolivariana*, 3 Volumes (Caracas, Ministerio de la Defensa, Dirección de Artes Graficas, 1993)

Lynch, John, 'British Policy and Spanish America 1783–1808', in *Journal of Latin American Studies*, Volume 1 (1969)

Lynch, John, *Simon Bolívar: A Life* (London, Yale University Press, 2007)

Muir, Rory, *Tactics and the Experience of Battle in the Age of Napoleon* (London, Yale University Press, 2002)

Pérez, Gabriel Carmargo, 'Cuna, Muerte y Sepultura de Coronel Jaime Rooke', in David R. Iriarte, *Reportario Boyacanense* (Madrid, 1981)

Pitt Lennox, William, *Three Years with the Duke or Wellington in Private Life. By an Ex-Aid-de-Camp* (London, Saunders and Otely, 1853)

Rourke, Thomas, *Man of Glory: Simon Bolivar* (London, Joseph, 1940)

Scott, Drusilla, *Mary English: A Friend of Bolivar* (Sussex, The Book Guild, 1991)

Sinclair, David, *The Land That Never Was: Sir Gregor Macgregor and the Most Audacious Fraud in History* (Paw Prints, 2008)

Tribin, Sotomayor, and Armando, Hugo, *Guerras, enfermedades y médicos en Colombia* (Bogotá, Escuela de Medicina Juan N. Corpas, 1997)

Vergara y Velasco, Francisco Javier, *1818: (Guerra de Independencia)* (Bogotá, Librería Americana, 1897)

Vila, Manuel Pérez, *Vida de Daniel Florencio O'Leary* (Caracas, 1957)

Villa, Antonio Rodriguez, *El teniente general don Pablo Morillo primer conde de Cartagena, marqués de la Puerta (1778–1837)* (Editorial America, 1920)

Wilson, Ben, *Decency & Disorder: The Age of Cant 1789–1837* (London, Faber and Faber, 2008)

Zamoyski, Adam, *Holy Madness: Romantics, Patriots, and Revolutionaries, 1776–1871* (London, Phoenix Press, 2001)

INDEX